KEYWORDS IN EDU
POLICY RESEAF
A Conceptual Toolbox

Andrew Wilkins, Steven J. Courtney and Nelli Piattoeva

First published in Great Britain in 2024 by

Policy Press, an imprint of
Bristol University Press
University of Bristol
1–9 Old Park Hill
Bristol
BS2 8BB
UK
t: +44 (0)117 374 6645
e: bup-info@bristol.ac.uk

Details of international sales and distribution partners are available at
policy.bristoluniversitypress.co.uk

© Bristol University Press 2024

British Library Cataloguing in Publication Data
A catalogue record for this book is available from the British Library

ISBN 978-1-4473-6009-4 hardcover
ISBN 978-1-4473-6010-0 paperback
ISBN 978-1-4473-6011-7 ePub
ISBN 978-1-4473-6012-4 ePdf

The right of Andrew Wilkins, Steven J. Courtney and Nelli Piattoeva to be identified as
authors of this work has been asserted by them in accordance with the Copyright,
Designs and Patents Act 1988.

Cover design: Robin Hawes
Front cover image: Shutterstock/Kryuchka Yaroslav
Bristol University Press and Policy Press use environmentally responsible
print partners.
Printed and bound in Great Britain by CPI Group (UK) Ltd, Croydon, CR0 4YY

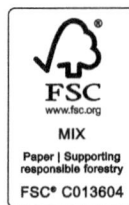

FSC
www.fsc.org
MIX
Paper | Supporting
responsible forestry
FSC® C013604

A love letter to a field of inspiration

Contents

Contents

About the authors

Andrew Wilkins is Reader in Education Policy and Director of Research in the Department of Educational Studies, Goldsmiths, University of London. He is a policy sociologist with research interests in education policy, comparative education and education governance.

Steven J. Courtney is Professor of Sociology of Education Leadership at the Manchester Institute of Education (MIE), University of Manchester. His research uses critical approaches which seek to explain and theorise education policy and educational leaders' identity and practice, as well as the relationship between these. He is currently Co-Editor-in-Chief of the journal *Critical Studies in Education*.

Nelli Piattoeva is Professor of Sociology of Education at Tampere University, Finland. Her research focuses on the changing means of the governance of schooling (for example, datafication) and on the role of formal education in societal governance (for example, schools as sites of nation-building). She is Co-Director of the Laboratory of International Assessment Studies. At Tampere University, she leads an interdisciplinary Research Centre on Transnationalism and Transformation (TRANSIT).

Introduction

A key dilemma for writers, be they poets, philosophers or researchers, is how to give meaning to the world when there are so many interpretative repertoires to articulate and learn from. To speak or to write is to participate in a symbolic economy where meaning is negotiated and mobilised through the availability of scattered discursive resources. Writing, in essence, is that dynamic, productive site where meaning is continually made, normalised and contested. A related dilemma for writers therefore concerns the why of said meaning. Taking a postmodernist perspective to its logical conclusion, meaning is arbitrary in the metaphysical sense that it lacks any ontological fixity to speak of. It has no essence or origin, or at least its origin has no status beyond the 'exteriority of accidents' (Foucault, 1998, p 146). Meaning at best reflects the interplay between spontaneous action and reproduced habits of culture. Postmodern cynicism aside, meaning is not entirely free-floating or symbolic. It represents pragmatic, engaged attempts at sensemaking. In other words, meaning making can be characterised as essential epistemic work, a form of 'anchoring' that is vital to human cognition and abstract thinking (Eagleton, 2003, p 59). Consider the importance of meaning to human efforts at coping with complexity or making social reality amenable to capture by unique and historically contingent systems of signification and belonging.

The dilemma here, then, concerns the symbolic and material consequences that result from deploying certain discursive resources (words, imagery, tropes, arguments) over and against others in our productions and representations of the world. If we accept the view that there is no such thing as neutral writing, and that writing only makes sense through the provision of shared meaning, it is incumbent on writers to take responsibility for the habits and choices that shape their constructions of reality. This includes recognising what is at stake when we write. After all, writing is about taking positions. Why do we write? For whom do we write? What is to be gained or lost from writing in a particular way? What kinds of disagreements must be struggled over, negotiated, held apart or brought together to achieve particular kinds of writing? As Bacchi (1999) reminds us, problems and solutions are not arrived at indiscriminately through the identification of some pre-existent, transcendental nature. Rather, these terms represent struggles to define and successfully limit the discursive boundaries for containing the possibilities through which certain things (practices, relations, processes) come to be represented, either as social facts or risk objects to be classified and regulated. In other words, problems and their solutions emerge through 'the subtle valuing and imposition of particular futures' (Douglas, 1992, p 10) based upon political and ethical struggles to make certain versions of reality more thinkable, analysable or defensible.

Our observation is that the field of education policy research is fraught with ambiguity and contestation owing to the different ways in which policy making and policy worlds are theorised according to tacit assumptions about epistemology

1

(the study of knowledge and knowing) and ontology (the study of truth or reality). In many cases, these theorisations carry within them 'an assumption of or bring to bear a perspective of coherence or rationality or planned order' (Ball, 2021, p 5). These exercises in reasoning are not exclusive to any particular branch of theory since they are evident across the spectrum of thinking that animates education policy research at the time of writing, from social constructivism to critical realism and positivism. The tendency to overestimate the rationality or dominance of policy making and policy worlds is not restricted to the 'empiricism' of the 'policy sciences' (Lerner and Lasswell, 1951), for example, with its emphasis on 'positivistic methods assuming a political neutrality' (Pillow, 2003, p 146). It is not uncommon for realist and poststructuralist researchers to commit similar categorical errors in their thinking about policy worlds in order to achieve some normative prescription for reality, one that fits with their own understanding or hopes for what is or should be (Wilkins, 2021). Meta-narratives like neoliberalism or governance and governmentality are seductive precisely because they are consoling and give coherence to specific grievances and discontents (Barnett, 2005). That is to say, said meta-narratives provide researchers with a set of 'fixed' objects, structures and relations against which other forms of action (and non-action) can be judged morally and politically. Moreover, and even more seductively, they provide researchers with a new metaphysical language for describing and navigating messy social realities.

But messiness, we argue, should remain the object of study if we are to grapple with the dynamics of emergence and contingency through which things are formed and contested, namely the 'promiscuous entanglements [that] crystallise different conditions of possibility' (Ong, 2007, p 5). Rather than use theory to overcome or suspend such messiness so that social reality can be more exclusively amenable to moral judgement or made more rationally comprehended as expressions or functions of wider systems and structures, it seems more appropriate, indeed politically necessary, to use theory to 'displace presumptions of structural coherence and determination' (Baker and McGuirk, 2017, p 431). This is because structuralist claims to oppression/domination typically risk reducing political and social change to a residual effect of undifferentiated power structures and relations, in effect obscuring 'the ways individuals act creatively for reasons of their own to create new forms of power' (Bevir, 2010, p 426). This has implications for how we theorise policy making and policy worlds. Importantly, it requires us to open up that analytical space in which agents can be found translating, resisting and refusing the power through which they are solicited to act and think in particular ways (Holland and Lave, 2001), making the possibilities for change more readily understood.

This means, on the one hand, taking seriously the interpretative repertoires through which social actors give meaning to the world and the locally adapted translations and refusals of power that might flow from these ideological struggles over meaning. These discursive resources, in essence, provide the political possibilities for resistance and change. As Foucault reminds us (2002b), '[a] reform is never anything but the outcome of a process in which there is conflict, confrontation, struggle, resistance' (p 457). On the other hand, it means remaining circumspect of any claims to essentialism or structural determinism that reify the messiness of social reality through an appeal to abstract structures of domination and power, be it globalisation or neoliberalism. Context-sensitive readings of power and agency often require new inventions and combinations of theories that are empirically useless elsewhere.

Linguistic philosophy teaches us that we can never attain unmediated access to truth since judgements and evaluations inevitably suffer from problems of signification owing to the ways in which language and communication function to constitute, rather than simply reflect, reality. Discursive psychology makes a similar argument regarding language use, 'best understood as the personal enactment of communal methods of self-accounting, vocabularies of motive, culturally recognisable emotional performances and available stories for making sense' (Wetherell and Edley, 1999, p 338). In this sense, language and communication are deeply epistemic insofar as they 'seek to resonate with, speak to, and work upon common conceptions of the world' (Alasuutari and Qadir, 2019, p 2). Language and communication are not the exclusive property of individuals or a universality since they derive their intelligibility from mediating and affirming a structured social existence that is intimately historical and cultural. As Holland and Lave (2001) point out, '[j]ust as we author ourselves by repeating the words of others, we are frequently in the process of enacting ourselves through the culturally identified activities of others' (p 15). Similarly, writing is not a window into the world, but a historically contingent affirmation of reality made possible by the assimilation of interpretative resources considered to be recognisable and meaningful to others. According to Billig (1996), to engage in speech or writing is to participate in the ideological history of affirming, displacing and negotiating the discursive themes available to us.

This book brings together diverse theories and concepts to document the intellectual history and contributions of education policy research. These theories and concepts, we argue, can be considered the major discursive themes or canonical narratives that have shaped the development of education policy research as a field of study, at least at the time of writing. On the one hand, education policy research may be characterised as a discipline or sub-discipline of education in the limited sense that it has 'object[s] of study' and 'accumulated specialist knowledge' not 'shared by another discipline' (Krishnan, 2009, p 9). These objects of study may include structures and processes that are specific to education, be it teaching, assessment or governance. On the other hand, according to Krishnan (2009, p 9), 'disciplines use specific terminologies or a specific technical language adjusted to their research object' as well as 'have developed specific research methods according to their specific research requirements'. There are specific strands of education policy research shaped by positivist thinking which, we argue, satisfy this definition of discipline. The expansion of randomised controlled trials in the UK and US (Torgerson and Torgerson, 2001), for example, point to a growing tradition of positivist education policy research that mobilises a recognisable technical language inspired by statistical analyses and deductive logic, a specific kind of 'technical-instrumental practicality' directed at producing 'specific social arrangements' (Jessop and Sum, 2016, p 105).

At the same time, education policy research more closely resembles a field than a discipline, assuming we adopt the position that a central focus and task of education policy research (broadly understood) is to make explicit the relationship between policy and politics (Wilkins, 2023), namely the ways in which power and claims to knowledge are inscribed in policy decisions and policy effects (Prunty, 1985; Popkewitz, 1991). In other words, we refute the idea that an independent social reality can be comfortably observed, tested and verified using the value-free instruments of a foundational positivist ontology. Our broader definition of and approach to education policy research is animated by, albeit not confined to a suite of intellectual traditions which, while admittedly European-centric in their origins and perspectives, continue to provide inspiration for education policy scholars today. These traditions, collectively known today as 'education policy sociology' (Ozga, 1987), emerged in the 1980s and 1990s as a reaction to and critique of the prevailing political and economic orthodoxy of that time, namely neoliberalism. In the spirit of this tradition, which seeks to provide education policy scholars with unique vantage points through which to exercise a reflexive disposition (Ball, 1994) and/ or commitment to anti-oppressive struggles (Troyna, 1994), this book not only describes the various theories and concepts that make up the field of education policy research, what we are calling 'keywords', but provides the reader with useful reference points and orienting positions for defining and situating their engagements with the field.

These keywords range from lofty concepts like 'genealogy' and 'topology' to more defined, often more problematic terms like 'deliverology' and 'microcredential'. In some cases, we have included sub-disciplines of education, political science, sociology and geography as representative keywords, such as 'cultural political economy' and 'policy trajectory analysis'. We regard these keywords (98 in total) as indispensable forms of knowledge in the contemporary field of education policy research at the time of writing, both as objects of analysis and tools of investigation and meaning making.

The vastness and richness of the history of education policy research means that, inevitably, there are omissions in this book for which we take responsibility. In researching the book, we were introduced to a wide range of terms recommended by colleagues working across the disciplinary spectrum, from education and sociology to geography and social policy. Many of these terms have been included here as keywords. Inspired by Raymond Williams' 1976 classic text *Keywords: A Vocabulary of Culture and Society*, we have selected and classified these terms as keywords in two related senses: 'they are significant, binding words in certain activities and their interpretation; [and] they are significant, indicative words in certain forms of thought' (2015 [1976], p xxvii). Terms like 'instrument' and 'rationality', for example, are significant binding words in that they represent vehicles or modalities for condensing some very complex social, political and economic processes, as described in the book. Through their capacity to 'bound together certain ways of seeing culture and society' (Williams, 2015 [1976], p xxvii), they emerge as detached albeit politically potent signifiers for thinking through the dilemmas and morass of contemporary education policy problem representation. On this definition, we selected to omit a range of terms which we judged at the time of writing to be the opposite of binding or indicative words, namely loose or broad words that were not in-and-of-themselves distinctive from an ontological or epistemological standpoint. Moreover, they were terms that could be easily bundled with the keywords already provided in the book and therefore did not warrant their own separate entry. For example, we noted that there are a large of number of *contextualising terms* that seek to describe the framing through which policy is configured, translated, contested or theorised, either vertically through meso and micro relations and institutions, and/or horizontally through wider macro movements and formations:

> policy agenda, policy apparatus, policy arena, policy capture, policy centre, policy configuration, policy context, policy design, policy environment, policy field, policy forum, policy framework, policy landscape, policy language, policy level, policy logic, policy mantra, policy nexus, policy paradigm, policy propaganda, policy settlement, policy site, policy space, policy spin, policy web, policy window, policyscape.

We also noted that there are a large number of *prescriptive and normative terms* that seek to circumscribe policy making and policy worlds according to New Public Management and economic models, measurements and functions of input/output and success/failure:

> policy design, policy development, policy directive, policy dissemination, policy evaluation, policy formulation, policy goal, policy guideline, policy innovation, policy monitoring, policy objective, policy outcome, policy panacea, policy production, policy reception, policy recommendation, policy remedy, policy solution.

Lastly, we observed through our research and conversations with colleagues that there are a wide number of *adjectival terms* used to describe the action, process or movement of policy and/or the tensions, hybridities and assemblages resulting from these activities:

> policy alienation, policy change, policy congruence, policy craft, policy emplacement, policy enablement, policy engagement, policy entanglement, policy flow, policy formation, policy hyperactivity,

policy importation, policy manifestation, policy move, policy revolution, policy shift.

Given the looseness of the above words as contextualising, normative or adjectival terms for describing policy making and policy worlds, we elected not to engage with them separately as keywords but instead weave them into the general narrative of the text as appropriate meaning-making devices for supplementing our descriptions of messy policy realities. It is also important for us to explain our rationale for omitting certain theories of policy found in the political sciences and public policy and administration literatures more generally, namely punctuated equilibrium theory, information processing theory, policy feedback theory and systems theory, among others. First and foremost, we are not claiming to offer an exhaustive account of the multitude of theories of policy available and their specialised vocabularies, applications and co-development vis-à-vis other disciplines. This is neither practical nor desirable for a writing project of this size and scope. Our aims for writing this book are far more modest and realistic. Principally, we want to offer the reader a suitable degree of comprehension of selected keywords that at the time of writing are established, in vogue or nascent in the field of education policy research.

At the same time, we want to explain our political and personal choices for shaping the structure and content of the book in this way; choices which deliberately exclude any desire or claim to produce some kind of totality or exhaustiveness of the field. We consider ourselves 'critical' scholars working within and across traditions of policy sociology, critical sociology of education and political sociology, among others. This has profound implications for how and why we do education policy research. While these traditions vary in terms of their histories and applications, they are united through their criticism and scrutiny of certain kinds of thought and reasoning that currently appear to dominate spaces and practices of education, most recently the vagaries of neoliberalism from quality improvement technologies to standardised testing regimes. This includes a shared commitment to enacting similar kinds of analytical and political work that, in the tradition of sociology, strive to make the normal exceptional and the mundane strange.

Following Jessop and Sum (2016), who use the terms critical and criticality to describe an attitude that moves beyond (and against) positivist orientations to research that primarily assesses 'the empirical validity of factual analysis or the technical-instrumental practicality of specific social arrangements' (p 105), we align ourselves with a 'policy scholarship' that emphasises the 'historical, theoretical, cultural and socio-political setting[s]' (Grace, 1995, p 12) that give rise to policy problems and their solutions. Therefore, our work differs from positivist conceptions of policy research as developments in 'scientific problem-solving rationality' (Simon et al, 2009, p 4). In other words, we are not convinced by any positivist epistemology which claims observations and facts can be comfortably separated from interpretations and values. Nor do we view policy problems and solutions as predefined by an independent reality waiting to be discovered through rational means of calculation and objectivity. Rather, we adopt a discursive view of policy making and policy worlds as the outcome of political influence, agitation or control in which competing forces struggle for the strategic occupation of dominant positions and relations.

At the same time, we are not opposed to the idea of rationality, but rather mindful of claims that there are limits to reason contained within certain models of rationality, including economic and sociological models of rationality. A categorical error and symptom of classical sociological thinking, for example, is to assume that culture, norms and practices are circumscriptions of individual behaviour (Bevir and Brentmann, 2007) and therefore can be translated into tidy forms through the provision of bifurcations and distinctions, namely individual/ collective, consumer/citizen, private/public. These analytic devices condense some very complicated relations and processes, however. Worse, they obscure those active, dynamic spaces in which meaning is resolved contingently through the articulation and combination of seemingly contradictory and incompatible practices, in effect obviating the need to better understand the essential meaning-making practices underpinning them. These concerns with 'ontological plurality' (Addey and Piattoeva, 2022, p 9), namely the diverse practices through which people derive and produce meaning about the world, reflect our commitment to poststructuralist thinking and interdisciplinary thinking more generally.

In essence, this book is designed to give the reader a range of starting points and entry points through which to engage with the plurality of positions that make up the crowded field of education policy research. To be more specific, we anticipate that the book will serve as a vital conceptual toolbox to assist:

- complex learning and teaching;
- wider and background reading and knowledge building;
- critical scholarship and research;
- interdisciplinary thinking and writing; and
- theory development and application.

While rich and expansive, the language of education policy research can appear extremely dense and opaque owing to its complicated relationship to different political movements and intellectual histories (Wilkins, 2023). Increasingly, students and researchers are invited to think and write about policy making and policy worlds without sufficient knowledge of these movements, their histories and the various 'turns', 'breaks' and 'continuities' underpinning their elusive formation. This book therefore is designed to give readers some firm footing on which to comfortably navigate this messy terrain with a view to conducting further, wider, more in-depth reading and learning. On this account, this book is not a history or genealogy of education policy research. Rather, it is an attempt to carve out a conceptual toolbox that educators, researchers and students can use to supplement their learning and understanding, making it appropriate for personal, teaching or research use.

Keywords

A

Activism

All research enables change; activist education policy research seeks explicitly and primarily to achieve specified changes to educational arrangements, practices, cultures or structures to alleviate the effects of disadvantage. Yeatman (1998) provides a useful definition of a policy activist as 'anyone who champions in relatively consistent ways a value orientation and pragmatic conception of policy which opens it up to the appropriate participation of all those who are involved in the policy process, all the way from points of policy conception to delivery on the ground' (p 10).

This definition, with its focus on values and participation, signifies a shift from how policy activism was first conceptualised by Heclo in the 1970s (in Smyth, 2012). Here, the policy activist 'was a kind of knowledgeable policy technocrat who was prepared to carefully watch developments' (Smyth, 2012, p 180). Intellectually, the activist disposition in policy research originated with the Frankfurt School in Germany, which advanced a critical approach to scholarship that 'aim[ed] to go beyond simply understanding and critiquing social, political and economic relations, towards seeking to change the world' (Savage et al, 2021, p 308). An important strand of critical education policy sociology continues this activist tradition (see, for example, Apple, 2013; Blackmore, 2014; Gorski and Zenkov, 2014). Whether it is called (socially) critical or activist, such policy research intends 'taking aim at both the ideological and practical work of schooling [and/or higher education] and connecting it to the wider structural issues that dominate public education' (Tilleczek, 2012, p 254).

Activism in policy research may be achieved in several ways, singly or together. One form of discursive achievement is through employing a methodology centred on co-construction where individuals or groups affected by a particular dimension of oppression contribute as partners in the research design and/or research process. For example, Tilleczek (2012) 'committed to working with and for young people to collectively make fissures visible to those in policy and decision-making positions' (p 254). Co-constructing or co-producing research can also be used as a sort of self-reflexive activism whereby power imbalances located in higher education might be problematised and disrupted to the wider benefit of communities and education (Duggan, 2021).

The principle underpinning and legitimating co-construction as activism is the inclusion of marginalised actors affected by a given policy in the development of and/or research into that policy. This principle is found also in research that does not extend quite so far as co-construction, but instead aims to enable such voices to be heard in some way in or through the research. For Smyth (2012), this counts as activism because the bar for such inclusion has been set so low in education policy, during a still-continuing era characterised in the Global North by market reforms, intense accountability and a technicised construction of education. Smyth (2012) argues that children in particular have been treated largely as the deficient objects of policy research and interventions, rather than as participants in processes of policy development. Smyth (2012) therefore calls for 'approaches to educational policy that are avowedly more activist in including the views and lives of young people, which in turn means opening up schools to being more democratic and participative' (p 180). For Smyth (2012), then, activism is a disposition that, once activated, will extend beyond policy to include and inform practices and attitudes within schools themselves. Policy research and policy development are inseparable and mutually constitutive.

Another method is to generate insights through research that further an activist political agenda. This is an approach exemplified by Taylor (2004) through an investigation and deconstruction of Education Queensland's reform agenda that uses critical discourse analysis (CDA; see entry on 'Critical discourse analysis'). Taylor (2004) argues that the power relations and structures upon which activists must focus are reproduced through language and discourse. Consequently, researchers who specialise in the application of CDA are well placed to contribute to a form of activism that draws on these skills to produce insights which may translate into political advances. Taylor's (2004) fundamental argument applies beyond CDA to include a range of research methods and instruments.

A third method makes use of policy activist networks, which for Yeatman (1998) comprises 'policy insiders' in state agencies working closely with 'policy outsiders' (p 16) in the community. Apple (2013) recommends a similar tactic, acting with progressive movements as one of his nine tasks for critical educationalists. Or researchers can themselves work to engage policy- or decision-makers, as Tilleczek (2012) did, through meetings, advisory-group roles for key people and the production of interim reports. The research team 'spent time following up with policy people to track implementations into the school system' (Tilleczek, 2012, p 255), thereby expanding the research process into a space more often conceptualised as impact.

Further reading

- Apple, M. (2013) Can education change society? New York: Routledge.
- Horkheimer, M. (1972) Critical theory: selected essays, New York: Seabury Press.

Actor-Network Theory

Actor-Network Theory (ANT), one of the most established approaches in the field of Science and Technology Studies, was originally developed in the 1980s by Michel Callon, Bruno Latour and John Law to understand scientific practices, innovation and technological change. In the decades since, an interdisciplinary collective of researchers has taken it to new research sites including the study of education policy. ANT could be placed under the label of poststructural research, but one crucial difference lies in its attention to the heterogeneity of actors contributing to phenomena and its symmetrical treatment of humans and non-human and material and semiotic elements. Despite the name, ANT is not a theory in the sense of explaining how the world is, but an ensemble of sensibilities that offers a 'toolkit for thinking about and charting the heterogeneous practices of association that make up the social' (Law and Singleton, 2014, p 380). ANT has thus challenged theory-centric approaches by emphasising social reality as an ongoing chain of practices to observe. Working through rich qualitative empirical cases, ANT seeks to generate knowledge about human and non-human agents without a priori defining their world-building capacities.

The hyphen in 'actor-network' problematises any distinction between agency and structure. All actors – individuals and large organisations – are network effects, that is, the effects of the relations that have provisionally constituted them (Law, 2004). The question then is: how is the network assembled, what makes the network and how is it sustained? For ANT, some ordering of the network will be strategic (intentional) but there will also be non-strategic orderings. However, the question of individual intentionality is of little interest to ANT; rather, it traces actions or practices that may result in certain intentions in a non-essentialist manner.

Power is a central term for ANT, but power is perceived as a relational accomplishment rather than a resource readily in one's possession. Instead of using power to explain certain outcomes, ANT asks how power is produced, what and whose labour makes power possible. Latour (1986) defines this as a translation model of power that assumes no inertia to account for the spread of an idea or a policy. Power is instead viewed as a consequence of collective action (Latour, 1986). This also means that power is a fragile accomplishment and that it could be otherwise. This is because power-making involves an intense and contingent relational activity of translation – another central concept for ANT – that signifies the enrolling, convincing and enlisting of actors (see entry on 'Translation'). Translations result in but are not the starting point of a situation in which certain entities exercise power over others (Callon, 1986). As Gorur et al (2019a) write, this not only captures ANT's view of power and politics but epitomises its politics of hope.

The resources required to constitute and make relations of power durable can be human and non-human. The term non-human may refer to a range of actors including animals, plants, environments or technologies. ANT emphasises that humans and non-humans are closely intertwined and therefore actors could often be examined as hybrids (Michael, 2017). The 'non-humans may participate as delegates of humans … [assisting] humans in gaining the ability to act at a distance. Non-humans are thus deeply implicated in technologies of governance' (Gorur, 2015c, p 90). ANT has been unjustifiably criticised for attributing agency to non-humans. To be clear, non-humans are not understood as possessing 'agency'; rather, their agency (as well as humans' agency) is considered a 'distributed effect of relations among other heterogeneous entities' (Baiocchi et al, 2013, p 327).

In education policy research, studies inspired by ANT have paid attention to the role of numerical indicators, theories and digital technologies in enabling or sometimes also undermining intended policy change. Interested in the making of scientific knowledge and scientific evidence, education scholars have followed the making of authoritative knowledge within and about education (Gorur, 2014). Working with the concept of performativity, Law (2004) stresses that social scientific methods are not merely describing but actually producing the realities they claim to describe. Subscribing to the notion of radical symmetry, some researchers have thus turned their attention to making explicit their own knowledge-making practices through autobiographical accounts of PhD research or experiences of peer review in education policy research. Here, knowledge-making is viewed as a process of enacting associations between heterogeneous elements, highlighting scientific practices as messy, and calling on (policy) researchers to be more open and analytical about what worlds their practices of research bring into being (Addey and Piattoeva, 2022).

Further reading

- Beech, J. and Artopoulos, A. (2021) Actor-network-theory and comparative and international education, in T.D. Jules, R. Shields and M.A.M. Thomas (eds) The Bloomsbury handbook of theory in comparative and international education, London: Bloomsbury, 429–446.
- Latour, B. (2005) Reassembling the social, Oxford: Oxford University Press.

Advocacy

Advocacy may refer to the actions of civil organisations engaged in mobilising specific forms of power over and against the state in order to balance the interests of different members of society. In concrete terms, policy advocacy work is studied from the perspective of established and emerging networks of intermediary organisations who 'increasingly play a policy-oriented function in urban contexts, including disseminating information and/or research to policymakers, or actual policy advocacy' (DeBray et al, 2020, p 64). Advocacy therefore captures the commitments of stakeholders, user groups and organisations working at different levels and scales (national and international) to give voice and representation to specific groups and priorities, in effect helping to steer policy reform towards particular ends. The resultant formations are what we might call policy advocacy groups, for instance, local parent advocacy groups, national social movements, trade unions and non-governmental organisations (NGOs).

Yet policy advocacy groups are not restricted to civil organisations, namely charity and not-for-profit organisations. The disparate interests and tactics that make up some policy advocacy groups point to a blurring and traversing of public, private and charity ambitions and agendas. Some policy advocacy groups operate at the intersection of a wide variety of interests that transcend or bring together the public and private, including intermediary actors like brokers, contractors, consultants, advisors and researchers. Hogan (2015) refers to these policy actors as intermediary organisations and actors or 'boundary spanners', namely people with 'high network capital' (p 307) capable of spanning and bridging the interests of the public and the private.

Similarly, Lubienski (2018) demonstrates the role of intermediary organisations and networks as actors engaged in the work of 'convening' and 'agenda-setting' (p 161) on behalf of policy makers. This includes joining up and 'connecting research producers with users, often by way of selecting, interpreting, packaging and promoting particular research' (p 160). Through research on the role of national and global connections and networks sustaining the global education industry, Rönnberg (2017) makes a similar set of observations concerning the ways in which key policy advocacy workers 'engage in the global buying and selling of both policy and related educational goods and services' (p 235), which include 'pitching and branding' strategies that work to situate the brand image and moral authority of certain key large for-profit education providers within the 'wider frame of egalitarianism and equality' (p 244).

This has led to a burgeoning interest in the role of policy advocates in diminishing or enhancing democratic processes, those that 'disable or disenfranchise or circumvent some of the established policy actors and agencies' (Ball, 2008, p 748). Rather than view policy advocacy groups in the traditional sense as civil organisations, they can be viewed as strategic alliances and supplements to the political power of the state and/or the for-profit agenda of private corporations and philanthropic groups that undermine 'civic capacity' (DeBray et al, 2020, p 64) including locally driven politics and citizen engagement or community building. Carvajal (2022), for example, documented the influence of NGOs on policy spaces in Chile aimed at building consensus around matters that 'served to legitimate government interests and adapt the Chilean market-oriented education system into a more tolerable form' (p 738).

In education, policy advocacy groups have taken on a variety of forms owing to the growth of 'corporatisation' and 'exogenous privatisation' in these sectors, from charter management organisations, think tanks and research institutes to media outlets, school reform organisations or what Rönnberg (2017) calls 'edu-preneurs' and 'edu-businesses' (p 244). Piazza (2019), for example, observes the growth and influence of particular kinds of policy advocacy networks and groups in the US, namely education upstarts and Education Reform Advocacy Organisations who do the discursive-political work of the state by promoting reforms that help to incentivise the kinds of school transformation that enable 'a neoliberal model for public education' (p 307). Amiel et al (2022) have made a similar set of observations through their study of two international organisations – the European Union and the Organisation for Economic Co-operation and Development – in which they show how 'entrepreneurship education' (referring to the promotion of learning organised around the development of the 'soft skills' based on improved self-control, resilience, communication and teamwork) emerges from a form of policy advocacy directed at shaping higher education reform in national education policy-making spaces.

Further reading

- Olmedo, A. (2013) Policymakers, market advocates and edu-businesses: new and renewed players in the Spanish education policy arena, Journal of Education Policy, 28(1): 55–76.
- Winton, S. (2018) Challenging fundraising, challenging inequity: contextual constraints on advocacy groups' policy influence, Critical Studies in Education, 59(1): 54–73.

Affect

The recent 'affective turn' in political studies has pointed towards the political weight of affects. Ahmed (2004a, 2004b) invites us to bypass questions about what affects are and instead to ask what they do, that is, how they are used, circulated, differentiated and stabilised, and how they attach individuals to communities and spaces. This view also challenges the way affects and emotions are territorialised as residing 'inside' the individual, as standalone entities amenable to introspection and expression (Ahmed, 2004a). They also form an 'economy' (Ahmed, 2004b, p 119) in which they may be mobilised for political and economic purposes. Literature focused on the affective dimensions of education policy remains sparse (Pitton and McKenzie, 2022). Emerging research delves into the questions of how policy is done, how actors are moved by policies' affective dimensions and how affective responses move, translate or impede reforms and policy. Attention to atmospheres, emotions, (gut) feelings, attunement and moods, for example, questions some ontological premises of policy research, such as rationality, cognitivism or individualism.

Staunæs (2018) argues that 'ugly' feelings, such as envy, are in fact central and moreover infrastructural to forms of neoliberal government; that is to say, they interconnect policies and reforms, measurement technologies and visualisations of performance with classroom practices and bodies of individual students. For instance, shame is formed, sustained and circulated through education standards, and naming-and-shaming is indispensable to standardisation (Brøgger and Staunæs, 2016). Naming refers to the way a scorecard system produces a plane of comparison which makes it possible to compare achievements across countries through colour coding (from dark green = excellent performance, to red = little progress has been made). The colour coding as a mechanism of shaming incites 'low achievers' to implement given standards to be relieved of the disgraceful tag. In this way, affective resonances function as 'vectors of control' (Sellar, 2015b).

Analytics of affect spans different levels from affective conditions of contemporary life to affective dimensions of individual encounters. Understood in this way, studying affect challenges education policy research methodologically: first, how to study something as fleeting and embodied as an affect; and second, how to demarcate the context of one's study. Pitton and McKenzie (2022), for example, theorise affect 'as an object-target for apparatuses of power, as bodily capacities emerging from encounters that are not reducible to apparatuses of power, and as collective conditions which structure and influence, as well as flow from, those encounters and apparatuses' (p 529).

Affect thus forms an important relay between programmes and strategies of government and autonomous individuals: 'to govern through how someone is sensing oneself and to manipulate how they relate to this sensing. Not in a predictable, controlled way, but by affecting in a dynamic, agenda-setting manner' (Brøgger and Staunæs, 2016, p 230). Equally, Staunæs (2018) evokes the concept of environmentality (after Brian Massumi) to argue that the physical milieu might be understood to be strategically shaped to vitalise and govern through intensities rather than identities. These examples show how affect contributes to sticking subjects, standards and infrastructures together, forming a collective, the members of which enjoy a degree of autonomy. Jobér's (2022) research on industrial fairs for teachers shows exactly how policy actors work on those whom they seek to govern, not through traditional types of persuasion involving political agendas, evidence or resources, but by engaging and enhancing affective atmospheres and the emotional states of public events.

While these studies point to the critical role of affect in the unfolding of policies, other researchers examine affective reactions as forms of precognitive critique emerging in the field. Staunæs (2018) offers a productive concept of affective and affirmative critique, characterised 'as an effect of the trans-corporeal entanglement' (p 419). This form of critique is neither a prerogative of the researcher nor research subject but is immanent in the researched field, pointing to important analytical strategies that hold out the potential of challenging the prevailing order of things.

Further reading

- Stage, C. (ed) (2015) Affective methodologies: developing cultural research strategies for the study of affect, London: Palgrave.
- Zembylas, M. (2022) Theorizing 'affective infrastructure' in education policy: articulating new political imaginaries for a more equitable future, Journal of Education Policy. DOI: 10.1080/02680939.2022.2157048

Alignment

Policy alignment connotes coherence between policy rationales and visions, content, goals, technologies and actors in and across systems of education. Both governments and intergovernmental organisations, such as the Organisation for Economic Co-operation and Development (OECD), depict alignment as a desirable objective that fosters efficiency, equity and overall improvement through harmonisation. Savage and O'Connor (2019) discuss how the policy alignment agenda in research has both normative and critical strands. The former is embedded in technical rationality and promotes policy alignment alongside standards-based reforms, data interoperability and intergovernmental coordination. Research may focus on evaluating existing alignments to identify successes and failures and propose solutions, for example. Such research has many commonalities with the policy agendas promoted by the OECD that sees it as a 'fix' for policy fragmentation and diversity in intergovernmental decision-making that are commonly described as problems. Here alignment is treated not only positively but also as a merely technical challenge without potential risks such as decontextualisation or high costs.

The critical strand looks at alignment from two intertwined perspectives. First, it focuses on its normative agenda, namely the explicit and implicit assumptions and goals behind policy alignment, and what considerations and solutions it foregrounds or leaves out. Second, it interrogates the actual practices and results of alignment, that is, which actors or policies are linked together and how. These may include 'alignment of processes and procedures, alignment between policy instruments and mixes, and alignment concerning the form and content of policies' (Savage and O'Connor, 2019, p 816). Alignment thus involves both technical elements, such as assessment and curriculum, and social elements such as individual and collective actors working cooperatively.

Savage and O'Connor (2019) examine the policies of alignment in federal countries and Australia in particular. Alignment reforms are not unique to the federal states yet they are interesting cases for education policy research because principles of alignment are contradictory to the underpinning rationales and the design of federal systems. In Australia, alignment was fostered by the establishment of new agencies to coordinate national reform initiatives through cooperation, curriculum, testing, data interoperability, and incentives through funding and professional standards for teachers designed to bring together state systems that were previously disconnected and autonomous. However, evidence points to gaps between the desirable (as imagined by federal policy) and the actual (as experienced by state policy actors). Contradictory to their stated design, these policy initiatives created new tensions or fuelled old ones concerning the roles and responsibilities of different actors, accountability and power in decision-making.

Phelps et al (2011) further demonstrate the centrality of common performance indicators and data collection systems as tools of alignment in another federal context, the US. During a period of economic recession, the targeted federal investment for education services increased, yet this funding distribution was accompanied by performance indicators that state and local recipients of federal funds were required to report on. This included state governments being charged with developing state-wide education data systems to collect highly individualised data on student performance. The aggregation and representation of said data functioned not only to create possibilities for improved relays or alignment between federal and state policy making, but enabled continuous monitoring and surveillance systems that federal government could use to legitimate decisions about allocation of state funding.

Phelps et al's study therefore demonstrates how federal demands for improved data collection and monitoring systems at the state level can be interpreted as political exercises in securing improved federal–state alignment. Phelps et al's (2011) evaluative study of the implementation of individual learning plans across state governments is also a good example of the normative implications attached to these kinds of policy alignment agendas. Moreover, their conclusions suggest that federal–state alignment typically suffers from misalignment resulting from competition between federal and state leaders to demonstrate capacity for problem solving or strong histories of local control over education.

Further reading

- Coburn, C.E., Hill, H.C. and Spillane, J.P. (2016) Alignment and accountability in policy design and implementation, Educational Researcher, 45(4): 243–251.
- Thomas, M.A.M. and Xu, R.-H. (2022) The emergence and policy (mis) alignment of Teach for Taiwan, Journal of Education Policy, 38(4): 686–709.

Anthropology

Despite its long-established interest in societies under colonial administration, anthropology lacked any focused attention on issues of policy making and policy worlds. Anthropology's traditional focus on marginalised communities would later be supplemented and enriched through a focus on explaining the role of policy professionals and elite organisations as distinct cultures inhabiting and reflecting historically unique policy worlds. Anthropologists would later define policies as socio-cultural practices (Hamann and Rosen, 2011) that create relations, meanings, subjectivities and spaces, and in this way, shape the worlds that people inhabit. A central concern for anthropologists of policy is to critique policy studies that viewed policy as linear, rational and neutral. The rise of globalisation and neoliberalisation has further intensified this turn among anthropologists and their expanded focus on the interconnections between local, national and global processes and the changing role of the state (Blasco and Vargas, 2011).

Policy lacks a concise definition owing to the complex and contradictory ways it is defined and mobilised across geopolitical landscapes and histories. When understood as an anthropological phenomenon, policies can be studied as cultural texts, classificatory devices and narratives that condemn or justify a present or imagined future, and therefore serve as rhetorical devices (see entry on 'Rhetorical analysis') and discursive formations in the construction of reality. On this account, policies may serve as modalities for the articulation of values, norms and principles in a given society. Anthropological studies of policy share a similar concern with using policy as a framing for tracing the configuration of dominant taken-for-granted principles governing a given society (Shore and Wright, 1997). Anthropologists typically focus on arguments and evaluations (or repertoires and tropes) that underpin policy making and therefore are critical of scholarly approaches and 'vernacular' explanations of policy as scientifically driven or simply common-sensical. From an anthropological perspective, policy is considered an effect of and a means to exercise power and orchestrate political effects that might include the exclusion of particular worldviews and policy options, the delegitimisation of opposition or the creation of categories and ideal types that normalise certain types of behaviour. In terms of the policy process, anthropology closely observes the constellations of actors, events and power structures that shape and guide policy decisions and their implementation. In other words, policy anthropology is the study of processes and relations that animate the production and implementation of policy, bearing in mind that the distinction between policy and practice, or origin and implementation, is artificial and analytical rather than empirical. Here, policy is not understood to follow an abstract model but is situated in historically and culturally contingent contexts that can be studied through an anthropological sensitivity to time and place. These concerns with context extend to empirical understandings of the construction of the local and to the sense-making activities that shape individual interpretations and experiences. This includes a deep phenomenological concern for lived experienced as a method and unit of analysis.

Anthropological studies have been carried out by researchers spending long periods of time with the researched subjects, which includes conducting participant observations as primary methods of data collection. However, interest in policy raises questions about the meaning and boundedness of field(work), previously understood in anthropological literature to connote an enclosed setting, usually a small, non-western society or Indigenous culture. More recently, interest in the way that policy 'moves', 'travels' and unfolds across and within different time-space constructs has led to anthropological experiments in multi-sited studies that decouple geographical and analytical categories (Hamann and Rosen, 2011). These anthropological studies of policy typically incorporate 'emic' and 'etic' perspectives that make critical reflexivity both possible and desirable and which disrupt traditional distinctions of the insider–outsider to unsettle any presumption of the boundedness of the research sites or the possibility of complete detachment and 'objectivity' on the part of the researcher. Anthropology's distinctive commitment to *holism*, for example, means that phenomena are always examined as a productive property of context. For instance, anthropological studies of policy not only follow the views and experiences of various social actors but also examine the socially circulating discourses that act to constrain and envelop the context-creating activities of social actors. Blasco and Vargas (2011) further suggest that the holistic perspective should also account for the economic, political and cultural forces that shape the state and its policies in relation to local contexts, actors and institutions.

Different from many other approaches to policy, anthropology's distinguishing feature is that the analyst is not external to the phenomenon but is situated as an embedded subject rather than a detached observer. On this understanding, the 'me' of the analyst is crucial to anthropological studies of policy since it shapes what gets observed, what gets left out and how observations are interpreted and reported (Hamann and Rosen, 2011).

Further reading

- Okongwu, A.F. and Mencher, J.P. (2000) The anthropology of public policy: shifting terrains, Annual Review of Anthropology, 29: 107–124.
- Wedel, J.R., Shore, C., Feldman, G. and Lathrop, S. (2005) Toward an anthropology of public policy, The Annals of the American Academy of Political and Social Science, 600(1): 30–51.

Archaeology

Despite its widespread application as a methodology, the archaeological method outlined by Foucault (1972) does not describe a prescriptive toolbox for research. In fact, the archaeological method used in education, namely policy archaeology (Gale, 2001), takes its inspiration from anti-foundationalist and anti-metaphysical traditions centred on investigations (or excavations) of the contingent regularities and relations that make possible the organisation of ideas over time and space. This includes a focus on the field of intelligibility (or episteme) through which ideas and thought systems are giving meaning and representation; in other words, 'the constitutive grid of conditions, assumptions, forces which make the emergence of a social problem, and its strands and traces, possible' (Scheurich, 1994, p 300). Here Foucault (1991) describes the archaeological method as historical investigations of the various elements that make up the conditions of possibility for the emergence of ideas and thought systems, namely the statement, discourses and the archive.

Understood from a broadly Saussurian sensibility, Foucault (1972) argues that the statement, which refers to 'atoms' or 'elementary forms of discourse' (p 80), acquires its authority (moral, ethical or otherwise) through its relationship to other statements, through their 'coexistence, their succession, their mutual functioning, their reciprocal determination and their independent or correlative transformation' (p 29). Discourse, on the other hand, shapes the complicated and uneven distribution of certain statements. In effect, discourse can be understood to define the discursive boundaries that make possible the ways in which some statements acquire certain authority in some contexts and not in others. In other words, the inclusion and exclusion of certain statements in different contexts can be read as a function of discourse, of the 'conditions of possibility or impossibility' (Bourke and Lidstone, 2015, p 835) that precede the production and circulation of meaning.

Hence, Foucault (1972) invites us to consider the omissions and silences (see entry on 'Silence') that typically accompany some statements and the interplay of rules and regulations that precede and limit their effects (and non-effects): 'as well as seeing discourse as constituted by statements that cohere, it is also important to analyse those excluded and the complex mechanisms that allowed this to happen' (Bourke and Lidstone, 2015, p 835). At the same time, despite the structuralist orientation of the archaeological method, Foucault (1972) challenges the idea that statements are only expressions of the homogenising effects of a singular or dominant discourse. Instead, Foucault (1972) investigates the historical transformation of ideas as expressions of contests over meaning, as the succession or interruption of ideas over time marked by breaks and ruptures in the specific rules governing the elevation or subjugation of certain knowledges.

On this account, Foucault encourages us to observe the ways in which different interests conflict, collide and converge to produce contested and contradictory discourses. And lastly, Foucault (1972) uses his archaeological method to locate the function and modification of statements within a 'general system' or 'archive' (p 131) that specifies 'the rules that have allowed what can be said (or not said)' (Bourke and Lidstone, 2015, p 838). In this way, 'archaeology describes discourses as practices specified in the element of the archive' (Foucault, 1972, p 131).

The archaeological method is evident through a range of education policy studies. Bourke and Lidstone (2015) use the archaeological method to understand the development of professional standards for teachers in Australia as meanings that are contingently resolved through historically and culturally produced events and objects that limit 'what is said and what can be seen in a set of social arrangements', with the outcome being a 'set of prescribed professional standards' (p 849). Policy archaeology, according to DeBeer (2015), is therefore a useful methodology for understanding how different forms of intervention enable certain events, objects and ideas to be 'nameable and describable' (Foucault, 1972, p 41) as 'problems' requiring interventions, remediation and solutions – or what Scheurich (1994) calls the 'social construction of problems' (p 297). In this vein, DeBeer (2015) utilises the archaeological method to trace the emergence of education policy in Ontario between 1965 and 1978 to show the multiple, contradictory discourses at work in the construction of meanings of disability. Similarly, Vakirtzi and Bayliss (2013) trace the role of medicalisation and psychiatric models of childhood more generally to show the discursive conditioning and emergence of 'the autistic subject' (p 5). More recently, Grimaldi and Ball (2021) have used the archaeological method to address how graphical user interfaces function as 'epistemic surfaces' or fields of events for the spatial and temporal governing of digital interaction between learners and education providers, with a unique focus on the different kinds of 'educational freedoms and form of autonomy' (p 116) made possible by these digital and virtual interactions.

Further reading

- Walton, G. (2010) The problem trap: implications of policy archaeology methodology for anti-bullying policies, Journal of Education Policy, 25(2): 135–150.
- Wiebe, C., Nguyen, A.-K. and Mattheis, A. (2021) Visualizing technocratic power: a cyber-archaeological analysis of the US National Education Technology Plan, Discourse: Studies in the Cultural Politics of Education, 42(2): 282–294.

Artefact

Artefacts are central to any research methodology since they guide how researchers produce and interpret 'data' through their investigations of the social and material world. According to Plowright (2011), there are four main characteristics of artefacts:

1. Informational artefacts which enable the researcher to record and store information.
2. Presentational artefacts, typically denotative in character, which act as medium for the presentation and communication of information to others.
3. Representational artefacts, typically connotative in character, which function to contextualise information for the purpose of capturing the experiential or historically and culturally contingent character of that information.
4. Interpretational artefacts, which move beyond denotative and connotative meaning to enable the researcher to frame information through a particular set of interpretative frameworks and related thick descriptions that capture the 'interpretation or translation of that experience' (p 95).

Understood from a Foucauldian perspective, artefacts can be considered discursive and material forms of communication or 'carriers of discourse' (Maguire et al, 2011, p 598), as modalities for the production, delineation and circulation of meaning. Souto-Otero and Beneito-Montagut (2016) make a similar observation in their study of the impact of datafication on education where they conceptualise digital artefacts as representational and communicative devices for 'the collection, cleaning, classification, display and retrieval of education-related data' (p 15). According to Hepworth (2014), visual communication artefacts, such as advertisements, logos, computer and smartphone operating systems, photographs, and websites, provide a cognitive and visual mapping or grid by which we may navigate the world and make sense of it. Moreover, they signify 'governing properties because they are inherently communicative, and communication is inextricably bound together with power, knowledge and governance' (Hepworth, 2014, p 281). In this sense, artefacts are inextricably linked to power since they function to 'persuade, argue and absorb ideological biases' (Hepworth, 2014, p 281). Similarly, Wilkins (2012) shows how school-choice practices are mediated through a visual field of choice made possible by specific artefacts, namely school brochures and websites that function as meaning-making devices in the symbolic and material work of indexing and differentiating schools in a local field of choice.

In their study of the role of multinational corporations and small- to medium-sized entities in the provision of health and physical education to public schools, Enright et al (2020) demonstrate how claims to and embodiments of expertise are held together both discursively and materially through the circulation and promotion of 'artefacts and resources' (p 206), such as digital platforms and various facilities and equipment that work to uphold the 'performance of expert activity' (p 208). Here, then, Enright et al (2020) adopts the concept of artefact to show how expertise is discursively reproduced by different kinds of devices, resources and institutional arrangements that are generative of wider networks of power and influence. Similarly, Shiroma (2014) adopts a policy network analysis of various technical artefacts (blogs, websites, online courses, videos and other media) to show how a specific regional network in Brazil, the Partnership for Educational Revitalization in the Americas, strategically influences public opinion and education policy decisions through building consensus between various participating organisations and actors both local and national.

According to Lambert et al (2020), artefacts also create spaces for subjects to engage in active processes of interpretation and revision, thereby multiplying the spaces and practices through which the human and the non-human world come together through mutually constitutive forms of interaction and meaning making. Through their study of web-based curriculum content, including guidance materials, textbooks, programmes of work and lesson plans, Lambert et al (2020) show the performance capacity and effects of artefacts as 'complex, ongoing processes of text production, negotiation, selective appropriation and re-representation' (p 260). This perspective can be characterised by the emergence of new materialist scholarship that calls for 'matter itself is to be conceived as active, forceful and plural rather than passive, inactive and unitary' (Lemke, 2015, p 4).

In their study of policy enactments in schools, Maguire et al (2011) also draw attention to 'the discursive artefacts and activities that make up, reflect, and "carry" within them the key policy discourses that are currently in circulation in English schools' (p 597), with a specific focus on school handbooks, school websites, posters and school diaries as artefacts for the representation and translation of discourse. However, Maguire et al (2011) remind us that artefacts do not carry any decontextualised (fixed) meaning which can always be read and understood in the same way by everyone, thus moving away from any claims to matter as representational or naturalistic. As Maguire et al (2011) argue, 'the sense viewers make of them depends upon cultural assumptions, personal knowledge, and the context in which the picture is presented' (p 608). Similarly, Souto-Otero and Beneito-Montagut (2016), in their study of the datafication of education, avoid claims to 'technological determinism, whereby technology determines changes in social relations. Instead, we see the use of technology as socially constructed: human action shapes technology' (p 15). Implicit to these perspectives is an emphasis on the polysemic nature of visual and technical artefacts, namely the idea that artefacts are culturally and historically embedded and need to be analysed within the broader social context in which they are produced, circulated and consumed (Pink, 2005).

Further reading

- Lambert, K., Alfrey L., O'Connor, J. and Penney, D. (2021) Artefacts and influence in curriculum policy enactment: processes, products and policy work in curriculum reform, European Physical Education Review, 27(2): 258–277.
- Pieters, J. (2004) Designing artefacts for inquiry and collaboration when the learner takes the lead, European Educational Research Journal, 3(1): 77–100.

Assemblage

Assemblage is an anti-structural concept that stresses emergence, heterogeneity and decentredness as essential to the formation of things (Marcus and Saka, 2006). Li (2007) defines assemblage as a 'gathering of heterogeneous elements consistently drawn together as an identifiable terrain of action and debate' (p 266). These heterogeneous components span 'humans, materials, technologies, organisations, techniques, procedures, norms, and events, all of which have the capacity for agency within and beyond the assemblage' (Baker and McGuirk, 2017, p 428). In addition to mapping the various elements that compose different assemblages, researchers typically ask how they are arranged, with a view that similar elements can generate different effects depending on the nature of the arrangement. In education policy research, assemblage thinking has been used to understand how assemblages steer individuals and groups in particular directions to achieve specific ends. Here, the analytic of assemblage is used to trouble the idea of policies and governance as external, totalising forces, and instead view them as a combination of diverse elements that (e)merge in local situations and are therefore always on the move. The analytic of assemblage therefore has been essential to addressing some of the limitations attached to concepts of policy transfer, policy borrowing and policy diffusion (see entries on 'Transfer', 'Borrowing' and 'Diffusion'), acting as a necessary corrective to rational-technical, institutionalist and state-centric accounts of policy and governance (Savage, 2020). Here, the objective is not to merely describe the productive elements and relations that form different assemblages, but to trace their performative effects and what they may (not) accomplish.

Assemblage thinking has its roots in philosophy and poststructural theory, indebted in the main to the philosophical writings of Gilles Deleuze and Félix Guattari, complexity theory introduced by Manuel DeLanda, and Bruno Latour's works on Actor-Network Theory (see entry on 'Actor-Network Theory'). Given this complex philosophical history, research that adapts the notion of assemblage tends to vary depending on its philosophical and theoretical anchoring, and whether assemblage is used ontologically, conceptually or methodologically. The commonalities between assemblage thinking in Deleuze and Guattari and Actor-Network Theory include a relational view of the world with an emphasis on entanglement between the social and the material and a topological perspective of space seen here as a product of (intense) relations between entities rather than an objective description of distance or proximity (Müller and Schurr, 2016). Yet there is also value in seeing these diverging approaches as different and complementary with a potential for cross-fertilisation. For instance, Actor-Network Theory embedded approaches can learn much from the productive forces of affect and desire so central to Deleuze and Guattari and their adoption of assemblage as fluid, elusive and producing unexpected effects and potentialities. Actor-Network Theory, on the other hand, perceives assemblage as identifiable socio-material networks, and offers many rich concepts to examine empirically how relations form and stabilise in practice (Müller and Schurr, 2016).

Savage (2020) usefully traces the development and application of assemblage thinking in education policy mobilities research, which is linked to the generation of new understandings of how policies move and combine in particular spaces and times in the context of transnational flows. Moreover, assemblage thinking has been used to develop knowledge of how policies de- and re-assemble, thus capturing the ambiguity and politics of policy making and how policies are subject to continuous disruption and change. For education policy researchers, assemblage thinking has been essential to showing how elements of policy configurations, technologies and rationalities are made to cohere in order to establish vital relays between the political goals of governments and the formal autonomous actions of subjects. Lunde and Ottesen (2021), for example, undertake a visual network analysis of education policy documents to examine how governments seek to promote educational digitalisation in Ireland and Norway. By purposefully positioning performance data as a central actor in the assemblage, governments in these contexts seek to enhance the use of digital technologies among school leaders and teachers. At the same time, assemblage thinking has helped to disentangle the role of governance and governing in daily life. Paananen and Grieshaber (2022) conducted ethnographies of early childhood education institutions to analyse the (unintended) consequences of policy. Here, they show how relations form between organic, non-organic, social and methodic strata to enable the governance of children and teachers. These configurations vary depending on who, what and why (in relation to each other) different elements are brought together (or held apart) in the assemblage. Paananen and Grieshaber (2022) also argue that the socio-material density of the assemblage matters: dense assemblages produce more interruptions in engagements with children specifically and create diminished opportunities for pedagogical expertise to take precedence compared to less dense assemblages where there is more space for the teacher to reconcile competing agendas.

Further reading

- Thompson, G., Sellar, S. and Buchanan, I. (2022) 1996: the OECD policy-making assemblage, Journal of Education Policy, 37(5): 685–704.
- Youdell, D. (2015) Assemblage theory and education policy sociology, in K.N. Gulson, E.B. Petersen and M. Clarke (eds) Education policy and contemporary theory, London: Routledge, 110–121.

Attraction

Policy attraction (Brent Edwards, 2013), as well as cross-national attraction (Ochs and Phillips, 2002; Davis et al, 2020), has been defined by the scholar most associated with its development, David Phillips, as the first of four proposed stages in policy borrowing (Phillips and Ochs, 2003). The other stages in policy borrowing being decision, implementation and internalisation/indigenisation (Phillips and Ochs, 2003). The elucidation of policy attraction came in response to a perceived explanatory deficiency of the term 'policy borrowing' (see entry on 'Borrowing'). As Phillips (2006) notes, 'there are very few cases indeed where the direct borrowing of policy by one country from another can be demonstrated through actual implementation' (p 556). Attraction, in this perspective, is initiated always by the reforming policy actor and may be located in any or all of Ochs and Phillips' (2002) six foci of educational policy, which they later conceptualised as '"externalising potential" in the target country' (Phillips and Ochs, 2003, p 453). These are:

1. policy philosophy;
2. policy goals;
3. strategies for policy implementation;
4. enabling structures;
5. educational processes; and
6. educational techniques (Phillips and Ochs, 2003, p 453).

Phillips (2000) argues that the impulse for attraction may derive from:

1. [s]erious scientific/academic investigation of the situation in a foreign environment;
2. [p]opular conceptions of the superiority of other approaches to educational questions;
3. [p]olitically motivated endeavours to seek reform of provision by identifying clear contrasts with the situation elsewhere; and/or
4. [d]istortion (exaggeration) ... of evidence from abroad to highlight perceived deficiencies at home. (p 299)

This conceptual framework has been used in a range of studies exploring cross-national (or policy) attraction. These include Davis et al's (2020) research that focused on the media discourse concerning Programme for International Student Assessment (PISA) in four countries: Australia, Finland, Japan and South Korea. The aim of this investigation was to illuminate these countries' 'context of attraction' (p 309). Chung et al (2012), also drawing on this framework, problematises the implementation of the master's in teaching and learning qualification, in which England borrowed unsuccessfully a similar policy from Finland.

However, the policy attraction model has generated critique for failing to encompass the diverse possibilities involved in policy formulation insofar as this formulation is influenced by national and international actors. For instance, Brent Edwards (2013) incorporates policy attraction into a four-part model called 'international processes of education policy formation (IPEPF)' (p 22). This model results from Brent Edwards' (2013) review of the literature, and so each of its four parts derives from elsewhere. Specifically, following policy attraction, Brent Edwards (2013) draws on the work of Archer (1984) and Spreen (2004) to add first policy negotiation. This in turn is comprised of three phases: external transactions, in which national groups critical of current arrangements use external actors to negotiate with the state, and in which policy makers derive legitimacy for their reforms from invocations of global education discourses. The second phase in policy negotiation is political manipulation, in which 'groups that are in the process of gaining political power are able to conceive and push through policies that generally have not been produced by "local policy experts"' (Spreen, 2004, p 108). The third phase in policy negotiation is internal initiative, in which local accountability prompts policy makers to recontextualise their proposed policies so that it is better adapted to the target site. Brent Edwards (2013) identifies key differences between policy attraction and negotiation, including the way in which the latter takes into account a range of actors and also involves a higher degree of contestation.

Brent Edwards' (2013) third element of IPEPF, following policy attraction and negotiation, is policy imposition, which functions globally to enact through neocolonial power relations the structures and practices of the Global North onto developing countries, thereby reproducing these relations. The final element of IPEPF is policy hybridisation, which, in drawing upon postmodernism, refutes the global/national binary in units of government as well as the notion of a 'linear and hierarchical relationship between knowledge and power in IPEPF that reflects countries' positions in the world system' (Brent Edwards, 2013, p 32). Policy hybridisation therefore 'problematises the other IPEPF perspectives by questioning assumptions regarding locus of viability, structure and influence. That is, it emphasises the (potential) diversification of structures, the modification of relationships among actors, and the unpredictability of IPEPF that stems from the intersection of multiple, multidirectional, and, perhaps, untraceable forces' (Brent Edwards, 2013, p 32).

Further reading

- Phillips, D. (2004) Toward a theory of policy attraction in education, in G. Steiner-Khamsi (ed) The global politics of educational borrowing and lending, New York: Teachers College Press, 54–68.
- Spreen, C.A. (2004) The vanishing origins of outcomes-based education, in D. Phillips and K. Ochs (eds) Educational policy borrowing: historical perspectives, Oxford: Symposium, 221–236.

Automation

The Merriam-Webster Dictionary provides three definitions of automation:

1. a technique of making an apparatus, a process or a system operating automatically, that is, involuntarily or aided by a machine;
2. the state of being operated automatically; and
3. an automatically controlled operation of an apparatus, process or system by mechanical or electronic devices that takes the place of human labour.

These forms of automation are intrinsic and vital to the kinds of digital technologies that increasingly pervade contemporary education systems and operations. However, due to the novelty of the subject, exact definitions and empirical observations of automation in education at the time of writing are scarce. Critical research on educational digitalisation discusses automation as a risky development, necessitating multiple lines of inquiry. Critical approaches underline the agentic nature of automation and remind us that technologies can be produced in alternative forms. Critical scholars of digital education urge us to think about what the prefix of 'edu' in educational automation should mean and how it could guide actualisations of automation instead of being determined by it.

Examples of educational automation include surveillance and monitoring systems (for example, facial recognition), decision-support technologies (for example, systems for automating grading and group-formation), personalised learning, and complexes of 'smart schools' operating through sensors and measures that modulate everyday activities. Automation therefore is both implicit (for example, in the inner operations of digital technologies or institutional automations that most staff are typically not aware of) and explicit and detectable, such as the aforementioned facial recognition which functions more or less invisibly. The shifting nature of automation's (in)visibility is therefore a central concern for critical scholars of digital education (see entry on 'Digital education').

The history of automation can be traced to the industrial revolution and the replacement of manual work by machines. Automation does not make human labour obsolete, however; rather, it produces new types of work to be carried out by humans. Examples include data labelling for artificial intelligence and teachers and students acting in machine-readable ways to fit with standardised forms of perception and measurement. Automation thus reconfigures teachers' work by generating new tasks that effectively alter the mundane performances of pedagogy. For instance, teachers are incited to coordinate, moderate and facilitate student engagement through the provision of digital educational platforms (Perrotta et al, 2021). Procurement and outsourcing to automated systems and platforms run by multinational (ed)tech corporations also bring new actors to the planning and implementation of educational processes and environments. Increasingly, education researchers are turning their attention to the consequences of automation for changing professional sensitivities and modes of judgement in the field of education.

Education researchers are also interested in the implications of automated systems for thinking about responsibility and accountability. These issues have been addressed under the rubric of data fairness and justice since automated systems rely on the production and analysis of digital data traces that reproduce and amplify deep-rooted societal inequities such as racism, ableism and sexism (Sahlgren, 2023). This has raised questions about how responsibility and accountability ought to be redistributed between teachers, managers and producers of automated technologies in automated decision-making and learning.

Automated systems claim to ease social interaction and reduce the burden of mundane tasks to make time for meaningful human relationships. Yet the logic of automation, which claims to reduce frictions, may lead to fewer interactions with other people (Selwyn et al, 2023). It is therefore crucial to consider the impact of these emergent operational logics on pedagogy and learning as relational processes and spaces that are traditionally oriented to the task of socialisation and living with others. These issues also link to concerns with how automation might recast the subject. Automation actively constructs subjects as self-identical and predictable as well as locates subjects within relations of individualised interaction with personalised technology (Selwyn et al, 2023). Predictive technologies are designed to anticipate action and intervene in advance to prevent unwanted events, for example. In this manner, automated systems close down possibilities as they locate students on an expected trajectory rather than an open path. The risk here is that ubiquitous automation would render the subject obsolete since subjects' knowledge of themselves would be made subordinate to or even replaced by how they are 'known' by the machines.

Selwyn et al (2023) therefore argue that researchers must interrogate presumptions and promises of educational automations as technologies sold to educators and administrators with strong promises of progress, convenience and improvement across pedagogical and administrative domains. Beyond effects on pedagogy or management of education, automation also changes relations and forms of governance exercised in, on and through education. These deep-seated changes to education practice have subsequently brought certain normative-ethical claims and assumptions into focus as points of debate and contestation, namely which tasks ought to be automated and which should we delegate to machines.

Further reading

- Hayes, A. and Cheng, J. (2020) Datafication of epistemic equality: advancing understandings of teaching excellence beyond benchmarked performativity, Teaching in Higher Education, 25(4): 493–509.
- Selwyn, N., Hillman, T., Bergviken-Rensfeldt, A. and Perrotta, C. (2023) Making sense of the digital automation of education, Postdigital Science and Education, 5: 1–14.

B

Borrowing

The term borrowing has for a long time been a central focus of research in the field of comparative and international education. Due to this disciplinary anchoring, the topic of borrowing has typically been studied in a cross-border manner with a focus on how countries and their governments borrow from the tried-and-tested policy arrangements of other countries. There are two strands of borrowing research worth mentioning here. There is, on the one hand, the normative and applied strand of borrowing research that focuses on studying evidence of 'best practice' and the effective transfer and implementation of those practices to other contexts perceived to be in need of reform or improvement. Steiner-Khamsi (2014) argues that the goal of applied research is to provide solutions to identified problems, namely the optimal class size or the optimal frequency for prescribing student tests that enhance the quality of education. On the other hand, there is the analytical strand of borrowing research that situates borrowing as a phenomenon in-and-of-itself worthy of critical attention. Here the focus shifts towards studies that concern how and why borrowing occurs within and across particular spaces and times (Steiner-Khamsi, 2014). The focus of this entry concerns the latter strand of borrowing research.

Different generations of borrowing researchers have focused on distinct topics, from early research that investigated the choice of reference societies in national policy reforms, to more recent studies that analyse, among other things, harmonisation processes facilitated by international organisations such as the European Union. In these studies, the term borrowing is typically accompanied by another term, namely lending, used here to refer to the policy influencer rather than its opposite, the policy recipient. Such binary distinctions may be considered too simplistic to capture the complex realities of borrowing, however, including the actions of those who facilitate or impede such processes. Educational borrowing can also be used to denote a specific mechanism of deliberate and often linear education (policy) transfer (Perry and Tor, 2008) (see entry on 'Transfer'). Additional terms can be used to represent or stand in for such processes, including the terms reception and translation (Steiner-Khamsi, 2014). The term translation is used to capture the political, economic and cultural reasons that might explain the appeal of imported reform packages and policy or ideas from the perspective of the recipient governments. The term translation signifies something qualitatively different, namely the local adaptation, modification or reframing of that which is imported (see entry on 'Translation').

Borrowing references either specific policies in identifiable countries or empty signifiers such as globalisation and 'international standards' in moments of domestic political contestation (Steiner-Khamsi, 2014). Borrowing therefore offers potential solutions to protracted policy conflict among advocacy groups where it performs a catalysing, mediating or certifying role in domestic policy battles. This observation marks an important distinction between discursive or symbolic and factual borrowing, that is, borrowing occurring on the level of policy talk versus actual borrowing of identifiable policies and practices for domestic implementation. As domestic contexts play a pivotal role in the act of borrowing, all borrowing should be considered necessarily selective, according to Steiner-Khamsi (2014). In developing country contexts, the economic aspects of borrowing appear central as a requirement of borrowing is the take-up of loans and grants from development agencies, making borrowing coercive rather than voluntary in some cases. Related to these observations, Takayama and Apple (2008) remind us of the participation of policy borrowing in western cultural imperialism. Another economic dimension to consider is the intensification of trade in and export of educational products and services, which induces voluntary alignment with international standards.

The translation side of borrowing is another important aspect of this literature as it focuses on local meaning making and implementation of borrowed policies. In contrast to neo-institutional accounts of borrowing that emphasise global diffusion, reception and translation studies shift attention towards variation, in effect undermining claims that policy borrowing occurs through equal and homogenising diffusion (see entry on 'Diffusion'). Instead, reception and translation studies show how similar things will mean and look different upon translation. In the same vein, studies working within a Luhmanian theoretical framework focus on the impact of borrowing on existing structures, policies and practices through the provision of concepts of replacement, hybridisation and reinforcement in order to better theorise the temporary outcomes of internalisation (Steiner-Khamsi, 2014).

While the previously mentioned research has a focus on explicit borrowing, that is, cases where there is an explicit reference to the sources of influence (actors, networks, projects, organisations) that make up travelling reform packages, Waldow (2009) introduces the concept of silent borrowing to highlight those instances where there is non-explicit reference or non-acknowledgement of those sources. This is an important observation since borrowing is largely a process of policy legitimation. Any explicit reference to sources of influence deemed by the recipient government/people to be 'undesirable' would in effect delegitimise and endanger the proposed changes, as was the case for educational reforms in Sweden (Waldow, 2009). Furthermore, Waldow (2009) observes a parallel between the silence of policy makers about the sources of their proposed reforms and the similar lack of acknowledgement of foreign influences by academic researchers examining these changes through the lens of endogenous factors.

Further reading

- Clapham, A. and Vickers, R. (2018) Neither a borrower nor a lender be: exploring 'teaching for mastery' policy borrowing, Oxford Review of Education, 44(6): 787–805.

- Steiner-Khamsi, G. and Waldow, F. (eds) (2012) World yearbook of education: policy borrowing and lending in education, London: Routledge.

Bricolage

Developed by the French anthropologist Claude Levi-Strauss, the term bricolage is used to capture the active process through which actors assemble seemingly incompatible elements, or traverse, straddle and combine seemingly incommensurable domains and sites, in order to bring about new forms of innovation in thinking and practice. More generally, bricolage describes the ways in which previously uncoupled or divided elements are gathered together to form a new provisional unity or composite that exceeds previous forms and formations. Bricolage is thus useful to tracing the emergence and multiplicity of things, objects, networks and relations as the unique products of complicated alignments, accommodations and co-existences. Bricolage has therefore been used in a variety of ways across multiple disciplines to name, describe and signify different kinds of conceptual and practical work, from 'epistemological bricolage' (Freeman, 2007, p 490) to 'policy bricolage' (Wilder and Howlett, 2014, p 183) and 'institutional bricolage' (Carstensen, 2015, p 156).

According to Carstensen (2015), bricolage is particularly useful for making sense of how value systems and institutional logics come to be recomposed and restabilised in new contexts, and therefore requires that the analyst (or bricoleur) is directed towards 'interpretive openness' (p 413) in their study of the emergence and multiplicity shaping different phenomena. Carstensen (2015) uses the historical example of the economic crisis of 2007–2010 to demonstrate the usefulness of bricolage as a methodological tool for explaining the conditions of possibility that give rise to changes during and following these tumultuous periods. In contrast to conventional 'synchronic', 'institutionalist' or 'structuralist' accounts of social change, in which change might be theorised as a 'lack of enforcement on part of rule makers and strategic non-compliance by rule takers' (Carstensen, 2015, p 156), bricolage is helpful for understanding social change as the unique product of creative processes of redeployment and recontextualisation among policy actors, namely 'efforts to reinterpret what an institution can mean under changed circumstances and which novel institutional elements can potentially be added to the institutional mix to respond to crisis' (p 140).

Freeman (2007) adapts the concept of bricolage to describe how learning takes place among public health policy makers and practitioners working in Scotland and the US. Here, Freeman (2007) observes the process of traversal and assembly through which policy makers and practitioners work within and across different epistemological terrains, each with their own traditions and forms of reasoning, to adapt meaning to accommodate new potentialities and projects. These epistemological terrains span the 'rational, scientific', the 'managerial' and the 'social and political' and therefore do not automatically map onto each other as complementary knowledges, but rather conflict, collide and sometimes converge to reveal unique forms of 'epistemological bricolage' (Freeman, 2007, p 490).

Wilder and Howlett (2014) produce a similar set of arguments regarding how policy making is sometimes resolved contingently through an appeal to different kinds of motivations and interests: 'policy proposals are not bound by dominant, interlocking and coherent sets of ideas, but are rather the products of ideational "bricolage" in which policymakers cobble together paradigms in a disjointed process of ideational construction' (p 189). Similarly, Gulson (2007) makes use of the concept of bricolage to challenge conventional binary thinking that reproduces overgeneralised assumptions about the macro and micro as separate and isolated entities or sets of self-contained relations. More specifically, Gulson (2007) adopts the Foucauldian concept of 'neoliberal spatial technologies' as a 'conceptual and descriptive bricolage' (p 180) to show how macro trends are reinscribed and reproduced through micro relations, thus revealing the mutually constitutive formation of these seemingly disconnected elements.

Through a study of national quality assurance systems in higher education in Taiwan, Hsieh (2016, p 885) observes the significance of 'policy entrepreneurs' to rearticulating local traditions as part of wider national and global education reforms, thus enabling new quality-assurance policies and arrangements to take place through the 'mechanism of bricolage'. Maroy et al (2017) make a similar set of observations through their comparative study of changing accountability systems in France and Quebec. Hence, they acknowledge the diverse ways education policy making and reform succeed through a continuous process of bricolage, of decontextualising ideas from their original sources and recontextualising them in new contexts, namely 'the translation of ideas, narratives, instruments and approaches discussed or introduced elsewhere, and which lead to redefinitions or re-articulations in light of rules, values, conventions and practices which have already been institutionalised' (Maroy et al, 2017, p 104). The concept of bricolage therefore is useful in challenging ideal-rational models of policy making and related concepts of 'policy transfer' and 'policy borrowing' which give the impression of policy moving uniformly across geopolitical spaces subject to the right rational incentives and settings. Stone (2017), for example, demonstrates the haphazard, uneven development of policy owing to the 'messy interpretative processes' (p 55) or bricolage through which policy problems and their solutions are recomposed in the context of localisation which concerns 'the local adaption, indigenisation and modification of policy into new formats' (p 56).

Further reading

- Barzanò, G. and Grimaldi, E. (2013) Discourses of merit: the hot potato of teacher evaluation in Italy, Journal of Education Policy, 28(6): 767–791.
- Collier, S.J. and Ong, A. (2005) Global assemblages, anthropological problems, in S.J. Collier and A. Ong (eds) Global assemblages: technology, politics, and ethics as anthropological problems, Malden, MA: Blackwell, 3–21.

Broker

There are two principal interpretations of brokering in the education policy literature. In the first, knowledge is brokered as part of knowledge-mobilisation processes for use in policy and other domains. This knowledge is mostly produced through research. In the second interpretation, policy positions themselves are brokered for deployment leading to advantage or mutually satisfactory compromise within a political arena. There are considerable overlaps between the literature on policy brokers and those on policy entrepreneurs and on policy intermediaries (see entries on 'Entrepreneur' and 'Intermediary').

Exemplifying the first position, Cooper (2014) positions brokering as an integral feature of knowledge mobilisation or 'intentional efforts to increase the use of research evidence … in policy and practice at multiple levels of the education sector' (p 29). Cooper (2014) focuses on what are called 'research brokering organisations' (RBOs), that is, 'third party intermediaries whose active role connecting research producers and users is a catalyst for knowledge mobilisation' (p 30). Cooper (2014) investigated 44 RBOs, including university research centres, think tanks and advocacy groups, and identified eight brokering functions within the sample. These brokering functions are described as:

1. linkage and partnerships;
2. increasing awareness;
3. increasing accessibility to research;
4. influencing policy;
5. increasing engagement with research;
6. organisational development;
7. implementation support; and
8. capacity building in researching institutions and groups.

Cooper (2014) also identified six brokering strategies used to achieve these aims: first, research products including reports and policy briefs; second, capacity-building strategies including toolkits and online tutorials; third, non-research strategies including strategic plans and advocacy; fourth, events strategies including conferences and awards ceremonies; fifth, network strategies including e-bulletins and social media; and sixth, media strategies including press releases and blogs. Despite the identification of advocacy as a key strategy, and influencing policy as a key function, Cooper (2014) follows Honig (2004) in not engaging in a discussion of brokers' positioning within power structures and relations and how brokers may enact agency that will limit that of others and marginalise non-advocated positions. Brokering in both accounts is constructed as being free of (self-)interest and uncontentious, a matter largely of facilitation and mediation. Nonetheless, this fundamental approach has generated scholarship through wider adoption (Cooper and Shewchuk, 2015).

Exemplifying the second interpretation, Ingold and Varone (2012) locate brokering within 'a political subsystem composed of participants who regularly seek to influence policy within that subsystem' (p 319). Ingold and Varone (2012) define a subsystem as being 'composed of advocacy coalitions whose members can include legislators, agencies, and interest groups, as well as researchers and journalists; these all coordinate with one another based on shared beliefs' (p 319). Brokers play an important role in seeking stability in the subsystem and mediating between actors with differing positions to achieve compromise. Where the focus is on such subsystems, the 'advocacy coalition framework' (ACF) is most often used to investigate policy change within them. The ACF was developed by Sabatier (1988) to explain change processes within a named policy subsystem, focusing particularly on the role of policy beliefs and policy brokers. Sabatier (1988) considered the latter as uniquely able to produce or influence change within relatively stable system parameters, and so the ACF enables a consideration of the interplay between this stable context along with the changeable external events and the equally changeable constraints and resources of subsystem actors. Subsequent contributions have focused on refining, adapting or building upon the ACF model, for example, in showing empirically how brokers in a subsystem promote learning that leads to change (Howlett et al, 2017). Contributions have also focused on using the ACF to explain new instantiations of policy change or new arenas where it is happening. For instance, Ingold (2011) adapted the ACF to illuminate and deconstruct the role of brokers in a case of legislative stalemate between two coalition camps in Switzerland. A detailed study of the range of applications of the ACF has been undertaken by Weible et al (2009).

Potential areas of instability warranting brokers' intervention are characterised by Howlett et al (2017) as threefold: competing definitions of the policy problem; competing views of appropriate instruments to address these problems; and competing politics regarding policy components. There is debate in the literature about whether such interventions arise from brokers' beliefs or interests (Ingold and Varone, 2012). It seems that studies focusing on policy actors' interests (for example, Mintrom and Norman, 2009) are as likely to see these as policy entrepreneurs as brokers.

Further reading

- Grek, S., Lawn, M., Lingard, B., Ozga, J., Rinne, R., Segerholm, C. and Simola, H. (2009) National policy brokering and the construction of the European Education Space in England, Sweden, Finland and Scotland, Comparative Education, 45(1): 5–21.
- Hodge, E., Childs, J. and Au, W. (2020) Power, brokers, and agendas: new directions for the use of social network analysis in education policy, Education Policy Analysis Archives, 28(117).

C

Community

The concept of community in education may refer to a wide range of formal and informal arrangements or collective movements, from classrooms, parent forums and management groups to professional, discursive and epistemic groupings that embody multiple histories and contexts. These collectives may be grounded in culture, policy making, science, nation-states or economic systems. In addition to communities being thought of as entities spanning scales from the local to the global, they may also be empirically studied as arrangements that are subject to multiple national and transnational influences. Increasingly, researchers have turned their attention to critical questions about which communities are acknowledged and made visible in research and which ones remain invisible or even marginalised. This includes a related focus on which communities influence agenda-setting and policy and how. The critique of human-centrism (anthropocentrism) in education research, for example, demonstrates how non-human communities affect and are affected by policy.

One of the most popular definitions of community can be traced to the seminal work of Anderson (1991) and his historical investigations of the emergence of nationalism and nation-states. Anderson (1991) describes the nation as an imagined horizontal comradeship irrespective of inequality and exploitation experienced by its members. Here, Anderson (1991) examines the different historical processes (including education) that create the conditions of possibility for these imagined communities to take shape. The nation as a community can be considered anonymous in the sense that its members will never meet all other members. Yet, according to Anderson (1991), these members imagine the nation as something confined to a finite space known as the sovereign state. This notion of 'imagined communities' has emerged within empirical studies beyond any singular interest in nationalism, following Anderson's (1991) claim that communities can be 'distinguished, not by their falsity/genuineness, but by the style in which they are imagined' (p 7) and that many communities will be defined by imagination because they are temporally and spatially unfixed. Stables (2003), for example, characterises the school as an imagined discursive community, one that is mobilised by students and teachers but also by those who are not directly connected to it, such as politicians. The imaginary quality of the school means that it cannot be described through pre-specified observable variables. For Stables (2003), this observation has important implications for policy: only those directly belonging to the school are best placed to discern its complex dynamic, albeit tendentially and partially through the provision of contingent historical relations and practices.

Interest in communities is rooted in the realisation that non-state actors shape policy processes and outcomes, and that the state is not the only actor guiding policy making and the construction of policy worlds. Another important implication of this thinking is that communities are increasingly transnational, operating at the intersection of domestic and international spheres. Peter Haas (1992) therefore mobilises the term 'epistemic community' to connote 'a network of professionals with recognised expertise and competence in a particular domain and an authoritative claim to policy-relevant knowledge within that domain or issue-area' (p 3). Epistemic communities therefore are not limited to scientists or researchers but consist of professionals from a variety of sectors, networks and organisations with varying epistemological commitments and priorities. These actors share certain normative and causal beliefs as well as notions of validity, for example. Examining the Organisation for Economic Co-operation and Development (OECD) through the lens of epistemic community and culture, Kallo (2021) analyses how the OECD as an organisation compensates for the limitations of its formal mandate and reliance on discretion in the absence of legislative capacity. To achieve this compensatory work, the OECD secretariat has extended its discretionary authority by constructing influential networks that reach beyond the secretariat to span national administrations and research institutes; a practice directed towards achieving legitimacy of claims through establishing cross-epistemic community consensus.

The human-centricity in community thinking has been recently questioned in Silova's (2021) work in comparative and international education, however. Silova (2021) points to research on education policy transfer that is premised on a binary assumption of global and local and where, typically, the global is defined through narrow definitions of communities as intergovernmental organisations or transnational civil society networks. Working from a decolonial and more-than-human perspective, Silova (2021) observes what is 'empirically missing' from these accounts, namely women, Indigenous knowledge systems, non-humans, and many 'others' whose knowledge suffers omission or active marginalisation within official narratives of global community.

Further reading

- Dunlop, A.C. (2017) The irony of epistemic learning: epistemic communities, policy learning and the case of Europe's hormones saga, Policy and Society, 36(2): 215–232.
- Millei, Z. and Imre, R.J. (2010) Rethinking transition through ideas of 'community' in Hungarian kindergarten curriculum, in I. Silova (ed) Post-socialism is not dead: (re)reading the global in comparative education, Bingley: Emerald, 125–154.

Consultant

Policy consultants have been defined as 'non-state, private-sector, profit-driven actors that are nevertheless involved in the policy process through (usually) contractual arrangements with state agencies' (Prince, 2012, p 195). In education policy, Gunter and Mills (2017) call them 'knowledge vendors, who seek to make gains within the economy (and hence socially, politically and culturally) through … "knowledge utilisation"' (p 65). Gunter and Mills (2017) identify three major groupings of consultants. The first is corporate consultants, namely those who are employed by often large-scale corporations such as Pearson. This form of consultant originated with the rise of scientific management in the US before becoming established in the UK through American-established firms in the 1920s. Corporate consulting 'started to establish itself as a multi-billion [dollar] industry when the large international accounting firms began to move into consulting' (Saint-Martin, 1998, p 328). The second category of consultant identified by Gunter and Mills (2017) comprises researcher consultants such as James Tooley and Michael Fullan, referring to those employed in universities and 'who build and use their reputations to develop [consultancy] activities and reputations' (p 34). The most successful of said consultants may achieve the status of guru, according to Eacott (2017). Finally, Gunter and Mills (2017) identify professional consultants, who are typically teachers 'who relocate their practice from salaried employment in a school and/or local public administration services into private business' (p 47).

The arguably increasing use of consultants reflects the shift from the autarkic to the service state whose function concerns commissioning rather than providing services (Howlett and Migone, 2013). The increased use of consultants reflects also growing contractualism as a basis for relationships involving the state and as a mechanism for operationalising them. Concerns therefore have been raised where service states become consultocracies and where consultants take important policy decisions or contribute to the way in which policy problems are framed and understood or decisions taken (Gabriel and Paulus, 2015). However, in a consultocracy, they do so outside of normal democratic processes and with limited accountability. In this capacity, consultants may thereby influence education policy in ways that reproduce corporate and managerialist agendas (Gunter and Mills, 2017).

Policy knowledge produced through consultancy has been in demand internationally, albeit unevenly, owing to New Right governments' need for private-sector management knowledge in order to operationalise, first, New Public Management in public-services provision (Saint-Martin, 1998), and second, privatisation (Gunter and Mills, 2017). In addition to these policy drivers, there are also structural motivations for states to use consultancy-produced knowledge: the hollowing-out of the state, which contributed to what detractors term its responsive deficiencies in the face of a 'new, fast-paced world' (Prince, 2012, p 190), has further enabled consultants' access to and influence upon political agendas. This influence is mutual: policy consultancies 'are specific organisational forms that are shaped by the conditions of their emergence' (Prince, 2012, p 196). The relationship within which consultants and the state are enmeshed is therefore better conceptualised as a network than as dyadic. This means that consultants are simultaneously part of the reason for, as much as the answer to, any present tumult in political landscapes internationally.

Consultants' functions in the policy arena are multiple. For Prince (2012), this function is to construct networks in which consultants are positioned as legitimately knowledgeable – largely through their location in economic and above all capitalist knowledge regimes (Gunter and Mills, 2017). Through these networks, consultants are to make sense of a chaotic world by inviting and structuring contributions from policy stakeholders. This structuring is vital and may happen 'through connections and interfaces that shape the possible engagements … [or] through audit procedures which discipline a particular group' (Prince, 2012, p 198). Second, and recursively, they are expected to deploy their legitimated knowledge in ways that build and reinforce such networks. Other consultancy functions include 'supplying needed technical skills; symbolic impression management; legitimisation and change management' (Howlett and Migone, 2013, p 243).

Consultancy operates within a policy-science framing (see entry on 'Policy science'), which constructs knowledge 'as a neutral set of facts and procedures … to be implemented "into" or "onto" a situation and people, and then objectively monitored and measured' (Gunter and Mills, 2017, p 66). Educational arrangements, environments and practices are thereby constructed as functional problems to be solved. That which cannot be reduced to this conceptualisation is not addressed, including notably questions of power and how this is interplayed with education policy.

The consultancy model has been taken up more widely in education to structure the practices and identities of even public-sector education professionals, particularly those constructed as occupying leadership roles in England. Headteachers and principals deemed successful are eligible to be accredited as national leaders of education, for example, whose expertise is available for purchase on a consultancy basis to other schools. Whole-system professional learning is, in effect, reduced to exchange relationships. Consultants have therefore, in this case, contributed to the formation of education policy that is predicated on and reproduces consultancy.

Further reading

- Arnaboldi, M. (2013) Consultant-researchers in public-sector transformation: an evolving role, Financial Accountability and Management, 29(2): 140–160.
- Weller, P., Bakvis, H. and Rhodes, R.A. (1997) The hollow crown: countervailing trends in core executives, New York: St. Martin's Press.

Context

In education policy research, the notion of context is invoked to signify or capture those various conditions that overdetermine how policies or ideas are mobilised and recontextualised in certain environments. Through their investigations of policy enactments in secondary schools, Braun et al (2011) describe context both as 'a set of objective conditions' and 'subjective "interpretational" dynamics' (p 588), thus pointing to two distinct interpretations of context. Furthermore, Braun et al (2011) differentiate several useful conceptualisations of context: situated contexts, used to refer to locale, school histories, pupil intake and community settings; professional contexts, used to refer to value systems, teacher commitments/experiences and management organisation; material contexts, used to refer to staffing, costing, buildings, technology and infrastructure; and external contexts, used to refer to local authority support (or lack of), regulatory and funding arrangements and pressures and expectations flowing from school inspection and league table positioning. Research focused on explaining the peculiarities and nuances shaping policy enactment (see entry on 'Enactment') at the institutional level therefore make good use of these interrelated concepts of context to better understand the various structural and relational elements overdetermining policy formations. From this perspective, context is a complex, dynamic force (as well as useful analytic) that works to locate understandings of policy processes and choices within multiple levels of macro, meso and micro influences.

Gorur et al (2019b, p 301) criticise some traditional social science approaches for assuming, perhaps unreflexively, that 'context' resembles a static container that prescribes or circumscribes action. Moving beyond this overly deterministic view of context, Gorur et al (2019b) develop a relational understanding of context as emergent, contested and relationally produced. Adopting this approach to context, Gorur et al (2019b) examine how the Programme for International Student Assessment (PISA) as a standardised measurement of learning outcomes is enacted across multiple countries and their unique geopolitical contexts. The challenge for PISA, as Gorur et al (2019b) see it, is to create a universalising standard that, on the one hand, appears internationally comparable, that is, sufficiently standardised to claim uniformity or equivalency. On the other hand, PISA is designed to be locally relevant, that is, sensitive and responsive to varying contextual differences. This contradictory task of producing 'contextualisation' and 'standardisation' creates a dynamic characterised by simultaneous contextualisation of standards and standardisation of contexts.

The implication here is that context is transformed from a matter of fact (operating as a predetermined explanatory lens in comparative research) into a matter of concern (Sobe and Kowalczyk, 2018). Here, we can observe how school context against the background of PISA interventions are relationally (re)produced at the intersection of some strange alignments. Understood in this way, we should avoid interpretations of context as a neat, bounded container, one that is habitually and unproblematically equated to discursive constructions of the nation-state or culture. Instead, as Sobe and Kowalczyk (2018) show context is better understood as a messy, overdetermined assemblage composed of diverse actors, projects, networks of influence flowing horizontally (locally) and vertically (nationally and internationally). These topological explorations of context demonstrate how schools and school systems emerge as instantiations of spatio-temporal 'fixes' that are constituted relationally at the intersection of national and international flows of power (Hartong and Piattoeva, 2021). This argument does not imply that we should abandon the nation-state as an object of study, however. On the contrary, it is important to remain attentive to how formations of the nation-state (or 'national imaginaries') shape and are shaped by relations of power that are external to it, namely the supranational of school systems under PISA (Sobe and Kowalczyk, 2018).

Similarly, Piattoeva et al (2019) problematise those realist, essentialist understandings of context that undermine the contingency and emergence of the formation of things. To make sense of overdetermination that shapes constructions of context, Piattoeva et al (2019) insist on making practices of contextualisation the focus of empirical inquiry. 'Contexting', an approach inspired by Actor-Network Theory, is used here to show how social actors re-present 'reality' in order to produce spaces of imagination that echo and redeem their own interests and claims to power. Piattoeva et al (2019) argue that policy makers and researchers alike bring contexts into being through the provision of scattered discursive resources, for example. Similarly, we can observe those discrete forms of contextualisation that are performed by international organisations, individual policy makers and experts at different levels to make policies contextually resonant. In other words, translations of policies imply translations of contexts, and policies and contexts are constantly and endlessly inscribed and reinscribed through this process.

Researchers in the field of comparative and international education have made similar calls for improved understanding of practices of context, contexting, contextualisation and context sensitivity in research and policy practice. The urgency and timeliness of this call makes sense at the time of writing given the rise to prominence of standardised assessments across the globe and the central role of intergovernmental organisations, think tanks and supranational EdTech business proposing identical solutions to complex and contextually diverse educational challenges.

Further reading

- Bartlett, L. and Vavrus, F. (2019) Rethinking the concept of 'context' in comparative research, in R. Gorur, S. Sellar and G. Steiner-Khamsi (eds) Comparative methodology in the era of big data and global networks, New York: Routledge, 187–201.
- Singh, P., Thomas, S. and Harris, J. (2013) Recontextualising policy discourses: a Bernsteinian perspective on policy interpretation, translation, enactment, Journal of Education Policy, 28(4): 465–480.

Convergence

In traditional political science, the term convergence is defined as 'the tendency of societies to grow more alike, to develop similarities in structures, processes and performances' (Keer, 1983, p 3). This tendency is decided by the degree to which societies adopt a 'progressively more industrial infrastructure' (Bennett, 1991, p 216), and in turn, societies that adopt and emulate specific policy instruments and goals for coping with the complexity arising from such industrial infrastructure. Industrial infrastructure can be understood in a variety of ways, but here it is used to signify the unique development of political and economic systems under globalisation and the growth and adoption of various governing strategies by societies seeking to enhance their capacity to improve efficiency and strengthen accountability and transparency under these conditions. In education, for example, different national education systems, despite their geopolitical variance, make use of similar performance indicators and output controls to improve monitoring and quality improvement, namely corporate measures of accountability, comparative-competitive frameworks and standardised testing regimes.

These formations therefore point to evidence of a global convergence of education policy, one that is arguably sustained and incentivised by the involvement of 'transnational policy communities' (Bennett, 1991, p 215) who aim to locate schools and school systems within wider systems of 'commensurability, equivalence and comparative performance' (Lingard et al, 2013, p 542). On this account, when studied through the lens of globalisation, convergence signifies an important analytic shift away from methodological statism and nationalism as units and methods of analysis, namely 'limiting one's analysis to state policies and politics within the state and assuming a fixed linkage between government and territory in a single nation' (Simon et al, 2009, p 38). Rutkowski (2007), for example, shows how intergovernmental organisations, such the World Bank, the Organisation for Economic Co-operation and Development and the United Nations Educational, Scientific and Cultural Organization, affect national education policy making through a combination of 'soft laws' (p 233), 'loans, aids and grants' (p 234), 'policy knowledge' (p 238) and 'experts' (p 240).

On the other hand, describing this as evidence of the homogenising effects of global policy influence, or 'global isomorphism' (Takayama, 2012, p 505), can lead some to assume something about the structural coherence and determination of policy enactments (see entry on 'Enactment'), namely that a static relationship exists between policy and practice in which global policy processes fit seamlessly with practices of self-governance within subnational and national policy contexts. Indeed, some education policy researchers remain circumspect of concepts like policy convergence and policy emulation to the extent that they risk producing reified and homogeneous accounts of global policy influence that omit something important about the sensitising contexts through which policies emerge, are contested and remade. The related concept of institutional isomorphism, which studies the degree of 'homogenisation' across different institutional environments as evidence of coercive, mimetic and normative or 'isomorphic change' (Hauptman Komotar, 2022, p 648), is similarly criticised for neglecting local environments and the 'diverse modes of their operation at different levels of analysis' (p 649).

Through a comparative study of the national standardisation of curriculum across the US and Germany, Hartong (2015) demonstrates the disproportionate influence of 'market mechanisms and external influence' led by 'industrials or philanthrocapitalists' on the implementation of national standards in the US, compared to Germany 'where the regime is much more internally controlled by educational professionals (teachers and state administrators)' (p 26). In a similar vein, Takayama (2012) compares the development of national testing regimes in Australia and Japan to show globally circulating policy discourses are translated at the national level in ways that are 'simultaneously similar and different' (p 505) owing to their unique path dependencies.

So while some global policy formations point to evidence of convergence, the disparate motives and interests shaping their emergence may highlight something more nuanced and profound, namely that policy is the continuous management of tensions and contradictions between global and national forces. Related to this, argue Lingard and Rawolle (2011), is the degree to which a nation-state can mobilise sufficient 'national capital' to mediate the pressures of globalisation, such as 'democratic governance' (p 492), and effect different outcomes based on its own strategic and normative interests. As Wilkins et al (2024) outline in their comparative study of five countries, New Public Management (NPM) tends to hold and endure within different national policy spaces through the unique (non-)interaction of various actors, networks and projects. In other words, while NPM represents a global movement or strategy in applied public choice theory and neoclassical economics, there are various iterations of NPM across the globe which are the product of historically situated processes in which global drivers and logics are resolved and accommodated contingently within path dependencies and value systems specific to nation-states and their cultures.

Further reading

- Veiga, A., Magalhães, A. and Amaral, A. (2019) Disentangling policy convergence within the European Higher Education Area, European Educational Research Journal, 18(1): 3–18.
- Yang, R. (2010) International organizations, changing governance and China's policymaking in higher education: an analysis of the World Bank and the World Trade Organization, Asia Pacific Journal of Education, 30(4): 419–431.

Criticality

The terms criticality and critique are central to much policy research, particularly studies that position themselves as researching *about* policy rather than *for* policy

(Ozga, 2000). Critical policy scholarship and critical policy sociology (see Molla, 2021 and Savage et al, 2021 for overviews) reflect these kinds of epistemic commitments where the empirical focus may concern, for example, the role of elite ideologies and unequal power relations in the formation of policy. These kinds of empirical studies – what might be described as 'critical scholarship' – signal a shift away from scholarship focused on positivist conceptions of evidenced argumentation. As Molla (2021) argues, 'critiquing is not about mere objecting; it rather means problematising assumptions and beliefs underpinning the objective appearance of reality and subjective meaning systems associated with the external representation' (p 9).

Savage et al (2021) point out that the term 'criticality' and its derivatives – critical argumentation/reflection/thinking – are taken for granted, however. To maintain a critical orientation, argue Savage et al (2021), requires constant interrogation of the meanings attached to these forms of analytical work and, contrastingly, what might be considered 'non-critical' scholarship. This seems especially important at the time of writing with the rise and dominance of evaluation culture, market mechanisms and economic rationality as determinants of education processes, together with the use and abuse of critique more widely as a purely subjective stance that can be weaponised for many different purposes (think, for instance, of Trump's climate denialism) (Raffnsøe et al, 2022). This is what Masschelein (2004) terms the trivialisation of critique or the transformation of critique into modalities for the exercise of power. Critique can also be understood to be spatially and temporally organised and mobilised. Critical policy sociology emerged in the 1980s as a reaction to Thatcherism in the UK and Reaganism in the US, for example. The necessity for critique at this time/place was brought into sharp focus by the rise of new political settlements that sought to repurpose the role of the state in the macroeconomy as well as reimagine citizenry through neoliberal forms of governmentality (Savage et al, 2021).

To explain what is meant by criticality, we might consider what is to be gained by enacting critical research or becoming a critical researcher (Savage et al, 2021). Critical researchers typically pursue different kinds of normative commitments and outcomes when challenging dominant power structures. At the same time, despite these divergences in normativity or political alliance or opposition, they are united by their commitments to broader emancipatory goals that include fostering equalities and social justice. Engagement in these types of political-analytical work require both a nuanced understanding of the contingency and emergence of structures and processes together with a normative-practical appreciation for the formulation of viable/credible alternatives as sufficient means to undermine or displace them (Molla, 2021). On this account, while the majority of those working in higher education can be considered people who are committed to research, there are specific individuals who occupy a more activist position through doing research and who use research as opportunities to produce tangible change in policy and education. At the same time, regardless of whether someone self-identifies as an activist researcher, there are policy sociologists and sociologists of education who produce similar kinds of work, namely work that carefully disentangles the discursive formations that make possible certain imagined futures and therefore remind us of the possibilities of change. Bacchi's (2016) investigations of policy representation and problematisation is a key example of this kind of work as it demonstrates the ways in which policy problems and their solutions are framed by value systems that are historically contingent and therefore open to challenge and revision.

A key dilemma for those thinking with/in criticality is the question of whether critique can claim to stand outside of that which it criticises. In other words, to what extent is critique already implicated in the structures and discourses that form the object of its critique? What are the implications of this for knowledge production? A requirement of engaging with and performing criticality therefore is an exercise in continuous, moving self-reflection. Scholars can be understood to enact politics through the formulation of research questions (with their tacit assumptions), the active selection of theories as interpretative lenses for sense making and the differentiation and valuing of subject matters that count or can be discounted. The claim that it is possible to exercise critique from a supposedly neutral, detached vantage point is therefore deeply problematic for critical scholars.

In envisioning the future of critique, Raffnsøe et al (2022) distinguish between negative and affirmative critique, while warning that these labels are not meant to pass judgement, claim preference for one over the other or present the two as binary and mutually incompatible. Raffnsøe et al (2022) view 'negative critique' as one way in which scholars exercise critique through examining 'assumptions in order to prove which ones are false' (p 194). Negative critique, in this sense, seeks to function within a sufficient distance from that which is critiqued. This form of critique can be traced to early modernity and the emergence of the Enlightenment project, an intellectual movement that sought to disrupt the metaphysical language of religious authorities and dogma that dominated at the time. In contrast to negative critique, affirmative critique produces the conditions for imagining and intensifying the possibilities for what can or should be, at least from the normative perspective of the analyst, and therefore presents critique as something immanent to, rather than independent of, the object under critique. Rather than privilege detachment, dispassion and rational objectivity, affirmative critique emphasises 'the specificity of the response to the world' (Raffnsøe et al, 2022, p 207).

Further reading

- Editorial Team (2020) The fatigue of critique? On Education, Journal for Research and Debate, 3(9): 1–2
- Zembylas, M. (2022) Affirmative critique as a practice of responding to the impasse between post-truth and negative critique: pedagogical implications for schools, Critical Studies in Education, 63(2): 229–244.

Critical discourse analysis

Critical discourse analysis can be situated within a wide number of analytical traditions (interpretivism, social constructivism, poststructuralism and discursive theory, to name a few), all of which challenge the foundational ontology of positivism, namely the idea that statistical and experimental methods based on deductive logics and meta-analysis can be used to empirically test and verify causally determined social facts. Unlike the policy sciences that emerged in the 1950s (see Lerner and Lasswell, 1951), which relied mostly on deductive methods of reasoning for producing knowledge about society, critical discourse analysts reject the idea that observations and facts can be comfortably separated from interpretations and values, and instead seek to uncover the ways in which policy discourse works to actively construct and transform policy worlds through the provision of meaning.

Critical discourse analysis differs from many variants of poststructuralist discourse theory, namely dialogical analysis, rhetorical analysis, conversation analysis and narrative analysis, all of which are concerned with the study of language as discursive accomplishments and interactional achievements that carry or serve certain dialogic, anticipatory and ideological usages (Billig, 1996), be they practices of fact construction, methods of accounting for the self, or the management of stakes and interests. According to Fairclough (2013), critical discourse analysis differs from these approaches, with their exclusive focus on language or talk as the primary units of analysis for the study of meaning, since it favours a critical realist understanding of the relations between 'discursive and material elements of social life' (p 177), thus aligning it more closely with the argumentative turn or the discursive turn (see entry on 'Interpretive policy analysis'). This is fundamental to what Wodak and Meyer (2009) term the 'constitutive problem-oriented, interdisciplinary approach' (p 2) of critical discourse analysis, namely 'de-mystifying ideologies and power through the systematic and retroductable investigation of semiotic data (written, spoken or visual)' (p 3). Moreover, according to Fairclough (2013), critical discourse analysis is 'normative and explanatory critique' (p 178): rather than simply describe social reality, critical discourse analysis assesses it according to agreed-upon definitions of social justice or a just society, as well as seeks to explain social reality as effects of wider social structures and ideologies, with an explicit focus on 'discursive strategies for the maintenance of inequality' (Van Dijk, 1993, p 250).

In this same critical vein, Stankiewicz (2022) adopts critical discourse analysis to capture the discursive strategies of academic workers involved in the 'revolt of the humanities' (p 494) that took place in Poland in the years 2013–2015, pointing specifically to the liberatory potential of these grassroots movements for producing new forms of political identity and political opposition. Similarly, Taylor (2004) uses critical discourse analysis to 'further social democratic goals' (p 436) by revealing the marginal discourses and silences that frame discussions of equity in Australian education policy texts. Critical discourse analysis therefore includes a political-strategic focus on critiques of ideology and domination through using critical explanatory models to examine the specific (extra)semiotic and institutional fixes that achieve 'relative permanence and stability in orders of discourse' (Taylor, 2004, p 181). This means recognising the overdetermination of texts and subjects by socially circulating discourses, which in effect provide the conditions of possibility for their (non-)emergence and contestation. 'This is another way of saying that texts are instantiations of socially regulated discourses', according to Janks (1997), 'and that the processes of production and reception are socially constrained' (p 329).

At the same time, it is important to be circumspect of any argument which suggests there is a direct or determining relationship between subjects, structures and discourse in which subjects emerge only as bearers of governmentalities or global hegemonies. It is naive to assume that power is effortlessly reproduced at the level of discourse, for example, 'because control is imperfect and incomplete in the face of contradictory systems, contested positions and contentious subjects' (Clarke, 2004, p 3). Therefore, we always need to insist on the instability and unpredictability of its appropriation and reproduction. While many proponents of critical discourse analysis are likely to share this view, there is a strong bias among some to conduct studies of ' "top-down" relations of dominance [rather than] "bottom-up" relations of resistance, compliance and acceptance' (Van Dijk, 1993, p 250). This is evident through Berkovich and Benoliel (2020), who adopt critical discourse analysis to make explicit how the Organisation for Economic Co-operation and Development (OECD) deploys certain 'discursive maneuvers' (p 501) through its texts on teacher quality to achieve some normative control of the discursive boundaries shaping different understandings and representations of desirable and undesirable teaching. According to Berkovich and Benoliel (2020), the OECD achieves this normative reworking of teaching quality through constructing the teaching profession as a 'problem' in several ways. Moreover, the activity of problematising teacher quality in this way serves to strengthen the influence of the OECD as expert provider of solutions for the remedial work of correcting these identified problems.

Further reading

- Fairclough, N. (1995) Critical discourse analysis, London: Longman.
- Lim, L. (2014) Ideology, rationality and reproduction in education: a critical discourse analysis, Discourse: Studies in the Cultural Politics of Education, 35(1): 61–76.

Critical race theory

Critical race theory is both a suite of theoretical claims and a social movement, in effect providing a form of anchoring for centring the ways in which race serves as a meta-organiser of privilege and oppression. Critical race theory originated in the US as a development of Critical Legal Studies with its theoretical founders being mostly legal scholars who saw the law as a primary yet under-explored mechanism for maintaining White hegemony. Concerning the foundational assumptions of critical race theory, Zamudio et al (2011) identify five. First, race matters. Race is a first-order social structure that organises all elements of the social world to oppress people of colour and minimise their contributions to society. These elements range from beliefs, identities and relationships through to institutions and policies. Racialism often operates invisibly because it is endemic and vast, or in ways that are refracted through class, gender and other structures. Second, history matters. Contemporary manifestations of racial inequality build upon others that have come before to normalise them. This belies the fluidity and contestability of race. Third, voice matters. Racialism can be countered through supplying alternative narratives to the dominant ones that centre White hegemony. This means that it is important to foreground minority perspectives that offer tools to critique and deconstruct race as a power structure. Fourth, interpretation matters. Critical race theory is normatively and purposefully interdisciplinary so that the movement can benefit from diverse insights. And finally, praxis matters. Praxis is where critical theory informs actions that promote social justice. Critical race theory provides the critical theory that puts this into action, which explains why it is a movement as well as a lens for viewing the world.

Critical race theory identifies Whiteness as the core problem that prompts its work, and so places responsibility on White people and their institutions to enact change to eradicate racialisation, rather than on 'people of colour'. This has produced the sub-field of critical Whiteness studies, which operationalises this shift in focus. In education policy research, for instance, critical Whiteness studies has been used to examine the discursive construction of Whiteness in Norwegian policy documents concerning the notion of cultural diversity. In Fylkesnes' (2019) study, the purported aim of the documents to promote social justice is belied by their collective discursive positioning of Whiteness as superior, with student teachers discursively impelled to become 'political actors of assimilation' (p 405). This underscores an important assumption of critical race theory: the issue is not just explicit racism, serious as this is, but also the often-unconscious ways in which even superficially well-meaning White actors and institutions nonetheless persistently reproduce Whiteness as superior, owing to the normalisation and internalisation of racialised scripts and narratives. Critical race theory is clear that the consequences of such actions are still racist, and indeed, although sometimes unintentional, are still 'non-accidental' (Gillborn, 2008, p 6), constituting a 'conspiracy' through 'concert of action for a common purpose' (p 192) to maintain White supremacy.

In education, many such actions reproduce White supremacy. One important example is assessment, which according to Gillborn (2008), '[c]ritical race theorists have long identified ... as one of the key mechanisms by which current inequalities are reinforced and legitimised' (p 91). This is because 'the "assessment game" is rigged to such an extent that if Black children succeed as a group, despite the odds being stacked against them, it is likely that the rules will be changed to re-engineer failure' (Gillborn, 2008, p 91). This is achieved partly by setting (tracking in the US) whereby students are grouped with others on the basis of what teachers deem to be similar or equivalent abilities. However, as Gillborn (2008) points out, other factors are also considered, including attitude and behaviour, and these are particularly susceptible to racist interpretations. Black children are therefore more likely to be taught in lower sets where access to higher-tier versions of examinations in subjects like mathematics is impossible. Tiering is where different versions of examinations are produced, most often one version for higher- and one for lower-attaining students. This latter group cannot achieve a high grade if they sit a foundation-tier examination. The perception of Black children as axiomatically less intelligent is grounded in 'racist pseudo-science', according to Gillborn (2008, p 110), that constructs IQ testing falsely as a test of intellectual capacity and potential, rather than as a test of learned tactics, dispositions and skills. Specifically, IQ testing privileges those learning achievements most often acquired by White children. This exemplifies a tendency for racism to be refracted through seemingly objective and techno-rational processes and discourses, as in where racist opposition to a new Muslim school is concealed within and enabled by technical municipal planning procedures that foreground any other reason than racism for rejecting the school (Gulson and Webb, 2012). Critical race theorists aim to illuminate and counter such forms of unspoken and unacknowledged racism.

Further reading

- Gillborn, D., Rollock, N., Warmington, P. and Demack, S. (2016) Race, racism and education: inequality, resilience and reform in policy and practice, Birmingham: University of Birmingham.
- Troyna, B. (1987) Beyond multiculturalism: towards the enactment of anti-racist education in policy, provision and pedagogy, Oxford Review of Education, 13(3): 307–320.

Cultural political economy

Cultural political economy is an interdisciplinary approach to the study of relations between the economic and political in the context of the cultural turn. Here the cultural turn encompasses those analytical traditions that are concerned with the study of semiosis (or meaning making) and a concomitant orientation to 'argumentation, narrativity, rhetoric, hermeneutics, identity, mentalities, conceptual history, reflexivity, historicity, and discourse' (Jessop, 2010, p 337). Given the variety of cultural turns and definitions of political economy, there is no singular definition of cultural political economy shared by academics, albeit a number of important dominant strands can be observed through Jessop's

(2010) modelling of cultural political economy. Here, cultural political economy is concerned with, among other important foci, the 'movement from social construal to social construction and their implications for the production of hegemony' (Jessop, 2010, p 336). Social construal refers to how subjects assimilate meaning, a process called selective apperception, while social construction captures the enduring formations of these assimilations at the level of subjects and meso-level structurations, namely identities (or habitus) and institutional logics. In both cases, there is an emphasis on variation, selection and retention to take account of the contingency of social formations and structurations as unique products of disparate motives and interests specific to different sites and peoples.

Cultural political economy is also interested in existential questions of 'complexity reduction' (Jessop, 2010, p 336), namely the role and necessity of spontaneous habits of culture to how subjects comfortably navigate the vicissitudes and uncertainties of inherently unstable social worlds. On this account, cultural political economy also has a concern 'with the interdependence and co-evolution of the semiotic and extra-semiotic' (Jessop, 2010, p 336) and, more broadly, 'the dialectic of semiosis and structuration' (p 336). Cultural political economy therefore avoids neat binaries and tidy entry points (agency over structure, discursive over material) to examine 'the interdependence and co-evolution of these interrelated semiotic (cultural) and extra-semiotic (structural) moments in complexity reduction' (Jessop, 2010, p 339). This includes combining semiotic and extra-semiotic analysis to describe and explain how competing regional imaginaries and different kinds of region-building come to be selected and retained across different territories and scales. Verger et al (2017), for example, adopt cultural political economy to 'capture such multi-scalar and multi-factorial interplay in the worldwide privatisation of education', with a unique focus on how 'educational privatisation advances through polymorphic processes that are contingent to structurally and strategically selective contexts, as well as to locally inscribed political and institutional dynamics' (p 758).

In other words, cultural political economy sidesteps the theoretical trap of structuralism and social determinism which assigns too much agency and power to either actors or structures, and instead recognises the 'the co-evolution of semiosis and structuration' (Jessop, 2010, p 340), namely the fragility of macro-social configurations and micro-social relations as mutually constitutive features of enduring projects to cope with/reduce complexity. In education policy research, cultural political economy is applied in various ways, principally as an analytical tool for tracing the development (and non-development) of specific policy assemblages across different geopolitical contexts in the context of a deeper understanding of the three 'evolutionary mechanisms' proposed by Jessop (2010, p 336): variation, referring to the fluid development of discourses and practices owing to continually emerging crises and challenges; selection, referring to the active take up and prioritisation of some discourses over others; and retention, referring to the institutionalisation and integration of said discourses and practices into durable social constructions.

Camphuijsen et al (2021) adopt cultural political economy to make sense of the variation, selection and retention of test-based accountabilities in Norway through a focus on 'the contingencies, events and actors involved in policy change, and identification of mechanisms inducing or restraining institutional change' (p 626). Similarly, Higgins and Novelli (2020) use cultural political economy to examine the variation, selectivity and retention (Jessop, 2010) of global education reforms in conflict-affected societies, with a specific focus on the peacebuilding interventionism of UNICEF in Sierra Leone and their efforts to develop the 'Emerging Issues' (EI) curriculum for teachers (2007–2008). Higgins and Novelli (2020) observe the EI curriculum to be 'a product of various processes of selectivity' (p 17) which they link to strategies 'deployed to advance particular construals' (p 7), including the 'regulating and controlling [of] behaviours and creating subject positions' (p 7). Adopting the same variation-selectivity-retention analytic framework, Moschetti et al (2020) use cultural political economy to better understand historically and culturally the relatively underdeveloped role of educational private sector actors as influencers and mediators in public-policy debates about education reform in Uruguay, which they partly link to enduring, inherited institutional landscapes. As Moschetti et al (2020) explain, 'Uruguayan society and policymakers share an array of policy "imaginaries" around the idea of education that has proven and continue to prove very resistant to exogenous forces' (p 381). At the same time, Moschetti et al (2020) acknowledge that, despite Uruguay's 'historical resistance to the privatisation agenda' (p 387), there are continuing attempts among civil organisations, think tanks and other organisations – those characteristic of private sector interests – to articulate a crisis narrative which the authors characterise as typical of 'variation', 'linked to situations in which popular discontent gains momentum' (p 373).

Further reading

- Robertson, S.L. and Dale, R. (2014) Towards a 'critical cultural political economy' account of the globalising of education, Globalisation, Societies and Education, 13(1): 149–170.
- Skerritt, C. and Salokangas, M. (2020) Patterns and paths towards privatisation in Ireland, Journal of Educational Administration and History, 52(1): 84–99.

Cycle

The policy cycle is an idealised approach to policy research/implementation within the political and administrative sciences that has both analytical and normative dimensions. Analytically, it pursues an economic rationalistic understanding of policy by dividing the process into neat, divided, sequential stages of a cycle. Normatively, it communicates expectations of democratic policy making. The policy cycle is typically divided according to pre-defined nodes or units, namely agenda-setting, policy formulation, decision-making, implementation and evaluation (possibly leading to termination) (Jann and Wegrich, 2006) with the cyclical dimension connoting ordered progression and feedback loops between the different stages. The agenda-setting stage is defined by problem recognition and issue selection, which informs (even predetermines) the diverse possibilities for problem representation and the kinds of solutions deemed desirable. At this stage of the policy cycle, Bacchi's (2012) concept of problem representation is useful for explaining the discursive conditions that frame the identification and articulation of phenomena (objects, practices, processes, peoples) as 'problematic' and in need of correction, intervention or improved control. In doing so, it becomes possible to trace the contingent regulations and relations that shape problem and agenda-setting. Moreover, it opens up possibilities for refuting the so-called objective nature of such processes or processes secured through any firm appeal to scientific evidence or public concerns.

During the policy formulation and decision-making phase, the identified problems are transformed into government programmes that often include objectives and blueprints or programmes of action. In contrast to economic rationalistic models that emphasise policy decision-making as sites of consensus, rational calculation or scientific modelling, a problem representation approach (Bacchi, 2012) allows us to empirically study these sites as outcomes of political agitation, mutual adjustment and bargaining among differently positioned actors.

The implementation phase, namely the point at which policy is realised (or not) in practice, captures the non-linear, dynamic character of policy formation. In a typically top-down manner, policy implementation studies have focused on deviations of implementation. However, this approach – criticised for its normative assumptions and appeals to hierarchy, statism and linearity – has been challenged by bottom-up perspectives that seek to explain the activities and contexts of agents of policy implementation. Bottom-up approaches to policy implementation studies, in effect, have displaced state-centred perspectives of policy in favour of approaches that emphasise policy processes as contingent and ongoing accomplishments achieved through the interdependence and interaction of actors operating in specific contexts. In education policy research, this perspective is evident in Bowe et al's (1992) conceptualisation of policy as a continuous process of making and remaking initiated by school actors actively contributing to the creative articulation, mediation and translation of policy initiatives. At the same time, this perspective has been criticised for downplaying the role and authority of the state in policy implementation (Hatcher and Troyna, 1994).

The last phase of the policy cycle focuses on policy evaluation and termination as ideal phases that are not necessarily present in all policy processes. Policy evaluation connotes evaluation of policy outcomes and reworking of policy design according to appraisal. Evaluation may also take place during other policy phases, leading, for instance, to policy redesign during agenda-setting. Evaluation studies, for example, is a field of inquiry committed to the development of tools for testing policy options and their impact in controlled settings to enhance rational, evidence-based decision-making. However, these controlled settings are proxies or aggregates for the real world and therefore evaluation studies face criticism that, despite claims to objective science, their methods are composed of tacit (normative) assumptions regarding how policy implementation should work on the ground. Evaluation results can be affected by the position and interests of those actors made responsible for developing the evaluation tool or engaging with its results, for example. Furthermore, some studies demonstrate that the promise of policy design and implementation upon initial piloting and evaluation merely postpones or prolongs the execution of unwanted policies (Jann and Wegrich, 2006).

Despite its popularity within the political and administrative sciences, the policy cycle has been criticised for, among other things, its deep attachment to ideas of rationality, linearity and hierarchy, together with its dichotomising of politics and administration and failure to engage with the messy realities of policy phases, including the iterative ways in which policy phases overlap and interpenetrate one another. Owing to these overly rationalistic attempts to represent policy processes as the (linear) formation of distinct phases of action, the policy cycle can be accused of misrepresenting, worse obviating, the realities of policy making. This includes criticism that the policy cycle pays insufficient attention to the networked, translocal nature of policy making or the role and influence of social actors as policy interlocuters and brokers who work beyond national state boundaries (Minh Ngo et al, 2006). Despite these criticisms, it is important to bear in mind that researchers who deploy policy cycle in their investigations do so as a heuristic device rather than as a theoretical model for determining relations of causation. More recently, the policy cycle has shifted away from an exclusive focus on explaining the input of political systems on shaping policy design, and shifted instead towards a focus on the output of policy design in terms of documenting its unintended consequences and how it affects particular groups of people and their interests (Jann and Wegrich, 2006).

Further reading

- Dery, D. (1984) Evaluation and termination in the policy cycle, Policy Sciences, 17: 13–26.
- Santos, Í. and Kauko, J. (2022) Externalisations in the Portuguese parliament: analysing power struggles and (de-)legitimation with Multiple Streams Approach, Journal of Education Policy, 37(3): 399–418.

D

Decoupling

Decoupling is one of several ways in which organisations might resist (or not) external, so-called 'institutional' pressures to be and act in a certain way (see, for example, Coburn, 2004), with other possibilities ranging from enthusiastic adoption, through grudging acceptance and avoidance, to refusal. In this spectrum, decoupling is a form of avoidance. It originated as a mechanism to explain lack of intra-organisational change in the literatures on institutional theory, with landmark contributions from, among others, Weick (1976) and Meyer and Rowan (1977). Weick (1976) pointed out that rational theories of change in organisations, including schools, often fail to account for what actually happens there and what might motivate it. Weick (1976) subsequently developed the notion of 'loose coupling' to indicate the ways in which 'coupled events are responsive, but that each event also preserves its own identity and some evidence of its physical or logical separateness' (p 3).

Meyer and Rowan (1977) built on Weick's (1976) insight by suggesting that a binary exists between those two elements of an organisation that are most often loosely coupled or decoupled. The first element consists of the organisation's structures, which grow to reflect the demands of the environment or what Meyer and Rowan (1977) call the 'institutional rules' (p 340) where institutional refers to beyond the organisation. These rules 'function as myths which organisations incorporate, gaining legitimacy, resources, stability, and enhanced survival prospects' (Meyer and Rowan, 1977, p 340). (In other framings, these institutional rules would constitute the policy landscape to be resisted, accommodated or embraced). The second element, decoupled from the first, consists of the technical realm of routine work activities within the organisation, which may operate according to quite different logics or imperatives. This means that 'conformity to institutionalised rules could promote the long-term survival of the organisation without necessarily increasing its efficiency or technical performance' (Oplatka, 2004, p 149).

Taking up this analytic in relation to education, Oplatka (2004) notes that 'one aspect of schools' conformity to socially legitimated changes and innovations is that their organisational structure and processes mirror the norms, values, and ideologies institutionalised in society' (p 148). In many states and jurisdictions internationally, these ideologies contemporarily will be largely grounded in market-based logics. Following this argument, schools become isomorphic with their marketised environment, despite that environment being socially constructed. Meyer and Rowan's (1977) idea of foundational myths underpinning institutional rules resonates in education, where adherence to the so-called 'standards agenda', a key element of the Global Education Reform Movement, has been called a matter of belief rather than evidence (Gunter, 2012). Any adherence to this agenda apparently and variously demonstrated by professionals in schools (often those in roles constructed as leadership) is therefore a symbolic act. Its audience is simultaneously the state (or the inspector on its behalf), and also parents- and children-as-consumers. For these audiences, such symbols are both more available and more easily incorporated into wider of discourses of what it means to be a 'good school' than information concerning what Meyer and Rowan (1977) consider discretely as the technical domain, decoupled from the symbolic myths of the institutional. In other words, it is considered much easier for a parent to grasp the symbols of effective schooling, such as a good inspection outcome or consistent use of a particular school uniform, than it is to understand and interpret what happens in the classroom regarding pedagogy and relationships. This interpretation, while focusing on the wrong features through displacement, nonetheless brings tangible benefits to the school through enhanced recruitment and reputation, both of which are meaningful in the market logic prevailing in many jurisdictions. This prompts school leaders to focus their attention on enhancing the symbolic, or more accurately in the case of schooling, the institutional over the substantive, decoupling the former from the latter and preventing real, in other words technical, change. One way in which this is achieved is through school actors' adoption of language that conforms to the marketised institutional environment. As Oplatka (2004) puts it, '[s]chools described in legitimated vocabularies are assumed to be compatible with defined, and often collectively rationalised myths and institutional rules' (p 149). This explains the corporatised language that is often revealed in school policies and data from school leaders' accounts (Courtney, 2015).

Decoupling as applied to schools relies on a conceptualisation of provision in which teachers function largely independently of, or at least without any need to take account of, the wider environment. Decoupling is largely a strategy adopted purposively by those professionals in roles constructed as leadership, who buffer teachers and teaching from these environmental influences. This view has been challenged, for example, by Coburn (2004), who argues that teachers are influenced by extrinsic notions of what constitutes good practice, but that they 'actively mediate these pressures in a process that is framed by their pre-existing beliefs and practices, which, in turn, are rooted in past encounters with institutional pressures' (p 212).

Further reading

- Bromley, P. and Powell, W.W. (2012) From smoke and mirrors to walking the talk: decoupling in the contemporary world, Academy of Management Annals, 6(1): 483–530.
- Hasse, R. and Krücken, G. (2015) Decoupling and coupling in education, in B. Holzer, F. Kastner and T. Werron (eds) From globalization to world society: neo-institutional and systems-theoretical perspectives, New York: Routledge, 197–214.

Deliberative policy analysis

Deliberative policy analysis can be considered part of a long tradition of using social-scientific research methods to achieve wider public–policy goals, specifically those directed towards building and sustaining political and social processes that are democratic, participatory and inclusive. The policy sciences which emerged in the 1950s (Lerner and Lasswell, 1951) shared a similar value orientation, intimately linked to the 'democratisation of society' (Simon et al, 2009, p 3) with its commitment to producing knowledge that could assist governments in optimising the effectiveness of state administration and organisational structures in the service of public life. The policy sciences were strictly positivist, empiricist and functionalist in their methodological and epistemological assumptions, however, and therefore represented a continuation of the Enlightenment project with its emphasis on the application of a 'scientific problem-solving rationality' (Simon et al, 2009, p 4) for producing objective and universal accounts of social change.

Similarly, deliberative policy analysis shares a strong normative commitment to democracy or pluralistic policy making, to be precise. This includes the pursuit of knowledge which can enrich understandings of democratic processes and in effect strengthen capacity to improve democratic conditions and outcomes. Unlike the policy sciences of the 1950s and 1960s, however, deliberative policy analysis does not aim to produce knowledge exclusively in and for the service of the state or in the name of improvement and evaluation, nor does it insist on positivist methodologies for capturing and producing knowledge about the world. Taking inspiration from the discursive or argumentative turn in policy analysis and planning (Fischer and Forester, 1993), deliberative policy analysis is largely a reaction to and rejection of the positivist fervour of those policy research traditions that produce knowledge as experiments in testing and affirming technical efficiency and the 'technical-instrumental practicality of specific social arrangements' (Jessop and Sum, 2016, p 105) and which therefore are dedicated 'to the development of methods and practices designed to settle rather than stimulate debates' (Fischer, 2003a, p 211).

According to Fischer (2003a), policy research traditions that seek to divorce interpretations from values, or which uphold policy making and policy worlds as privileged spaces of rationalist planning, represent an 'epistemological misunderstanding of the relation of knowledge to politics' (p 211). This is a view shared by many education researchers working in 'policy sociology' (Ozga, 1987), otherwise known as 'sociology of education policy' or 'critical policy sociology', who challenge positivist assumptions that 'the optimal solution for policy problems is a value-free activity' (Simon et al, 2009, p 10). Relatedly, they resist those rationalistic methodologies that claim to construct objects, ideas and processes as 'policy problems' through the provision of value-free knowledge or which separate out the legitimacy and authority of different interests and obligations from the value judgements or hierarchies of knowledge that give them meaning (Bacchi and Goodwin, 2016).

Moreover, to deny the relationship of politics to policy is to overlook how policy making and policy worlds function as contested spaces in which policy problems (or ideological dilemmas) are negotiated through the provision of meaning. Echoing this, Fischer (2003a) argues 'policy politics is itself about establishing definitions of and assigning meaning to social problems' (p 216), and therefore seeks to make explicit, rather than reify or de-socialise, the very ontological and epistemological a prioris (or argument-as-givens) that frame the discursive boundaries for policy debate.

Deliberative policy analysis therefore is a post-empiricist orientation to policy research that uses informal logic to 'probe both the incompleteness and imprecision of existing knowledge' (Fischer, 2003a, p 220). This does not mean deliberative policy analysis is post-empiricist in the sense that it fails to engage with policy worlds in ways that can be empirically knowable. Rather, it aims to demonstrate the very limits of empiricism and of empiricist assumptions that such a policy world can be known in advance, with a commitment to the permanence of agonism, namely deliberation and debate, that allows ethical and political subjects to continually become other than current systems, structures, practices and discourses allow or plan for. As Fischer (2003a) explains, 'rather than rejecting the empirical, the issue here concerns its relationship to the normative' (p 223). In this vein, Boossabong and Chamchong (2019) use deliberative policy analysis to examine the role of a think tank in Khon-Kaen, Thailand that worked with the municipality to design and facilitate deliberative forums. While Boossabong and Chamchong (2019) acknowledge the influence of deliberative policy analysis literature on the design of these forums, they conclude that the deliberation forums themselves lacked the 'ideal-type deliberation rooted in the Habermasian logic of communicative action' (p 484). Similarly, Escobar and Elstub (2017) adopt deliberative policy analysis in their discussion of 'mini-publics' to outline the potential of using democratically innovative approaches to strengthen citizen participation in matters of public interest, from science and technology to health and education. These innovations in participatory governance range from citizens' juries to consensus conferences and deliberative polls, all of which seek to empower citizens through learning, support and deliberation to engage in complex issues about making good collective decisions. In their study of the development of adult literacy, numeracy and English for speakers of others languages (ESOL) in England from the 1970s to 2000, Hamilton and Hillier (2007) also use deliberative policy analysis to similar effect by tracing a chronology of the key changes impacting policy developments during this time, which they link to the ascendency and interaction of multiple interest groups (central government, grassroots movements and local authorities) competing to shape the policy narrative.

Further reading

- Li, Y. and He, J. (2016) Exploring deliberative policy analysis in an authoritarian country, Critical Policy Studies, 10(20): 235–246.

- Maarten, A., Hajer, M.A. and Wagenaar, H. (eds) (2009) Deliberative policy analysis: understanding governance in the network society, Cambridge: Cambridge University Press.

Deliverology

Deliverology is a strategy for implementation (see entry on 'Implementation') devised by Michael Barber (see Barber, 2007), who was appointed to lead the Prime Minister's Delivery Unit from 2001 for the UK New Labour government. Deliverology became the privileged state strategy for effecting widespread public services reform and inspired homologous approaches internationally (Pring, 2012). Deliverology aimed to recouple the policy environment with practice through a tightly focused 'delivery chain' (Barber, 2007, p 85) from the minister through to the desired policy outcomes. In education, this meant that ministerial intentions were designed to influence practice in the classroom through intervening upon not only teachers' pedagogies but also their professional priorities and even identities. The aim was to raise pupils' attainment in standardised tests and public examinations. The mechanism through which the delivery chain was operationalised was raising standards through accountability, from teacher through school leaders to the state, in high-information contexts. The inspiration and template was 'very much ... the business world' (Pring, 2012, p 748).

Considerable resources and roles were marshalled to participate in the delivery chain. Collectively, these have been described as a 'very public technology of performance – made up of league tables, national averages, comparative and progress indicators, Ofsted ... assessments and benchmarks. These together are intended to instil into schools ... a "performance culture" constituted and reinforced by a "policy technology"' (Ball et al, 2012b, p 514). Across the public services, this technology was part of a wider 'audit culture' that uses numbers to know, evaluate, compare and control; it is 'a complex of surveillance, monitoring, tracking, coordinating, reporting, recording, targeting, motivating' (Ball et al, 2012b, p 525). Key to how this functioned in schools was a newly corporatised cadre of school leaders, enculturated through the National College for School Leadership (NCSL) to believe in the need for and to deliver a range of targets. Concerning this, Gunter (2012) argues that 'leadership was constructed and promoted as the means of suturing together a vast array of interventions in the curriculum, staffing, lesson planning and assessment, and to evidence success or be accountable for failure' (p 5).

The 'standards agenda' was a response to 'an historically contingent, fragile but commonsensical political rationality' (Ball et al, 2012b, p 514), with the 'need' to demonstrate improvement in public services, supported by a 'rhetoric of necessity' (Ball et al, 2012b, p 518). The British government at the time, New Labour, saw this as being most obviously achieved through rising performance measures, where the measurable was consequently privileged over the intangible and explicitly related to improving the nation's economic productivity and competitiveness, often linked to matters of social inclusion (Raffo and Gunter, 2008). Epistemologically, this framing is positivist, which is used in education research by the school effectiveness and school improvement (SESI) part of the field. SESI field members were commissioned by the NCSL to undertake research, whose findings were epistemologically pre-disposed to align with NCSL's agenda and hence disseminated as best practice. Dissenting voices were, however, ignored, further enabled by the networks within which Barber operated (see Gunter, 2012).

Deliverology takes from SESI the assumption that education acts as a simple policy system, with clear and predictable causal outcomes that are linked in a direct and linear manner to 'input' behaviours from actors along the delivery chain. Its functions are best understood as a science in this framing, rather than a *social* science, and the most appropriate metaphor for the system is a 'machine' (Diamond, 2021). This perspective can be contrasted with a view of education as complex and full of unpredictable elements, with context and culture influencing practice and outcomes more than deliverology allows for, alongside many unintended consequences (Diamond, 2021). One such consequence was the construction of particular groups as appropriate recipients (or not) of intense focus regarding interventions. A key target for much of the New Labour period (1997–2010), for example, was the proportion of pupils gaining grades A–C in at least five subjects in their secondary-phase examinations (later, these five had to include English and Maths). This incentivised an intense focus on those pupils on the C/D borderline at the expense of, for example, those predicted Bs or Fs but who wanted to improve (Ball et al, 2012b). This differentiated focus is also classed and racialised. A further consequence of the performativity that operationalised and outlasted deliverology was harm to the identities and values of teachers (Ball, 2003) and school leaders (Courtney, 2016). This included symbolic violence to 'students' souls' (Ball et al, 2012b, p 522) where children are subject to 'depersonalisation' (Pring, 2012, p 750) and valued by the state primarily because they 'help the school maintain its reputation' (p 749). The standards agenda therefore is not only totalising: 'students are also encouraged to monitor themselves and parents are encouraged to monitor their children' (Ball et al, 2012b, p 523). It is even totalitarian, and teachers 'whose practices fail to conform … are disappeared' (Courtney and Gunter, 2015, p 410). Where deliverology is enacted, what it means to be a teacher or educational leader and do teaching or leading is defined by the state, whose vision is reductive and instrumental.

Further reading

- Gewirtz, S. and Cribb, A. (2020) Can teachers still be teachers? The near impossibility of humanity in the transactional workplace, in A. Brown and E. Wisby (eds) Knowledge, policy and practice in education and the struggle for social justice: essays inspired by the work of Geoff Whitty, London: UCL Press, 217–232.

- Gunter, H.M. (2008) Modernisation and the field of educational administration, Journal of Educational Administration and History, 40(2): 161–172.

Dialogue

Dialogue in policy processes comprises meaningful and purposeful engagement between two or more stakeholders to achieve a policy goal. Within this broad framework exist many considerations, including those concerning form, participant selection, participant representativeness, purpose and power relations. Bangura (1997) identifies five models of policy dialogue. They are corporatist, technocratic, global sustainable pluralist, power sharing, and entryist. The first three are most pertinent to education policy, either through the way in which they reveal the underlying ideological context or how major global agreements are reached, and so are described here.

Bangura (1997) defines corporatism as 'a system for managing socio-economic conflicts in which organised interests are brought into the governmental policymaking process to facilitate debate, bargaining and compromise over key issues that affect the performance of the macro economy, the livelihoods of workers, and the process of industrial accumulation' (pp 57–58). The primary actors are generally restricted to governments, organised labour and employers' groups, each of whom exercises relative autonomy to advocate respectively and as equal partners for the economy, labour and capital. Conceptually predicated on Keynesian economic theory, corporatism foundered in the post-welfarist world of the 1980s onwards. Corporatism was the ideological foundation upon which the dialogues took place that produced welfarist education policies internationally, including non-selective education. Corporatism was replaced by technocracy, which 'questions, very fundamentally, the theoretical discourse of Keynesianism and the corporatist agenda of involving vested interests in the policymaking process' (Bangura, 1997, p 62). Ideologically neoliberal, technocracy allocates resources according to market conditions, and its primary actors are technocrats, constructed as disinterested, but expert in the aims and mechanisms of the market. These actors are located in government, but particularly in global financial institutions such as the International Monetary Fund and the World Bank. These latter organisations are dominant globally since financially struggling governments typically enter into dialogue with them to secure loans to subsidise their struggling economies. Explicit here is the link with education, which is constructed as a service – and not necessarily a public one – to be delivered effectively, but mostly efficiently.

Bangura's (1997) final model most pertinent to education is global sustainable pluralism. This aims 'to create a new global socio-economic and political order that would be sensitive to the basic needs and diversity of the human and natural world, as well as to the question of their sustainability' (Bangura, 1997, pp 70–71). Equitable education counts as a basic need in this formulation. The model is largely operationalised through global summits: examples in education are the 'Education For All' World Education Forum summits (previously World Conference on Education for All) aiming to achieve the UN's Sustainable Development Goal 4 on that theme. Weaknesses of the model include ambiguity concerning the identity and power of stakeholders; it is not clear who these might be, how representative they are nor how they might affect change once they return from the summit. Lewin (2011) has argued further that 'target setters live in different worlds to target getters' (p 575) and that this gap has widened as targets are phrased ever more precisely in response to interpretative variety and poor outcomes on the ground. For Chabbott (2003), the relationship between 'target-setters' and 'getters' is less causal: the former are enculturated epistemologically into practices where the generation of frameworks and objectives along with accompanying guidance is normalised and discrete. Its purpose is intelligibility to and within the like-minded summit-going community rather than to those whose practice on the ground it is ostensibly intended to influence.

Policy dialogue happens at micro as well as macro levels. Williams (2011) argues that in the form of public deliberation or dialogue, it 'can contribute significantly to effective public management' (p 254), including where policy is an intended outcome. This, Williams (2011) suggests in his theory of change, is for several reasons, of which the first is increasing understanding of decisions among affected groups. They are then more likely to accept these decisions, having participated in their formulation and contributed a valuable perspective. Arguably, this produces better decisions and policies, which generates more commitment to them as well as anticipating opposition. What Williams (2011) calls implementation is enhanced through participation, which enables participants to grow and develop. Next, social pressure means that the previously unpersuaded are encouraged to accept the decision, enhancing team identity; this widescale acceptance produces greater legitimacy for the policy. Overarching considerations include how power functions in that context, how expertise is distributed, how goals are understood, and what information and constraints are evident.

Further reading

- Blackmore, J. (1995) Policy as dialogue: feminist administrators working for educational change, Gender and Education, 7(3): 293–314.
- Dryzek, J. (2016) Deliberative policy analysis, in G. Stoker and M. Evans (eds) Evidence-based policymaking in the social sciences: methods that matter, Bristol: Policy Press, 229–242.

Diffusion

Policy diffusion is thought to happen when 'an innovation is communicated through certain channels over time among the members in a social system' (Rogers, 2003, p 5). This means that policy convergence in different jurisdictions (or municipalities, regions and localities) owing to a shared experience, an economic crisis for instance, would not constitute policy diffusion. Policy diffusion has conceptual overlaps with a range of other terms, including policy borrowing, policy transfer and policy learning (see entries on 'Borrowing', 'Transfer' and 'Policy learning'). Unlike these related terms, however, diffusion does not foreground within its definition the role of human agency, although clearly this is semantic coyness: such agency must underpin its operationalisation (and in fact reappears in more developed iterations, see Shipan and Volden, 2008). Policy diffusion is neutral in its construction of the policy object; an innovation need not be an improvement, at least not for all. Diffusion is also ambiguous (or malleable) regarding mechanism and actors. Diffusion studies reflect the disciplinary location of the researcher, for example, and so may include qualitative approaches across the social sciences (Sugiyama, 2013), geography and anthropology (Strang and Meyer, 1993). These studies focus on identifying motivations grounded in sociologically or ideologically shared norms and values. Nonetheless, there is also a strong strand within policy diffusion studies that privileges quantitative approaches that seek to identify patterns across measurable dimensions (Eta and Mngo, 2020), including network analyses (Strang and Meyer, 1993). This framing may produce in some researchers, specifically those epistemologically disposed to think in this way, assumptions that those diffusing policy are motivated by rationality, and concomitantly, may lead such researchers to construct rejected innovations as being irrationally motivated (Eta and Mngo, 2020).

Theoretical developments in quantitative policy diffusion studies have focused upon addressing its definitional ambiguities and silences, which Strang and Meyer (1993) categorise through the theorisation of adopters, diffusing practices and mechanisms. Concerning mechanisms, for instance, significant work has been undertaken on the roles of learning, competition, imitation and coercion, with some researchers (Shipan and Volden, 2008) exploring the relationships shared by these mechanisms with wider conditions, including spatio-temporal 'fixes' and arrangements. Learning is constructed as a positive, agentic process in which policy makers seek to address a policy problem by scanning for examples of 'good practice' elsewhere and learning from those experiences. Challenges to learning therefore include understanding what success looks like in other locations. Observed retention of the policy over time is an often-used proxy. A second mechanism is economic competition. The prevalence of economic competition in the wider literature is partly explained by the fact that much policy diffusion research is located in federal contexts such as the US, Australia or Canada, where any diffusion happens (or not) over boundaries that are political but not economic, and so where economic impact over these borders is easily affected and felt. This is less likely to occur across national boundaries, unless supranational conditions are privileged (for example, through the European Union). A third mechanism is imitation, where, unlike in learning, the object is to resemble the original policy maker rather than achieve the policy objectives. In other words, imitation is actor-oriented, whereas learning is action-oriented.

A fourth policy diffusion mechanism is coercion, which can be affected directly through, for example, imposing or threatening economic sanctions or newly challenging conditions. Indirect coercion may be achieved through third-party (sometimes international) institutions, such as the World Bank.

Sociological approaches to policy diffusion focus their attention on change 'as a function of social context and relations to others' (Sugiyama, 2013, p 37). Social structures that link actors across jurisdictions are seen as likely to produce shared understandings of policy problems and potential solutions. Such structures range from formal professional associations to informal networks: the qualifying criterion is that they operate as an epistemic community 'where actors' intersubjective meaning and their desire to gain legitimacy in the eyes of their peers shape policy choices' (Sugiyama, 2013, p 39). Importantly, this framing introduces a credible alternative to the rationalistic approach to understanding the acceptance or rejection of policy innovation.

A further approach to understanding policy diffusion is ideological, in which shared belief systems lead to the adoption of policies across boundaries. This element can be interplayed with others described here. As Gilardi (2010) points out, 'recent theoretical work on learning suggests that ideological positions and prior beliefs on the effectiveness of policy alternatives limit the influence of new information and tie policymakers more or less firmly to their original policy stance' (p 652).

Further reading

- Chisholm, L. (2007) Diffusion of the national qualifications framework and outcomes-based education in Southern and Eastern Africa, Comparative Education, 43(2): 295–309.
- Weyland, K. (2009) Bounded rationality and policy diffusion: social sector reform in Latin America, Princeton: Princeton University Press.

Digital education

The ubiquity of data science and 'big data' to sorting, classifying and measuring everyday decision-making, from minor, day-to-day decisions about who to date, where to eat and how to travel, to major political and economic decisions about finance, labour industries and security, is central to modern life. The visualisation, modelling, auditing, assessment and reporting of human behaviour through datafication and digitalisation is also a key component of modern education systems, driven by neoliberal competitive logics designed to fabricate schools as purveyors of quantified metrics, and therefore compel their participation in the reproduction of school systems as navigable units of 'commensurability, equivalence and comparative performance' (Lingard et al, 2013 p 542). This shift towards 'governance by numbers' (Piattoeva and Boden, 2020) has not only created the conditions for further commercialisation of education services and its 'assetisation' to extract economic value. It has also given rise to more pervasive, post-panoptic forms of surveillance, management and performance measurement of staff and students and their configuration into 'data-driven subjectivities' (Gorur and Dey, 2021, p 69).

Digital education describes both an object of study and an interdisciplinary field of study that straddles multiple disciplines (science and technology studies, software studies, network analysis, critical data studies and sociology, among others) to study the role and impact of data and datafication and related, complementary trends (adaptive learning technologies, cloud computing, automated teaching technologies, artificial intelligence, machine learning, blended learning, learning analytics, platformisation, predictive modelling, usage tracking, flexible and customised learning, sentiment analysis, and online simulation environments) on the emergence and development of new information tools and governing knowledge in the field of education. Here datafication refers to 'the rendering of social and natural worlds in machine-readable digital format' (Williamson et al, 2020, p 351) and therefore describes the unique process through which different processes, practices, objects and experiences are represented and given meaning by data-collection machines. Digital-education researchers call attention not only to the risks posed by such data-collection machines, namely their method of using an automated reductionist logic to record, manipulate and distribute data, but also the danger of presenting such machines as neutral, technical instruments for making judgements about the social world or 'blackboxing'. Digital-education researchers therefore argue for better scrutiny, theorisation and problematisation of data-collection machines owing to the way certain actions, behaviours or opinions acquire meaning according to automated value judgements prefigured by the system and its designers.

Dodge and Kitchin (2007), for example, point to those forms of algorithm regulation performed by software systems that operate with very limited human intervention – a new form of governance they call 'automated management' (p 264). Similarly, Williamson and Eynon (2020) highlight the automated formation of artificial intelligence and related computational processes that include machine learning, adversarial networks and deep learning: 'developing machines that can learn from their own experience, adapt to their contexts and uses, improve their own functioning, craft their own rules, construct new algorithms, make predictions, and carry out automated tasks without requiring control or oversight by human operatives' (p 224). Hence many people working in the field of critical data studies call for improved participatory methods by which complex chains of external mediation made possible by stakeholder involvement can give broader public legitimacy to these data-collection machines, a form of technical agonism that works to relocate the 'prefiguring judgement' (Williamson et al, 2020, p 353) underpinning these systems among communicating publics to enable trust, improve transparency and facilitate more plural forms of expertise (Swist et al, 2017). This includes opening up avenues through which users of technology can challenge the 'limiting and demoralising standardised customisation' (Roberts-Mahoney et al, 2016, p 416) by which their autonomy is circumscribed to fit with predetermined order functions.

Related to this is an emphasis on critical data literacy. Critical data literacy moves beyond a concern with the development of skills required to use data and digital media, such as structuring data or creating data visualisations, to the generation of a more profound awareness of and critical reflection on big data systems and their risks. These risks may include the impact of algorithmic profiling and predictive systems on reinforcing discrimination, disadvantage or 'digital in/exclusion' (Selwyn et al, 2020, p 2), to threats to personal privacy and protection posed by the aggregation and cross-referencing of data sets by large commercial corporations and political organisations (Sander, 2020). Underpinning this critical data movement is a commitment to enabling 'data citizens' and forms of 'data citizenship' that place children and young people at the centre 'of alternative and emancipatory technologies and technological practices' (Robertson and Tisdall, 2020, p 60). Critical data literacy therefore represents a continuation of critical pedagogy: the creation of emancipatory forms of knowledge and the interrogation of knowledge structures.

Through a study of India's Unified District Information System of Education, a data platform that publishes district- and school-level data, Gorur and Dey (2021) draw attention to the iterative and regulative function of these data platforms as 'ontologically productive' (p 69), that is, as platforms that compel among users certain forms of engagement with technology that produce 'relations of unequal power and hierarchy, relations of trust and distrust, and relations of closeness and distance' (p 78). Related to this is the enactment of new forms of education governance through digital technologies in which new forms of governing are made materially and ontologically possible by the recursivity of data as something that both captures and produces social and political effects: 'Such recursion means that digital database technologies not only represent educational settings and subjects as data-sets, but also that the data actively change them' (Williamson, 2016a, p 124).

Further reading

- Grimaldi, E. and Ball, S.J. (2021) The blended learner: digitalisation and regulated freedom − neoliberalism in the classroom, Journal of Education Policy, 36(3): 393–416.
- Thompson, G. and Cook, I. (2017) The logic of data-sense: thinking through Learning Personalisation, Discourse: Studies in the Cultural Politics of Education, 38(5): 740–754.

Digital policy sociology

Digital policy sociology is the interdisciplinary study of different iterations of the digital from the perspective of various theories, concepts and methods taken from socio-technical systems, science and technology studies, software studies, the sociology of statistics, and critical data studies. These iterations of the digital, of digital systems and digital use are too numerous to list here, but include information and communication technologies, social media, big data, artificial intelligence, computational decision-making, computer-mediated communication, and nanotechnologies, to name a few. A central focus of digital policy sociology concerns the emergence and influence of the digital as discursive and material technologies or artefacts that mediate and augment different forms of social interaction, social structures and social relations. More widely, a recurring focus of digital policy sociology and for critical scholars of digital technologies concerns the policy rationalities that give rise to and strengthen demands for algorithmic forms of governance in the field of education (Gulson and Webb, 2017b), which represent 'an emerging, next-generation iteration on the logics of transnational, comparative modes of "governing by numbers"' (Williamson, 2021, p 368).

The ubiquity of computation and machine learning as mechanisms for the acceleration and expansion of categorisation and social sorting has also led to a focus on the impact of digital forms, systems and technologies on the perpetuation and intensification of different kinds of inequality, disadvantage and 'social embedment' (Hartong, 2021, p 34), such as the discriminatory effects of bias algorithms (for example, racial profiling) on the reproduction of ontogenetic, racialised bodies. This means challenging the prevalent view of data, metrics, numericisation or algorithms as neutral products of automatic calculation or simply technical, that is, beyond human influence, manipulation or unconscious bias, and instead making explicit and political what Hartong (2021) calls the 'ambiguous production logics behind data platforms' (p 36), namely the implicit value judgements and hierarchies of knowledge embedded in the computations, approximations and representations flowing from the design of data tools and infrastructures. Ratner et al (2018), for example, demonstrate the extent to which data visualisations of national test data in the field of education are contingent products of 'situated circumstances and negotiations' (p 33) shaped by the interests of civil servants. This includes drawing attention to the meaning making inherent to said technologies, namely their ontological capacity to make visible, normalise and naturalise different kinds of subjects (see Gorur and Dey, 2021).

As critical scholars of digital technologies observe, the process of collecting, encoding and recording data is a mode of politics itself since it involves the allocation of values and identification or construction of 'problems'. At the same time, scholars of digital policy sociology and digital sociology more generally emphasise the 'affordances' of technologies as digital innovations of the social, namely the ways in which technologies invite certain actions and value orientations, and therefore limit the ways in which actors reflexively engage with digital technologies. This means acknowledging the governing power of 'algorithmic regulation' (Introna, 2016) to augment and mediate what is seen and valued by human beings. On the other hand, critical policy sociologists working in the field of digital data studies emphasise the historically and culturally unique forms of human–machine interaction and learning made possible by new data technologies. 'This understanding', according to Fussey and Roth (2020), 'acknowledges both the materiality and influence of things but avoids technological determinism' (p 664). Selwyn (2013), however, cautions against any over-optimistic view of the context-sensitive development of technologies as learner-centred: 'there is little evidence of digital technologies leading to an increased diversification of learning opportunities. If anything, technologies such as the Internet can be associated with a distinct entrenchment of existing provider interests' (p 203).

Hartong (2021) and others (Gorur, 2015b; Landri, 2018) have made similar observations through their studies of the various aspects of enactment and materiality made possible by digital data platforms and infrastructures, especially the ways in which data, transparency and prediction work to make schools and school systems amenable to calculation and the authority of governing institutions (Piattoeva, 2015). Adopting a topological perspective to make sense of how digital education platforms implicate schools in practices that produce space-times, Hartong (2021) observes the ways in which digital school performance platforms in the US introduce digital forms of compulsory visibility that work to locate schools materially and discursively within practices and relations that are compatible, commensurable and comparable with wider systems of education governance. Moreover, these digital school-performance platforms, which schools use to register, represent and compare their educational performance relative to other schools, reinforces 'what is seen and valued by schools' (Hartong, 2021, p 35). At the same time, Hartong (2021) avoids arguments of technological determinism which reduce the school to a digital imprint of wider systems of control and domination. Hartong (2021) acknowledges the extent to which digital school-performance platforms are centrally designed by governments to be a composite of replicable and transferable digital tools that can 'operate within particular (yet dynamic) boundaries' (p 36), yet 'foster a more context-sensitive and careful modeling and understanding of data (relations), including utilising a greater diversity of platform data, as well as more customised and interactive platform designs' (p 35). Other researchers note the ontological politics of digital data platforms as technologies for improving surveillance and control of subjects through the availability of 'data-driven subjectivities' (Gorur and Dey, 2021, p 69).

Further reading

- Kitchin, R. (2017) Thinking critically about and researching algorithms, Information, Communication and Society, 20(1): 14–29.
- Thompson, G. and Cook, I. (2015) Becoming-topologies of education: deformations, networks and the database effect, Discourse: Studies in the Cultural Politics of Education, 36(5): 732–774.

Discourse analysis

Discourse analysis represents a shift away from a structuralist and linguistic view of language as logocentric, whether it is structural anthropology (the comparative study of human cultures) or semiotics (the study of sign systems). From a structuralist perspective, written and spoken language is a self-contained relational structure, meaning that each component of speech or text (whether viewed from the perspective of phonology, morphosyntax or semantics) is a sub-set of a much wider web of interrelated components or chain of signifiers. In this context, the general meaning of language can be traced to its location in a logical order that precedes and regulates the subjective use of language.

Discourse analysis offers up a poststructuralist view of language that is less interested in explaining the ascribed meaning of language with reference to some underlying rational structure. Instead, discourse analysis maintains a focus on the substantive aspects of language and language use (articulatory, conceptual, pragmatic) as forms of social action or signifying practices aimed at the discursive achievement of certain ends. This includes a focus on talk, text, verbal interaction and communicative events as performances directed at producing specific effects and produced for particular occasions. In contrast to the logocentrism of structuralist theories of language, in which language is studied as a lens through which to map the structure that precedes and governs language use and its ascribed meaning, discourse analysis is foundationally and methodologically poststructuralist, relativist and interpretivist. A focus of discourse analysis concerns how language produces meaning which is always performed, resisted, naturalised, normalised and contested. Poststructuralist theories of language thus refuse a structuralist view of subjects as exclusively bearers of discourse and instead allow for a view of the 'agentic production of discourse' (Bacchi, 2000, p 52). Therefore, concerns with the truth or falsity of statements are typically suspended in discourse studies. Instead, discourse analysts are concerned with the 'work' or 'action' of discourse as constructions or discursive accomplishments of 'interactional achievements' (Wood and Kroger, 2000, p 148); as a pragmatic, active, engaged or 'designed activity' (Wetherell, 2001, p 17) directed towards bringing about certain effects.

As Foucault (1981) argues, 'discourse is not simply that which translates struggles or systems of domination, but is the thing for which and by which there is struggle' (pp 52–53). From this perspective, discourse has no centre or structure – a locus, origin or permanent settlement from which it derives its meaning (see Anderson and Holloway, 2020). Language only takes on the appearance of something fixed or stable when disparate elements come together through labour and work to form a facile synthesis that works to substitute discourse for truth. Foucault (1977) therefore describes discourse as a 'discursive formation' or 'regime of truth': an open, contingent and unstable set of sites and practices through which subjects pursue truth claims that function as a partage between true and false statements. In other words, discourse does not simply reflect reality but actively constructs it to legitimate ways of seeing, evaluating and describing reality, and therefore constitutes a movement or site for the realisation of specific social, political and economic ends. As Britzman (2000) observes, discourses 'authorise what can and cannot be said; they produce relations of power and communities of consent and dissent, and thus discursive boundaries are always being redrawn around what constitutes the desirable and the undesirable' (p 36). From a policy perspective, discourse represents engaged, pragmatic attempts to set in motion specific enunciative strategies aimed at constructing particular versions of reality as well as directing human action towards specific ends. Policy discourse thus represents a discursive economy of language: it brings into perspective different ways of construing and acting upon social reality in order to effect change.

A discourse analytic reading of education policy speeches and texts stresses the importance of language to the discursive framing of policy problems and solutions (Bacchi, 2000) and to the hegemonic production and circulation of meaning and power more generally. Here, policy language is studied as not only stipulative and iterative (capable of producing new meaning through argumentative and rhetorical practices of transposition and abridgement) but as something constitutive and regulative (representing engaged attempts to represent certain speaking positions as 'troubled' or authorised, or to validate specific claims to knowledge and truth). Policy texts represent dynamic spaces through which policy makers and politicians seek to articulate and mobilise reform (Wilkins, 2023a). Maguire et al (2011), for example, adopt a Foucauldian understanding of discourse to explore policies as discursive strategies for making up particular kinds of visions of the 'good school' and 'good teacher'. Similarly, Raaper (2017) combines Foucauldian discourse theories with Fairclough's practical tools of analysis to show the differential applications and development of assessment policy in Scotland and Estonia and their interdiscursivity (combination and co-articulation) with wider globally circulating norms.

Further reading

- Courtney, S.J. and Mann, B. (2021) Thinking with 'lexical' features to reconceptualize the 'grammar' of schooling: shifting the focus from school to society, Journal of Educational Change, 22: 401–421.
- Woo, E. (2023) What is the problem represented to be in China's world-class university policy? A poststructural analysis, Journal of Education Policy, 38(4): 644.

Dispositif

Dispositif (or apparatus) is both an object and method of study. To describe something as a dispositif is to recognise the provisional conceptual identity or unity of that object as an ensemble of heterogeneous parts whose apparent seamlessness is the crystallisation of problematic alignments, unique combinations and 'promiscuous entanglements' (Ong, 2007, p 5). Similarly, to investigate something as a dispositif is to recognise the incompleteness and open-endedness of that object as a composite of various properties and capacities that are unique to historically contingent processes of 'gathering and dispersing' (Anderson and McFarlane, 2011, p 125). These active processes of gathering and dispersing, of recomposing and restabilising, of fixing and fitting, take on various forms owing to the context-sensitive ways in which they are fashioned through intermediating materials and agents – actors, networks, ideas and projects – as well as different temporal, spatial and scalar relations and practices. To study dispositifs therefore is to document the ways in which particular elements and entities are brought together or 'stabilised and set to work in multiple domains' (Rabinow, 2003, p 55). This includes a focus on how 'mobile relations of power' are sustained and reproduced through coarticulation and combination of various elements that 'intersect, permeate, modify and produce subjectivities in concert with material objects and practices' (Bailey, 2013, p 810). As Foucault (1980) explains, dispositif is the study of objects as 'a thoroughly heterogeneous ensemble consisting of discourses, institutions, architectural forms, regulatory decisions, laws, administrative measures, scientific statements, philosophical, moral and philanthropic propositions' (p 194).

In this account, dispositif describes the 'shift from the study of objects to the practices that produce them' (Walters, 2012, p 18), with a unique focus on the fragility and instability of objects as bound to multiple determinations and conditions of possibility, and therefore 'subject to changes in direction, bifurcating and forked, and subject to drifting' (Deleuze, 1992, p 159). This means paying close attention to what is being 'obscured and made possible' by dispositifs in a particular field (Salter, 2008, p 244). This also means avoiding deterministic arguments concerning the structural coherence of objects as linear, universalisable, patterned or homogeneous, and instead attending to the fracture, traction and repair of objects under different historical and geopolitical circumstances to capture the 'operational logics, forces and dynamics at play in a specific configuration of power relations' (Dillon and Lobo-Guerrero, 2008, p 272). The analytic of dispositif therefore is important to transcending 'traditional analytical dualisms between micro-macro, internal-external and local-central' in order to capture the interconnections of actors, networks and projects through the mobile apparatus (Power, 2013, p 528).

Moreover, it requires paying close attention to the complicated distribution and unevenness of objects as composites or properties of 'fragile relays, contested locales and fissiparous affiliations' (Rose, 1999, p 51). Dispositifs, then, are not studied as the sedimenting effects of predefined sequencing or the residual effects of rational consensus, perfect control and system design since this would imply an internal coherence or predictability to the distribution and patterning of objects. Rather, dispositifs are understood to be the contingent regularities and relations that make possible the interactive elements through which objects and subjects emerge and cohere: 'in a way they "rectify" the preceding curves, they draw tangents, fill in the space between one line and another, acting as go-betweens between seeing and saying and vice versa, acting as arrows which continually cross between words and things, constantly waging battle between them' (Deleuze, 1992, p 160). Dispositifs, therefore, can also be studied as techniques in ordering reality and rendering it in particular ways. As Salter (2008) observes, dispositifs denote a constellation of continually moving, interacting sets of objects, actors, practices and institutions that register a 'capability for governance, or the disposition of a field towards a mode of governance' (p 248).

Bailey (2013) adopts the concept of dispositif to trace the various discourses, objects, practices and rationalities that make up the policy apparatus or 'policy dispositif' (p 807). For Bailey (2013), policy dispositifs represent 'strategic struggles over the meaning and governing of education' (p 809) and therefore describe the discursive and material developments in the 'socio-technical formation of government' (p 809). More specifically, Bailey (2013) observes how Teach First, a UK-based social enterprise focused on teacher training, develops as a strategic and tactical arm of much wider macro-policy dispositifs linked to government policy designed to shape teacher subjectivities in particular ways, namely as 'exceptional leaders'. At the same time, Bailey (2013) stresses the non-linearity of this relationship as a movement or interaction that permits 'unending possibilities of transformation and "flight"' (p 811). Similarly, Hartmann and Komljenovic (2021) apply the concept of dispositif to trace the dispersion and gathering of employability-related activities and structures across different universities in response to wider European policy reforms, with a specific focus on employability as 'strategic dispositif' (p 4) interlinking the needs of labour markets.

Further reading

- Bussolini, J. (2010) What is a dispositive?, Foucault Studies, 10: 85–107.
- Thomas, O.D. (2014) Foucaultian dispositifs as methodology: The case of anonymous exclusions by unique identification in India, International Political Sociology, 8(2): 164–181.

Divergence

Policy divergence describes increasing disharmony between previously aligned policy landscapes or agendas across jurisdictions (see, for example, Greer, 2006), or between policy intentions and enactments at 'street level' (see Gofen, 2014). In the case of the former, (inter)national sense, divergence is therefore a feature of policy studies in particular sorts of sites; for instance, of those focusing on the effects of devolution in the four 'home nations' of the UK; or on the effects of Brexit. Such instances of disharmony must be intended, but do not necessarily have to be completely new policies. Legislative bodies may diverge from one another through actively choosing new policy directions, as was the case when Wales abandoned the school league tables and standardised testing that characterised the English education system. Divergence may also occur through legislative bodies opting not to follow the policy initiatives of another legislative body. This took place when Scotland, Northern Ireland and Wales declined to introduce English-style academies (state-funded independent schools) into their raft of provision.

Divergence can also be shown to occur in other ways, namely following a period of (voluntary or forced) convergence when the particular features of a policy assemblage do not themselves align with jurisdictions' distinctive historical features and dispositions. When the conditions promoting or forcing convergence dissolve, the former differences typically re-emerge. Such a case was described by Dobbins (2017) in a study of higher-education governance in Poland and Romania following the fall of communism in 1989. In this example, marketisation was largely resisted in Poland owing to a persistent underlying Humboldtian tradition, namely one focused on academic autonomy. In Romania, a historical disposition towards state control of universities meant that the state was able to implement numerous features of marketisation that aligned with western notions of the 'effective university'.

It is important to note that divergence is in constant interplay with convergence (see entry on 'Convergence') and that the direction of travel is rarely persistently one-way only. For example, Dobbins (2017) identifies a degree of re-convergence in Polish and Romanian higher education; and Wales re-introduced some of the audit-based features of the English system following a so-called Programme for International Student Assessment (PISA) shock. Moreover, the factors motivating policy divergence are strong, despite superficial analyses overstating the case for convergence owing to the effects of marketised globalisation and the supranational homogeneity of citizens' expectations. Greer (2006) summarises these countervailing pro-divergency factors as follows: First, despite apparent national-level convergence (for example, through common legislative features), there will be divergence at the local level owing to the unpredictable clash between policy and context. More fundamentally, Greer (2006) points out that four elements must cohere for a policy to come about: 'problem, politician, policy and power … a successful policy must respond to a problem that puts the issue on the agenda, be proposed by advocates who frame the idea correctly, correspond to a politician's strategy for partisan advancement, and be appropriate in light of the power and position of the government' (p 165). The chances of these elements aligning in different contexts are so slight as to make policy divergence highly likely, even undesirable.

These examples of policy divergence all concern Greer's (2006) national-level analytical framework (albeit operationalised by actors along the policy chain). To supplement this, Gofen (2014) develops the notion of 'street-level divergence' where those actors charged with carrying out policy have the final say in what it looks like. This framing tends to align with a policy implementation rather than a policy enactment perspective (see entries on 'Implementation' and 'Enactment'). The mediating role between so-called policy maker and policy taker is influenced by a range of factors, which Gofen (2014) categorises as either pertaining to the street-level policy actor's choice or as an inevitable consequence of typical policy implementation. Regarding choice, Gofen (2014) draws on the literature to identify three foundations: rationalism, ethics and professionalism. A policy actor may decide rationally to diverge from policy intentions or aims 'as a coping mechanism to overcome barriers to job performance such as limited resources and stressful work setting' (Gofen, 2014, p 475). Or dissonant interests may prompt divergence. Ethically motivated divergence may occur when street-level actors have moral or value-based disagreements with a policy framing, and 'bend, break, or ignore rules to provide justice for their citizen-clients' (Gofen, 2014, p 476). Finally, the requirements of professional standards may provoke divergence in cases where such standards would otherwise be compromised by implementing the policy in the expected way.

Understanding street-level divergence as an inevitable outcome of any attempt to 'do policy' comes closer to policy enactment than choice-based explanations. This is because it recognises 'factors such as skills, habits, values, motives, loyalties, and the inevitable incompleteness of relevant knowledge' (Gofen, 2014, p 477). Fully accepting a policy-enactment framing would largely or entirely negate the concept of street-level divergence itself since, for policy-enactment scholars, all actors involved in policy are policy makers and so the starting point from which divergence is measured is blurred. Privileging some actors as policy makers and categorising others as policy takers is a conceptual error in an enactment framing.

Further reading

- Birrell, D. (2009) The impact of devolution on social policy, Bristol: Policy Press.
- Morphet, J. and Clifford, B. (2014) Policy convergence, divergence and communities: the case of spatial planning in post-devolution Britain and Ireland, Planning Practice and Research, 29(5): 508–524.

Drift

According to Hacker and Pierson (2010), policy drift is a strategy whereby public policy is intentionally prevented from adapting to new contextual conditions. This means that policies held in stasis produce changed social and/or economic outcomes for certain constituencies or groups over time. The actors who are pro-stasis need not be highly visible, yet axiomatically have the power or authority within the political system to achieve their objective. This may be owing to their status and/or connections, or to their organisational ability to exploit veto rights. In all cases, drift is achieved in the face of opponents' recognition and advocacy of alternatives. In summary, Hacker and Pierson (2010) argue that 'drift requires (1) policies whose effects change due to shifting circumstances,

(2) recognition of this change, (3) availability and awareness of viable alternatives, and (4) nonmajoritarian reasons why those alternatives are not adopted' (p 170).

For Galvin and Hacker (2020), policy drift need not involve obstruction. They argue that the very challenge of maintaining policies may mean that sufficient legislative support may not be summonable across political divides to effect change, or priorities may be focused elsewhere. An example of policy drift in England concerns university tuition fees, which at the time of writing have been purposively capped at £9,250 per annum since 2017. This represents a series of reductions in real terms to university funding. It is viable to increase the cap in line with inflation, yet the UK government finds it politically and economically expedient to maintain it. A further example, from the US, concerns the way in which an intended policy intervention into promoting equity in schooling was overtaken by and subsumed into a growing discourse regarding teacher quality, measured through high-stakes accountability and audit (Griffen, 2022).

Hacker and Pierson's (2010) definition represents the latest stage in the increasing conceptual development undertaken mostly by Hacker, alone or with colleagues: earlier versions left open the possibility of apolitical or inadvertent drift, for instance. It has been used as the foundation upon which a range of supplementary contributions have been made, addressing questions unasked in Hacker's formulations, in effect giving rise to more nuanced, historically contingent positions on drift. Some of these contributions are set out in what follows.

The gap regarding the ways in which actors respond to policy drift, and how their agency may be conceptualised, is addressed by Kay and Baines (2019). Kay and Baines (2019) start out from the premise that policy drift may be largely or wholly inadvertent, an observation derived from an ambiguity in a former iteration of drift offered by Hacker (2004). Yet despite claims to accident and serendipity, this notion of inadvertency is fundamental to Kay and Baines' (2019) conceptualisation of policy drift since it successfully disaggregates drift from responses to drift. Kay and Baines (2019) use an evolutionary metaphor to suggest two further mechanisms for responses to its effects, besides reversal or maintenance. The first is acclimatisation, in which actors are thought to accept the changed conditions produced by the drift. The second is adaptation. Here, actors are positioned as undertaking a more fundamental re-organisation of the self in order to occupy the new terrain for the long term.

Galvin and Hacker (2020) further contribute to these debates by identifying and addressing a research gap concerning the political effects of policy drift. Galvin and Hacker (2020) argue that policy drift creates new conditions that don't just advantage or disadvantage existing actors, but which motivate the creation of new groups or the emergence of new actors to respond to the altered policy landscape. Such groups or actors are likely to be representative of those disadvantaged under the changed conditions. In this sense, policy drift is 'mobilising', according to Galvin and Hacker (2020, p 218). However, policy drift is also limiting because it structures these new actors' agency around the still-existent static policy. The only recourse is 'patches and workarounds' that 'invariably create new complications and problems, which in turn generate new policy dynamics' (Galvin and Hacker, 2020, p 218).

Further reading

- Béland, D. (2007) Ideas and institutional change in social security: conversion, layering, and policy drift, Social Science Quarterly, 88(1): 20–38.
- Béland, D., Rocco, P. and Waddan, A. (2016) Reassessing policy drift: social policy change in the United States, Social Policy and Administration, 50(2): 201–218.

E

Elite

Identifying putative elites is a key but problematic task because observing that a sub-set of a population functions as an elite insofar as policy formulation is concerned is easier than identifying who the members of that sub-set are. It seems that elite identification is a product of the intellectual and conceptual framework that is deployed to do so. Kakabadse et al (2011), for instance, typologise elite identity according to four theories. In classical theory, elites are composed of 'people who have the highest indices in their branch of activity ("the strongest, the most energetic and the most capable") within society' (Kakabadse et al, 2011, p 3), which means that the constitution of elite groups is liable to change. In critical theory, elites are a product of 'access to wealth and power' (Kakabadse et al, 2011, p 3), which makes them hard to displace. In democratic theory, elites are those whose acquired skills are deployed or deployable for the common good. Elites can consequently be removed through democratic processes. In network theory, elites are constituted through 'strong social, political or professional ties', and so membership is 'evolving [and] dynamic' (Kakabadse et al, 2011, p 3). There is considerable literature that identifies a shift from economic through corporate to education elites, whereby actors made powerful through and within a capitalist landscape move their attention to the framing of public policy in ways that suit their interests. This means that elite actors are not obliged to directly participate in policy making but they may influence it through supranational institutions like the World Trade Organization (Gaus and Hall, 2017). This phenomenon, like its underlying neoliberal ideology, is global yet enacted locally by those acting in ways that reproduce a neoliberal orthodoxy (Courtney, 2017b; McGinity, 2017). In practice, it is not possible to disentangle the reproduction of neoliberalism from neoconservatism, whose definition foregrounds the reproduction of advantage and so is central to any discussion of elites.

Regarding the question of elite motivation, Genieys and Smyrl (2008) identify the immanent tension and paradox by posing the question as follows: 'why would individuals who, by definition, have done well for themselves under a given institutional and policy system, wish to alter it?' (p 22). They argue that a partial answer may lie in the Weberian concept of *Herrschaft* which 'designates a specific relationship in which one party has the right to issue orders and the other the duty to obey them' (Genieys and Smyrl, 2008, p 28). The elite motivation is therefore 'the reasonable and legitimate expectation of being obeyed' (Genieys and Smyrl, 2008, p 28). This is complicated by the inevitable existence of competing elite groupings, which makes it 'extremely unlikely that a single cognitive framework will ever become altogether hegemonic' (Genieys and Smyrl, 2008, p 31). Elite participation in policy making can become institutionalised over time, lessening the urgency of a focus on motivation (it happens because it has always happened). In South America, for instance, institutions imported bureaucratic systems from Spain and Portugal that privileged technocratic competence (and hence the creation of policy elites) over public participation (Montecinos, 1993). As elsewhere, elites produced in this way do not constitute a homogeneous group and so '*Técnicos* and politicians lack shared interpretive frameworks to address the tension between the logic of politics and that of policy decisions' (Montecinos, 1993, p 27). Researchers who locate elites and their interests in neoliberal networks of power identify the retention and reproduction of that power as a primary motivation. Further, if it is assumed that different elite factions are constantly and inevitably competing for dominance in any system, then the struggle is potentially never-ending, which is strongly motivating for participants.

Finally, on the question of the mechanisms by which elites exercise their influence on policy, Genieys and Smyrl (2008) draw attention to the notion of the 'référentiel' (p 23), a normative discursive construct that frames rational thinking on a given topic. Like any successful intervention into discourse, it implies both an act and source of power, and so is political. The role of elites in relation to *référentiels* is not to impose them (they cannot), but to act as mediators who both interpret and manage the framing of *référentiels*, and who then engage in 'explanation and application' (Genieys and Smyrl, 2008, p 23) to ensure they take hold and endure. This conceptualisation is congruent with scholarship that co-locates elites with neoliberalism. Here, the *référentiel* concerns the purposes of, and concomitantly, the accepted practices within education and its leadership, and is constructed through elite interventions to be axiomatically primarily economic. Maintaining this construct is hard work and is enabled through discursive dominance at multiple levels of policy making.

Further reading

- Gunter, H.M., Hall, D. and Apple, M.W. (eds) (2017) Corporate elites and the reform of public education, Bristol: Policy Press.
- Kakabadse, A. and Kakabadse, N. (eds) (2012) Global elites: the opaque nature of transnational policy determination, Basingstoke: Palgrave Macmillan.

Embodiment

Embodiment refers to the diverse ways in which education policy concerns itself with or treats social actors as material and corporeal through the construction, stigmatisation or essentialisation of their bodies as the object or subject of policy. Most obviously, this pertains when education policies are concerned with physical processes or outcomes, as is the case with the 'obesity discourse' and its normative treatment in schools (Evans and Davies, 2012, p 617). In this instance, the body functions as a site of, and mechanism for, knowledgeabilities concerning what it means to be normal and what those deemed wanting must change in themselves in order to comply. Such regulatory treatments are consequently strongly psychologised and individualised, with bodies constructed as problematic along one or more arbitrary dimensions of difference. Constructing bodies in this way, with public policy as an instrument, is an exercise in and of power, which requires theorisation. Evans and Davies (2012), for instance, call the imposed meanings that regulate bodies 'perfection codes' (p 620) and note that they reflect corporate rather than educative interests. Evans and Davies (2012) also point out several major problems with the pathologisation of certain bodies, including cultural insensitivity and the over-simplification and subjectification of issues arising from complex, structural conditions.

Evans and Davies' (2012) research speaks to a wider effect of this sort of embodiment; the hierarchisation of learners as objects of education policy according to features denoting their socio-economic status or their ethical or moral value. These are written into bodies in proxy fashion as corporeal characteristics, such as race or gender. This process may stigmatise, as is the case with the teen mothers who are the focus of Pillow's (2015) contribution. Pillow (2015) notes that in the US, 'teen pregnancy has been and remains clearly linked with racialised discourses of Blackness including deficit theories that pathologise Black women, Black youth, and the Black family' (p 61). The moral censure of Blackness is superficially redirected onto the more acceptable object of the pregnant teen. Here, bodies are coded and recoded in multiple ways that are nonetheless unambiguous because social actors undertake such pseudo-corporeal readings all the time.

Bodies can therefore be thought of as corporeal and material entities used to mark out and index certain students through policy as being educable or ineducable. For Pillow (2015), the policy message is that teen mothers are ineducable. This is articulated through diverse products of the associated policy regime (see entry on 'Regime'), including how teen mothers' low attendance is treated and what support is put into place to help them graduate. Gunter (2019) makes a wider claim, that children are segregated for their learning in England 'based on the promotion of "biopolitical distinctiveness" espoused through superiority-inferiority binaries' (p 2). Specifically, 'the construction and conservation of segregation is located in a complexity of eugenics and structural technologies (such as supply of and demand for school places)' (Gunter, 2019, p 13). Embodiment functions differently in Pillow's (2015) and Gunter's (2019) examples than in Evans and Davies (2012). For Evans and Davies (2012), the focus on the body and its discursive treatment is explicit. In contrasting, yet complementary fashion the work of Pillow (2015) and Gunter (2019) exemplify a wider strand in policy in which the embodiment is implicit or even concealed. This is possible owing to a feature of the presently dominant ideological underpinning of neoliberalism in western(ised) nations, namely that which tends to abstract and disembody policy in its ostensible pursuit of a technical, rational approach. This approach is implicitly gendered, made evident by the ways in which rationality is discursively allocated to masculinity and masculinised bodies, and hence normalised and invisible. Consequently, where bodies are brought into view, it is often because they are female or feminised (or gender non-specific) and so are inherently problematic or at least misaligned with the default. A related strand of policy literature is concerned with bringing bodies back into policy studies through a focus on policy actors as embodied agents, as entrepreneurs (Ball, 2017) or resisters (Courtney, 2017a), for example. An important effect of this work is to materialise neoliberalism and connect it with people's histories and desires.

The assumptions about bodies and embodiment in policy work therefore require problematisation through a range of methodological and theoretical tools. Pillow (2015), for instance, uses queer theory (see entry on 'Queer policy analysis') and queer critique to shift the focus requiring problematisation from teen mothers to the policy landscape that constructed them as deficient. This provides a new starting point (of the teen mother as worthy of the best educational experience) just as starting from the assumption of the equal educability of all children produces structures of provision that are more like comprehensive than selective schooling. From these perspectives, embodied approaches to policy work need not be individualised, as Bansel (2015b) argues that what is embodied is discursive as well as corporeal. Consequently, the embodied subject is inherently and inevitably relational, capturing a unique, agentically influenced combination of variously accepted or resisted discourses that are intelligible across fields. This has important implications for notions of generalisability in qualitative policy scholarship: two people may well never be the same, yet neither are any two in a given society mutually unintelligible.

Further reading

- Newton, T. (2003) Truly embodied sociology: marrying the social and the biological? Sociological Review, 51(1): 20–42.
- Wright, J. and Harwood, V. (eds) (2009) Biopolitics and the 'obesity epidemic': governing bodies, Abingdon: Routledge.

Enactment

Central to some education policy studies is the adoption of the analytic of enactment and a corresponding refusal of and challenge to representations of policy implementation as linear, top-down and smooth. In rational policy literature, for example, policy is sometimes seen as a problem-solving activity limited by the 'closed preserve of the formal government apparatus of policy making' (Ozga, 2000, p 42). The analytic of enactment is used instead to trace the context-sensitive arrangements through which policy is 'encoded' and 'decoded' (Braun et al, 2011, p 586) within 'institutionally determined factors' (p 586) that include school-level capacities, resources and unique interpretations or value systems. Empirically, this means documenting the recontextualisation of policy within different education organisations, schools in particular, with a thick description of the role of local actors, such as teachers, students and other staff, as influencers and interpreters of policy in those spaces. In these contexts, actors are perceived as both agents and subjects of policy who inhabit and perform policy in ways that are commensurate with different interests and goals as well as limited by specific capacities and resources (Ball et al, 2012a). From this perspective, the analytic of enactment involves a shift away from static concepts like 'policy acceptance' and a shift towards dynamic concepts like 'resistance and subversion within ad-hoc, borrowing, re-ordering, displacement, innovation, and re-invention processes' (Candido, 2020, p 131). Policy can be read as discourse, for example, and therefore is not a tidy script with clearly defined boundaries and demarcations for modelling practice. Typically, policy is messy and untidy as it oscillates between the dictates of state authority and the flexibilities and discretions of small government and local actors, with the implication that policy pronouncements and guidelines range from the directive to the suggestive. The analytic of enactment therefore stresses the messiness of policy as assemblages of 'different realities with all the attendant contingencies' (Fenwick and Edwards, 2011, p 723).

Alongside its main focus on the agency of social actors as people who practice policy and therefore represent the principal vehicles for its (im)mobilisation, the analytic of enactment emphasises the importance of recontextualisation made possible by the diversity and multi-layered nature of the socio–institutional settings through which policy unfolds. Policy makers typically develop education policy with an 'ideal' image of those contexts that complement and supplement its successful implementation. In reality, these policy environments are rarely analogous or resemble the ideal. Braun et al (2011) further note that local actors are often confronted with multiple policy objectives and goals, both present and past, which are rarely compatible or mutually reinforcing in terms of their values and effects. Thus, contexts are not only marked by the idiosyncratic nature of local settings but also by the possibility of simultaneously present policies being processed and affecting, sometimes undermining, each other.

Heimans (2012), studying vocational education in Australia, draws attention to the contextual and material aspects of policy enactment. Emphasising the processual, emergent qualities of policy actors as the co-function and co-articulation of policy enactments, Heimans (2012) undermines a static view of policy actors as fixed, unchanging or preceding policies. Researchers divide processes of policy enactment into two key elements: interpretation and translation (Ball et al, 2012a; Verger and Skedsmo, 2021). Interpretation signifies the decoding of policy mandates through individual and collective sense-making. Individual interpretation is entangled with personal biographies and situatedness or so-called 'subjective interpretational dynamics' (Ball et al, 2012a, p 21). Collective interpretation, on the other hand, is thought to result from the provisional agreements and settlements flowing from the interactions and negotiations between a broad range of internal and external stakeholders holding diverse interests. Translation, therefore, is the active process of adjusting, modifying or reframing policy as well as operationalising it into concrete actions, instruments and materials (see entry on 'Translation'). Translation is a process of engaged adaptation framed by the formal autonomy of policy actors operating within local needs and constraints. Local responses to national policy mandates are therefore more likely to be complementary or supportive when there is strong alignment (see entry on 'Alignment') between the stated policy objectives and the pre-existing values systems and professional identities shaping local projects and politics. Moreover, there is evidence of policy alignment where stated policy objectives are considered by local policy actors to be fair, useful and valid (Verger and Skedsmo, 2021). In other cases where there is evidence of policy misalignment, policies tend to be evaded, gamed or enacted only symbolically, as Verger and Skedsmo (2021) summarise in the case of accountability policies.

Studying secondary schools in the UK with a focus on three policies (personalised learning, performance standards and behaviour management), Ball et al (2012a) identified four partially interconnected elements that shape policy enactment: situated contexts; professional cultures; material contexts; and external contexts. Situated contexts emphasise locational and historical embeddedness which impacts, for instance, student intake; professional cultures embody the professional values of teachers or school leaders as well as the school's ethos; material contexts include buildings, budgets and digital infrastructures; and external contexts range from local to national level expectations and pressures. By nuancing explanations of the contexts that shape policy enactment, Ball et al (2012a) demonstrate why it is insufficient for studies of policy enactment to focus only on one set of dynamics at the expense of others, assuming we want to account for the complexities of context (see entry on 'Context') as a variable in policy enactment.

Further reading

- Takayama, K. (2012) Exploring the interweaving of contrary currents: transnational policy enactment and path-dependent policy implementation in Australia and Japan, Comparative Education, 48(4): 505–523.
- Wikström, P., Duek, S., Nilsberth, M. and Olin-Scheller, C. (2022) Smartphones in the Swedish upper-secondary classroom: a policy enactment perspective, Learning, Media and Technology. DOI: 10.1080/17439884.2022.2124268

Entrepreneur

The notion and importance of the policy entrepreneur was popularised by Kingdon (1984), who conceived policy formation as a fairly linear, emplotted process characterised, first, by agenda-setting, and then by challenges to that agenda that take the form of a proposed alternative. Contestation between these two elements produce a policy proposal that is then put to those with authority to make the final decision. Kingdon (1984) called those who succeed in advancing the policy agenda in this way 'policy entrepreneurs', characterised as persons who exemplify particular persistence and authoritativeness. It is important to note that Kingdon (1984) distinguishes between policy formation (linear) and policy agenda-setting (complex and contingent). To explain the latter, Kingdon (1984) developed multiple streams analysis.

Considerable scholarship was later developed to expand on the concept, characteristics, activities and cultural/political significance of policy entrepreneurs beyond those associated with multiple-streams approaches. For example, King and Roberts (1992) added several psychological traits to the personality profile of policy entrepreneurs, arguing that in terms of their interpersonal style, they are respectful, tolerant of differences and open to others' views, yet at the same time hard to convince. Moreover, they are characterised as largely ethical with a preference for using understated methods. Concerning how policy entrepreneurs express their power, King and Roberts (1992) observe that they prefer collective over positional approaches and depend on personal resources including intellectual and social capital as well as considerable industriousness. Policy entrepreneurs act upon core values that are grounded in duty, according to King and Roberts (1992, adapted from Table 2, p 184). Drawing on Schumpeter's elucidation of entrepreneurialism more generally, Roberts and King (1991) extrapolate to claim that in policy too, entrepreneurs' primary function is innovation in context; that is to say, the idea adopted by policy entrepreneurs need not be wholly new but must be properly aligned with the target context. This means that policy entrepreneurs often use bricolage to construct new policy solutions: they select from across a range of current practices or transpose practices to new fields (Verger, 2012). By focusing upon entrepreneurs' 'willingness to take risks' and objectives of 'creating and moulding agile, flexible organisations to meet the challenge of change', Roberts and King (1991, p 149) locate policy entrepreneurialism explicitly within the neoliberal paradigm implied by its name.

A less specifically ideologically charged description of the policy entrepreneur's function focuses on the establishment of what Verger calls 'new programmatic ideas' (Verger, 2012, p 111). This is 'a technical idea that provides the interpretation of a policy problem and prescribes a precise course of action to solve it' (Verger, 2012, p 110). This analysis locates the activities and functions of policy entrepreneurs at the level of discourse as well as practice in supplying an authoritative interpretation. Consequently, while this analysis disaggregates entrepreneurship from any particular ideology, it constructs it as an instrument of power more generally, one that might serve any number of ideological purposes. Verger (2012) argues that 'policy entrepreneurs contribute to building the causal beliefs that constitute the cognitive basis of programmatic ideas, packaging the programmatic ideas in a way that makes them appealing to a range of audiences, disseminating these new ideas among practice communities and pushing for them to be implemented in particular contexts' (p 111). From this perspective, policy work could hardly be achieved without policy entrepreneurs.

Most research locates policy entrepreneurship in individuals within organisational units. For Roberts and King (1991), this may be anywhere 'outside the formal governmental system' (p 152), including 'international organisations, think tanks, universities, or big consultancy firms, which are located at the interstices of business, governments, and academia' (Verger, 2012, p 111). Such individualised, psychologised and often market-oriented constructions of policy entrepreneurs are contested by research that locates entrepreneurship as potentially performed by certain bureaucratic institutions or organisations. For instance, Nay (2012) argues that the UNAIDS Secretariat displayed key features of policy entrepreneurialism, that is, those concerned with exercising influence over policy. Nay (2012) develops this key observation to conceptualise three (interrelated) strands of influence. First is what Nay (2012) calls prescriptive influence, which is used to refer to 'a capacity to elaborate regulatory rules and norms with an impact on policy-building processes, policy instruments and management rules' (p 56). The second is technical influence, defined by Nay (2012) as 'the development of specific technical instruments and skills by which the administration increases its capacity to assist policy actors to establish agreements, design programmes and implement decisions' (p 56). The third is cognitive influence, which is 'the capacity to gather, integrate, shape, publicise and circulate information and knowledge used in international public policies' (Nay, 2012, p 57). In other words, policy entrepreneurs frame the policy problem in ways that make it more amenable to the solution they proffer. This is a power-laden act, and so as Verger (2012) notes, successful policy entrepreneurship is more likely to be associated with institutions that are authoritative and credible.

Further reading

- Adams, B.E. (2007) Citizen lobbyists: local efforts to influence public policy, Philadelphia: Temple University Press.
- Mintrom, M. and Luetjens, J. (2017) Policy entrepreneurs and problem framing: the case of climate change, Environment and Planning C: Politics and Space, 35(8): 1362–1377.

Environmental and sustainability policy analysis

Environmental and sustainability policy analysis is used here as an umbrella term to articulate and condense a variety of research and pedagogical approaches (environmental education, education for sustainable development and climate change research) that call for improved education, evidence-based policy and ecological literacy concerning the impact of human activities on the natural environment. This includes promoting an ethics of care and responsibility towards nature in which 'nature has intrinsic value, giving it priority over things that only have contingent, instrumental value' (Bonnett, 1999, p 315), what is sometimes called 'environmental stewardship' (Wals and Benavot, 2017, p 4). Moreover, environmental and sustainability policy analysis develops in tandem with a strong commitment to democracy, plurality and the value of diversity, meaning respect for diverse viewpoints that are specific to particular value/cultural positions. This not only means 'recognition of the value position inherent in the views of all who use the term [sustainability]' (Bonnett, 1999, p 315) but challenging 'dominant anthropocentric, scientific and "Western" materialist ways of viewing the world to include local and indigenous perspectives' (Wals and Benavot, 2017, p 4).

While nature-conservation education can be dated back to the 19th century, environmental and sustainability policy analysis combines the priorities of nature-conservation education and sustainability education, which emerged during the 1960s. Environmental and sustainability policy analysis developed through conservation ecology and urban studies in the 1970s and 1980s in response to climate scientists who warned of the Anthropocene, a new geological era in which human activities are undermining the planet's capacity to self-regulate. Environmental and sustainability policy analysis therefore arises from a pressing need to develop robust policy responses and education programmes, both formal and informal, that position the environment (including plants, animals, land and the atmosphere) as essential for the sustainability of future generations, alongside housing, food, health, employment and basic schooling.

While acknowledging the importance of learning for sustainability, Aikens et al (2016) helpfully draw attention to the polyvalence surrounding the term sustainability owing to its interpretative openness, namely the ways in which it has been co-opted, reimagined and deployed to achieve a range of economic purposes and goals (also see Wals and Benavot, 2017). This includes a 'resourcist turn' in sustainability education (Aikens et al, 2016, p 12), namely managing resources for human survival or economic development. For example, in their study of how the language of sustainability is adopted and mobilised within Canadian post-secondary education policy making, McKenzie et al (2015) highlight the 'neoliberalisation of sustainability in education policy', namely the 'sustainability focus of corporate social responsibility work in schools' (p 326). Moreover, Aikens et al (2016) demonstrate that sustainability emerges in a competitive policy environment where there are multiple forces competing for dominance of education and its purpose (also see Rickinson and McKenzie, 2020).

The result is that sustainability education becomes subordinated, placed at the margins or made into subjugated knowledge within a policy and institutional landscape that values individual attainment and competition as the means and ends of education. Moreover, some critics point to the complicity of some education systems, notably western models of education, in the perpetuation, even popularisation of environmental destruction, namely through its contribution to 'pervasive "industrial mind-sets" that steer students towards individualism, materialism and hyper-rationality' (Wals and Benavot, 2017, p 4). In response, Van Poeck and Lysgaard (2015) argue that scholars of environmental and sustainability policy analysis should not be only concerned with perfecting findings, advice and solutions that promote best policy and practice, but should address the politics–policy relationship framing the field of environmental and sustainability policy analysis, namely 'the complex underlying factors that influence which policies may be developed, emulated, passed on, or passed over' (p 3).

The impact of environmental education has achieved mixed results across different geopolitical spaces and scales. In a review of literature from the Global North and Global South, Aikens et al (2016) observed widespread evidence of limited roll-out of environmental education as a resource and competency of a cross-curricular programme. In most cases, environmental education is conflated with environmental science and, emerging through science education exclusively, therefore lacks a strong presence in the social-studies curriculum (Aikens et al, 2016). For Wals and Benavot (2017), the most successful approaches to sustainability education policy implementation occurs when there is a 'whole school' or 'whole institution' (p 6) approach that integrates responses to environmental challenges at every level rather than through piecemeal or 'bolt-on' and 'built-in' approaches. The 'ecologisation' of education (Posch, 1999, p 342) can therefore take place on two levels: the 'social/organisational level', where policies are geared towards developing the agency of pupils and teachers as stewards of the environment or developing critically reflective spaces for their engagement in the politics of environmentalism; and the 'technical/economic level', where infrastructure is ecologically re-engineered and directed towards saving resources and reducing waste.

Further reading

- Læssøe, J., Feinstein, N.W. and Blum, N. (2013) Environmental education policy research – challenges and ways research might cope with them, Environmental Education Research, 19(2): 231–242.
- Robottom, I. and Stevenson, R.B. (2013) Analyses of environmental education discourses and policies, in R.B. Stevenson, M. Brody, J. Dillon and A.E.J. Wals (eds) International handbook of research on environmental education, New York: Routledge, 123–125.

Epistemology

Epistemologies are both theories and means of knowledge production, or how we know what we know. They speak to 'the fundamental relationship between the knower and what can be known' (O'Reilly and Kiyimba, 2015, p 7). Different epistemologies construct education policy and its objects, modes of investigation and aims in sometimes mutually incompatible ways. As Biesta and Burbules (2003) put it: 'If one assumes, for example, that knowledge can provide us with information about reality as it "really" is, and if one further assumes that there is only one reality, then one might conclude that there is eventually only one right way to act' (p 2). The epistemological allusion is to positivism, which applies the scientific method to the social sciences from a belief that the social world shares with the natural an objective reality. Positivist researchers, for example in the school-effectiveness field, use tools and methods through which they aim to capture and measure different features of this reality, which is external to them as researchers. This attempt at capture may be thwarted by imperfections in the sampling, tools or methods, or by biases in the researcher. Biesta and Burbules (2003) contrast this epistemological approach with post-positivism: 'If, on the other hand, one believes that the world of human action is created through action and inter-action, and the knowledge is intimately connected with what people do, then new knowledge opens up new and unforeseen possibilities, rather than telling us the one and only way to act' (p 2).

Such 'unforeseen possibilities' may include a focus on participants' subjective experiences, which is enabled through an interpretivist epistemology. The relationship between researcher and researched can be theorised (demarcated, troubled, made interrelatable) in several ways through a variety of epistemological positions and commitments:

1. *Hermeneutics*, with its focus on how specific experiences speak to (and may even serve to redeem and echo) participants' cultural and social context.
2. *Critical realism*, with its focus on how structures such as patriarchy or capitalism may exist independently of actors' constructions of them and may even have agency themselves.
3. *Social constructionism*, with its focus on the role of language and discourse in people's continuous construction of the social world in which there is no external 'real' social reality.
4. *Social constructivism*, with its focus on the interplay of language and discourse with power relations and their (non-)effects, namely the ways in which socially constructed knowledge informs others' learning and cognition without fundamentally troubling the notion of an external reality.

Researchers' selection of research question, methodological choices, constructions of key terms, and features of the research are therefore all enabled or precluded by their epistemological stance. A key measure of rigour in policy research is the alignment of researchers' claimed epistemology with their methodology, methods, instruments, conceptualisations and choice of concepts. So, ideally, the social-constructionist researcher avoids terms that conjure up a positivist epistemology (and vice versa). For example, 'data collection' implies conceptually that data exist prior to their 'gathering' by researchers, rather than being co-created with them as constructionists believe. The use of 'findings' implies that key messages exist in the data before the act of analysis which the constructionist researcher undertakes. Anderson and Holloway (2020) uncover the extent of this alignment in their study of education policy research. Here, the use of discourse analysis serves to 'illuminate the ways in which different theoretical frameworks, methodological paradigms, and epistemological vantage points comprise research stances that represent different conceptualisations of discourse, policy, and the relationship between the two' (p 189). Their analysis highlights significant instances of misalignment, where claimed or implied epistemology is contraindicated by other elements of the research. This is a problem for rigour in the field, since as Anderson and Holloway (2020) note, 'complications in terms of theoretical and analytical coherence might prevent the promise we expect of from our collective and individual work' (p 215). For this reason, the objectives of, for example, policy sociology (see entry on 'Policy sociology') are not achievable through a positivist lens, whereas randomised control trials make sense only in this paradigm.

Epistemologies are not politically neutral but are closely bound up with questions of power, since accepted 'ways of knowing' privilege those actors who practise these ways as 'knowers' and marginalise or silence those whose ways differ. This is true of all epistemologies, whether or not they claim a focus on power, as critical researchers do (Courtney et al, 2021b). Epistemologies themselves are differentially valued in the field, with positivist knowledge often preferred over that generated through post-positivist approaches (Ozga, 2000; Duarte, 2021). This is because of the positivists' discursive capture of the legitimate goals of education research through the notions of usefulness and improvement. As Ozga (2000) notes, 'research should be useful, but usefulness is not a straightforward concept, and enhancing pupil performance, while desirable, is not a sufficient description of the proper and legitimate concerns of education research' (p 5). Refutations of hegemonic epistemologies that silence important voices and perspectives include feminist standpoint epistemology (Rixecker, 1994) and queer theory (see entry on 'Queer policy analysis'). Finally, a focus on epistemology itself diminishes other ways of being human that cannot be reduced to what is known or knowable, for instance, 'the practical, the aesthetic, the ethical, or the religious dimensions' (Biesta and Burbules, 2003, p 15).

Further reading

- Marsh, D. and Stoker, G. (eds) (2010) Theory and methods in political science (3rd edn), Basingstoke: Palgrave Macmillan.
- Popkewitz, T.S. (1984) Paradigm and ideology in educational research, Barcombe: The Falmer Press.

Event

An event can reference a concrete occasion or a happening taking place in a particular place and at a delimited time that has a stated purpose or outcome, such as a conference, a lesson or a tradeshow. But an event is also, in a poststructural sense building on Gilles Deleuze and Michel Foucault, a loose, spontaneous assemblage of actors, both human and non-human, distributed in time and space. The event as assemblage (see entry on 'Assemblage') refers to compositions momentarily produced to achieve provisional arrangements or directions considered meaningful or significant. The provisionality of the event as assemblage means that it is continuously undergoing change through a process of becoming (Gulson and Webb, 2017b). When studied from the perspective of a poststructural sensibility of *eventalisation*, events can be conceived of as the combination and co-articulation of multiple determinations that, despite their outward appearance of connection or uniformity, 'may not be as internally coherent and unassailable as they often seem' (McCann, 2011, p 146). A particular actualisation of an event, for example, can be considered one possibility among many others in an endless stream of yet-to-be-realised possibilities. This suggests that events can always be otherwise should forces come together, cohere and endure in ways that make such assemblages possible, if only tendentially and provisionally since 'relations may change, new elements may enter, alliances may be broken, [and] new conjunctions may be fostered' (Anderson and McFarlane, 2011, p 126).

In the same vein, Jobér (2022) and Player-Koro et al (2018) conceptualise the events of educational trade fairs as 'policy events' or instantiations of the complex relations between education policy making and governance. Here, new modes of government and governing are not conceived in terms of power over education being confined to the state or to the market, but rather, in a capillary sense, exercised through distributed networks involving heterogeneous actors. These types of tradeshows are held across the globe in multiple countries and regions, opening up shared spaces or meeting points for the interaction of corporate and state policy actors, on the one hand, and local school authorities and teachers on the other. These tradeshows, often focused on selling education technology products and services, not only create possibilities for trade in education products, but create essential interactive environments for the circulation, insertion and promotion of ideas, knowledge, policies and practices. Another effect is to 'disable or disenfranchise or circumvent some of the established policy actors and agencies' (Ball, 2008, p 748) through addressing teachers or local authorities directly with ready-made technological solutions and pedagogical ideas for concrete classroom situations. At the same time, such events offer central venues for the social labour required to sustain and extend networks of diverse policy players. Thus 'trade shows are best understood as sites of symbolic, performative and practical policy work' (Player-Koro et al, 2018, p 692). Moving beyond any exclusive concern with events sponsored by established policy actors and commercial players, additional research in these areas could highlight the significance of counter-events where said hegemonic ideas are contested and alternatives debated.

These emerging fields of inquiry have also turned attention to teachers' experiences of said events, namely their shifting positionalities as policy subjects within wider networks of power, as well as a focus on the varied interests and logics underpinning the promotion and circulation of ideas at these types of events. Jobér's (2022) study of the World's Leading Education Show in London, for example, points to the ways in which policy actors work on those whom they seek to govern not (only) through traditional types of persuasion involving political agendas, evidence or resources, but also through engaging and enhancing affective atmospheres and emotional states. From this perspective, the education tradeshow as event constitutes an essential modality for facilitating various forms of affective governance, in some cases leaving teachers in a state of awe (Jobér, 2022). These attempts at affective governance can be traced to the specific design of the different interactive components of the tradeshows, from the hands-on demonstration sessions, lectures, and talks with teachers and vendors, to the celebratory-focused social events.

Using the same discursive logic, Gulson and Webb (2017b) adopt the term 'policy event' to study the creation of an Afrocentric Alternative School in Toronto, Canada. For Gulson and Webb (2017b), the 'policy event' is both a conceptualisation of policy and an approach to studying how policies come into being. Rather than focus on the event as the 'resultant formation (the apparatus, the regime, the technology) which appears settled, potentially even complete' (Li, 2007, p 264), Gulson and Webb (2017b) frame the event using a poststructural epistemology to show how the school as event is overdetermined by multiple influences spanning different times and spaces as well as subject to diverse narrations from multiple actors. Gulson and Webb (2017b) therefore point to the intensity and fragility of the school as event with a focus on 'the gaps, fissures and fractures that accompany processes of gathering and dispersing' (Anderson and McFarlane, 2011, p 125). Moreover, this approach allows us to question the Cartesian binary logic that is central to notions of cause and effect, linearity or the centrality of human intentionality found in some policy studies. By theorising the event as the 'product of multiple determinations that are not reducible to a single logic' (Collier and Ong, 2005, p 12), Gulson and Webb (2017b) stress the incompleteness, indeterminacy and ad-hocery of education policy, and therefore complicate dominant views of policy making and implementation as a techno-rational instrument in the improvement of schooling.

Adopting a different perspective, Pereyra et al (2018) demonstrate how the event can be understood as something that is complementary and supplementary to the mediatisation of policy (see entry on 'Mediatisation'). To do this, Pereyra et al (2018) draw our attention to the publication of the Organisation for Economic Co-operation and Development's (OECD) Programme for International Student Assessment (PISA) results, which are characterised here as a media phenomenon and orchestrated media event. As Pereyra et al (2018) demonstrate, PISA as a media event unfolds in several ways. As part of the OECD's deliberate communication strategy, PISA's results are launched on the same day in a concerted manner across countries in a ceremonial, broadcasted occasion. This builds anticipation and interest in the results across national contexts while retaining the OECD's capacity to steer the spread and interpretation of results. PISA as an event further unfolds through social media with the aid of retweets and commentaries, in effect creating a recursive logic that helps to centre the authority of PISA and the legitimacy or urgency of its results.

Further reading

- Menashy, F. (2016) Understanding the roles of non-state actors in global governance: evidence from the Global Partnership for Education, Journal of Education Policy, 31(1): 98–118.
- Zourabichvili, F.K. (2012) Deleuze: a philosophy of the event: together with the vocabulary of Deleuze, translated by K. Aarons, G. Lambert and D.W. Smith, Edinburgh: Edinburgh University Press.

Experimentation

Experimentation in relation to education policy refers to two distinct phenomena, with each of these dividing genealogically further down its branch. The first major categorisation comprises experiments where an education policy is introduced with little or none of one or more of the following: political support, evidential support from research or evidential support from enactment elsewhere. The policy is therefore an experiment in the sense that its potential effectiveness is not established. This sort of experiment is particularly associated with ideological stances by policy makers and has been characterised as experimentation in the sense it serves as 'a distinct approach to governing' (Huitema et al, 2018, p 144). The second major categorisation concerns experimentation as research method. However, even here there are diverse approaches. Some interpret this method differently, for instance, with or without randomisation as a necessary condition. Experiments have limitations and attract valid critique concerning fundamental questions of, inter alia, epistemology and ontology.

Policy experiments that merit the name because they are evidenced either insufficiently or not at all are reasonably widespread in jurisdictions experiencing or enacting what Sahlberg (2011) has called the Global Educational Reform Movement (GERM). This is a suite of related reforms that focus on 'curriculum development, student assessment, teacher development, technology-assisted teaching and learning, and proficiency in basic competencies (i.e., reading mathematical, and scientific literacy)' (Sahlberg, 2011, p 176). GERM is promoted by private-sector actors and institutions whose interests it serves, and so it is underpinned by an explicit commitment to competition, apparent autonomy and choice, and by an implicit acceptance of privatisation, both exogenous but particularly endogenous. Such a commitment, demonstrated by policy makers globally to various degrees, travels primarily through ideology rather than evidence. The firmest believers with the means to realise their commitment tend to become 'laboratories' of untested policy ideas; experiences there subsequently provide sufficient grounds for others to adopt these ideas or not. Notorious examples of such laboratories include England from the 1980s, where experimental work to create quasi-markets inspired reformers globally (see Finkelstein and Grubb, 2000). Another laboratory was New Zealand, which earned the name twice; once following its 1935 adoption of Keynesian welfarism and then again in 1984, when it converted to a form of neoliberalism that was 'the most radical of any undertaken in an industrialised nation' (O'Neill, 2015, p 831). Laboratories need not be nation-states or even jurisdictions, however. Williamson (2012) characterises the third sector as 'perhaps the paradigmatic decentralised laboratory' (p 776) in its creation and promotion of 'an "experimental" curriculum policy' in its role as 'an intermediary between government and market' (p 776). Huitema and colleagues (2018) argue that what unites all these cases is their reliance on a conceptualisation of experimentation as 'an approach to governance', whose aim, following Dewey, 'is to try out new approaches in practice' (p 146). However, while Dewey saw this process of 'probing, trial and error' as 'a central phenomenon in democracy and ethics' (Huitema et al, 2018, p 146), in a neoliberal context, it is arguably less democratic.

Policy experiments as a research method are often described by their practitioners and perceived by research funders as the gold standard in the social sciences, reflecting these groups' (and arguably, many societies') privileging of positivism relative to social constructionist knowledge production. Experiments may be defined as a sufficiently resourced method that draws on an intervention theory and an explicit hypothesis to evaluate one novel idea at a time using participant randomisation between control and intervention groups to test the effectiveness of that intervention. However, as Adams (2020) points out, in education, 'operationalising "novel" in a meaningful way is not feasible given that almost all education reforms have been tried somewhere else before' (p 32). In education, therefore, 'novel' may mean 'novel in this context'. Much of the attraction of experiments to policy makers lies in their apparent objectivity, yet politics and values suffuse all aspects, from the selection (and hence problematisation) of their focus through to how the results are interpreted and the effect of the experiments on discourse (re)production (Huitema et al, 2018).

Experiments have limitations, even when accepted on their own terms. For instance, they may be poorly designed or resourced, or their political basis may be deliberately obviated or shift during the experiment. The requirements of the method arguably mean that relatively few subjects are amenable to proper treatment and illumination through experimentation, although many more are attempted. More fundamental questions may be asked about the appropriateness of the positivist paradigm in which they are located to many issues in education, which are better addressed through constructionist or other poststructuralist methodologies.

Further reading

- Berk, R.A., Boruch, R.F., Chambers, D.L., Rossi, P.H. and Witte, A.D. (1985) Social policy experimentation: a position paper, Evaluation Review, 9(4): 387–429.
- Sadoff, S. (2014) The role of experimentation in education policy, Oxford Review of Economic Policy, 30(4): 597–620.

Expertise

The term expertise is used vernacularly to signify something qualitatively unique, new, useful or significant about the opinions, judgements, perspectives or 'know-how' of a person or organisation with notable or recognised skills in, and learning of, a profession, craft or branch of scientific or technical knowledge. Expertise, therefore, is the social configuration or interpretative frame resulting from the organisation, delineation and valuing of 'different ways of knowing the very same thing' (Carr, 2010, p 18). While the role of experts and expertise has been crucial to the development of modern systems of government (Foucault, 2008), it has arguably become even more important to the repurposing of the role of government in the macroeconomy, namely providing the mainstay for emerging forms of 'networked governance' (Srivastava and Baur, 2016) that work to displace the role of traditional government authorities as principal overseers of the economy and welfare.

Contemporarily, the ubiquity of expertise has been attributed to several interconnected trends. On the one hand, the rapid acceleration of interconnections and flows between diverse localities and nations brought about by globalisation has created ever-increasing new demands for knowledge about the multi-causality and multi-dimensionality of nations and cultures within the context of emerging economic risks and ontological insecurities. On the other hand, and related to this, is the rise of global corporations, supranational organisations and international political and economic unions (from the Organisation for Economic Co-operation and Development to the European Union). This rise has challenged the old orthodoxy that power or knowledge production could or should be studied from a single vantage point or isolated entity such as the nation-state or government. And finally, the shift from 'government to governance' (Rhodes, 1996), in which top-down authority exercised through state power is thought to be supplanted by new flexible modes of governing defined by plural and dispersed forms of power, has multiplied the domains to be monitored and controlled, in effect increasing demands for improved calculation and prudent management by governance experts.

These contexts not only challenge the epistemology of state authority as best placed to respond to the diversity and complexity flowing from processes of modernisation and globalisation, but uniquely have created the conditions for the mobilisation of new knowledge actors and authorities in the form of think tanks (see entry on 'Think tank'), expert and consultative committees, public policy labs, social enterprises, consultants and consultancy firms (see entry on 'Consultant'), advocacy organisations and charities. As Lingard (2016) observes, some experts span different professions, sectors and knowledge disciplines in order to extend their 'involvement and enhanced impact' (p 32) in these areas, acting as boundary spanners or boundary organisations in the process. Similarly, Williamson (2014) notes how, in traversing and combining the demands of these areas, experts emerge as mediators and cross-sectoral intermediaries who labour to 'produce, brand and market their ideas as unique new policy packages in order to appear innovative and to mobilise political, public and media support simultaneously' (p 227). This highlights the ways in which expertise can be understood to be distributed, dispersed and networked.

From a conceptual or methodological perspective, expertise therefore serves as a useful analytical or heuristic tool for making connections between changes in macro, micro and meso relations and practices. From a postmodernist, social constructionist or relativist perspective, for example, expertise represents attempts to construct and authenticate ways of seeing, evaluating and describing reality, and therefore is helpful in making sense of the subtle ways in which power operates through discourse or ideology, namely through the authoritative allocation of value to speaking, acting and knowing in certain ways. Expertise seeks to purport truths about who we are or what is worth knowing; confer value on particular objects, actors and projects as true, valid or valuable; produce relations of power built around communities of consent and dissent; and therefore is generative of the very discursive boundaries that set limits around certain speaking positions and value judgements considered acceptable, scientific or credible. Expertise therefore works at the intersection of power and knowledge and can be considered a product of processes that are both 'repressive and productive' (Carr, 2010, p 18) since they work through dividing practices that separate social actors into distinct epistemological, knowing subjects as experts or laypeople.

Bajenova (2019) observes how the expansion of the European Union has been accompanied by new demands for technical and political knowledge from European think tanks acting as sources of expert knowledge and policy advice. Bajenova (2019) documents the ways in which think tanks assume the 'use of academic, publicity and political forms of capital, which differentiates them from other forms of knowledge providers' (p 67), thus pointing to expertise as a form of labour that sustains its legitimacy through mobilising distinct forms of capital, and familiarity with artefacts (see entry on 'Artefact') and resources, that work to index and therefore instantiate already existing preferred knowledge or know-how. Expertise has also been usefully conceptualised by Grek (2013) and Lawn (2013) as political tools of education governance, either as productive sites for guiding and enforcing education policy decisions through 'mediation, brokering and "translation"' (Grek, 2013, p 696) or as epistemic communities for giving objectivity and rigour to knowledge systems that enable new forms of governing of education centred around 'assessment and testing' (Lawn, 2013, p 118).

Further reading

- Normand, R. (2010) Expertise, networks and indicators: the construction of the European strategy in education, European Educational Research Journal, 9(3): 407–421.

- Wilkins, A. (2017) Creating expert publics: a governmentality approach to school governance under neo-liberalism, in S. Courtney, R. McGinity and H. Gunter (eds) Educational leadership: theorising professional practice in neoliberal times, London and New York: Routledge, 97–110.

F

Fast policy

Since the 1980s, political and social scientists have been documenting the technological, economic and cultural effects of globalisation. Globalisation has given rise to a multitude of ontological and economic possibilities, from instantaneous communication to cross-border trade of physical commodities. Globalisation has therefore been studied at various scales and levels, from micro-qualitative studies observing the impact of resettlement on refugees and the emergence of hybridised local cultural identities, to macro-quantitative studies examining the impact of transnational capital mobility, trade liberalisation and international outsourcing on national industries.

Another significant impact of globalisation has been the intensification and compression of policy movement around the globe, held together by the involvement of 'intermediary' actors in the brokering, mediation and translation of relationships and exchanges between governments and agencies. This enables a range of intergovernmental and interagency pragmatic policy borrowing and fast-tracking policy decision-making to occur. The result is the translocal and cross-scalar flow and insertion of new global policy networks at the subnational and national level made possible by the expansion of multilateral organisations and international political and economic unions, such as the Organisation for Economic Co-operation and Development (OECD), the World Bank and the European Union.

On the one hand, the increased mobility of policy ideas across the globe is, according to Peck and Theodore (2015), evidence of 'fast-policy regimes' (p 3) or 'compressed policymaking moments' (p xvi). These are mobile, fluid, transnational policy spaces in which intermediary actors and agencies spanning transnational corporations, philanthropic organisations, professional bodies and business communities work through long-distance interconnections to broker new kinds of cross-national political and institutional connections. Their aim is to influence and profit financially from the packaging and selling of 'what works' or 'best practice' solutions to different countries (Bartlett and Vavrus, 2016). While fast policy can give the impression of policy ideas moving seamlessly across national borders and subnational spaces more or less intact, Peck and Theodore (2015) warn against 'reading off' these processes as evidence that policy ideas are recontextualised and implemented according to interests or motivations that can be traced to some principle design, singular logic or predefined sequencing. To do so, argue Peck and Theodore (2015), is to study policy movement within a positivist, rational-actor framework that offers only reified, homogeneous accounts of policy change.

Instead, Peck and Theodore (2015) draw attention to the 'institutional heterogeneity and contending forces' (p xxiv), which act as sensitising contexts for the assemblage and recomposition of fast-policy mobilities (see entry on 'Mobility'). Here, fast policy can be studied empirically as the contingent product of local politics and projects including infrastructuralisation (the interplay of capacities, structures and logics), topologisation (the configuration and ordering of practices according to measurement, metrics, ranking and comparison), spatialisation (the production of social and political space) and scalecraft (the learning and application of scalar practices, fixes or reconfigurations), all of which point to the fragilities and relays that make up policy mobilities. Hence, in the global education policy literature, fast-policy mobilities are sometimes framed as complicated expressions of local–global interactions, what is called 'vernacular globalisation' (Appadurai, 1996) or 'localised globalism' (de Sousa Santos, 2006).

Hardy et al (2021) draw on the concept of fast policy to explain how key aspects of Finnish education – early childhood, basic/compulsory education and vocational education – have moved from a policy moment characterised by slow, steady, thoughtful investment in 'teachers and principals' (p 775) as agents for change to one characterised by 'intensification and fragmentation' (p 780). Here, policy decisions are ripped out of their social context through an exclusive concern with efficiency and best practice. The result is that certain private actors and processes are privileged over others in these contexts. The need to manage policy decisions through decontextualised, prescriptively coded forms of evaluation created unique opportunities to valorise the 'cogency of business-models in educational contexts' (Hardy et al, 2021, p 782). Lewis and Hogan (2019) also examine the unique demands created by fast-policy environments in New South Wales, Australia, namely fast-tracking decision-making and rapid programme roll-out guided by evidence-based policy. In one case study, they observe how international edu-businesses, like Pearson, are able to leverage their position as impartial technical experts and 'big data' providers to package and sell 'what works' solutions through the provision of services that combine educational performance data sourced from the OECD, the International Association for the Evaluation of Educational Achievement (IEA), the United Nations and the World Bank, to enable governments to locate their schools within wider webs of commensuration, equivalence and comparison in a global context. As Lewis and Hogan (2019) observe, 'Pearson has created an infrastructure that allows unprecedented policy mobility, joining up and condensing education data into one easy-to-read format' (p 10).

Similarly, Williamson (2019) shows the importance of Silicon Valley to fast-policy environments as a unique topographical zone and outcome of 'relations that have sedimented into specific technical, economic, and cultural patterns of innovation and production' (p 284). Through their commitment to developing technology-enhanced approaches to learning and teaching, such as personalised learning technologies derived from the application of code and algorithms, Silicon Valley emerges as a condition and effect of fast-policy regimes, marked by 'compressed development and implementation horizons, by iterative forms of deference to best practice and paradigmatic models, by enlarged roles for intermediaries as advocates of specific policy routines and technologies, and by a growing reliance on prescriptively coded forms of front-loaded advice and evaluation science' (Peck and Theodore, 2015, p 4).

Further reading

- Alirezabeigi, S., Masschelein, J. and Decuypere, M. (2021) Disentangling fast school policy at a slow pace, in C. Addey and N. Piattoeva (eds) Intimate accounts of education policy research: the practice of methods, London: Routledge, 169–184.
- Hardy, I., Rönnerman, K. and Beach, D. (2019) Teachers' work in complex times: the 'fast policy' of Swedish school reform, Oxford Review of Education, 45(3): 350–366.

Feminist policy analysis

A key focus of feminist policy analysis, and related disciplines like feminist comparative policy or feminist critical policy analysis, concerns using theoretical and methodological approaches which are explicitly feminist, and therefore anti-foundationalist, interpretivist and/or poststructuralist in orientation, to make visible the role of gender and of gendering to policy-making processes and outcomes. This includes using feminist perspectives and hybridised feminist positions (liberal feminist, Black feminist, socialist feminist, radical feminist, empirical feminist, postmodernist feminist) to challenge the accepted constructs, methodologies and concepts that make up policy studies as a discipline, especially those approaches that (un)intentionally construct a prioris using gender bias that disproportionately affects women and/or are positivist (so-called neutral, dispassionate, detached, objective and technical) in their appraisals of policy problems and their solutions.

In this respect, feminist policy analysis can be considered overtly political and unapologetically ideological with its focus on using research to promote policies that further women's interests through challenging the implicit androcentrism shaping state politics and administrative arrangements (Kenway, 1990). This includes a focus on strengthening gender (as well as race, queer, sex and social class) equality through promoting 'culturally appropriate social and educational policy' (Gonzalez, 1998, p 99) and pursuing difference through a 'quest for equality [not] being based exclusively on men's terms' nor based on a homogeneous category of 'women' but which balances the 'interests of specific groups of girls and those of girls in general' (ten Dam and Volman, 1995, p 212).

According to Bensimon and Marshall (2003), the starting point for any feminist policy analysis is a 'standpoint feminist epistemology' that acknowledges 'the idea that knowledge is socially situated' (p 343) and therefore the primary unit of analysis for any feminist policy analysis is the lived experience of gendered (and racialised, classed, sexed) subjects within changing historical and cultural moments. A unique analytical focus of feminist policy analysis concerns using experimental, alternative methodologies, such as policy archaeology, genealogy, narrative and oral history, to uncover how bodies of gender and colour are positioned, summoned and regulated in those moments through dominant policy discourses. Pillow (2003), for example, adopts a feminist genealogy (see entry on 'Genealogy') to show how the body, that inescapable frame of reference in the formation of subjects, emerges as a site of intervention and control for various authorities: 'The teen pregnant body is a site of state regulation and control not only of the teen mother, but also a site for the regulation and reassertion of societal norms, morals and values on issues such as female sexuality, single-parenting, welfare, birth control and abortion' (p 149).

In contrast to the foundational ontology of positivism, which claims that causally determined social facts can be observed, tested and verified using value-free knowledge, feminist policy analysis turns the analysis on its head by problematising the very 'practices and decisions that are assumed to be gender neutral in order to show that they can and do result in perverse consequences for women' (Bensimon and Marshall, 2003, p 344). In other words, it is by refusing to evaluate 'women on the basis of male norms' (Shaw, 2004, p 58) and through placing women's experiences at the centre of policy decisions that policy analysis assumptions and methods properly address those dimensions of 'silence, taboo topics, hidden injuries, nonevents, and nondecisions' (Shaw, 2004, p 69) that are uniquely female.

Feminist policy analysis therefore draws attention to the various forms of 'epistemic injustice' (Blackmore, 2022, p 623) brought about by policy-making decisions and processes, supposedly gender-neutral in design and their effects, that disproportionately affect and disadvantage women. In a study of higher education institutions, Blackmore (2021) demonstrates the impact of corporate restructuring and research policies for women who, by virtue of their commitments to an ethics of care and justice, find themselves responsible 'for the domestic labour of quality assurance, curriculum and pedagogy while men dominate the external face of the university in research, internationalisation and advancement' (p 629). Similarly, radical feminist critiques of the state focus on the complicity of administrative and governance arrangements, in particular the reproduction of different dimensions of society as public and private, in sustaining conditions and relations that support 'the patriarchal family, its judicial and other arrangements concerning matters of rape, domestic violence, pornography and reproductive technology, and its involvement in militarism and warfare' (Kenway, 1990, p 57).

It is here that radical feminists and social feminists depart from the liberal feminist position that social change can be affected positively through state-actioned, piecemeal reform or incrementalism, and therefore present 'a more malleable view of state patriarchy and argue that certain state arenas may be appropriate sites for feminist action' (Mazur, 2016, p 2528). For racial feminists and socialist feminists, the state apparatus is preordained to operate through assumptive worlds that always already privilege men, with the result that 'the interests of women and the interests of the state intersect and, most often, contradict each other' (Shaw, 2004, p 59). Similarly, feminist policy scholars, sometimes called empirical feminists, are considered by Mazur (2016, p 2527) to have a more 'moderate agenda', seeking to work with rather than against 'the scientific arena', compared to 'many feminist scholars who seek to transform or revolutionise the study of politics'. Black feminists or women scholars of colour also note the blindspot in feminist political work, namely the failure of White middle-class women to 'recognise their own race privilege' (Weiler, 2008, p 501) and the contribution of the feminist activism of women of colour to the women's liberation movement across the globe.

Further reading

- Bensimon, E.M. and Marshall, C. (1997) Policy analysis for postsecondary education: feminist and critical perspectives, in C. Marshall (ed) Feminist critical policy analysis II: a perspective from post-secondary education, London: Falmer, 1–21.
- Jenkins, F. (2014) Epistemic credibility and women in philosophy, Australian Feminist Studies, 29(80): 161–170.

Framing

Framing is the discursive construction of a policy subject or object in order to render particular modes of thinking and action about it appropriate or inappropriate, to establish an expectation either of agency or inactivity from particular actors in relation to it, and to summon a particular reality, or regime of truth, within which certain perceptions, emotions and experiences are enabled and others precluded. Frames structure agency through changing perceptions and constructions of the terrain within which agency happens, and so are political. Framing occurs at several levels in regard to education policy. First, framing occurs through depoliticisation and concomitant decision-making about how certain educational matters may be framed as best located with individuals or families rather than in the political realm, and so, thus privatised, cease to be policy objects at all (Gunter, 2019). They are framed out of public consideration, in other words. Depoliticisation and the framing that is an integral part of it is a strategy undertaken by jurisdictions with legislative powers in order to delegitimate political and democratic forms of action and marginalise political actors.

Second, the fundamental notions of what policy is and how it should be 'done' have been framed in two major and contrasting ways, called policy science and policy sociology (see entries on 'Policy science' and 'Policy sociology'). These framings influence, inter alia, understandings concerning the scope of policy analysis (that is, *with* versus *without* historical, ideological, political and cultural contextualisation); the relationship between policy and effect (that is, linear, direct and measurable versus complex and contingent); and how policy gets 'done' (that is, implemented versus enacted) (Adams, 2016). The question of who undertakes such framing is a matter of membership of particular epistemic communities.

Third, framings alter how a given policy object is interpreted. In this sense, framing is a strategy undertaken by a range of actors, including policy entrepreneurs, think tanks or networks (see entries on 'Entrepreneur', 'Think tank' and 'Policy network analysis'), the media or policy makers, whose aim is the normalisation of a desired construction of the policy problem and solution. In this sense, framing may be seen as 'a mode of meta-governance' (Milana, 2016, p 218). New frames cannot normalise what is unfamiliar or threatening to stakeholders' interests; instead, to succeed, frames draw and build on existing assumptions in the target or in cognate fields, or, more often, on stories about the social world. These new '"causal stories", i.e. explanatory frames' (Verger, 2012, p 112) and the policies that derive from them must also demonstrate consistency and coherence in relation to one another, notwithstanding their often-haphazard assembly through processes of 'bricolage, transposition, and translation' (p 112). This, according to Verger (2012), enables the production of convincing diagnoses of the policy problem, and also of prognoses, in other words policy prescriptions, that are more liable to generate approval from the public, or from 'practice communities' through being 'framed in a way that makes them familiar, feasible, and perceived as a superior policy solution' (p 112).

For Verger (2012), what is framed is not simply the object of policy, but rather 'new programmatic ideas' (p 111) about that object, that is, the whole discursive package from interpretation of the policy problem through to the solution. Related to this wider point is a narrower one concerning what van Lieshout et al (2012) call 'scale framing', which they use to refer to 'the process of framing a phenomenon on a certain scale' (p 164). Framing a potentially national policy problem as uniquely local, for instance, summons different actors and locates them as differentially powerful within decision-making structures. An example of this in education is the way in which national, or arguably global, marketised conditions produce problems for its leadership that are discursively scale-framed as best solved through individuals developing and demonstrating entrepreneurial leadership (see Courtney, 2020).

Fourth, certain professional roles within education may be discursively imbued with particular attributes and features; in other words, the role itself may be framed through policy-derived expectations such as regulatory standards, or ideal versions may be constructed through policy, including professional standards. This process has been elucidated in relation to the role of the school leader and how role framing may influence actors' identities as policy subjects. This may be interpreted through a psychology lens using role theory, which is 'a cognitive schema that defines behavioural expectation attached to the role' (Berkovich and Benoliel, 2021, p 42). An example from sociology adapts MacIntyre's (2013) notion of the 'character' to argue that role-holders engage more or less self-reflexively with a policy-framed leader character to produce a range of identity possibilities (Courtney and McGinity, 2020).

Further reading

- McDonald, L. (2013) In their own words: US think tank 'experts' and the framing of education policy debates, Journal for Critical Education Policy Studies, 11(3): 1–28.
- Serrano-Velarde, K. (2015) Words into deeds: the use of framing strategy in EU higher education policy, Critical Policy Studies, 9(1): 41–57.

G

Genealogy

Originally developed by French social theorist and philosopher Michel Foucault, the concept of genealogy aims to trace 'the details and accidents that accompany every beginning' (Foucault, 1998, p 144). For Foucault (1998), genealogy recognises that every idea and thought system is conditioned by 'its jolts, its surprises, its unsteady victories and unpalatable defeats' (pp 144–145). Genealogy therefore 'rejects the meta-historical deployment of ideal significations and indefinite teleologies. It opposes itself to the search for origins' (Foucault, 1998, p 140). Inspired by German philosopher Friedrich Nietzsche, who through his writing on morality and religion opposed metaphysics and the search for the origins or essences of things (in German 'Ursprung'), Foucault described ideas and thought systems as the 'exteriority of accidents' (Foucault, 1998, p 146), meaning that what comes to stand in for, or represent, truth is only ever the 'outcome of a process in which there is conflict, confrontation, struggle, resistance' (Foucault, 2002, p 457).

Genealogy therefore concerns the mode of dissension by which some ideas and thought systems acquire the status of 'truths' – universal ideals, value systems or normative assumptions. Here, mode of dissension refers to that dynamic, generative, productive space in which ideas and thought systems are struggled over by cultures and interest groups through invasions, ploys, omissions and silences. In this sense, genealogy differs from traditional historical methods of inquiry where, typically, ideas and thought systems are studied chronologically or sequentially as the culmination and expression of a linear-rational search for truth. On this account, genealogy views ideas and thought systems as the contingent product of struggles over meaning, struggles that tend to be concealed or violently suppressed through appeals to 'reason', 'rationality' or 'morality'. Genealogy therefore aims at denaturalising ideas or thought systems taken to be timeless and rooted in a fixed and unchanging reality, 'making it so that what is taken for granted is no longer taken for granted' (Foucault, 2002, p 456).

In education policy research, genealogy has been used to great effect to undermine a view of global policy processes as moving uniformly and predictably across nations, spaces, places, institutions and peoples. Instead, genealogy emphasises the ruptures and breaks that characterise the uneven development of policy processes and their complicated distribution and refraction, with a focus on the volatility of policy goals and dilemmas as the serendipitous outcome of specific geopolitical configurations and their unique flows and connections as 'temporary policy settlements' (Gale, 2001, pp 389–390). In this account, genealogy stresses the 'frequent disruptions, uneven and haphazard processes of dispersion' (Tamboukou, 1999, p 203) through which policy is made and unmade. This includes a focus on how policy is socially and politically mediated, selected and transformed on the basis of consensus formation among temporary alliances and local politics and projects.

More broadly, genealogy has been adopted by education policy researchers as a heuristic tool to trace the ever-deepening relationships between education and the interests and influence of businesses and economic prerogatives, but more specifically to outline the modes of reasoning or 'discourses' through which new modes of governance are grafted onto education problems and solutions. Through a study of the rise of 'quantified child', Smith (2017) uses genealogy to demonstrate how certain trends in global education policy making have intersected and combined to rationalise and normalise the quantification or datafication of children (see entry on 'Digital education'). Here, quantification and datafication refer to the ways in which subjects and practices acquire the provisional conceptual identity of numbers as a condition for their monitoring and management.

Adopting a similar approach, Dahlstedt and Fejes (2019) use genealogy to trace the emergence of 'entrepreneurship education' within Swedish curriculum reforms during the 1990s and 2010s, with a focus on what problems such reforms are intended to solve and their effects in terms of shaping and recalibrating students as flexible, problem-solving, adaptive, learning subjects. Similarly, Hunkin (2016) uses genealogy to trace a history of the discourse of 'quality' in early childhood reform policy in Australia in order to show its implicit and explicit links to human capital theory, while Olmedo and Wilkins (2017) also use genealogy as a method to trace constructions of the parent through English education policy discourse. Here the focus concerns how parents are (differently) summoned in the role of consumers, governors and producers to support and supplement market-based education system design.

Further reading

- Courtney, S.J. (2021) A genealogical analysis of charisma in leadership, in F. English (ed) The Palgrave handbook of educational leadership and management discourse, Cham: Palgrave Macmillan, 1–19.
- Tamboukou, M. and Ball, S.J. (2003) Genealogy and ethnography: fruitful encounters or dangerous liaisons?, in M. Tamboukou and S.J. Ball (eds) Dangerous encounters: genealogy and ethnography, Bern: Peter Lang, 1–36.

Governance

Alongside other major signifiers like neoliberalism, governance is one of the most cited concepts in contemporary political and social theory. Used primarily as descriptive noun to denote the various economic, political and social changes affecting government and civil society in Anglophone countries since the 1990s, and later to describe similar observable changes in countries in the Global South, the term governance has been translated across various geopolitical contexts as a useful analytic for tracing the changing relationship between citizens and the state under globalisation. A focus of governance studies includes tracing the various rationalities and tactics deployed by governments as coping mechanisms for managing and responding to the complexity and diversity flowing from processes of globalisation, including deindustrialisation, ontological insecurity, hyperconnectivity, multiculturalism, translocalism, risk consciousness or detraditionalisation (see Giddens, 2002). These coping strategies are diverse, and take on different forms and logics according to the inherited institutional landscape in which they emerge, but they all share a unique focus on mobilising non- and extra-statal actors and organisations, specifically those from the private and charity sectors, as policy interlocutors and policy spanners who can help create vital relays between government aspirations and the everyday actions and decisions of public actors and organisations operating in decentralised contexts.

Since the 1980s and 1990s, governments in mostly Anglophone countries have responded to globalisation by carving out spaces in which to reimagine the role of government in the macroeconomy, namely one that promotes global alignment, capital mobility, fiscal responsibility and the rights of citizens as consumers. This has included weakening the role of traditional structures of government with a democratic mandate, considered to be too inefficient or costly, and more generally displacing a view of the moral necessity for a social democratic state and its various affordances, from economic protection of individuals and groups against the unintended consequences of capitalism to government-subsidised mass social programmes. Instead, the new role of government, sometimes called the 'small state', 'small government' or 'devolved government', has been to fully privatise (denationalise) public assets and services or contract them out to private companies and charities.

On this understanding, a useful definition of governance is what Rhodes (1996) describes as 'governing without government' (p 652), namely the displacement of government as principal overseer of public-service delivery and management. Governments persistently and actively set rules and manage expectations intended to shape the way public organisations and individuals conduct themselves, a process Cooper (1998) calls 'governing at a distance' (p 12). This is evident through the raft of provisos, incentives, directives and guidelines intended to shape how public actors and organisations conduct themselves. Governance, in this sense, refers to those various governmental programmes 'designed to improve conditions by which change can be affected or limited to serve different political, economic and environmental aims' (Wilkins and Gobby, 2020, p 311). It can also be conceptualised in more controversial and negative terms to signify the abrogation of state responsibility and its reluctance to protect individuals and organisations against some of the worst excesses of unregulated markets.

Governance therefore denotes the shift away from vertical structures of top-down government and the shift towards horizontal, flexible networks of bottom-up government. Governance points to a disaggregation of state power, sometimes seen as necessary to remove the 'clunky command or instrumental contract relationships' (Davies and Spicer, 2015, p 226) that limit the capacity of organisations to innovate, and the mobilisation of new intermediary organisations, policy networks and policy communities working 'consensually' towards conflict resolution or trust building with stakeholders (Klijn, 2012).

Owing to its unique capacity to articulate and condense a wide variety of economic, social and political trends, and the different ways it is deployed normatively and conceptually to achieve different kinds of analytical and political work, the term governance can sometimes suffer from loose or indiscriminate use, resulting in some confusion over its meaning (Wilkins, 2021). From a deliberative-interactive perspective (Kooiman, 2003, p 33), governance is considered essential to producing 'interactive learning' environments that are essential to communicative reasoning and to enabling diverse peoples to arrive at mutually influencing sets of goals and ideals. At the same time, governance can be conceptualised from a Gramscian perspective (Davies, 2012, p 2694) as 'integral to neoliberal hegemonic ideology and strategy' since it derives its legitimacy from creating vital relays between the ambitions of governments and the formally autonomous operations of public institutions, that is, through 'trying to improve coordination of governments with the other actors who are necessary to deliver services or implement policies' (Klijn, 2012, p 213). Similarly, from a governmentality perspective, governance can be conceptualised as formal and informal modes of power for administering, managing and intervening upon the behaviour of others in order to cultivate spaces and relations for the realisation of particular modes of participation and self-governing among citizens (Wilkins, 2016).

Further reading

- Bevir, M. and Rhodes, R.A.W. (2006) Governance stories, London: Routledge.
- Eagleton-Pierce, M. (2014) The concept of governance in the spirit of capitalism, Critical Policy Studies, 8(1): 5–21.

Governmentality

During the 1970s, Michel Foucault presented a series of lectures at the Collège de France that traced a genealogy of the modern state through a historical reconstruction of the role of disciplinary institutions and power within different phases of liberal societies, from Ancient Greece to modern neoliberalism. Central to these analyses was the concept of governmentality (not to be confused with governance – see entry on 'Governance') which Foucault (2008) used to describe the 'rationalisation of governmental practice in the exercise of political sovereignty' (p 4). By this, Foucault (2008) meant the ways in which governmental power is made both practical and technical within specific organised practices as methods for upholding and affirming the political power of liberal authorities. Foucault's antihumanism and rejection of the idea of a sovereign, self-originating subject, or what is sometimes called the 'Cartesian subject', also led him to philosophical-based historical investigations of the constitution of the subject as a discursive effect of the 'institutionalisation' of liberal rule through judicial and political forms of state power. Here, Foucault locates a history of the subject within the history of the formation of modern state power, thus marking out important analytic spaces for tracing 'the multiple and diverse relations between the institutionalisation of a state apparatus and historical forms of subjectivation' (Lemke, 2007, p 44).

In this framing, Foucault (1982) characterises 'government' as 'modes of action, more or less considered or calculated, which were destined to act upon the possibilities of action of other people' (p 790). Governmentality, therefore, is concerned with how different kinds of historical subjects come to be represented (or not) within specific judicial, economic and political programmes. This includes a focus on the conditions and practices that crystallise (or not) to make various forms of governing possible, namely 'the technologies through which governing is made practicable and the forms of rationality ... that render domains and problems of government thinkable and analysable' (Dean, 1998, p 26). To take one example, Foucault observed a historically significant transformation in the problem of government in early modern Europe, roughly the period spanning 1500–1800, during which time the modern state emerged through the 'invention and assemblage of particular apparatuses and devices for exercising power and intervening upon particular problems' (Rose, 1999, p 19). Foucault refers to the invention of 'modes of objectification' and 'dividing practices' as key 'techniques for assuring the order of human municipalities' during this time (Foucault, 1977, p 218).

Government therefore differs from sovereignty since, according to Foucault (1991), 'it is a question not of imposing law on men, but of disposing things; that is to say, of employing tactics rather than laws' (p 95). Yet sovereignty and discipline are not displaced by the modern art of government but recast within a concern for 'problems of self-control, guidance for the family and for children, management of the household, directing the soul, and other questions' (Lemke, 2007, p 45). Governmentality, in other words, is the study of specific arrangements in which government introduces new possibilities for agency and relations to the self while at the same time utilising that agency for its own objectives (Rose, 1999). This also means acknowledging the complicated ways in which subjects are incentivised to work on them themselves, not through duress or compulsion but 'through "interest" and "curiosity" to improve themselves' (Perryman et al, 2017, p 754).

Various education researchers have adopted the analytic of governmentality as a useful lens for framing studies of policy making and policy travel, especially in the dynamic context of neoliberal policy logics. Bailey (2015), for example, highlights the importance of educational charity Teach First and its Leadership Development Programme as technologies of and ancillaries to government. Bailey (2015) draws attention to the 'managerial discourse of resilience which is inscribed into the Teach First competencies and values' (p 233), characterised as 'one such site where subjectivity and conduct are potentially shaped' (p 234) according to a vision of a responsible and enterprising self. Gobby (2013) mobilises a governmentality perspective to similar effect through demonstrating the influence of neoliberal government on the Independent Public Schools (IPS) programme in Western Australia. Here, Gobby (2013) documents the various subject positions and forms of knowledge (entrepreneurial agency, performative culture and corporate know-how) inscribed and made possible by the IPS programme, or what Tikly (2003) describes in the context of South African education reform as the 'decentralisation of responsibility for risk management' (p 69). As Gobby (2013) describes it, 'school self-management functions as a regime of government and self-government through which power is exercised on, through and by principals' (p 283). Other researchers have examined how the same policy logics have been extended to and translated as part of 'the practice, perception and self-crafting of teachers' (Perryman et al, 2017, p 754).

Writing about education reform in Queensland, Australia, Goodwin (1996) similarly acknowledges this shift to corporate managerialism, which is defined as a 'technology of control' (p 73) through which government exercises greater forms of scrutiny over others by virtue of their commitment to reinventing themselves in the approved-of image. Hay and Kapitzke (2009) adopt a governmentality perspective to produce a similar set of observations about education reforms in Queensland, Australia, where it is argued that 'industry school partnerships are an improvised technology for pursuing particular objectives of government within globalised and globalising contexts' (p 214).

Further reading

- Larner, W. (2000) Neoliberalism: policy, ideology and governmentality, Studies in Political Economy, 63: 5–25.
- McKee, K. (2009) Post-Foucauldian governmentality: what does it offer critical social policy analysis?, Critical Social Policy, 29(3): 465–486.

H

Historiography

Conventional approaches to the study of history, sometimes called historical method or traditional historiography, rely on using guidelines and techniques borrowed from archaeology to write histories of the past. These techniques include drawing on primary and secondary source material as well as employing 'source criticism' to determine the reliability of source material and acceptable oral traditions, often with a probabilistic approach to 'drawing generalisations – inferring patterns – from individual studies to make more generalised claims about the world' (Priem and Fendler, 2019, p 614). Combined, these techniques in writing history also provide the tools to 'story' history through accurate account-giving that builds up a reliable picture of the past events and their environments. Tamboukou (1999) warns, however, that historical methods of accounting for the past tend to operate within certain ontological and epistemological a prioris that include a naive Enlightenment view of past events that overestimates the rationality of history as 'continuous development, progress and seriousness' (p 208). In other words, historical methods can sometimes suffer from a strict teleological view of knowledge production as cumulative, linear, progressive and inevitably and unendingly striving for improvement and betterment of peoples: history moves through periods of time or stages of development (from 'barbarism' to 'civilised', for example) in which 'new' knowledge builds on 'old' knowledge to correct inaccuracies, to overcome error, to combat bad information or ignorance, or to rewrite false accounts. For radical revisionists of history, this acceptance of liberal progress is not only naive but serves 'as a rationalisation for the inequitable status quo' (Kincheloe, 1991, p 234).

As du Gay (2003) reminds us, historical methods may suffer from the 'logic of overdramatic dichotomisation' (p 664) in which past events (and their relation to the present or some imagined future) are presented chronologically and sequentially through an epochalist reading of social change as discrete moments in the singularity of place and time. It is important to acknowledge that social change can be the result of ruptures and shifts made possible by unique historical agents and environments, thus equating elements of social change to situated happenings. However, it is equally important to avoid reducing social change to tidy temporal representations of 'old' and 'new' or 'past' and 'present', or to commit the hermeneuticist error of restricting meaning to the interpretative model that was prevalent at the time. This also means avoiding any presumption of self-evidence and natural order in which there are things waiting to be found. The historically informed study of education policy development, for example, should therefore not be treated simply as an 'empirical question' of the study and verification of 'true' and 'false' statements, according to Gale (2001), since 'much rests on the meaning or possible meanings that we give to policy' (p 383). In other words, the interpretative categories and frameworks that make up our understanding of past events and how we 'read' and 'write' policy history, themselves the contingent products of truth regimes and researchers' stances on realism, positivism and pragmatism, need to be interrogated as much as the object of study. To do otherwise is, according to Kincheloe (1991), to commit to 'naive ideological assumptions which hide contradictions, limit understanding of how meaning is produced, dispersed, and received, and mask the power relations such processes entail' (p 241).

Hence, Tamboukou (1999), following Foucault, insists on a genealogical historiography that takes seriously 'the workings of those practices in which moral norms and truths about ourselves have been constructed' (p 208). This means avoiding any claims to the self-evidence of secondary or primary source material as indicative of the 'truth' of a past event or the proper reasoning by which origins and hidden meanings or ideologies may be uncovered. Instead, a genealogical historiography opens up that analytical space in which claims to truth or reason can be deconstructed as the 'outcome of a process in which there is conflict, confrontation, struggle, resistance' (Foucault, 2002, p 457). In other words, genealogical historiography is not a search for the origins or essences of things – that is, ideas or thought systems which can be claimed to be universal or categorical in some meaningful transcendental or metaphysical sense. Genealogical historiography aims to 'historicise social constructions' (Cavanagh, 2006, p 422) through observing the ways in which particular ideas and thought systems are deployed and brought together (or subjugated) in order to purport truths about who people are, should be or are destined to be. This means the substitution of truth for discourse and a focus on 'the tensions, contradictions, and diversity of frameworks that constitute the meanings of the terms as they are being used' (Priem and Fendler, 2019, p 612).

Drawing on psychological, medical and psychoanalytic literature sourced from the early part of the 20th century, Cavanagh (2006) combines queer perspectives with genealogical historiography to trace the pathologising of White, female, spinster teacher personality profiles as 'queer or gender-variant' (p 438). Here Cavanagh (2006) demonstrates that the idealised figure of women and womanhood at the time – 'white, genteel, domesticated, heteronormative femininity' (p 422) – was normalised through an explicit gender and sexual regulation and 'othering' of 'historically specific subjects with gender and sexual identifications yet to be fully understood' (p 438). In the same radical revisionist spirit of genealogical historiography, Grimaldi and Landri (2019) deploy what they call, borrowing from Gale (2001), a 'critical policy historiography' (p 4) to understand how Early School Leaving has been mobilised as a social problem in the Italian context since the Second World War. Through highlighting the competing national and international political rationalities that have jointly and separately shaped the emergence and construction of said social problem,

Grimaldi and Landri (2019) characterise these developments as 'an unstable process of continuous policy problematisation, design and adjustment' (p 15).

Further reading

- Guldi, J. and Armitage, D. (2014) The history manifesto, Cambridge: Cambridge University Press.
- Mockler, N. (2017) Early career teachers in Australia: a critical policy historiography, Journal of Education Policy, 33(2): 262–278.

I

Implementation

Policy implementation 'may refer to anything meant to happen after an intention or aspiration has been expressed' (Hupe, 2014, p 166). However, it has largely been constructed in the sub-field of implementation studies as having certain common features. These include a rejection, or under-emphasising, of the role of theory; an assumption of rationality in the actors involved; a strict conceptual division of labour between policy makers at the 'top' and implementers at the 'bottom'; a reliance on a technical interpretation of the mechanisms of implementation; and an understanding of the relationship between the elements in a causal chain as linear and direct. Implementation in this positivist perspective is amenable to being rendered as broad-brush diagrammatic models comprising, for instance, wheels, cycles or one of the latter in a series of sequential or perceived causal stages.

Such simplistic models cannot capture the complexity of the social and political interactions involved in policy processes. Neither can the conceptual and theoretical tools used in most implementation studies satisfactorily explain how policy 'gets done'. Consequently, the sub-field, which emerged following Pressman and Wildavsky's (1973) landmark publication, is characterised by disputes. For instance, the field engaged in a long-lasting debate regarding whether policy implementation should be seen as 'top-down' or 'bottom-up'. A 'top-down' perspective is concerned with how faithfully, effectively and efficiently a policy is translated into practice from the hierarchical apex, where it is formulated, to the chalkface, and by which mechanisms. Any deviations from the original policy intention are problematised and the implementer blamed for them. Concomitantly, the values and actions of the policy maker are accepted uncritically and adopted as the starting point of the implementation study. Hupe (2014) describes 'mainstream implementation studies' (p 170) as typically 'top-down' and tending to be explored through single case studies. 'Bottom-up' implementation studies are concerned, on the other hand, with the motivations, experiences and actions of those who are meant to be doing the implementing. These actors are characterised by Lipsky (1980) as 'street-level bureaucrats'. Far from wilful non-compliance, bottom-up studies demonstrated the diverse influences on actors as they engage with policy. For instance, especially in education, professionals 'on the ground' may have professional codes, standards or cultures that are poorly understood or devalued by government policy advisors, and which are not factored into policy making. Or the full extent of implementation requirements from diverse sources may be impossible to achieve, necessitating prioritisation and selectivity.

There are important exceptions to this generalisation of under-theorisation. Nudzor's (2009) recontextualisation within implementation studies of policy as text and discourse, for example, enables a proper focus on power. Notwithstanding such exceptions (and in fact, Nudzor's [2009] study is located liminally between policy implementation and enactment), the contestations over the way in which implementation is fundamentally conceptualised both help define the terrain and also explain why 'for the majority of academics, the study of implementation has become a "yesterday's issue"' (Hupe, 2014, p 166). Moreover, the positivist assumptions underpinning implementation studies meant that it is often regarded as 'largely descriptive and poorly integrated into mainstream policy theorising' (Howlett, 2019, p 406). Attempts to move the field on from this state have included a focus on several new theories, yet all have weaknesses. Game theory, for instance, centres on iterative decisions to coerce or persuade in order to achieve implementation compliance. However, game theory does not provide a satisfactory theory of power that might explain differences between implementing actors' capacity to resist. Principal-agent theory equates the politician/administrator relationship with the principal/agent one that is demonstrated between lawyers and clients, or doctors and patients, 'in which the principal is dependent on the goodwill of the agent to further his or her interests when it may not be in the interests of the agent to do so' (Howlett, 2019, p 410). However, like game theory, principal-agent theory did not produce theorisations that aligned well with those in mainstream policy studies. The same problem cannot be applied to the use of instrument choice theory in implementation studies which constructs implementation as the effective selection and deployment of one or more policy instruments, which protagonists of the theory saw as the correct object of evaluation. Instrument-choice theory, however, confronts neither the processual nor mechanistic questions underpinning the top-down/bottom-up debate (Howlett, 2019).

The core ideas underpinning thinking about and insights into how policy 'gets done' are not reducible to only those interpretations found in implementation studies. They extend and have arguably also evolved into policy enactment, governance studies and network analysis (see entries on 'Enactment', 'Governance' and 'Policy network analysis'), among others, where they may deal with theories of power concerning why social actors act as they do within complex policy-informed and power-laden structures of professional relationships. Nonetheless, the policy field's core concern with what might loosely be known as the 'implementation' part of the policy process persists, regardless of how this part is named, conceptualised and translated into objects of study.

Further reading

- Barrett, S.M. (2004) Implementation studies; time for a revival? Personal reflections on 20 years of implementation studies, Public Administration, 82(2): 249–262.

- Cairney, P. (2009) Implementation and the governance problem: a pressure participant perspective, Public Policy and Administration, 24(4): 355–377.

Indigenous policy analysis

Indigenous policy analysis is concerned first with how Indigenous peoples in postcolonial societies are represented and promoted through legal and legislative frameworks. Second, Indigenous policy analysis maintains a more specific focus on the contribution of those frameworks and their concomitant organisation of rights and obligations to ensuring Indigenous peoples are central (rather than peripheral) to policy-making processes and outcomes. Indigenous policy analysis draws on and combines a wide variety of theories and analytical approaches to make sense of these dynamic processes, including decolonising race theory, tribal critical race theory and critical race theory. Some scholars, including Burgess et al (2022), suggest that decolonising race theory offers a more meaningful set of heuristic tools for capturing the voices of Indigenous peoples compared to, say, critical race theory since the latter retains a strong focus on racialised stereotyping as method for underscoring self-identification (or self-determination) while the former 'understates the role of culture, inherent connection and obligation to Country and positioning as "colonised" which are prioritised by Indigenous Australian scholars' (p 3). According to Burgess et al (2022), a place-based, country-centred values and knowledges that prioritise a construction of 'First Peoples as sovereign beings, rather than racialised beings' (p 3) are central to Indigenous peoples' claims to self-determination. Decolonising race theory therefore refuses, or at least problematises in the context of other generative, relational and sometimes contradictory modes of identification, race-informed dichotomous thinking and binary logics in order to capture the 'diversity of Indigenous peoples, knowledges and life worlds' (Burgess et al, 2022, p 3).

A central focus of Indigenous policy analysis and Indigenous research is the promotion of legal and legislative frameworks as well as participatory policy making and action research that recognises Indigenous peoples' right to self-determination. This includes a focus on the value of Indigenous voices and knowledges to the design and improvement of public services and public life more generally. In Australia, for example, governments have long recognised the limited success of using rational-technical approaches to engaging Indigenous Australian peoples in the policy-making process, and instead shifted their attention to using participatory, stakeholder models to engage Aboriginal user groups in progressive problem solving focused on strategic and operational change. Similar kinds of participatory public engagement projects can be observed around the world, from Citizens' Juries in the US to Planning Cells in Germany and Citizens' Assemblies in Canada. These forms of participation and action also extend to the classroom. Drawing on a study of the Aboriginal cultural mentoring programme in New South Wales, Australia, Burgess et al (2022) show the importance of embedding Indigenous stories and skills in the classroom to challenge the hegemony of settler-colonial histories and knowledge and to enable 'teachers and students the opportunity to engage with multiple and complex knowledge systems' (p 10). At the same time, similar policy initiatives rolled out in other Australian states, such as the National Partnership Agreement on Remote Service Delivery (NPARSD), have proved less effective. Designed to improve experiences of state services for Indigenous Australian peoples, the NPARSD initiative ultimately failed owing to accountability flowing upwards to the minister rather than, as imagined in the original plans, downwards towards Indigenous user groups.

According to Brown (2020), the result is an inadequate space for the expression of 'authentic otherness' (p 410) since it reproduces those forms of epistemic injustice that render Indigenous peoples' knowledges and voices peripheral to the policy-making process. In a similar vein, Regalsky and Lauri (2007) demonstrate how the Bolivian government denies genuine spaces for the recognition and promotion of Andean peoples through a superficial method of 'interculturality' (p 242) designed to deny Indigenous customary law and local knowledge through the superimposition of Bolivian state political authority in Indigenous schools.

Similar efforts to decolonise education can be observed during the first Lula administration (2002–2010) in Brazil, where the government sought to challenge the 'Eurocentric-based ethnocentrism' (Guimarães, 2015, p 940) underpinning Brazilian basic education through promoting public policies and affirmative action centred around Afro-Brazilian and Indigenous culture. In Taiwan also, policy initiatives designed to promote forms of Indigenous education can be observed. Yet, as Chen (2016) shows, these interventions fall short of realising their aims owing to their lack of commitment to culturally responsive teaching, namely the inclusion of Indigenous teachers in schools and the development of Indigenous teacher education that is pedagogically and epistemologically separate to general teacher education. In Guatemala too, policy initiatives focused on participatory action were introduced to redress the discrimination, exploitation and injustice of Mayan peoples. In practice, this meant the creation of education commissions open to participation from Mayan organisations. In most cases, however, the demands of Mayan peoples have been sorely neglected according to Poppema (2009), with many Mayan schools closing owing to lack of national financial support. In Chile, for example, a similar story of participatory action-driven policy change can be observed. Huencho (2021) notes that while Indigenous peoples in some Chilean states are protected and promoted under legal frameworks that recognise their right to self-determination, there has not been a corresponding change in their political recognition at the nation-state or constitutional level, in effect limiting their authority and autonomy to contribute meaningfully to public policies that affect them. As Huencho (2021) argues: 'the design of governance to recognise indigenous peoples and their demands is put into tension by not incorporating new rules, procedures, and also representation spaces appropriate to the diversity that these peoples represent' (pp 224–225).

Further reading

- Lea, T., Thompson, H., McRae-Williams, E. and Wegner, A. (2011) Policy fuzz and fuzzy logic: researching contemporary Indigenous education and parent-school engagement in north Australia, Journal of Education Policy, 26(3): 321–333.
- Rata, E. (2010) Localising neoliberalism: indigenist brokerage in the New Zealand university, Globalisation, Societies and Education, 8(4): 527–542.

Infrastructure

Education research on infrastructure takes its inspiration from an understanding of governance (see entry on 'Governance') as multiscalar and transnational movements or collectives made up of diverse actors spanning state and non-state organisations and interests. The formation and materialisation of infrastructures is typically explained with reference to the production of numerical data or other forms of evidence, most notably the collection, organisation and representation of evidence through digital means. These modalities for the expression of infrastructures can be understood to initiate or preclude policy change in diverse ways as well as function to steer schools and school systems at a distance and towards certain ends. Gulson and Sellar (2019), for example, describe infrastructures as not simply an underlying arrangement of technical objects and systems but also as embodiments for a variety of more intangible elements and practices, such as habits of thought, subjectivities and social practices. Understood in this way, infrastructure bears the imprint of social relations and cultures as well as contributes to their articulation and mobilisation. As a form of governance, infrastructure can similarly be understood as bearer and producer of various modes and relations of centralised and dispersed power (Gulson and Sellar, 2019). In this same vein, Sellar (2015a) traces the composition of data infrastructures to make explicit the 'relationships between different kinds of institutions, political agendas, scientific practices, education policies, modes of governance, measurement instruments and our own scholarly practices' (p 774).

Similarly, Saari (2012) adopts a socio-material approach to trace the ways in which actors form and reproduce infrastructures as networks. Saari (2012) notes, for example, the ways in which official policy documents work to position different institutions as producers of evaluation infrastructures for guiding the reform of compulsory schooling in Finland. This includes guiding said institutions towards specific activities of gathering, organising, analysing and circulating data on school reform experiments and achievement tests. The result is an evaluation infrastructure and system of visibility designed to limit the discursive boundaries for containing the different possibilities for representing evidence, specifically evidence that enables reform. Evaluation data emerged as the main driver for these infrastructures as they open up possibilities for the capture of behaviour through methods of calculation and measurement, and therefore the possibilities of reducing said behaviour to relations of comparison and equivalence so they could be assessed against the stated objectives of the reform. The resulting formation was a feedback system consisting of four stages: planning, instruction, results and evaluation. This evaluation infrastructure was underpinned by a closed circuit in which new stages of planning were guided principally by standardised data.

Schools and school systems can also be viewed as vital infrastructures to the functioning of societies: a recursive system that creates vital albeit fragile relays between central authorities and remote, devolved administrations, in effect making governance possible across dispersed sites, levels and scales. In education, however, the notion of infrastructure is typically discussed in relation to the rise of 'governance by numbers' (see entry on 'Numbers') where it concerns the spread and maintenance of evaluative instruments and data configurations, mediums and platforms as essential tools and technologies for emerging forms of digital governance (Williamson, 2018). In this context, infrastructure is used to refer to specific information systems 'designed to make data usable for organisational purposes, from local area networks to distributed cloud-based computing' (Gulson and Sellar, 2019, p 352). In other words, data infrastructures can be viewed as assemblages (see entry on 'Assemblage') that aim to give coherence, equivalency and comparability to otherwise diverse education systems separated by history, culture or space. Here, technical standards and tools of digital education can be considered agentic non-human actors that (together with agentic human actors) enable education policy and governance. For Gulson and Sellar (2019) and Hartong (2018), the emergence and consolidation of new data infrastructures also help to foster points of entry and networking for private actors keen to influence and profit from public education.

Education researchers also have addressed some of the methodological requirements and implications of studying infrastructures as provisional, dispersed, complexly entangled and decentred. One implication here being that the study of infrastructure as assemblage calls for new epistemologies that problematise the taken-for-granted binaries of agent and structure or actor and context (Piattoeva and Saari, 2022). These studies of infrastructure typically reference poststructural approaches, such as Deleuzo-Guattarian assemblage theory, in order to evade the entification of infrastructure as an 'it' with entry points and end points that can be neatly (and objectively) defined and whose borders or interconnections can be traced using diagrammatic representations, fixed timelines and network (cause-and-effect) models. Central to this notion of infrastructure as assemblage therefore is an aversion to definitional parameters and 'pregiven social categories' (Baker and McGuirk, 2017, p 428). The analytic of assemblage instead allows education researchers to highlight the constant coming-together of symbolic, material and social elements in the formation of data infrastructures. In these contexts, 'infrastructure' emerges simultaneously 'as an idea, an analytic, a descriptive lens, or an orientation' (McFarlane, 2011, p 206).

Building on these approaches to infrastructure, Espeland and Sauder (2016) observe through their study of media rankings of law schools in the US that the USN (U.S. News and World Report) emerges as a central infrastructure of tests and data instruments in the development of these trends. As Espeland and Sauder (2016) argue, law school ranking by media outlets like the USN constitute a major infrastructure determining faculty funding. In this way, infrastructures generate effects as well as structure social relations. More recently, education researchers have called for greater attention to be paid to the affective dimension of infrastructures (see entry on 'Affect') through more consideration of the different ways infrastructure is constituted by and productive of vital, visceral forces that operate beyond rationality and reflexivity. From this perspective, infrastructures can be viewed, on the one hand, as shifting modalities for the production, that is suppression, circulation and dispersion, of various affects. On the other hand, the role of affect can be considered essential to the sustainability of infrastructures (Sellar, 2015b).

This view of infrastructure 'as a process of "co-functioning" whereby heterogeneous elements come together in a non-homogeneous grouping' (Anderson and McFarlane, 2011, p 125) in effect renders the limits and multitude of effects of infrastructures elusive. Such elusiveness – what Brenner et al (2011, p 229) describe as its 'mercurial nature' – is precisely what leads some to criticise the analytic of assemblage. Specifically, criticism has been levelled against the lack of attention to structure within assemblage approaches to infrastructure and other phenomena. As Baker and McGuirk (2017) observe, the analytic of assemblage is deployed as an interpretative strategy to 'displace presumptions of structural coherence and determination' (p 431) in order that multiplicity, emergence and contingency are more central to the analysis of the formation of things. The danger here, as Bender (2010) explains, is that such approaches risk engaging in an 'indiscriminate absorption of elements into the actor-network' with the 'effect of levelling the significance of all actors' (p 305). Moreover, they neglect the sensitising effects of wider structural forces, namely 'historically entrenched, large-scale configurations of uneven spatial development, territorial polarization and geopolitical hegemony' (Brenner et al, 2011, p 233), which call for a more 'sustained account of this *context of context*' (p 234, emphasis in original).

Further reading

- Bouzarovski, S., Bradshaw, M. and Wochnik, A. (2015) Making territory through infrastructure: the governance of natural gas transit in Europe, Geoforum, 64: 217–228.
- Star, S.L. (1999) The ethnography of infrastructure, American Behavioural Scientist, 43(3): 377–391.

Institutional theory

Institutional theories originating in sociology, political sciences and organisational studies have recently emerged as a focus of education policy research. These institutional theories are various and span different theoretical approaches and analytical traditions. Yet despite their various internal developments, histories and applications, institutional theories share a commitment to certain ontological and epistemological a prioris, namely the assumption that individual actors, organisations or policies are scripted by their environments such as formal and informal institutions that persist over time. These institutions are thought to establish the conditions that shape the actions and decisions of actors as well as form their expectations of other actors' behaviour (Alasuutari, 2015). There are various meanings used to define institutions within the broad spectrum of institutionalist theories. Institutions are typically described, on the one hand, as compositions of rules, procedures, conventions and norms. On the other hand, the meaning of institutions has been extended to include cognitive scripts and symbolic systems which resemble definitions of culture. These various meanings reflect attempts to capture what we might call the constitutive elements of institutions, namely that which works to define, even constrain, what is considered appropriate or desirable for the field of action in which individuals and organisations operate.

One key variant of institutional theory is sociological institutionalism. Sociological institutionalism mainly addresses issues of macro-level diffusion and isomorphism through using (macro) cultural accounts to explain the conditions for the emergence of similarities in the development and organisation of societies among different countries. A classic example of isomorphism in education is the global development of the organisation of national education systems around age-based grade levels and subject-based curriculum. In pursuing a cultural explanation of these types of isomorphism, sociological institutionalism opposes rational choice institutionalism. While sociological institutionalism positions actors as imitators of a shared global script or world society (see entry on 'World culture theory'), rational choice institutionalism subscribes to a notion of actors as maximisers who operate within predictable or rationally calculable preference orderings, making them more likely to conform to institutional arrangements that secure personal advantage. Here the 'maximiser' refers to persons 'who always seek the biggest possible benefits and the least costs in their decisions' and who are 'basically egoistic, self-regarding and instrumental in their behaviour, choosing how to act on the basis of the consequences for their personal welfare' (Dunleavy, 1991, p 3).

Analogous to sociological institutionalism, historical institutionalism too stresses concepts of stability and convergence as the main drivers of change and development. But rather than locate elements of global isomorphism within a shared world society/culture, historical institutionalism foregrounds national differences in the formation of different, albeit similar, systems of governance, regulation or organisation as vital relays for sustaining global isomorphism. A central concept in historical institutionalism, for example, is path dependence, which explains how institutions preclude radical change and make certain policies persist. Part of the explanation lies with the development of bureaucracy that works to tame political change. In these contexts, path dependence acts as a self-reinforcing dynamic in which responses are used to strengthen the recurrence and continuation of a pattern. Change, then, can only occur at those rare moments of 'critical juncture' when multiple interests and forces intersect and combine to produce the conditions of possibility for new organisational pathways and policy choices.

There are other strands of institutionalist theorising worth noting here, specifically those that shift focus away from top-down accounts of organisational change and locate the focus instead more firmly within bottom-up explanations. Scandinavian institutionalism (Czarniawska, 1997; Sahlin and Wedlin, 2008) and discursive institutionalism (Schmidt, 2008), for example, have as their focus the processes of diffusion that enable, even compel, different kinds of organisational formations. At the same time, these approaches to institutional theorising place a strong emphasis on those moments of translation and rearticulation made possible by the strategic responses and practices among local actors engaged in processes of 'editing' institutional scripts. Discursive institutionalism is particularly useful here for highlighting the role of ideas, discourse and communicative interaction as fundamental drivers shaping organisational change and development. Ideas and communication can be understood to help legitimise policies by pointing to their appropriateness and relevance for the local context. The focus on ideas and communication brings into focus the essential actions of local actors as brokers or interlocutors for validating and communicating ideas that enable organisational development or disruption.

Scandinavian institutionalism subscribes to the notion that the spread and maintenance of models of world society/culture is made possible by the everyday labour of social actors engaged in translational activity; activity which, if successful on the ground and among actors and organisations, facilitates the circulation of global institutional scripts (Suárez and Bromley, 2016). In this framing, local actors are not represented as passive emulators of institutional scripts but, instead, positioned in active, dynamic roles as translators and mediators of institutional scripts. This includes the profound translational work of remodelling or repurposing global or national institutional scripts, so they are more responsive to situated problems that are historically or politically unique to organisations and their communities or clients. Such processes of translation and localisation make diffusion possible by rendering foreign items familiar and experientially domestic (Alasuutari, 2015). From this perspective, bottom-up approaches to institutionalism also address some of the limitations attached to sociological institutionalism, namely the decoupling that occurs when distinctions are made between formal adoption and actual implementation. Scandinavian institutionalists tend to avoid decoupling processes in this way as well as resist the binaries resulting from such thinking, namely presence/absence and real/imaginary. Instead, Scandinavian institutionalists focus on exploring those dynamic, dilemmatic spaces that fall in-between adoption and implementation wherein policy ideas are reworked and remodelled or repurposed through adaptation and translation (see entry on 'Translation'). Both discursive and Scandinavian institutionalism therefore make the agency of actors central to the analysis. Here, actors are viewed as sentient subjects who may selectively embody and perform interests drawn from institutional scripts. At the same time, their ideational capacity for creativity or contestation means that their actions cannot be reduced to institutional scripts.

Critiques of institutionalism are not uniform and vary according to which strand is under consideration. In general, criticisms of Scandinavian institutionalism and discursive institutionalism tend to be directed towards its stated preference for explaining stability and order over change. Sociological and historical institutionalism, on the other hand, are criticised for their emphasis on producing a monolithic view of institutional (world culture/society) scripts as developing in uniform ways, a view that undermines the active role of actors as translators and mediators of institutional scripts.

Further reading

- Amenta, E. and Ramsey, K.M. (2010) Institutional theory, in K.T. Leicht and J.C. Jenkins (eds) Handbook of politics: state and civil society in global perspective, New York: Springer, 15–39.
- Boxenbaum, E. and Jonsson, S. (2008) Isomorphism, diffusion and decoupling, in R. Greenwood, C. Oliver, K. Sahlin and R. Suddaby (eds) The SAGE handbook of organisational institutionalism, London: SAGE, 78–98.

Instrument

The focus on policy instruments is indebted in one sense to the Foucauldian interest in how power is exercised materially and discursively through concrete devices and practices. Set apart from traditional approaches to the study of policy instruments that prioritise stakeholders, ideas and institutions as embodiments or 'instruments' of policy, the study of policy instruments in governmentality studies draws on the Foucauldian notion of technologies of governance to explain the mundane mechanisms through which 'authorities … [seek] to shape, normalise and instrumentalise the conduct, thought, decisions and aspirations of others in order to achieve the objectives they consider desirable' (Miller and Rose, 1990, p 8). Technologies of governance as policy instruments can be viewed as modalities or moving assemblages that make different political programmes operable and capable of deployment. In other words, technologies of governance as policy instruments can be thought to represent strategies, practices and rationalities for managing populations or structuring public policies according to particular logics and goals (Le Galès, 2016). Technologies of governance as policy instruments can also be traced to the rise of intensification of various 'modes of objectification' and 'dividing practices' (Foucault, 2000, p 326), namely digital platforms, performance metrics and assessment frameworks which function as techniques for directing behaviour change and the transformation of human beings in (digital, performative, auditable) subjects (see entry on 'Digital policy sociology').

In contemporary policy sociology, the focus on policy instruments has helped to shape new understandings of the relationship between citizens and the state and the reshaping of the state or changes to public policy owing to trends in the wider macro-economic context of globalisation and internationalisation. This has shifted focus towards the study of broader questions concerning the relationship between mechanisms of governing and the governed in the context of global–national relations, that is, the development of concrete and discursive forms of managing national societies within transnational movements composed of various networks, actors, projects, ideas and organisations (Le Galès, 2016). These policy sociology approaches therefore challenge key assumptions about the neutrality of instruments or their indifference to political strategies. Lascoumes and Le Galès (2004) propose a typology of policy instruments that shape political relationships in line with different forms of legitimacy, for example. The five-type typology of policy instruments outlined by Lascoumes and Le Galès (2004) includes: legislative and regulatory; economic and fiscal; agreement-based and incentive-based; information-based and communication-based; and performance indicators, standards and best practices. In particular, the use of performance indicators, standards and best practices as a way to describe policy instruments has seen widespread adoption among education policy researchers since the 1990s and 2000s. These heuristic tools for describing policy instruments have attracted much attention for their application in explaining the shift towards the rationalisation of governance in the 1990s following globalisation (Wilkins, 2021) and the increasing reliance among governments on perfecting regulatory mechanisms to guide and shape behaviour change among citizens at a distance (Le Galès, 2016). In this sense, the choice among governments to deploy particular packages of policy instruments over others has major implications for understanding the formation and incongruity of public policies over time and space. Policy making and its effects, therefore, can be understood to be conditioned by the historical layering of multiple policy instruments and their evolution by inertia or purposeful redesign (Verger et al, 2019).

The study of instrumentation, that is, the development and deployment of policy instruments, shifts focus towards improved understanding of the discourses and interests or goals shaping policy makers' decision-making, including the range of intrinsic and extrinsic factors that condition instrument selection and impact. Verger et al (2019), for example, identify several factors that actively condition the selection and deselection of policy instruments destined for policy reform programmes. These include economic development and agreements; financial feasibility of instrument options; political affiliation and ideologies of the policy makers; and political-administrative regimes. The effects of policy instruments also need to be understood as geopolitically discrete and unique. Policy instruments like national large-scale assessments (developed to collect information) and test-based accountability instruments (developed to incite behaviour) appear to share similar rationalities in terms of their stated goals or outcomes but can produce very different effects depending on the political-administrative tradition of the national government in question.

It is also important to use geopolitical framings to understand the attraction of certain policy instruments, namely the active selection and deselection by which policy makers choose to deploy some policy instruments (or a combination of policy instruments) over others. Carvalho's (2012) study of the Programme for International Student Assessment (PISA) as a knowledge-policy instrument, for example, is helpful for disentangling how transnational policy tools acquire popularity and function within certain national policy contexts. PISA can be considered a policy instrument that combines and condenses some elements of the five-type typology identified by Lascoumes and Le Galès (2004), namely, information-based and communication-based and performance indicators, standards and best practices. However, the dynamics of these policy instruments, including their legitimacy, are resolved differentially and contingently in specific contexts owing to the ways in which different governments tactically deploy and rationalise these policy instruments to complement pre-existing political-administrative structures and goals (Wilkins et al, 2024). On this understanding, there is a necessary plasticity to the development and implementation of policy instruments within and across geopolitical contexts. PISA acquires its legitimacy among national governments as a policy instrument for perfecting programmes of regulation that enable governments to govern more effectively both nationally and internationally within wider networks of global competition. PISA's popularity as a knowledge-policy instrument can also be traced to its malleability to be adapted by national governments to serve and affirm their own specific geopolitical interests.

The production of a policy instrument is a complex matter owing to the wide range of actors and experts involved, from scientific and technical actors to managerial and political actors. These actors are engaged in policy production in multiple ways, both actively and passively. In the case of PISA, they contribute in different ways to PISA's circulation, maintenance, application and adaptation. These actors can be considered essential to the consensus that gives PISA its legitimacy as a knowledge-policy instrument and tool of governance. Yet, as already described, PISA is a shape-shifting entity as it moves through different geopolitical contexts and therefore remains inherently plastic. For instance, PISA extends its reach and influence globally by producing a wide range of publications and other informational products made to be relevant for a range of actors and a multiplicity of possible uses. These publications and products are intended to serve the diverse needs of a wide range of actors, from researchers, the media and policy makers, to bureaucrats and teachers, all of whom may choose to adapt these resources to serve different goals or outcomes. PISA, therefore, is not produced or applied in any singular way as its use is constantly subject to reinterpretation, decontextualisation and recontextualisation across geopolitical contexts. The suggestion here is that there are moments of both convergence and divergence in how PISA, and by extension policy instruments in general, is applied by different users defined by unique path dependencies and value systems (Carvalho, 2012; Verger et al, 2019).

Further reading

- Hannaway, J. and Woodroffe, N. (2003) Policy instruments in education, Review of Research in Education, 27: 1–24.
- Namian, D. (2020) Governing homelessness through instruments: a critical perspective on housing first's policy instrumentation, Critical Policy Studies, 14(3): 303–318.

Intermediary

Intermediaries can be used in a loose sense to refer to networks, actors and organisations or 'meso-level' entities that operate between national authorities, such as governments, and their constituent institutions, be they schools, health providers or social care and housing services. Intermediaries operate through different sites, levels and scales and through various forms of agency, from consultants and think tanks to non-human actors like data instruments and digital platforms. The rise of intermediaries in education policy can be linked to two entangled phenomena. The first phenomenon is the emergence of networked governance which connotes the shift in power from state institutions, including traditional structures of government, to complex constellations of state and non-state actors (see entry on 'Governance'). The second phenomenon is the rise of datafication and digitalisation as instruments and objectives of education policy making and implementation (see entry on 'Digital education').

Intermediaries function beyond, or are only partially connected to, the formal domain where we are likely to find political decision-making or traditional expert structures in action. In fact, intermediaries can be best understood as shape-shifting entities of a mercurial nature that 'criss-cross public, private and third sector borderlines and mobilise resources and ideas from across academic research, political thought, design, [and] media' (Williamson, 2015, pp 88–89). Being located in and contributing to complex governance networks, intermediaries not only blur the boundaries between the state, commerce and civil society, but reshuffle the distribution of roles and responsibilities across and between these domains. At the same time, intermediaries perform a range of new roles made possible by the increasing dependence of the education sector on the production, analysis and usage of 'big data' to track student performance, calculate teaching quality and monitor school management, inputs and infrastructure, among other oversight and intervention priorities. Yet these technical and social tasks are not neutral in the sense they lack 'prefiguring judgement' (Williamson et al, 2020, p 353). These technologies bear the imprint of human control and intervention, including the strict allocation of values (and non-values) that make automation of problem representation and identification possible in the first place.

Intermediaries are therefore intensively political in the sense that they circulate specific discourses, sell or promote material and ideational solutions, as well as endorse certain educational imaginaries at the expense of others. From this perspective, technical solutions designed or promoted by intermediaries can be understood as performative inasmuch as they nudge education practices towards certain interpretations and actions of problem representation, in effect closing down the possibilities for alternative visions.

Williamson (2015) identifies think tanks, social enterprises, policy labs and third-sector institutions as intermediary organisations that promote software technologies in the governance of public services. Similarly, Hartong (2016) highlights data transfer, visualisation and interoperability service providers as intermediaries whose technical expertise has become vital to enabling large-scale data technologies to work and meet the needs and competences of policy actors or school-level personnel. Hartong (2016) refers to these service providers as 'data mediators' who not only intensify demands for data-based governance in fields of education policy making and pedagogy but who simultaneously engender spaces and practices that make a necessity of certain data-based actors, tasks and roles.

Decuypere et al (2021) point to a similar set of observations about non-human intermediaries through a study of the digital education platforms like 'Google Classroom'. Platforms like these, argue Decuypere et al (2021), are programmed digital architectures that process complex user data in order to improve flows of information and interaction between individual end users and corporate and public bodies. Digital education platforms are therefore intermediaries by design and purpose. Yet their intermediary roles can be disentangled in more nuanced ways: digital education platforms enable and streamline activities of exchange between providers and users of services; their scripted architectures permit some forms of activities and exchanges that actively work to disable others; and by structuring attention, shaping decision-making and guiding cognition, they reconfigure how phenomena are seen and what remains unseen and therefore unaccounted for. Moreover, since it is the platform constructors and not teaching professionals who design and operate these digital education platforms, the role of teachers as experts is displaced to make way for new forms of expertise and expert knowledge, namely technical skills and competences.

The emergence and expansion of these intermediary actors and processes in the field of education is fraught with ambiguity. Teachers, on the one hand, can be considered targets of intermediary actors such as providers of software services and professionals enabling technical embedding and alignment. On the other hand, teachers, including school districts and individual schools, are increasingly called upon to act as intermediary actors in the spread and maintenance of these technologies, as intermediary platform actors. Google, for example, runs certification programmes for teachers, teacher trainers and innovators. These certification programmes are designed to shape the technical skills of teachers as technology users and enablers as well as construct visions of good school pedagogy in alignment with the values of 'Silicon Valley Culture' (Ideland, 2021). In these contexts, intermediaries bypass traditional legislative, educational or executive institutions to directly influence in-class or in-school processes. A key priority for future studies of digital education therefore is to document these slippery dynamics, namely how intermediaries navigate and adapt to the idiosyncrasies of micro contexts while promoting decontextualised solutions in the format of policies, ideas and concomitant hardware and software.

Further reading

- Lubienski, C. (2014) Re-making the middle: dis-intermediation in international context, Educational Management Administration and Leadership, 42(3): 423–440.
- Williamson, B. and Komljenovic, J. (2023) Investing in imagined digital futures: the techno-financial 'futuring' of edtech investors in higher education, Critical Studies in Education, 64(3): 234–249.

Interpretive policy analysis

Traditional policy analysis, such as the policy sciences (Lasswell, 1971) and related policy perspectives influenced by functionalism, instrumentalism and systems theory, reflect the ascendency of a positivist turn in the study of policy making, policy enactment and policy change. At the time of writing, there continues to be a strong positivist tradition in education policy research, with various studies making use of meta-analysis, deductive logic and experimental hypothesis modelling to produce empirically verifiable answers that are somehow perceived to be 'hardwired' into reality. The proliferation of randomised controlled trials (RCTs) in the UK and US (Connolly et al, 2018) reflects a neopositivist orientation to policy research, for example, with its emphasis on the quantitative evaluation of inputs and outputs to produce empirically verifiable answers that are relevant to policy makers.

RCTs aim to produce rigorous assessments of the effectiveness (and ineffectiveness) of specific interventions and programmes against a particular normative framework, ideally with a view to influencing policy change and steering policy outcomes towards optimal solutions that are efficient, cost-effective or equitable. RCTs therefore are driven by instrumental concerns about the 'technical-instrumental practicality of specific social arrangements' (Jessop and Sum, 2016, p 105) and the production of relevant knowledge in the service of policy, otherwise known as 'analysis for policy' (Simon et al, 2009, p 29). Furthermore, these approaches to policy analysis and policy change run the risk of assuming that the production of knowledge and facts are separate from the interpretations and values that give them meaning.

Like positivism, poststructuralism is the rejection of metaphysics and theism. Both positivism and poststructuralism challenge religious or spiritual explanations of social reality that exclude concerns with materiality and the sensory world.

However, unlike neopositivist methods which stress that 'the optimal solution for policy problems is a value-free activity' (Simon et al, 2009, p 10), poststructuralist and constructionist methods view knowledge production as intimately historical and cultural and therefore maintain a keen focus on the connections between the empirical and the normative. Following the same principles, interpretive policy analysis adopts a similar set of ontological and epistemological presuppositions to shift from deductive to inductive modes of inquiry about a particular phenomenon in order to challenge conventional neopositivist understandings of what can be known about that phenomenon, namely that unbiased research instruments provide us with unmediated access to a reality 'out there' that is objectively independent from the researcher. The linguistic turn – also called the 'argumentative turn' and the 'discursive turn' – instead forces 'analytic attention on the ways in which language itself constitutes the social "reality" analysts are studying' (Yanow, 2007, p 117).

At the same time, poststructuralism suffers from overestimating the coherence and dominance of structures as forces that constitute subjects in all kinds of ways, in effect leaving very little room for agency and reason. Instead, interpretive policy analysis favours hermeneutic analyses of the values, beliefs and actions of individuals as meaning-making devices. These function as forms of practical reasoning for shaping human behaviour and therefore favour a nonfoundational understanding of meaning that is 'consonant with the complex, contested world of public policy' (Wagenaar, 2006, p 437). For interpretive policy analysts, communication and argumentation are central to the analysis, in particular 'the processes of mobilising, utilising and evaluation of communicative practices in policy analysis and policymaking' (Fischer and Gottweis, 2013, p 426). This includes the use of multiple interpretetive frameworks (frame analysis, storytelling analysis, rhetorical analysis and policy narration, for example) to understand policy making and policy enactment as dynamic spaces for the framing and negotiation of problem definitions and policy settings. Moreover, it includes a strong normative commitment to democracy and making policy processes more action-oriented and inclusive through the provision of diverse rationalities and various forms of local reasoning (Fischer and Gottweis, 2013).

Developed under the auspices of continental philosophy and significantly influenced by Jürgen Habermas' theory of communicative action, interpretive policy analysis is less focused on how policy might work, at least from a technical or rationalist perspective of policy research as a problem-solving science, and more concerned with the messiness of policy problems as contested, contingent and contradictory. According to Fischer and Gottweis (2013), such 'wicked problems', which vary geopolitically, require workable solutions that can only be 'discovered with the assistance of informed deliberation capable of bringing about an exchange of competing views of governmental officials, politicians and the members of civil society' (p 429). Hendriks (2007), for example, mobilises the conception of 'praxis stories' to bring into view the meanings that citizens ascribe to their actions and experiences as meaningful, and in doing so seeks 'not to evaluate practice against theory' (p 294) but rather use these observations to generate a democratic theory of the policy process. Interpretive policy analysis is also useful for drawing attention to the shortcomings and incompatibilities of policy in terms of whether it addresses the needs of different stakeholders. Through a comparative study of lifelong learning policies in nine European countries, Parreira do Amaral and Zelinka (2019) use interpretive policy analysis to show how particular 'national cultural, social and political features are often bracketed out in the construction of the policies and their target groups' (p 418).

Further reading

- Aukes, E., Lulofs, K. and Bressers, H. (2018) Framing mechanisms: the interpretive policy entrepreneur's toolbox, Critical Policy Studies, 12(4): 406–427.
- Fischer, F. (2003) Reframing public policy: discursive politics and deliberative practices, Oxford: Oxford University Press.

L

Leadership

Educational leadership is a field that draws on differing disciplinary backgrounds with distinctive epistemologies that produce knowledge claims that are arguably mutually incompatible. Leadership knowledge intersects with policy in diverse ways that reflect its underpinning epistemology. Here, specifically, the field may be broadly understood as composed of functionalist and critical parts (see Gunter [2016] for a more detailed mapping). Functionalist scholars tend to locate their work in the school improvement and/or effectiveness tradition (see, for example, Leithwood and Jantzi, 2005). This draws on a positivist epistemology that is often explicitly atheoretical or even anti-theoretical (Courtney et al, 2018); the legitimacy of such research lies in its unmediated responsiveness to questions regarding 'what works' in education. Courtney et al (2021a) describe how functionalist researchers largely render professional practice through leadership models denoted by adjectives such as 'transformational', 'distributed' and 'system', which they deploy in an often unproblematised and normative manner. Functionalist assumptions include that leadership is an ontologically valid concept and is necessary to improve education, whose goal is to improve students' outcomes in standardised tests. Here, the leadership style/model is operationalised through the leader's vision, which inspires and motivates followers in ways that take little account of context. This decontextualisation is purposive: it enables an illusory universalism that underpins a leadership industry (Gunter, 2012). Privileged models change over time in a way that responds to state political agendas. For example, transformational leadership was imported from business into the field of education where it comprised a key mechanism for education reforms internationally. Charisma is integral to, but implicit within, this broader transformational model, with its focus on the single 'heroic' leader (see Courtney, 2021a). As heroism failed, the focus moved to distributed and then system models, all of which focus instrumentally on delivery and performance. Functionalist research into educational leadership is designed to be amenable to policy making through its claimed capacity to produce solutions to complex problems, for example.

The functionalist part of the field can be contrasted with the critical (Gunter, 2016; Courtney et al, 2021a; Courtney and McGinity, 2022). Drawing on social constructionism, critical scholars may problematise the very existence of leadership, noting that conceptual distinctiveness arrives only with the addition of the sort of adjectives mentioned earlier (Gronn, 2003). Leadership, for critical scholars, is an illuminative element of a wider policy-scholarship approach to research, which, for Grace (1995), 'brings back into the analysis of school leadership an historical and a contemporary sense of the ideological, power and value relations which shape and pattern school leadership in particular historical periods and in various cultural settings' (p 3). From this perspective, education policy is an important structural feature that contributes to the construction and constitution of leadership roles, practices and identities. In other words, critical scholarship reveals that the way in which educational leaders understand who they are and what they do is highly structured by extrinsic policy agendas (Wright, 2001). This leaves leaders to exercise meaningful agency only over what Wright (2003) calls 'second-order values' (p 140).

Adopting the same critical leadership lens, Gunter (2012) describes how the New Labour government (1997–2010) in England created 'believers' among existing and aspiring school leaders in its education reforms through controlling knowledge production regarding leadership. Here, the concept of 'leadership' and the role of 'leader' can be seen to be deployed to replace 'management' and 'manager' and achieve the state's instrumental goals concerning the intensification of professional accountability in return for raised standards and higher prestige. Other critical work has explored further features and consequences of this state-sanctioned construction of 'leader' and 'leading'. For instance, Hall et al (2013a) identify New Public Management as a targeted policy intervention into the identities of those in schools newly known as leaders, rather than managers. Significantly, these interventions draw on approaches, methods and aims that derive from the private sector, and so contribute to a continuing privatisation of educational leadership and leading (Courtney and Gunter, 2017).

A significant strand of critical, or policy-scholarship-oriented leadership research aims to problematise the conceptual labels that are used uncritically and normatively in the school-improvement literature. For instance, Hall et al (2013b) draw attention to the ways in which distributed leadership belies authority-based delegation; Courtney and Gunter (2015) reveal the totalitarian practices underpinning vision work in leadership; Fitzgerald and Gunter (2008) argue that teacher leadership is invoked to encourage teachers' involvement in the neoliberal reform movement; and Courtney and McGinity (2020) reconceptualise the contemporaneously normative system leadership as a manifestation of depoliticisation, with multi-academy trusts and their CEOs engaging in policy entrepreneurship (see entry on 'Entrepreneur'). Critical research into educational leadership therefore is less amenable to policy making than functionalist accounts of leadership owing to its refusal to simplify the social world. Policy is more important to the critical field as a key structural consideration in contextualising, conceptualising and interpreting what are constructed as 'leadership' practices and identities.

Further reading

- Courtney, S.J., Gunter, H.M., Niesche, R. and Trujillo, T. (eds) (2021) Understanding educational leadership: critical perspectives and approaches, London. Bloomsbury.
- English, F.W. (ed.) The Palgrave handbook of educational leadership and management discourse, Cham: Palgrave Macmillan.

M

Mediation

In policy studies, mediation refers to two distinct processes. Lúcio and Neves (2010) describe the first as being where two or more parties with unaligned positions engage with one another through a further, dispassionate and neutral participant (a mediator) in order to reach a mutually agreeable policy position. This position cannot be one that is predetermined by the mediator. For this aim to be realised, the mediator must be acceptable to the other parties and must typically not occupy a position of authority in relation to the negotiators or wield power within the mediation process. This process must be confidential and based on open-minded negotiation rather than on confrontation, as well as aim to anticipate future potential conflicts. Importantly, decisions are reached by the negotiators rather than the mediator, whose role is to facilitate their communication. The impetus to align diverging interests or goals may come from within or beyond the grouping (not including the mediator), but participation in all cases must be voluntary. This sense of mediation has applications beyond policy formation, and may be used to reconcile relationships between, for instance, institutions, nations, corporations or factions; between individuals within them, or between any of those former and their communities (Lúcio and Neves, 2010).

While mediation's earliest and best-studied examples are located in conflict studies, particularly regarding labour disputes, Lúcio and Neves (2010) identify strong possibilities for mediation 'as social and educational work' (p 486). Their justification lies in increasingly robust evidence that mediation may function as 'a communicative action' (Lúcio and Neves, 2010, p 486) whose deployment may strengthen and develop, rather than repair, relationships between subjects who may be conceived as proactive agents of social transformation. In this way, Lúcio and Neves (2010) argue that mediation as social and educational work aims to problematise and complexify, and through that to construct new social relations in a spirit of dialogue and sharing.

Mediation may be employed more or less formally and at different points in the policy process. Exemplifying the more formal end of the spectrum, the US has statutes that determine the use of specific conventions for public policy mediation for the creation and revision of regulations (Laws and Forester, 2007). However formal the context, mediation has acquired a substantial repertoire of evidence-informed techniques that promote success, including 'joint fact-finding' and 'integrative bargaining' (Laws and Forester, 2007, p 347).

The second major focus of applied mediation in policy studies is that of transformation through intercession. For example, a policy may be conceived in a certain way by state or federal decision-makers yet is enacted differently on the ground following intercession from local actors, or factors that might be local (for example, organisational) or global (for example, neoliberal). Therefore, in policy mediation, local culture or regulatory conditions are as likely to intercede into policy meaning making as the activities, agendas and dispositions of local school teachers, principals or headteachers.

Furthermore, the transformation implied by this sense of policy mediation may sometimes be more precisely understood as mitigation, in which the original policy goals or mechanisms might be deemed by local actors charged with their implementation or enactment to be potentially harmful or unwelcome. We refer to both 'implementation' and 'enactment' purposefully here, since, conceptually, the idea of mediation plays a different role in each paradigm. When thinking with 'policy implementation', any deviation from original policy intentions is a problem to be solved or investigated, depending on whether your role is focused on policy making or researching. By extension, anything that mediates those intentions is also liable to be constructed as problematic in this wider sense. Brain et al (2006), for example, appear to construct teachers' practice as 'the' key mediator between policy and practice, where it is singled out for typological exploration. On the other hand, a 'policy enactment' approach renders visible those routine, everyday policy processes comprising multiple and diverse interventions, intercessions and interpretations by a range of actors and conditions, and so policy mediation is a feature and not an irritant in this framing.

A more fundamental issue is that in many western-style liberal democracies and the jurisdictions that emulate them, the role of the teacher is increasingly reduced to being 'a technocratic implementer of policy' (Brain et al, 2006, p 412). In this context, any evidence of education professional values, dispositions or ways of knowing are susceptible to pathologisation as 'mediating factors'.

Further reading

- Ranson, S. (2011) School governance and the mediation of engagement, Educational Management, Administration and Leadership, 39(4): 398–413.
- Sussking, L., McKearnan, S. and Thomas-Larmer, J. (eds) (1999) The consensus building handbook: a comprehensive guide to reaching agreement, Thousand Oaks: SAGE.

Mediatisation

In the same way that professional and private lives are inundated by media-saturation, education policy too is increasingly shaped by the politics and influence of media representations or 'mediatisation'. Here, mediatisation is used to refer 'to the increasingly dominant influence of media in shaping public life and policy discourses, and an ongoing process by which actors gain relative power (such as governments, institutions, news media or global rankers) using media logics' (Shahjahan et al, 2022, p 225). On the one hand, mass media can be understood in a very limited sense as vehicles for delivering information that is objective and impartial. On the other hand, mass media functions as a dividing practice and mode of politics since it works to steer public attention, direct policy agendas and manufacture consent for particular forms of public opinion (Lingard and Rawolle, 2004). A key focus of critical policy sociology therefore is the role of mediatisation as discourses and framings for education policy debate, negotiation and dissemination. This includes a focus on the discursive role of mediatisation as ideological spaces for the invention and translation of new actors and processes in the field of education.

Ward (2015), for example, moves beyond a focus on how media influence public opinion to document 'the public discussion of issues that the media allows and on the incentives and capacities that political actors have to take part' (p 183). In the specific case of Australia, Ward (2015) observes how the media opens up crucial spaces for rival political parties to frame certain policy agendas as issues of public interest and debate – or what might be called the mediatisation or discursive framing of public policy agenda setting. On this account, what is omitted or silenced (see entry on 'Silence') by these discursive framings can be considered as significant as what is reported by the media. The issue of what is included and excluded from the mediatisation of public policy agenda-setting is particularly salient at the time of writing as more education policy issues and their solutions are being framed as matters of technical improvement and efficiency requiring highly specialised expertise (Ward, 2015).

The omnipresence of media as a modality or space for mediating public policy dilemmas can be explained, in one sense, by the transition to governance by networks and the multiplication and expansion of arenas where public policies are deliberated, negotiated and reconciled or held apart (see entry on 'Governance'). Shahjahan et al (2022), for example, point to the ways in which actors spanning different interest groups strategically use media for their own purposes, such as framing issues, garnering attention and legitimacy for specific issues and events, and intervening to decide what is (and what is not) newsworthy. Adding to these observations, Lingard and Rawolle (2004) document how, increasingly, mediations of education policy are recast through forms of 'de facto policy, policy as sound bite, media policy representations as deliberate political misrepresentations, and policy release as media release' (p 363). Moreover, Lingard and Rawolle (2004) specify that the logic of practice underpinning the journalistic field works to reconstitute policy through specific cross-field imbrications.

From the perspective of policy makers, the media represents significant opportunities to influence what is deliberated as matters of public interest. This is evident from the burgeoning number of public relations departments and employment of media consultants by governments, as well as the careful curation of media presence by state officials seeking to bolster support for particular kinds of policy reform. Political communication, in effect, has become increasingly professionalised and handled strategically by governments (Lingard and Rawolle, 2004; Ward, 2015). Here, then, we can observe how education policy and politics is co-constructed through mediatisation as various actors (political parties, advocacy groups and stakeholders) deploy media logics to achieve specific ends (Hamilton, 2017). At the same time, the media stands apart from government as an actor in its own right since it wields power, irrespective of government influence, to carve out the discursive boundaries for containing the language around what constitutes matters of public interest (Ward, 2015).

Education researchers have adopted the framing of mediatisation to achieve different kinds of analytical work in their descriptions of policy making and policy worlds both nationally and globally. Hamilton (2017), for example, draws on the example of international large-scale assessments administered by the Organisation for Economic Co-operation and Development (OECD) to show how the circulation and planned reception of these assessment results are strategically worked on by the OECD through the preparation of media releases and orchestrated media events. In a similar vein, Shahjahan et al (2022) explores the reception and recontextualisation of Global University Rankings in India to demonstrate how league table results gain traction in some national contexts through the use of affective mediations and translations by local actors. What these studies also reveal is the extent to which contemporary forms of mediatisation of policy are increasingly framed by the provision of numbers and graphic visualisations (see entry on 'Visual methods') that function as effective vehicles for the promotion, accessibility and usability of performance indicators, national and international assessments and cross-country comparisons.

What is sometimes omitted in education studies of mediatisation of policy, however, is the variability and mutation of the media across the globe in terms of the changing affective and normative ploys used to realise specific policy goals depending on the geopolitical region. For instance, the assumption among some that media presents antagonistic political views (Ward, 2015) may not apply to neo-authoritarian societies. Shahjahan et al (2022) therefore urge researchers of mediatisation of policy to look beyond westernised contexts to account for such misalignment. In the same vein, Shahjahan et al (2022) encourage us to move beyond any exclusive focus on the international rankings produced by the Programme for International Student Assessment to take account of the multiple ways in which the mediatisation of policy is exercised through affective and normative means on other platforms and technologies. Hamilton (2017), too, reminds us of the increasing diversification of media platforms and their growing importance to mediatisation of policy both nationally and globally.

Further reading

- Barnes, N., Watson, S. and MacRae, S. (2022) The moral positioning of education policy publics: how social media is used to wedge an issue, Critical Studies in Education.
- Hattam, R., Prosser, B. and Brady, K. (2009) Revolution or backlash? The mediatisation of education policy in Australia, Critical Studies in Education, 50(2): 159–172.

Micro-credential

Micro-credentials are complex terms that are not easy to define, as evident by the shifting meanings attributed to it within scholarly literature and the variety of organisational and administrative domains (from higher education institutions to transnational organisations) that have appropriated and infused it within their own specific social arrangements as markers of specific technical-instrumental achievements. One way to make sense of micro-credentials is to view them as short, competency-based units of recognition that deliver and certify learning in vocational and higher education domains that are not recognised alone as educational qualifications by relevant authorities. Timewise, micro-credentials take less than a full academic year to complete, and certification-wise, they account for less than a conventional credential (in the European Union, less than five European Credit Transfer and Accumulation System; see Pollard and Vincent, 2022). Micro-credentials may be further broken into digital or certificate badges, massive open online course or industry-recognised certificates, and when accumulated separately or in combination with others, may amount to a post-secondary qualification. From this perspective, micro-credentials are premised on and foster the idea that qualifications can be unproblematically reassembled from disaggregated components provided by different educational authorities and actors.

The introduction of micro-credentials is typically accompanied by many lofty promises of flexibility and independence from time- and place-restricted learning; wider recognition and attractiveness among employers who typically attach less worth to formal degrees; and the validation of skills and competences that are not certified by traditional degrees. Higher education institutions across the globe, for example, increasingly view micro-credentials as conduits to new sources of revenue while also fulfilling progressive promises such as widening access and promoting equality. Many of these assumptions are coming under greater investigation and scrutiny from education scholars working in fields of critical studies of education policy, curriculum and education digitalisation. Pollard and Vincent (2022), for example, argue that micro-credentials reinforce the precarious position of teachers by strengthening demand for casualised work. Moreover, while micro-credentials appear to hold out the possibility of improved employability, they have also been found to wield the adverse and contradictory effect of undermining such features as they rely on the production of quickly expiring skills and the promotion of 'an architecture of planned obsolescence combined with the perpetual return of workers to commodified e-learning' (Ralston, 2021, p 86). Lastly, argue Pollard and Vincent (2022), micro-credentials promote transmissive and transactive pedagogy based on passive reproduction and assimilation of knowledge and skills driven by profit.

Building on the sociology of Basil Bernstein and the continental *Didaktik* tradition, Wheelahan and Moodie (2021) claim that micro-credentials need to be properly contextualised as supplements to dominant discourses of human capital theory and employability. Micro-credentials, in essence, can be considered the latest tools of neoliberal governments and non-state actors such as think tanks, intergovernmental organisations, industry and philanthropies, determined to steer education towards a generic focus on human preparedness for the job market. Within human capital theory, for example, workers are positioned as responsible for making themselves adept to the volatility and pace of fast-changing job markets through continuous upskilling and retraining. Complementing this vision of learners as existing or soon-to-be workers, micro-credentials are organised around a narrow instrumental focus on specific task handling, role occupation and generic skills and competencies, such as problem solving or critical thinking. Micro-credentials, in other words, are designed to be 'stackable, additive, and commutative so the order of acquisition is irrelevant' (Wheelahan and Moodie, 2021, p 222). Viewed in another way, micro-credentials function to break the kinds of coherence, sequence and hierarchy that are typical of disciplinary knowledge and academic or vocational curriculum-based subjects. Through their emphasis on workplace discipline rather than scholarly discipline as an organising principle, micro-credentials prioritise knowledge relevance, knowledge transfer and knowledge application at the expense of knowledge for self-development, self-learning or even 'critical consciousness' (Freire, 1970). By reducing knowledge to ready-made, accessible bite-sized components, micro-credentials run the risk of transforming knowledge into a commodity to be consumed and valued only for its utility in securing self-advantage, financial gain and/or employment. While students of micro-credential learning accumulate specific skills relevant for specific tasks, they are not given access to epistemic skills needed to critically evaluate broader questions such as what knowledge is and how it matters. Rather, they are taught to be complicit and unreflective, and this has wider implications for professional identities and subjectivity.

Drawing on the work of Michel Foucault, Pollard and Vincent (2022) take up the question of subjectivity through a form of post-digital theorising that asks: how do we become subjects of knowledge through micro-credentials and how might new subjectivities emerge (or not) through different ways of doing micro-credentials? While Pollard and Vincent (2022) align themselves in many ways with the critique of micro-credentials, they also develop proposals on how to address this critique in order that micro-credentials might be made more inclusive and ethical. As micro-credentials are becoming omnipresent in the work of education at the time of writing, albeit in flux subject to changing attitudes towards their validity and usefulness, it is a timely move by Pollard and Vincent (2022) to shift from critique to concrete proposals of alternatives. To this end, Pollard and Vincent (2022) offer up three principles of alternative micro-credentials: embeddedness in the curriculum; alignment with the university mission; and pedagogy that fosters reflexivity on the political nature of discourse and how subjects are discursively fashioned. The first principle focuses on embedding skills deemed necessary for all students, such as academic skills, into the formal curriculum to ensure their equal and broad availability. The second principle calls for increased alignment between micro-credentials and the expressed values of universities, such as inclusion and flourishing, with the effect of undermining those neoliberal and instrumentalist values that are usually not stated in public missions but typically fostered in practice. The third principle builds on critical pedagogy to reinvent emancipatory learning practices based on surprise, creativity, playfulness and reflexivity.

Further reading

- Abramovich, S., Schunn, C. and Higashi, R.M. (2013) Are badges useful in education? It depends upon the type of badge and expertise of learner, Educational Technology Research and Development, 61(2): 217–232.
- Baker, D.P. (2011) Forward and backward, horizontal and vertical: transformation of occupational credentialing in the schooled society, Research in Social Stratification and Mobility, 29(1): 5–29.

Mobility

Policy mobility research can be traced to the interdisciplinary field of 'mobility studies' and economics, critical geography and sociology more generally which share an interest in the development of studies looking at how the world is constituted by physical, virtual, corporeal or imaginative movements of people, ideas, information and objects (Gulson et al, 2017). The ontology that foregrounds movement and mobility within and across these studies reflects the dynamics of policy making in emerging globalised time-space. Specifically, it is an unbounded, inductive ontology that emphasises the non-linear, fast-paced transfer of policies across locations; the growing interactions and interconnectedness of previously disconnected actors; and the establishment of novel spaces of governance such as transnational expert networks or online communities. Here, movement connotes a general displacement while mobility adds a concern with strategies and implications of such movement. Policy mobility research therefore problematises fixed notions of policy cycle (see entry on 'Cycle') to underscore the constitutive effects of ongoing processes of relation-making and space-making that mobilise policies. On this understanding, policy mobility research does not start from the position that policy worlds can be divided into hierarchical, pre-existent scales defined by political-administrative and geographical constructs of local, regional, national and global (see entry on 'Scalar policy analysis'). Instead, policy mobility research treats scales and sites as categories of practice that need to be explained as context-sensitive forms of action rather than deployed as second-order events or 'backdrop, location or passive context' (Clarke, 2019, p 195). These problematisations of linearity and scale help to distinguish policy mobility research from other strands of policy research, namely policy transfer and policy borrowing (see entries on 'Transfer' and 'Borrowing').

A key focus of policy mobility research is the study of how, why and to what extent diverse networks of actors contribute to policy content and movement. This includes a focus on the quality and integrity of relations (or nodes) in the network; the discursive/material means through which said relations are produced and sustained; and the ways in which policy 'moves' (and becomes contested, disrupted or translated) within these movements. Policy mobility research therefore traces the dialectics of policy movement through a recognition of the ways in which policy is co-constituted through local contexts and local projects. In this description, policy mobility research does not represent a rejection of the role of traditional government structures and actors in the policy-making process, such as the state or administrative structures and divisions (provinces, municipalities, districts) formalised in law and legislation (McKenzie and Aikens, 2021). Quite the opposite; policy mobility research remains sensitive to the significance and complexity of local characteristics as inscription devices for carving out spaces for policy change. However, policy mobility research does ask a different set of questions to those that notionally preoccupy theorists of state policy, namely how the state, alongside other actors, shapes policy (im)mobilities and how topologically mobile policies interact and combine with historically predefined yet shifting governing structures.

Another key driver of the unbounded ontology underpinning policy mobility research is a critique of methodological territorialism and methodological nationalism as framings for policy research. Here, policy mobility research offers up a dynamic concept of policy and power (as relational, fluid, networked, maintained through labour, and distributed in space) as well as subscribes to methodological propositions that permit similar kinds of analytical work. Alongside an interest in cases of successful movement, policy mobility research also considers absence or failure of movement and its causes. McKenzie and Aikens (2021, p 318) describe phases of policy (im)mobility as, for example, initial refusal or mutation into acceptable forms influenced by context-specific factors such as lack of motivation and funding, ideology and competing policy priorities and governing arrangements. Furthermore, Edwards et al (2020) offer helpful ways to understand how policies are experienced as more or less mobile for different individuals and groups. Using mobility theory to problematise fixed notions of spaces as geographically bounded entities, Edwards et al (2020) point to the (in)ability of some individuals to move through space owing to their unequal positions in socio-spatial arrangements. On this account, policy mobility research offers a number of methodologically important and theoretically innovative approaches to studying the movement of policy, its enactment and the unequal reception and effects of policy on individuals occupying different and historically unique geopolitical spaces.

Methodologically, policy mobility research is open-ended through its sensitivity to the fluidity and variegation of policy as a contingent product of historically and culturally unique regularities and relations. Policy mobility research also achieves this open-endedness through its articulation and combination of various analytical methods. These methods (and their application) include discourse analysis, various forms of network analysis (bibliometric, ethnographic, social), multi-sited ethnography that follows policies, ideas and people *in situ*, and comparative case studies that tease out the unevenness and differences of policy mobility across countries or levels and scales of governance. Policy mobility research also calls for inventive methods that include paying critical attention to the performative effects that occur using certain methods to represent and explain phenomena. Some methods have the effect of reinscribing dominant modes of knowledge production or, in some cases, overstating the integrity of relations between actors and organisations in a network. Consider, for example, the performative, reinscribing effects of using elites as sources of knowledge in the 'following the policy' approach or using the primacy of nodes to represent relations in a network. In this sense, policy mobility research strives to make explicit the active contribution of different actors to policy as enablers or disablers of its movement, as well as draw attention to the wider geopolitical framings that determine how policies move and/or become domesticated/institutionalised (Lewis, 2021).

Further reading

- Peck, J. and Theodore, N. (2015) Fast policy: experimental statecraft at the thresholds of neoliberalism, Minneapolis: University of Minnesota Press.
- Wood, A. (2016) Tracing policy movements: methods for studying learning and policy circulation, Environment and Planning A: Economy and Space, 48(2): 391–440.

Multiple-streams analysis

Multiple-streams analysis was developed by John Kingdon in his 1984 book, *Agendas, Alternatives and Public Policies*. Kingdon's (1984) multiple-streams framework seeks to explain the first two parts of which is identified as a four-part policy process: agenda setting and the elucidation of viable policy alternatives (the remaining parts being authoritative selection and implementation). That is, its objective is to illuminate 'why some subjects become prominent on the policy agenda and others do not, and why some alternatives for choice are seriously considered while others are neglected' (Kingdon, 1984, p 3). Kingdon (1984) developed his ideas in response to prevailing contemporaneous ideas about agenda-setting in policy making. Specifically, *rationalism* was rejected owing to its failure to capture how reality works. *Incrementalism*, Kingdon (1984) argues, is contradicted by evidence that policy change may happen suddenly. More important to Kingdon's (1984) model was Cohen et al's (1972) *Garbage Can Model* of organisational choice. While it arguably over-corrects for rationalism's limitations in constructing organisations as 'organised anarchies' (Cohen et al, 1972, p 1), Kingdon's (1984) model proved useful in its emphasis on 'the ambiguity of decision making' (McLendon and Cohen-vogel, 2008, p 32). Incorporating this idea led to a framework that rejected earlier cyclical or staged conceptualisations of policy formation.

Kingdon's (1984) insights into policy agenda-setting foreground two key elements. First is the way in which multiple (groups of) actors interact to have their interests privileged as policy. Second is the way in which the contextual conditions for agenda-setting, along with these actors, may be categorised as discrete *streams*. These streams may occasionally converge, which is a prerequisite to policy-agenda shift. Kingdon's (1984) multiple-streams framework comprises several primary concepts, including three categorisations of stream. The first is the *problem stream*, which refers to issues that present to decision-makers as requiring policy intervention. The identification, or construction, of problems is therefore tied to values. These problems may come to policy makers' attention through routine *indicators* concerning, for example, rising inflation or falling employment. Or a normally routine matter can become the target of specific attention through extra data-gathering, perhaps owing to a perceived but then-unevidenced change. This change in attention status may come about because of *focusing events* such as a crisis or disaster, including the arrival and spread of a new pandemic. Or it may come from *feedback*, including complaints.

The second element is the *policy stream*, which Kingdon (1984) explains through drawing on the biological metaphor of the 'policy primeval soup' (p 116). Following this metaphor, proto-policies and ideas swirl around among more-or-less connected members of a community of experts with particular agendas and varied specialisms. These ideas prosper or fade in a process analogous to 'natural selection' (Kingdon, 1984, p 117). Moments of prospering 'soften up' the public towards certain solutions, which may be amalgams of several proto-policies, just as molecules combine to spark life. Finally, the *political stream* is constituted of 'factors that influence the body politic, such as swings in national mood, executive or legislative turnover, and interest group advocacy campaigns' (Béland and Howlett, 2016, p 222). Such factors enable or preclude entire suites of policy through discursive dominance. These include, for example, a polity's disposition to fund or defund public services, including education, to invest in technological advances or to construct regulation as protective or destructive.

A key mechanism for encouraging certain ideas to prosper within the policy stream is the advocacy of *policy entrepreneurs*, Kingdon's (1984) next key conceptual contribution. Their role in this framework is more focused than in the wider literature on policy entrepreneurs that evolved from his work (see entry on 'Entrepreneur'). In multiple-streams analysis, policy entrepreneurs take advantage of, or create, temporally limited *policy windows* of opportunities in which streams converge. During these moments, entrepreneurs invoke certain problems and link them to their preferred policy solution in the context of amenable political conditions. These instances demonstrate considerable variability, and so 'an element of randomness thus is strongly present and can clearly be seen at work in the actions of policy entrepreneurs' (McLendon and Cohen-vogel, 2008, p 33), as well as seeming arbitrariness in the convergence or otherwise of streams. Policy windows, for instance, may be opened by policy entrepreneurs themselves, by focusing events or by institutionalised events such as elections.

The multiple-streams framework has been praised for its focus on the role of agency and contingency in agenda-setting and decision-making (Béland and Howlett, 2016) and for providing causal explanations for the first time (McLendon and Cohen-vogel, 2008). However, it has also attracted critique for its lack of attention to other parts of the policy process, notably implementation (Howlett, 2019), and for its ontological validity, that is, whether problem, policy and political streams exist as discrete entities (Brown, 2007). The framework has consequently been refined. Herweg et al (2015), for instance, incorporate new strands that foreground the role of political parties.

Further reading

- Ruvalcaba-Gomez, E.A., Criado, J.I. and Gil-Garcia, J.R. (2023) Analyzing open government policy adoption through the multiple streams framework: the roles of policy entrepreneurs in the case of Madrid, Public Policy and Administration, 38(2): 233–264.
- Santos, Í. and Kauko, J. (2022) Externalisations in the Portuguese parliament: analysing power struggles and (de-)legitimation with Multiple Streams Approach, Journal of Education Policy, 37(3): 399–418.

N

Narrative policy analysis

Narrative analysis in policy and the social sciences more generally has as its main focus the ways in which human subjects mobilise storytelling and the narrative form as a medium for producing meaning about the world and relations to the self. Politicians and policy makers, for example, deploy narratives through speeches and policy documents to achieve particular ends that include persuading the electorate of their vision, commitment or sentiment. Similarly, citizens assembled in a government council meeting addressing local councillors about a particular issue that is affecting them may draw on storytelling as an effective tool for communicating their preferences or grievances and discontents. In both cases, the narrative form of communication can be 'best understood as the personal enactment of communal methods of self-accounting, vocabularies of motive [and] culturally recognizable emotional performances' (Wetherell and Edley, 1999, p 338).

Policy as text or discourse can also be approached as narratives ('policy narratives') in the sense they reflect technologies, practices or rationalities of government (Bansel, 2015a). According to Chase (2017), narrative is the achievement of '[m]eaning making through the shaping or ordering of experience, a way of understanding one's own or others' actions, of organising events and objects into a meaningful whole, of connecting and seeing the consequences of actions and events over time' (p 421). A narrative approach to policy studies therefore closely observes how different, seemingly contradictory and competing discourses are brought together through the medium of narratives to communicate and represent definitions and practices of policy as well as policy problems and their solutions. Understood from this perspective, policies as artefacts do not reflect actually existing realities but rather reflect the political work of governments or other actors who actively seek to prefigure and contain realities to complement and realise particular ends. This includes mobilising policy as narratives in order to imagine and manage the possibilities for acting on and governing citizens as bearers of rights, obligations and duties (Wilkins, 2018) (see entry on 'Governmentality'). The narrative approach therefore concerns questions of power and refusal, namely how policy narratives function as modes for curating governing, on the one hand, and modes for inciting resistance, on the other hand. A narrative policy analysis foregrounds counter-narratives and subjugated narratives through normative and analytical commitments to making explicit evidence of resistance to dominant narratives and the production of alternative narratives.

Bansel's (2015a) approach to narrative policy analysis is unique for combining several theories: Foucault's notions of governmentality, discourse and subjectification; Ricoeur's temporality, narrative and identity; Massey's space and narrative; and Roe and Stone's narrative policy analysis. When combined, these modes of analysis open up possibilities for viewing narratives as both strategies of persuasion and technologies of government that are sustained by the fragile synthesis and coordination of normative discourses and discursive practices within particular spatio-temporal fixes. In this sense, policy narratives can be understood to be temporally and spatially situated. The policy narrative, in other words, is a form of emplotment: it works to create spatial-temporal orders in which difference and sameness can be imagined through the provision of storied histories of personal attachments and modes of belonging. Narrative prefiguration or emplotment therefore contains the possibilities to 'authorize what can and cannot be said; they produce relations of power and communities of consent and dissent, and thus discursive boundaries are always being redrawn around what constitutes the desirable and the undesirable' (Britzman, 2000, p 36). Narrative policy analysis makes the familiar strange through critiquing and problematising that which may be taken-for-granted as something normal, given or desirable. The implication here is that what may appear inevitable, objective and necessary can be construed in policy contexts as a function and outcome of the narrative. Hence, dominant policy narration demands critical deconstruction to make way for alternative methods of communicating and framing ideological dilemmas and policy problem representations.

Studies of policy as narrative also concern matters of identity or the self. Personal or institutional narratives typically revolve around versions of the self, of others and an imagined social world composed of interpersonal, cultural and historical relations and contexts (Chase, 2017). Kosunen and Hansen (2018), for example, document how identity is inhabited and performed through Finnish narratives of comprehensive education by influential national political actors. Kosunen and Hansen (2018) consider these narratives important as the authors of these scripts wield significant authority to configure spaces for the (re)imagination of policy history and its future. As Kosunen and Hansen (2018) observe, these authors produce narratives that selectively omit certain events in order to present a particular version of the history of Finnish comprehensive education. Moreover, the narratives of Finnish comprehensive education presented by these authors changed depending on the intended audiences, according to Kosunen and Hansen (2018), demonstrating the temporal dimension of storytelling as an anchor used to produce a narrative of historical continuity, progress or success.

Further reading

- Czarniawska, B. (2010) The uses of narratology in social and policy studies, Critical Policy Studies, 4(1): 58–76.
- Maguire, M. and Braun, A. (2019) Headship as policy narration: generating metaphors of leading in the English primary school, Journal of Educational Administration and History, 51(2): 103–116.

Neoliberalism

Despite neoliberalism now being elevated to something normative, intuitive and ordinary ('we are all neoliberal now' being a popular slogan), it is a notoriously slippery concept with a very complicated intellectual history and relationship to different political, cultural and economic projects. Like many popular '-isms' – feminism, spiritualism and universalism – neoliberalism is used as a shorthand to describe a movement or 'thought collective' (Mirowski, 2009, p 428). From a Marxist or political economy perspective, neoliberalism is signified by the entrenchment of economies and peoples within the grip of new forces of global capitalism, a form of 'restoration' that, according to Harvey (2005), involves elite groups of transnational actors pursuing new means of capital accumulation and class power through engineering patterns of consumption and debt (also see Duménil and Lévy, 2004). Neoliberalism can also be conceptualised from a Foucauldian or governmentality perspective (Rose, 1999) to represent those governmental programmes designed to fabricate new kinds of moral and ethical selves organised around virtues of competition and self-interest. Typically the 'neoliberal subject' is characterised by the economic-rational figure of 'homo economicus', namely the 'individualist fiction of the disembodied or unsituated human subject' (Gray, 2007, p 24) made popular through the classical liberal discourse of the 19th century and early 20th century, a time during which utilitarian principles and philosophies promoted the view of structures and individuals as effortlessly self-regulating under the efficient equilibrium of capitalism.

The muddiness and expansiveness of the term neoliberalism means that it has been used to explain the emergence of various governmental programmes around the globe, from Pinochetian authoritarian democracy and Thatcherite neoconservatism to Reganite economics and Blairite Third Way social democracy. Owing to its 'promiscuity (hanging out with various theoretical perspectives)' (Clarke, 2008, p 135), neoliberalism has also served as a useful analytic for describing the effects of these governmental programmes, from the transformation of citizenship (Johansson and Hvinden, 2005) to the production of new feminist subjectivities (Rottenburg, 2013). Neoliberalism also serves as a master narrative in everyday language for explaining transformations of work, travel or family, where increasingly they are seen as functions of market fundamentalism, corporatocracy or financialisation.

Like other meta-narratives that seek to make complicated social and political worlds easy to navigate and understand, neoliberalism is consoling according to Barnett (2005) precisely because it coheres specific grievances and discontents. Neoliberalism recasts social and political worlds around a vision of competing forces struggling for the strategic occupation or valorisation of different assets (as private and not public), rights (as consumers and not citizens) and relations (as competitive and not collaborative). The effect of this seductive, binary language is that certain people are well placed to position and elevate themselves and others morally and politically according to their role in that struggle.

Another effect of the popularisation of neoliberalism in academic and everyday language is an overestimation of the rationality and coherence of neoliberal projects, with the effect that very little appears to exist 'outside' neoliberal appropriation. Such indiscriminate use of the term neoliberalism is not only fatalist (even if it is consoling) but reduces 'the social' or 'the personal' (those spaces in which subjects can be found resisting, refusing, reinventing and answering back) to a 'residual effect of hegemonic projects and/or governmental rationalities' (Barnett, 2005, p 7). Moreover, it assumes 'that governmental practice in a plurality of sites flows uniformly from the big transformations produced by neoliberalism' (Newman, 2007, p 54) and therefore fails to consider the unevenness and variegation of neoliberal projects across the globe, specifically the ways in which policy 'moves' and 'travels' and comes to be revised and inflected within unique historical and geopolitical settings.

A dynamic conception of neoliberalism is therefore typically employed by education policy researchers, one that is sensitive to the contingent and messy geopolitical relations that are required to cohere in order to make neoliberalism possible. Here neoliberalism can be studied as 'mobile calculative techniques of governing that can be decontextualised from their original sources and recontextualised in constellations of mutually constitutive and contingent relations' (Ong, 2007, p 13). This means moving beyond synchronic, institutionalist or structuralist accounts of neoliberalism to capture the 'variety of neoliberalisms' (Plehwe, 2009, p 3) that exist and play out in different contexts. In their research on policy enactments in schools, Ball et al (2012a) analyse the 'creative processes of interpretation and recontextualisation' (p 3) through which neoliberal policy discourse is translated and implemented. Similarly, Wilkins (2019) details the ways in which certain academy schools in England simultaneously co-opt and transform key elements of neoliberal discourse in order to achieve partial congruence of multiple stakes, interests and objectives. In both cases, neoliberalism is situated against the background of locally situated dilemmas, obligations, normative commitments and dispositions. In other cases, researchers have called for the introduction of new concepts to take account of these messy accommodations and refusals of neoliberalism, namely 'postneoliberalism' (Springer, 2015), 'after neoliberalism' (Rose, 2017) and 'authoritarian neoliberalism' (Bruff, 2014).

Further reading

- Apple, M.W. (2017) What is present and absent in critical analyses of neoliberalism in education, Peabody Journal of Education, 92(1): 148–153.
- Castree, N. (2006) From neoliberalism to neoliberalisation: consolations, confusions, and necessary illusions, Environment and Planning A, 38(1): 1–6.

Numbers

A central tool of governing in higher and other phases of education (primary, secondary, college) is the use of numerical data collection instruments to monitor individual and institutional performance. These processes of monitoring, tracking and evaluation in effect work to locate education workers within fields of compulsory visibility or 'datafication', such as publication counts, rankings, impact indices and numerically calculated/datafied student feedback. Datafication is premised on the idea that progress in learning outcomes, research quality and work efficiency require rigorous quantitative data capture. Datafication is performed across multiple levels of governance from the individual to the global. Similarly, the production and analysis of data occurs within and across different levels of governance, with the effect of bringing local, regional, national, and global spaces and practices into relations of commensuration, comparison and equivalence (see entry on 'Digital education'). The phenomenon of data in education is often discussed through the prefix of 'big'. Doug Laney's widely used '3V' characterisation of big data as high-volume, high-velocity, and high-variety 'information assets' means that international large-scale assessments such as Trends in Mathematics and Science Study, Progress In International Reading Literacy Study and the Programme for International Student Assessment are not – in their inception or their typical uses – examples of big data (Sobe, 2018). Big data, often produced and analysed in real time with volumes of data that are too massive for human calculation, rely heavily on novel expertise and technological advances. Datafication thus generates complex data infrastructures as assemblages of expertise, technology, hardware and politics, enabling unprecedented methods of data collection, data transfer and data interoperability.

In this sense, data collection is not something new. The history of datafication can be traced to the development of statistics and reporting among centralised state administrations and the governance of colonial constituencies by metropoles. National and local government authorities, for example, use data as 'scientific evidence' to inform decision-making about performance evaluation and the allocation of budgetary funds, as well as enhance claims to the credibility of their political rhetoric. However, at the time of writing, numerical data is no longer exclusively produced for such work. Data serves multiple functions and effects within the public imagination, including, for example, inciting and mobilising students as consumers of education where they are directed towards using public ranking systems (or league tables) to make informed decisions about university choice in relation to perceived teaching quality (including staff-to-student ratio), employment prospects and research intensity (volume, income and reputation).

In education policy literature, the rise of datafication is used to denote the emergence of specific modes of governance that aim to foster new subjectivities intimately linked to practices of data use, from collection to measurement and monitoring (Grek, 2009). Espeland and Sauder (2007) theorise these trends in terms of reactivity: 'Because people are reflexive beings who continually monitor and interpret the world and adjust their actions accordingly, measures are re-active. Measures elicit responses from people who intervene in the objects they measure' (p 1). Academic work, for example, is at the time of writing increasingly subject to a plethora of measurements and metrics designed to constitute academic subjects as calculators, managers and tutors of data, namely data subjects and data objects. Consider the role of data technologies like Google Scholar listings of publications by citation and national assessment frameworks to determine research quality and impact. These data technologies rely on proxy measures and aggregates that, when combined, produce 'metric assemblages' that work on academic identities in specific ways, namely by inciting academics to perceive their own self-worth in the academy and the value of their work as reducible to and inseparable from the calculable form (Burrows, 2012). The shaping-by-numbers of educational spaces and organisations manipulates collective and individual subjectivities of people, giving rise to performance-evaluated teachers and test-oriented students.

In order to better understand how certain discourses and techniques come to exercise such profound influence over and across distant spaces and practices, what is sometimes referred to as tactics in governing-at-a-distance, education researchers highlight data circulation as a key modality in contemporary forms of governance. This includes a specific normative and analytical focus on data production (what is produced, by whom and how), data availability (who has access to data, and in what formats) and data use (who uses the data, how, what are the stakes attached to data use). This analytical shift towards data circulation has in effect given rise to new fields of study, including sociology of numbers and quantification of education, both of which retain a strong focus on how numbers are mobilised, circulated, consumed and contested (Gorur, 2015a). These fields of study are driven by deep epistemological questions about the normative and political dimensions of data circulation and production. Digital and data sociologists, for example, seek to explain the role of data engineers and data producers to defining policy problems and their solutions, as, increasingly, the incalculable becomes rendered into numeric forms. Furthermore, focus has shifted towards tracing the circulation, availability and use of data among teachers and local administrations in order to make clear the extent to which said actors are emerging as a residual effect of data projects and rationalities. The anxiety over the omnipresence of big data in contemporary societies across the globe sometimes assumes that said actors have become captured in governmental fields of data power. There is uncertainty and messiness to these processes, however, which make them crucial to study actual rather than assumed processes of governance by data (Selwyn, 2016).

Further reading

- Piattoeva, N. and Boden, R. (2020) Escaping numbers? The ambiguities of the governance of education through data, International Studies in Sociology of Education, 29(1–2): 1–18.
- Porter, T. (1995) Trust in numbers: the pursuit of objectivity in science and public life, Princeton: Princeton University Press.

O

Ontology

Ontology is the naming and categorisation of reality, or *that which is*. Pluralising it to ontologies aligns with post-positivist insights into the multiple and contingent conditions of reality. Ontological statements, including classifications, about *what is* draw on *how* we think we know (see entry on 'Epistemology'). Each of these two concepts requires and shapes the other. For example, an epistemological approach that draws on material semiotics 'argues that the practice of relations shapes and forms the actors caught up in them', that ontological realities '*are done in practices*' (Law and Singleton, 2014, p 384, original emphasis) or enactment. Since different actors engage in different practices, this means that in material semiotics, what might have been thought of as an ontologically singular entity or phenomenon from a positivist perspective, is instead necessarily plural. This is compounded by the insight that even over little time, the context within which practice takes place also changes, which in turn produces new realities. *That which is*, or the ontological object, can never be singular in material semiotics and similar epistemologies. This multiplicity goes beyond the interpretive, where it is understood that a single event will be experienced and interpreted in many ways that themselves acquire an ontological status; it suggests that what is being interpreted is already ontologically multiple.

Asking what education policy *is* may consequently be seen as a more ontologically challenging and politically charged question than it at first appears, bringing to the fore issues including reality versus representation. That is to say, policy-as-relational-practice (social reality) and policy-as-text (representation) are ontologically more imbricated than they are identical, and it is evidence of power functioning effectively and teleologically to have them understood as reducible to one another, and/or as the text having privileged status over embodied practices.

The power to impose ontological understandings of *what policy is* constitutes a power over reality, including how subjects make sense of themselves, and so ontological framings are simultaneously largely implicit in policy and policy studies and also fundamental to the creation and reproduction of epistemic paradigms, their communities and claims. Even the act of defining the features of ontology may be seen as a political act whose purpose is to shape the conceptual territory to suit a particular agenda. In this spirit, Webb and Gulson (2015) refute the inherent positivism of Law's (2004) five-part definition in positing that ontology is 'enmeshed with people ... not "out there" but produced in various times/spaces ... not anterior ... [but] multiple ... and ... non-representational' (p 23). For Webb and Gulson (2015), their definition is a rejection of an entire paradigm that has constructed policy as singular, independent and fixed, and that has contributed to a misplaced focus on 'what works' in education. Marshalling the resources of a policy research community to finding out 'what works' involves ensuring commitment to that intellectual project's ontological assumptions, the task of an ontological politics (Mol, 1999). Singh et al (2014) would hesitate to call this research, arguing that research should establish new ontological frames (itself ontologically political) rather than confirm existing ones. They insist that 'the doing of research is an "interference" [in] reality' (p 828).

All aspects of the policy process are influenced by ontological politics. For instance, control over naming *that which is* implies by abjection *that which is not*; that is to say, the silences of education policy (see entry on 'Silence'). Such ontological dominance also implies a concomitant control of discussions regarding purposes, mechanisms, roles, objects and values in education policy. Ontological dominance may be achieved discursively through reification; for example, by summoning in and through policy a cadre of professionals to be known (and to know themselves) as *education leaders* who should perform business–derived practices that are to be understood as leading. Or that which becomes defined and reified as policy-informing evidence gains that ontological status over other disregarded sources through a technocratic ontological politics that establishes the programmatic policy framing (Carusi et al, 2018).

Trans-jurisdictional ontological coherence, manifested in a material 'infrastructure of the policy ontology' (Brøgger, 2016, p 73) is important in enabling policy transfer, or diffusion, because it both implies a sufficiently shared understanding and set of assumptions about the policy and also supplies a common apparatus for operationalising it. In the case of the Bologna Process, for example, Brøgger (2016) notes that this infrastructure comprised 'an absence of "government" and decrees and the presence of "incentives" and standards' (p 79). Such infrastructure in turn performs ontological reification and reproductive functions.

Further reading

- Kung, S. (2018) The shifting space of ontology: appeals to crisis and the reformulation of nation, race, and biology in educational reform, Discourse: Studies in the Cultural Politics of Education, 39(2): 196–218.
- Mellaard, A. and Van Meijl, T. (2017) Doing policy: enacting a policy assemblage about domestic violence, Critical Policy Studies, 11(3): 330–348.

P

Partnership

The impetus to engage in partnerships in education can be interpreted as a rational response to the demands, constraints and effects of neoliberalism and globalisation. This is first because neoliberalism constructs the ideal agent as perpetually self-actualising an entrepreneurial and corporatised subjectivity. Substantive engagement with the commercial world and its actors through varied forms of partnership is an obvious way to operationalise this work and realise its product (Hay and Kapitzke, 2009). Partnership working exemplifies neoliberalism in a second way too. When the state privileges knowledge about education and its leadership and management that is generated by partners at the 'chalk-face' or 'service-user' level of practice, it implicitly marginalises expert knowledge generated in universities and local authorities or districts. Such expertise may be disregarded as overly bureaucratic or as representative of so-called 'producer capture'. This thinking arguably underpins much of the recent turn to so-called system leadership (see Courtney and McGinity, 2022). Here, as in other products of partnerships, the outcome may be constructed as 'an "organic" development initiated at the grassroots level' (Griffiths et al, 2009, p 197), yet in fact differs little from that desired by the state. Third, some partnerships are explicitly a function not just of neoliberalism but of privatisation. These arrangements, called 'public-private partnerships in education (ePPP)' (Verger, 2012, p 110), are the preferred mechanism of the World Bank and other supranational organisations for increasing privatisation in education systems internationally for purposes including enhancing provision and access, raising learning outcomes and introducing incentives (Verger, 2012). ePPP function, on the one hand, exogenously through providing a mechanism through which private-sector actors occupy roles and provide services in education. On the other hand, they function endogenously through privileging corporatised ways of acting and thinking, as well as corporatised understandings of educational purposes in those already working in education.

Globalisation also tends to produce partnerships. It does this first through invoking a deterritorialised relationship between abstract policy concepts, for example, between *global competitiveness* and *education*. Second, globalisation discursively privileges the attainment of a relationship between such concepts in policy and practice. Engaging in localised partnerships both concretises the abstracted relations and enables the performance of a causal relationship between the two. In this way, partnerships may be argued to 'solve the problems' of globalisation, which include 'the need for economic competitiveness, stimulation of innovation, and management of school to work transitions for young people' (Hay and Kapitzke, 2009, p 203). Imagined through the configuration of transnational relations, partnerships can also be understood as a key modality for carrying out the primary work of global actors' desire to hollow out the state.

This element of performativity speaks to 'the *symbolic dimension* of partnerships' (Dahlstedt, 2009, p 790, original emphasis). More fundamentally, partnering constitutes and represents a technology of governance (Hay and Kapitzke, 2009) in which the state sets out what is meant by appropriateness regarding choices of partner, as well as the mechanisms for and outcomes of partnerships. This delimitation of options by the state has been widely theorised using Michel Foucault's concept of governmentality (see entry on 'Governmentality'). From a governmentality perspective (Miller and Rose, 2008), the simultaneous promotion and discursive circumscription of partnerships in education by the state conceals its increasing power over the field behind an illusory sense of agency accorded to school or university-level actors when they partner. This illusory agency legitimises the policy approach that is produced from the partnership.

It is important to avoid the impression of determinism, however, when thinking of partnerships and their role in education. Gewirtz and Ozga (1990) point out that while the 'indirect rule' of a governmentality approach by the state avoids the resistance provoked by 'direct rule' (p 40), the illusory agency it instead depends upon 'fosters feelings of independence and becomes unmanageable' (p 41). Griffiths and colleagues (2009) similarly argue that while partnerships may intensify the steering capacity of the state, they remain 'complex "sites of struggle" that have the potential to be positive by empowering individuals to make decisions at the local level' (p 206).

The term *partnership* invokes equality yet acts of partnering are deeply inflected by power relations. Partners may not trust one another; there may be conflict concerning their roles or their interpretation of key concepts; particular stakeholders may come to the partnership with established dominance over policy making, demonstrated in some cases through facility with sanctioned policy terminology; or there may be cultural differences that impede smooth partnership functioning (Griffiths et al, 2009).

Further reading

- Cardoso, C.M. (2008) Government-Microsoft partnerships: supranational formulation in private and public policy, Globalisation, Societies and Education, 6(3): 241–264.
- Tooley, J. (2005) Management of private-aided higher education in Karnataka, India, Educational Management, Administration and Leadership, 33(4): 465–486.

Performativity

Performativity is a culture in which effectiveness and efficiency are privileged to the point of compulsion and judged largely through the quantitative comparison of inputs and outputs. Performativity is also a strategy for performing the achievement of such effectiveness and efficiency within these conceptual and discursive limits and at appropriate moments, such as during an inspection or in a quality-assurance return. It is not axiomatic that educational outcomes are amenable to being conceptualised only as measurable inputs and outputs, and so it is a considerable policy/discursive accomplishment to make these transformations and to mandate this interpretation across the field of education through rewards, but especially sanctions, such that professional practitioners feel (or *are*) obliged to conform. A key factor that contributes to this is the public nature of both the data and of the responses to them.

Performativity was first elucidated by Lyotard (1984), who contrasted and interplayed its two meanings: one signalled creativity and regeneration and the other referred to state or organisational regulation. The concept of performativity went on to be widely taken up in this latter sense by actor-network theorists (see entry on 'Actor-Network Theory') and was used to theorise gender by Butler (1990). Performativity was developed for use in education by Ball (2003), for whom it is one of the three policy technologies (along with the market and managerialism) that together operationalise a neoliberal global education reform package. This package is characterised by a dependence on numbers to make sense not just of education but the social world; and on control of public services, including education, through 'steering at a distance' (Ball, 2000, p 17). This political-technological work of steering at a distance is evident in the establishing an audit culture enforced through high-stakes accountability. The constituent technologies of this performative work make it a repudiation of the preceding tradition of welfarism, which was predicated on professionalism and bureaucracy. Performativity consequently erodes teacher and educational leader professionalism.

Ball's (2003) characterisation of performativity as a policy technology helps explain its compulsory nature, since such technologies consist in 'techniques and artefacts' (p 206) whose function is to order and direct human agency within relationships of power. Performativity is consequently more than a mode of governance; it is a theory of power, even totalising control, and so 'the issue of who controls the field of judgement is crucial' (Ball, 2003, p 216). Performativity therefore lends itself particularly well to analyses of state power, especially regarding school inspection. Perryman (2009), for instance, recognises inspection performances as fabrications constructed by school actors for the sole purpose of satisfying inspectors. Perryman (2009) develops the 'performance' element within performativity by emphasising the two roles of the performer and the audience.

However, belying the apparent superficiality invoked by the term *performative*, such acts of conforming may exceed the mere representation of value and instead come to inhabit it wholly. In other words, the field of judgement and its criteria may be internalised. In this way, performativity may involve subjects' identities, or even souls, notwithstanding the apparent and misleading objectivity of the artefacts and rationales underpinning it (Ball, 2003). Indeed, Ball (2003) argues that the primary object of reform is not educational structures or even practices, but rather the subjectivities of educationalists who are obliged to transform themselves into ever-self-actualising agents, always reform-ready. In this way, performativity inevitably produces instability in its subjects, since the precise nature of the reform to be enacted (or embodied) is liable to change, despite the investment made in each iteration. What matters is not so much the product as 'the constant act of performance, fabrication and construction, that is the constitution of worldly configurations in and through the production of knowledge' (Singh, 2015, p 372; see also Courtney, 2016). That said, Singh (2015) is drawing on a Bernsteinian rather than Ballian interpretation of performativity. In that former, the Lyotardian focus on novelty and re-creation is retained.

Researchers working within a socio-material approach understand performativity differently to the previous discussion on performativity as a principle or technique of neoliberal governance. In the socio-material approach, performativity connotes an onto-epistemological position that sees policies, knowledge or any other means of representing, describing and interacting with the world as productive (thus performative) of the realities they depict. In Actor-Network Theory, performativity implies that entities 'achieve their form as a consequence of the relations in which they are located' (Law, 2004, p 4). In other words, they are performed in, by and through relations. This means that all entities are a result of an ongoing process of assembling or relating and are thus potentially reversible and open for change. If durability is established, an actor-network scholar would ask: How is it achieved? Performativity moves beyond the critique of representation or untrue fabrication to claim that all representations are productive. They construct and add to the world rather than reduce or misrepresent it. For instance, Gorur's (2014) 'sociology of measurement' deploys performativity to understand how international comparisons of equity or large-scale assessments of learning outcomes such as the Programme for International Student Assessment constitute that which they measure through seemingly neutral calculations and comparison. Thus, performativity helps Gorur (2014) to examine the performative role of these measurement technologies – What do these measurements do? – rather than to ask whether or not measurements are accurate representations of the stable exterior 'realities', that is, equity or achievement, that they claim to portray.

Performativity is also deployed theoretically in linguistics, and from there in fields including organisational studies, to explain the way in which stories, narratives and words in organisations 'do not only describe but also bring into being the ideational schemes on which they are based' (Merkus and Veenswijk, 2017, p 1264). These discursive resources construct the reality that they depict, including the reification of theoretical abstractions. Merkus and Veenswijk (2017) describe how this applies to the realisation of New Public Management as well as arguably explains how the features of transformational leadership came to be embodied and observed in school leaders' practice and identities.

Further reading

- Gobby, B., Keddie, A. and Blackmore, J. (2018) Professionalism and competing responsibilities: moderating competitive performativity in school autonomy reform, Journal of Educational Administration and History, 50(3): 159–173.
- Teague, L. (2015) 'Acceptance of the limits of knowability in oneself and others': performative politics and relational ethics in the primary school classroom, Discourse: Studies in the Cultural Politics of Education, 36(3): 398–408.

Policy ethnography

Policy ethnography refers to the use of ethnographic methods to study the movement, translation and mediation of policy in different contexts. This includes using ethnographic methods to describe and explain the geopolitical, cultural, temporal and topographical features of those contexts as unique inscription devices for the shaping and enactment of policy. Ethnography can be traced to early anthropology and sociology and has as its focus the study of culture through inductive methods of reasoning that rely on the 'thick description' of events and activities. These enable understanding of the interpretive significance of values, beliefs and actions as framings that give meaning to everyday human behaviour and interaction or 'sociality' (the formation of social bonds). To conduct this kind of research, ethnographers typically engage in fieldwork characterised by long-term residence called 'immersion fieldwork' (Lewis and Russell, 2011, p 399) that allows for deep-dive, continuous observations of people's interactions with each other and their environments, with a focus on how such interaction is made possible by 'condensed expressions of meaning' or symbols (Fetterman, 2010, p 27) and 'repeated patterns of symbolic behaviour' or rituals (p 29). From a policy analysis perspective, this might entail using rhetorical, narrative, discourse, frame or speech analysis to 'reveal cultural myths in which policies are grounded' (Dubois, 2009, p 221).

Unlike conventional qualitative methods, such as interviews, focus groups and (non-)participant observations which typically insist on the researcher maintaining some form of 'appropriate' distance from the phenomena under investigation, usually under the pretence that such research sites can be better controlled or observed and documented 'objectively' (independent of researcher influence), ethnographic research develops through a view of social phenomena as 'uncontrolled' and 'haphazard' (Fetterman, 2010, p 37). Ethnography favours a nonfoundational and post-positivist understanding of research methods as overlaid with value orientations and interpretive strategies. Epistemologically and ontologically, ethnography takes seriously the production of knowledge as sites of contests over meaning. Ethnography recognises that the provision of meaning, which functions as a useful representational device for narrating unstable social realities, is precisely what enables researchers to construct both provisional and deterministic accounts of social change. As Hammersley (1994) observes, it can also be used selectively and politically 'as a way of "deconstructing" others' accounts' (p 153). The implication here is that 'ethnographers themselves are engaged in a process of "world construction" when they analyse data and write research reports' (Hammersley, 1994, p 153).

Ethnography therefore is well placed to appreciate the messiness of policy making and is 'consonant with the complex, contested world of public policy' (Wagenaar, 2006, p 437). Moreover, ethnographic researchers typically view those being researched as collaborators and partners in the generation of knowledge, thus helping to adapt research priorities to meet specific organisational priorities and service user needs. In a very practical sense, ethnography provides opportunities for progressive problem solving as it offers researchers and policy makers valuable tools for showing how multiple stakeholders ascribe significance to different viewpoints and actions as meaningful to their lives. Dubois (2009), for example, retains a faith in the capacity of ethnographic fieldwork to 'solve dysfunctions, improve efficiency or reduce the "democratic gap"' (p 221).

Ethnography that is more 'critical' in orientation, called 'critical ethnography', makes a moral and ethical necessity of this kind of political work by emphasising the responsibility of the researcher to use ethnographic methods to not only 'name and analyse what is intuitively felt' but 'to demystify the ubiquity and magnitude of power' (Madison, 2011, pp 13–14) (see entry on 'Criticality'). Dubois (2009), for example, adopts a critical policy ethnography to explore the 'power relations inherent in the legitimised political treatment of a group and in the imposition of meanings and myths' (p 223). The commitment to emancipatory goals and projects that is typical among critical ethnographers means acknowledging both the constraining effects of power on the possibilities for self-formation, and therefore a recognition of 'the complex ways they [subjects] are constituted within historically and culturally specific sites' (Tamboukou and Ball, 2003, p 8), but also that power is discourse and therefore functions as dynamic, productive spaces in which the contingently normal is permanently vulnerable to change. As Foucault (1998) reminds us, 'discourse transmits and produces power; it reinforces it, but also undermines and exposes it, renders it fragile and makes it possible to thwart it' (p 101).

Nichols and Griffith (2009) use policy ethnography to understand how Canadian principals and parents in British Columbia accomplish school governance with a focus on how strict policy guidelines provided by the provincial government are embodied (or not) through the speech and action of social actors; in other words, 'to discover the lineaments of the institutional in the experiential and to make those social relations visible' (p 242). Sutoris (2018) takes a more critical approach to policy ethnography by drawing attention to the problematics of scaling out, especially when national policies are devolved to the local level in ways that assume such policies are ethically universal and desirable. By highlighting the diverse rationalities and reasoning that make up the local, Sutoris (2018) highlights the potential of the 'ethnographic approach to illuminate the more contested aspects of scaling, especially its ethics' (p 406).

Further reading

- Avelar, M., Nikita, D.P. and Ball, S.J. (2018) Education policy networks and spaces of 'meetingness': a network ethnography of a Brazilian seminar, in A. Verger, H.K. Altinyelken and M. Novelli (eds) Global education policy and international development, London: Bloomsbury, 56–74.
- Blaustein, J. (2015) Speaking truths to power: policy ethnography and police reform in Bosnia and Herzegovina, Oxford: Oxford University Press.

Policy field analysis

Policy field analysis is rooted in Pierre Bourdieu's social theory and his thinking tools such as field, habitus, capitals, (logic of) practice and field effects. Bourdieu conceptualises society as composed of semi-autonomous, antagonistic fields that function as sites of ongoing struggles. These fields are loosely delimited and consist of positions occupied by agents (people and institutions) (Thomson, 2014) and may also contain sub-fields, all of which (to less or equal extent) are overlaid by the field of power. The relative autonomy of different social fields is thought to be a reflex of their distinctive logics of practice contained within and produced by the combination of the field's capitals; capitals which Bourdieu divided into economic, cultural, social, and symbolic (Thomson, 2014). The agents that occupy and traverse different fields embody dispositions – or habitus – that are developed in and expressive of practices that are generative of a specific field. Habitus as an embodiment of social history therefore 'provides the connection between agents and practices' (Rawolle and Lingard, 2008, p 731).

The logic that makes up specific fields is considered to impose certain limitations on what can be done, and what is done reproduces the field's logic in return. Moreover, the fields are understood to be positioned unequally, often reflecting power-laden hierarchies and asymmetries between their specific capitals, for example, economic capital versus cultural capital. Yet, as Rawolle and Lingard (2015) explain, the field of power upon which a society's norms, expectations and reward-and-punishment systems are predicated are not predetermined as 'economic capital or cultural capital or social capital but are a contingent mixture at particular points in time' (p 19). Moreover, there is a reciprocal relationship between the field of power and other social fields: they mutually affect each other in an ongoing process of co-construction (Thomson, 2014). To study a field, therefore, it is necessary to identify the triad of characteristic practices and their logics, dominant and dominating agents and their attributes, including the capital embodied by these agents.

Though Bourdieu's work addresses the role and organisation of schooling in society, it does not explicitly address education policy. Still, education policy scholars have found Bourdieu's concepts useful for approaching education policy analysis within a policy sociology framework. Rather than a focus on policy per se, Bourdieusian scholars typically mobilise the concept of the policy field; and instead of politics, the field of politics (Rawolle and Lingard, 2015). Here the concept of policy field functions as a methodological and theoretical heuristic rather than a grand theory and allows education researchers to examine how policies are affected by connections and overlaps between different social fields, and the processes of change produced by these synergies or lack of. Bourdieu's conceptual toolbox has also been put to use in facilitating improved understanding of the (dis)connections between policy and its implementation (Rawolle and Lingard, 2015). In this context, policy field and the school field can be understood as separate and functioning according to their own distinctive logics of practice. Policy is produced within a specific policy field and can therefore make claims to some imagined universality subject to its bureaucratic and internal logic. Yet the field of the classroom has its own specificity and, consequently, through cross-field effects, the gap between policy and practice typically emerges. Criticisms of this approach, as highlighted by Thomson (2014), mainly concern the problem of defining the borders of the field; the problem of there being too many fields and how to study them comprehensively; the problem of recognising, locating and understanding change where it occurs; and the lack of clarity on how the cross-field connections work to produce the domination of some fields over others, and to what effect.

Yu (2018) usefully draws on the policy field analysis to address a number of these concerns, namely, policy change and cross-field effects. Yu (2018) shows how education policy changes are produced through intertwined influences of multiple fields in a non-linear manner. Drawing on the example of China, Yu (2018) demonstrates that policies concerning the education of migrant children in public schools have changed dramatically as a result of changes in and cross-effects between population policy, the change of political leaders, the needs of the economic sector and the influx of migrant children. Cross-field effects have also been explored through research focused on the mediatisation of education policy (see entry on 'Mediatisation') resulting from changes to journalistic logic (Rawolle and Lingard, 2008). Rawolle and Lingard (2015) also show how the policy field can be conceptualised beyond the nation-state as a container of all social fields and instead located through global processes that include the evolution of a global commensurative space of measurement. Relatedly, Rawolle and Lingard (2015) show how cross-field effects and the relationship between national and global fields of education policy connect in a shared 'policy habitus' exhibited by both national policy makers and agents of international organisations such as the Organisation for Economic Co-operation and Development.

Further reading

- Ladwig, J.G. (1994) For whom this reform? Outlining educational policy as a social field, British Journal of Sociology of Education, 15(3): 341–363.

- Saarinen, T. (2008) Whose quality? Social actors in the interface of transnational and national higher education policy, Discourse: Studies in the Cultural Politics of Education, 29(2): 179–193.

Policy learning

Policy learning has been conceptualised in several ways, with consequences for how, in what circumstances, with what purposes, and by whom learning is understood to take place (Bennett and Howlett, 1992). It was first referred to by Deutsch (1966), who discussed the way in which governments might improve their learning capacity through drawing on feedback. The idea was later developed by Heclo (1974), who argued that policy learning is primarily undertaken by governments, although it need not be conscious. It is, for Heclo (1974), 'a relatively enduring alteration in behaviour that results from experience; usually this alteration is conceptualised as a change in response made in reaction to some perceived stimulus' (p 306). For Heclo (1974), learning is a product of environmental change, with the implication that it *must* take place if governments are to keep up with inevitable environmental changes, and so avoid policy failure or drift (see entry on 'Drift'). Bennett and Howlett (1992) draw on further contributions to set out five conceptions of policy learning, comprising 'political learning, government learning, policy-oriented learning, lesson drawing and social learning' (p 277). The foci of these five conceptualisations are similarly diverse. Some conceptualisations are oriented towards the subject of learning (or, who is learning, namely governments) or the object of learning (or, what is being learned, namely more effective policies or policy instruments). These conceptualisations seek to improve our understanding of those political processes that enable policies to succeed, as well as generate new understandings of how certain issues come to be accepted as policy problems. Other conceptualisations focus on the mechanisms for learning (or, how is learning taking place?). This may involve drawing on direct experiences of failure or on indirect experiences of *others'* failure.

This definitional complexity means that considerable scholarship in the field seeks to typologise policy learning or to develop existing typologies. For example, May (1992) distinguishes between policy learning, which may be either instrumental or social, and political learning. Instrumental policy learning is centred on the 'viability of policy interventions or implementation designs' (p 336), and so is intended to illuminate what went wrong or how to improve such that policy goals are reached in future. Social policy learning focuses on the 'social construction of a policy or problem' (May, 1992, p 336), with the aim of changing public expectations or redefining goals. Political learning concerns 'learning about strategies for advocating policy ideas or drawing attention to policy problems' (May, 1992, p 336). Here the focus is shifted towards explaining the political arena where ideas are debated and a concomitant focus on knowledge about how to move policies up decision-makers' agenda and to have them figure as important by the public. At its most extreme instantiation, this feature can speak to paradigmatic policy change (Hall, 1993).

Typologising further, Lange and Alexiadou (2010) identify four policy-learning styles in their empirical study of policy learning in the European Union: mutual, competitive, imperialistic and surface. Mutual policy learning is inclusive, contextualised, accommodating of alternative perspectives, and self-reflexive. It is not focused on knowledge generated through benchmarks and performance indicators, namely competitive policy learning undertaken through relying on the apparent objectivity of quantitative measures and their comparison. Imperialistic policy learning, on the other hand, is focused on advancing national interests and spheres of influence in and through education. Finally, surface policy learning happens when EU member states endeavour to protect their education-policy agenda from influence by other states or the Commission.

Researchers have investigated the relative merits of alternative fora or mechanisms for policy learning. These include the open method of coordination (OMC) employed within the European Union since the Lisbon summit in 2000, and laboratory federalism (Kerber and Eckardt, 2007). The OMC is a benchmarking process in which national policies are submitted to a central authority which evaluates them, identifies so-called best practices and makes recommendations to member states. While it is arguably more efficient than laboratory federalism, OMC is concerned solely with the diffusion (see entry on 'Diffusion') of existing policies. Further, it cannot be assured that what is 'best practice' in one jurisdiction would necessarily be so in others.

Laboratory federalism 'can be seen as an innovation system in which public policies are the object of innovation and imitation processes driven by decentralised experimentation, mutual learning and competition' (Kerber and Eckardt, 2007, p 233). Kerber and Eckardt (2007) argue that the lack of a central authority may produce better results since the success criteria are decentralised, more varied, and so the risk of being 'incorrect' is mitigated. Moreover, laboratory federalism produces policy innovations, unlike the OMC. However, an important risk is that jurisdictions learn in ways that constitute a 'race to the bottom' through distorted incentives.

Further reading

- Hodgson, A. and Spours, K. (2016) Restrictive and expansive policy learning: challenges and strategies for knowledge exchange in upper secondary education across the four countries of the UK, Journal of Education Policy, 31(5): 511–525.
- Tamtik, M. and Sá, C.M. (2014) Policy learning to internationalize European science: policies and limitations of open coordination, Higher Education, 67(3): 317–331.

Policy network analysis

Policy network analysis is the study of how different policy processes – policy making, policy enactment and policy delivery – come to be influenced by new moral and epistemic communities and knowledge networks operating within acentred, polycentric systems called 'networked governance', 'heterarchical governance' and 'polycentric governance'. These emerging systems of governance work to undermine traditional government structures and bureaucratic modes of governance, in effect opening up plural modes of governing in which federal, state or regional and local powers are supplemented, and in some cases substituted by 'intermediary associations' (Ranson et al, 2005, p 359) that span private, public and charity organisations (Olmedo et al, 2013). Policy network analysis therefore complements the 'governance turn' (Ball, 2009a, p 537) with its focus on how formal and informal relations of trust, consensus building, diplomacy and cooperation are maintained and reproduced in contexts where power is notionally disaggregated and interdependent (Stoker, 1998), rather than confined to some sovereign authority, namely government. This includes a focus on the interactions of state and non-state actors (private organisations, social enterprises, charities, non-profit venture funds, edu-businesses, and new philanthropies) and the networked effect of such interactions as enabling 'more flexible structures (heterarchies) where relationships, responsibilities, and processes of decision-making are shared in different instances by a heterogeneous group of old and new actors with different backgrounds, profiles, and interests' (Olmedo, 2017, p 73).

Following this description, a policy network 'can be understood as webs of relatively stable relationships that mobilise and pool dispersed resources so that collective action can be orchestrated towards the solution of a common policy goal' (Fataar, 2006, p 644). According to Olmedo (2017), policy networks function as extensions of government rule, albeit designed to instantiate new forms and modalities for the reorganisation of education governance: they 'represent the main driver for political change in legislating a landscape that creates the conditions for networks to develop around different aspects within the public sphere (e.g. organisation, co-funding, delivery, etc.)' (p 72). Policy network analysis therefore offers unique insights into the influence of different actors on 'policy interpretation and relay' (Player-Koro et al, 2018, p 682).

From an empirical standpoint, policy network analysis typically begins with 'the construction of a network of actors (known as nodes) where the lines connecting them (known as ties) represent shared information, knowledge and social capital' (Avelar et al, 2018, p 56). Researchers warn of the limits of network diagrams, however, namely that the construction of relationships between actors in a network through the visual representation of nodes and connecting lines brings to bear a perspective and a set of assumptions about the strength and intensity of those relationships. Such a perspective fails, for example, to provide any rigorous or measured account of the distribution of resources and capabilities in a network, the extent to which such networks are entrenched in asymmetrical power relations or the degree of epistemic homophily governing such relations; in other words, whether such relations are heterogeneous or homogeneous according to strict priorities and interests.

Moreover, by 'reading off' the programmes, events and social exchanges managed by these networked actors as evidence of their partnerships and collaboration, a policy network analysis provides a fixed temporal and topological reading of a set of relationships that are better understood to be overdetermined by fluctuating social and structural dynamics. As Ball (2008) remarks, by giving representation and meaning to social relationships through network diagrams (sometimes called 'sociograms'), policy network analysis can work to flatten and stabilise relationships that 'do not do justice to their messy, complex and dynamic nature' (p 748).

To overcome these limitations, education researchers typically supplement policy network analysis with ethnography (or 'network ethnography') to provide a thick description of those 'sites of knowledge exchange' and 'sites of persuasion' (Avelar et al, 2018, p 56) through which policy is mediated and transformed by the interactions of individuals and organisations. In the same vein, Adhikary and Lingard (2017) combine traditional policy network analysis or network mapping with an ethnographic focus to analyse the activities, events and interactions that make up the 'policy network' which has enabled conditions for the emergence of Teach for Bangladesh, a non-government organisation established in 2012 in Bangladesh and offshoot of US-based policy movement Teach for All/America. Through a critical policy analysis of interviews and nearly 250 web-based artefacts (including videos, newspaper articles, webpages and social media postings), Adhikary and Lingard (2017) document evidence of policy exporting and policy borrowing by tracing the 'networked relations of friendship, business connections, political power and position' (p 199) through which global philanthropic business prerogatives are recontextualised in Bangladesh. Similarly, Ball (2016) combines policy network analysis with ethnography to show the conditions (or conduits) that enable policy mobility across time and space, in effect providing an important toolbox of analytic and representational devices for 'following policy' (p 553) through an empirical focus on those conversations, meetings and social events that give 'network robustness' (p 557) to global–local interactions and exchanges. Policy networks therefore remain important sites for empirical observations of the 'wheres' and the 'doing' of 'policy work' (Player-Koro et al, 2018, p 682).

Further reading

- Rönnberg, L. (2017) From national policy-making to global edu-business: Swedish edu-preneurs on the move, Journal of Education Policy, 32(2): 234–249.
- Shiroma, E.O. (2014) Networks in action: new actors and practices in education policy in Brazil, Journal of Education Policy, 29(3): 323–348.

Policy scholarship

Policy scholarship can be located within a thought collective or movement that shares strong connections with policy sociology, critical policy sociology and sociology of education. Similar to these traditions, policy scholarship is a response to the limits of logical positivism, utility theory, systems theory and functionalism to policy research. Moreover, it is a direct challenge to the epistemological commitment of the 'policy sciences' (Lerner and Lasswell, 1951) and related policy-directed, positivist-oriented research to produce knowledge in the service of state administration and public policy through 'a science of policy forming and execution' (Lasswell, 1951, quoted in Wagner et al, 1991, p 8), albeit one lacking sufficient critique of the value judgements underpinning those policy goals and desired outcomes. Following the Second World War and the rise of welfare liberalism (Wilkins, 2023b), the policy sciences came to the assistance of governments in many western countries who required the knowledge infrastructure to support an expanded state bureaucracy that would offer citizens essential forms of security and protection against the unpredictable forces of capitalism. This included state administration of 'need' – what Rose (1999) calls governing 'the social' – made possible through the provision of new types of specialist knowledge and management tools. Underpinning these developments during the 1950s and 1960s was a focus on 'intelligence, design and choice' (Simon et al, 2009, p 3) and a concomitant technicist belief in policy processes as sites of rational calculus and planning driven by an intrinsic motivation for greater democratisation of society and the economy.

The policy sciences maintained an explicit value orientation to these ends, which it sought to help government realise through 'the improving of the concrete content of the information and the interpretations available to policymakers' (Lasswell, 1951 quoted in Wagner et al, 1991, p 8). Yet policy science, what Grace (1998) calls a 'recontextualised form of natural science' (p 204), appears to overestimate the rationality of policy processes as coherent and linear and policy solutions as objective and value-free. Moreover, policy science places too much faith in the Enlightenment ideal of a formal rational model that presupposes the shared capacity of individuals to operate from a position of 'perfect knowledge', to strive for a 'maximum position' determined by transitive preference orderings and to calculate the expected benefits and costs of actions in ways that are rationally self-serving. Policy science therefore operates through a standard rationality that is asocial and acontextual, one that precludes any engagement with the contingent relations and regularities that shape and pattern individual experience and need.

According to Grace (1995), policy science therefore neglects the 'historical, theoretical, cultural and socio-political setting' (p 12) guiding the formulation of policy problems and their solutions. This also means that policy problems, themselves the cultural and political artefacts of unique path dependencies and value systems, can only be properly responded to and understood in the 'relational settings' (Grace, 1995, p 3) that give them form and meaning. In contrast to policy science that 'excludes ideological and value conflicts as "externalities" beyond its legitimate remit' (Grace, 1995, p 3), Grace (1998) advocates for policy scholarship or 'critical scholarship' that takes seriously 'the limitations of technicism, the ideological and historical struggles behind "logic" and "sequence" and the problematics of objectivity' (p 204). Moreover, Grace (1998) enjoins us to resist policy science for the way it has become 'domesticated to the requirements of the state' (p 216). Similarly, Simon et al (2009) make a distinction between policy science and policy scholarship as a 'general opposition between analysis for policy and analysis of policy' (p 29).

A policy scholarship therefore necessitates a form of 'critical advocacy' that confronts the politics of policy making, namely 'the process and structures through which macro-societal expectations of education as an institution are identified and interpreted and constituted as an agenda for the education system' (Dale, 1994, p 36). Critical advocacy can be located in the rise of specific orientations to education policy research, be it a reflexive disposition (Ball, 1994) or a commitment to anti-oppressive struggles (Troyna, 1994). Through the use of theory 'as a sort of moving self-reflexivity' (Gregory, 1994, p 86), critical advocacy insists on ' "conceptual normative yardsticks" against which we can assess existing arrangements and envision future directions' (Molla, 2021, p 11).

Influenced by policy scholarship, education policy sociologists since the 1980s up until the present have turned their attention to documenting the ways in which power and claims to knowledge are inscribed in policy decisions and policy effects (Prunty, 1985; Popkewitz, 1991). This means no longer taking accepted policy discourse as 'the presupposition of analysis' but 'making the rhetoric itself the focus of what is to be understood and explained' (Popkewitz, 1996, p 27). Smyth (2010, p 125), for example, adopts policy scholarship to trace the rhetoric shaping social inclusion policy discourses in the Australian context, with a focus on how the language of 'targetology' and 'deliverology' not only works to conceal the macro-structural problems underpinning social inclusion but presents social inclusion as a problem to be fixed 'through technical and managerial means – ameliorative and punitive processes like accountability, transparency, marketisation, targets and heroic forms of leadership'. In the spirit of critical advocacy, Smyth (2010) presents an alternative model of understanding social inclusion based on 'richly descriptive narratives and biographies of the lives of those most directly and profoundly affected' (p 126).

Further reading

- Popkewitz, T. (2008) Cosmopolitanism and the age of school reform: science, education and making society by making the child, New York: Routledge.
- Whitty, G. (1997) Social theory and education policy: the legacy of Karl Mannheim, British Journal of Sociology of Education, 18(2): 149–163.

Policy science

Policy science is understood in the UK and Australia to be a procedural suite of strategies which enable the normative selection of a course of policy action determined by considerations of technical or rational effectiveness and efficiency, including cost-benefit calculations. Its formulation in the US is somewhat complicated by its originator, namely Lasswell's (1971) technicist and scientist definition of the political sciences of what is arguably 'a key critical feature — contextual orientation' (Torgerson, 2019, p 122). Here, we predominantly refer to the UK/Australian interpretation, which, as we set out here, takes up Lasswell's (1971) technicist element at the expense of contextual considerations.

Policy science is normative because 'the policy scientist really is a type of social engineer who makes instrumental decisions' (Fay, 1975, p 14) predicated on positivist onto-epistemological assumptions, all of which are invoked through the central term 'science', in other words, the natural sciences. This collocation is intended to confer rigour on the methods of policy science, yet as Yates points out in a review symposium, 'what is being called "science" or "evidence" in policy arenas is a form of research that ignores the complexity and messiness of the objects of its study: education and people' (Yates et al, 2011, pp 467–468).

The assumptions of policy science include, first, that social actors' practice and activities may best be conceptualised as generalisable and predictable behaviour. These normative assumptions about practice, in turn, reveal the strong reliance in policy science on psychological ways of producing and conceptualising knowledge. Second, policy science assumes that data may be described as having been collected rather than generated. This implies that the data pre-existed the act of its co-creation with the researcher. A third assumption is that data 'collected' in controlled settings (that is, through experiments) may usefully inform policy analysis, as if complex educational processes were reducible to variables (see Davies, 2004). Fourth, policy science constructs a reasonably unproblematic linear relationship between cause and effect. Following this, policy science further assumes that knowledge about policy analysis is additive, in the same way as it is in pharmacology, for instance, and hence is amenable to multiplier methodologies such as systematic literature reviews. The construction through such additiveness of 'a deductive chain of wider and wider generality' (Fay, 1975, p 21) means that policy science holds that policy action is, or should be, predictable, within limits (Fay, 1975; Geller and Johnston, 1990). Fifth, policy science, through its dependence upon so-called objective, measurable 'facts', understands theory as at best a distraction from the identification of such facts (whose significance is often held to be self-evident), and at worst as a polluting influence on interpreting policy 'facts'. Together, these assumptions produce a sixth dimension, that policy analysis should be undertaken within an implementation rather than enactment framing. In these ways, policy science may be contrasted with policy sociology and especially policy scholarship (see entries on 'Policy sociology' and 'Policy scholarship'), which, based on their post-positivist epistemologies, locate policy analysis and policy making in their ideological, cultural, historical and socio-economic contexts.

Policy scholarship and policy science exemplify and represent in policy studies opposing positions in what were labelled the paradigm wars (see Bryman, 2008), which fundamentally concern epistemology. Policy science (as also happens in positivist epistemic communities in other areas of education) seeks legitimacy for its knowledge claims through the apparent, but illusory objectivity of this underpinning positivism. Policy science is attractive to state and other decision-makers precisely because, in rejecting not only context but also values (Greenfield and Ribbins, 1993), it simplifies both problems and solutions and 'promises to "deliver the goods" in a technical and usable form' (Grace, 1995, p 3). Of more concern is the potential role of policy-science approaches in states' regulation of education institutions and of those who work there. For Courtney and Gunter (2017), policy-science approaches are implicated in the privatisation of education and its leadership through the way in which they are internalised as 'best practice' and idealised identities. Within the field, some researchers adhere all the more firmly to policy science in order to counter what they see as the 'considerable ideology masquerading as social science' (Levin-Waldman, 2005, p 524). From this perspective, which associates the critical researcher's explicit statements concerning positionality with partisanship, 'the use of statistical research and other methodologies steeped in social science is intended to give an imprimatur of neutral legitimacy to otherwise ideological and partisan goals' (Levin-Waldman, 2005, p 524). The paradigm wars rage on, it seems. It is also clear that for as long as governments require evidence upon which to draw to legitimate their policies or engage in 'the search for single templates' (Yates et al, 2011, p 468), or need a mechanism for regulating the practice and identities of education professionals, there will be a demand for policy-science approaches.

Further reading

- Cairney, P. and Weible, C.M. (2017) The new policy sciences: combining the cognitive science of choice, multiple theories of context, and basic and applied analysis, Policy Sciences, 50(4): 619–627.
- Webb, P.T. and Gulson, K. (2015) Policy, geophilosophy and education, Rotterdam: Sense Publishers.

Policy sociology

Policy sociology or 'education policy sociology' (Ozga, 1987) refers to a tradition of critical thinking among education researchers reacting to the prevailing orthodoxy that dominated economic and political thinking during the late 1970s and 1980s. During this time, economic liberals and political conservatives (collectively known as the 'New Right') outlined the blueprints for a minimal state characterised by fiscal responsibility and deflationary financial policies. These 'diverse skirmishes were rationalised within a relatively coherent mentality of government that came to be termed neo-liberalism' (Millar and Rose, 2008, p 211). Central to the vision of this mentality of government were public policies organised around restoring the explicitness of the price system of the market and of the figure of the consumer as a framework for public sector reform. Education policy in England, for example, was radically transformed during the 1980s and 1990s to reflect and uphold the ascendancy and dominance of this new hegemony in economic and political thinking. Education policies introduced during this time included consumer choice/voice, inter-school competition, league table and performance accountability, and deregulation leading to private-sector involvement in and sponsorship of public-sector organisations. These education policies therefore signalled a decisive break from the post-war political settlement called welfare liberalism (Wilkins, 2023b) that had developed between 1944 and 1979. Under welfare liberalism, citizens were granted access to welfare provision on the basis of rights rather than charity. In contrast, these rights and entitlements under neoliberalism were made conditional on people exercising responsible choice as consumers in a marketplace.

It is important to note that welfare liberalism developed on the basis of an expanded state bureaucracy that sought to better 'institutionalise' relations between citizens and the state so that citizens could be afforded new forms of security and protection against the crisis and conflicts naturally occurring within capitalism. In essence, welfare liberalism relied on new legal forms and measurements of 'competency' and 'entitlement' to develop its systems of governing, which in turn required new types of specialist knowledge and management tools. The policy sciences, which developed through the 1950s, occupied a central role in producing the knowledge infrastructure required to support welfarist liberal governments' technocratic vision. The policy sciences were primarily pragmatic, rational and positivist in orientation as they sought to produce knowledge that could be empirically tested and verified using meta-analysis, deductive logic and experimental hypothesis modelling. With their emphasis on 'the development of a science of policy forming and execution' and 'the improving of the concrete content of the information and the interpretations available to policymakers' (Lasswell, 1951 quoted in Wagner et al, 1991, p 8), the policy sciences represented a continuation of the Enlightenment project and its commitment to a 'scientific problem-solving rationality' (Simon et al, 2009, p 4). The explicit focus on evaluation and improvement underpinning the policy sciences, especially their strong commitment to science in and for the service of state administration and public policy, had a major influence on economic and social change in Europe and the US during the 1960s and early 1970s.

In response to these developments and inspired by post-Marxism and poststructuralism, education policy researchers in the 1980s turned their attention to documenting both the crisis of welfare liberalism and the limits of logical positivism, functionalism and systems theory to policy research more generally. Policy sociology represented a direct challenge to understandings of policy as a privileged space of rationalist planning, for example, what Prunty (1985) describes as 'guise of scientific precision' (p 133), namely the idea that policy problems can be defined objectively, indiscriminately and without recourse to certain value judgements or hierarchies of knowledge (also see Bacchi and Goodwin,

2016). This included a rejection of the foundational ontology of positivism that underpinned these perspectives, namely the idea that observations and facts can be comfortably separated from interpretations and values (Troyna, 1994; Taylor, 1997). Instead, policy sociology reconceptualised policy making and policy implementation as a contested and productive space for the 'authoritative allocation of values' (Prunty, 1985, p 136).

A focus of policy sociology therefore concerns the 'contexts of knowledge production' (Ozga, 2021, p 293), including which knowledge and whose values matter and are represented in policy. The result is a paradigm shift in thinking about policy that is overtly 'political', one that harnesses 'that analysis to an explicit political commitment to change things' (Troyna, 1994, p 72) and strives to 'expose the sources of domination, repression, and exploitation that are entrenched in, and legitimated by, educational policy' (Prunty, 1985, p 136). Policy texts in effect 'represent the outcome of political struggles over meaning' (Taylor, 1997, p 26). Another perceived danger of conventional positivist orientations to policy research was the absence of theory that 'leaves the researcher prey to unexamined, unreflexive preconceptions and dangerously naïve ontological and epistemological a prioris' (Ball, 1995, pp 265–266). Policy sociology therefore is the 'prioritisation of theory' (Ozga, 2021, p 297) and the possibilities it offers for 'a different language, a language which is not caught up with the assumptions and inscriptions of policymakers or the immediacy of practice' (Ball, 1997, p 269).

Further reading

- Dale, R. (1992) Whither the state and education policy? Recent work in Australia and New Zealand, British Journal of Sociology of Education, 13(3): 387–395.
- Gewirtz, S. and Cribb, A. (2002) Plural conceptions of social justice: implications for policy sociology, Journal of Education Policy, 17(5): 499–509.

Policy trajectory analysis

Policy trajectory analysis starts from the position that context is essential to understanding policy-making processes, including policy discourse and policy enactment (see entry on 'Context'). Following the poststructuralist tradition of policy sociology and policy scholarship, policy trajectory analysis strives to make sense of the messiness and 'localised complexity' (Ball, 1993, p 10) of policy production as non-linear, interactive and iterative. Policy trajectory analysis therefore represents a shift away from formal rational, functional and instrumental models of policy analysis, namely those reified and asocial accounts that neglect the essential 'relational settings' (Grace, 1995, p 3) that crystallise to produce different possibilities for the emergence of policy articulation over time and space. In this sense, policy production is formed through 'intertextual relationship or contexts' (Gale, 1999, p 399) that are historical, cultural and political. Policy trajectory analysis seeks to capture such intertextuality through a consideration of the 'discursive and strategic framing[s]' (Gale, 1999, p 402) that give coherence to policy settlements. At the same time, policy trajectory analysis connotes emergence, contingency and plurality since it describes policy settlements as always unfinished and incomplete – and therefore continuously open to challenge – owing to the 'ad hocery, negotiation and serendipity' (Ball, 1993, p 11) of policy production.

Policy texts therefore are 'discourse' that 'translates struggles or systems of domination' (Foucault, 1981, p 52): they represent engaged, pragmatic attempts by relations of authority and power to use culturally recognisable tropes and repertoires to ascribe meaning to particular actions as desirable or acceptable. Policy texts, in this sense, are 'highly specific discursive genre[s]' (Wetherell, 2003, p 25) since they represent dynamic spaces for the negotiation and management of tensions and contradictions (or ideological dilemmas) flowing from unique path dependencies and value systems. At the same time, policy texts are 'domains of interdiscursive struggle amongst discourses' (Gale, 1999, p 400) as they move through multiple sites, levels, organisations and actors that are discrete yet interconnected, each with their own selective interpretive frameworks for making sense of policy texts, thus pointing to 'gaps and spaces for action' (Ball, 1993, p 11). Policy trajectory analysis thus recognises the different forms of agency and creative negotiation performed by social actors at the point at which they are addressed or summoned by policy discourses, highlighting how 'discursive power is diffused in education' (Beech and Artopoulos, 2016, p 258). Relatedly and contradictorily, policy trajectory analysis also maintains a strong focus on the limits of those negotiations owing to the fact that policy discourse is 'a moving discursive frame which articulates and constrains the possibilities and probabilities of interpretation and enactment' (Ball, 1993, p 15).

This means remaining circumspect of traditional concepts like 'policy borrowing', 'policy convergence' and 'policy transfer', which appear to overestimate the homogenising effects of policy as uniform and linear or, conversely, underestimate the resilience of local contexts and the capacity of local actors to resist and reject policy demands. Policy trajectory analysis therefore shares a deep political and epistemological concern for the availability and provision of meaning that work to normalise, naturalise and contest policy-making processes. As Ball (1993) observes, policies are cultural and political artefacts whose meaning is contingent on the particular ways in which policy problems and their solutions are framed, interpreted and enacted: 'we can see policies as representations which are encoded in complex ways (via struggles, compromises, authoritative public interpretations and reinterpretations) and decoded in complex ways (via actors' interpretations and meanings in relation to their history, experiences, skills, resources and context)' (p 11).

Policy trajectory analysis is also strongly represented through contemporary trends in education policy research to trace the multiple enactments of global policy within nation-states and to think through policy movement as 'increasingly complex, pluri-lateral and cross-scalar' (Mundy et al, 2016, p 7). Here, the commitment is to 'deparochialise' (Lingard, 2006) education policy analysis by conceptualising policy making as translocal, mobile and networked (Wilkins et al, 2024). In this reading, policy is the co-function and co-articulation of multiple discourses flowing both vertically and horizontally as well as globally and nationally. Within this literature too is a context-sensitive appreciation for the unique path dependencies and value systems that give rise to adaptations and refusals of education policy. Policy trajectory analysis therefore is nestled within two readings of policy change as 'embedded' and 'travelling' (Ozga and Jones, 2006, p 1), with the former approach focused on how policy change is intimately wedded to national, regional and local politics and projects and the latter focused on contextualising policy change at the intersection of national and global influences.

Liasidou (2009) adopts policy trajectory analysis to capture the strategic and discursive framing shaping special education policy making in Cyprus with a focus on 'the diverse and contradictory values and beliefs vying for ascendancy' (p 107) within that policyscape. Similarly, Wilkins et al (2019) offer a comparative policy trajectory study to document the highly politicised contexts that have shaped the uneven development of New Public Management in four countries: Australia, England, Spain and Switzerland. Maroy et al. (2017) also adopt a policy trajectory analysis of education policy in France and Quebec to show how accountability regimes are the resultant formation of unique path dependencies, established or subverted state authority made possible by 'negotiations and struggles among actors' (p 16), and the capacity of those actors to translate policy in ways that are meaningful both nationally and internationally.

Further reading

- Edwards, T., Gewirtz, S. and Whitty, G. (1992) Whose choice of schools? Making sense of City Technology Colleges, in M. Arnot and L. Barton (eds) Voicing concerns, Wallingford: Triangle, 143–162.
- Johnson, D. (2006) Comparing the trajectories of educational change and policy transfer in developing countries, Oxford Review of Education, 32(5): 679–696.

Policy work

The way in which policy work is conceptualised is a function of policy analysts' epistemology and imagination. That is to say, how people arrive at evaluations and judgements about what constitutes 'work' in the realm of policy will depend primarily on how policy, policy processes and actors, and policy-work objectives are themselves understood. Such interpretations are both multiple and wide-ranging and can be a matter of epistemic community belief. Moreover, as Colebatch (2006) points out, 'it is not simply that one can draw more than one map: it is that the different maps are themselves part of the policy process, and that participants may use different maps in different contexts' (p 313). Colebatch (2006) identifies three maps in which policy is framed 'as authoritative choice, as structured interaction, and as social construction' (p 313). Each map or framing is useful for explaining the diverse influences (normative and epistemological) that shape how policy work is differently understood and mobilised as an object of investigation or presumption of character and duty.

First is *authoritative choice*. Colebatch (2006) describes this as a policy framing in which governments make decisions that become policy. Policy work may then be seen simply as government actors deciding and all other actors attempting to influence that decision. This is not how policy gets done, however, and so Colebatch (2006) suggests a second framing, *structured interaction*. This second framing recognises that multiple voices are in play during the policy process, both within and without government, 'contending for attention and resources and the ability to define the question' (Colebatch, 2006, p 314). In this paradigm, policy work concerns constructing and sustaining relationships between these voices or stakeholders. Colebatch (2006) argues that this framing assumes that policy problems pre-exist their proposed solution, which is identified as not always the case. Consequently, a third framing, *social construction*, acknowledges that some policy work must involve constructing and defining the policy object as a problem through meaning making.

Ball et al (2011) work within the epistemological boundaries of their conceptualisation of policy enactment (see entry on 'Enactment') in proposing an eight-part typology of policy actors in schools, defined by the work they do in relation to the policy process. These eight figures of the policy actor are as follows. First, *narrators* interpret, select and enforce meanings. This work is largely undertaken in schools by members of the senior leadership team. Indeed, the narration work of primary-school headteachers was later elucidated in more detail by Maguire and Braun (2019). *Entrepreneurs* advocate for certain policies and integrate them creatively. *Outsiders* are those actors located beyond the school and may undertake policy work concerned with collaborating, monitoring and entrepreneurialism. *Transactors* are focused upon monitoring and reporting and so are located in positions of responsibility at various points along a line-management structure. *Enthusiasts* may be found in any role and often 'embody [the] policy in their practice and are examples to others' (Ball et al, 2011, p 630). This touches on the work of *translators*, whose efforts to make the policy 'meaningful and doable' (Ball et al, 2011, p 631) may be through embodied modelling as well as through repackaging the policy by creating policy artefacts like posters or summary documents. The role of *critics* is twofold for Ball et al (2011). First, they point out the implications of policy for staff workload, and second, they are the repository of, and mechanism for, reminding the profession of alternative ways of being and doing. Critics hold the institutional memory of acting otherwise. Finally, *receivers* exhibit considerable compliance from a position of 'policy dependency' (Ball et al, 2011, p 632). They tend to be early on in their teaching career and are motivated by small-picture thinking regarding the need to get by in the classroom. Consequently, they are greatly reliant on translators' outputs and little disposed to policy creativity.

As an idealised typology, Ball et al (2011) note that one actor may fulfil different roles, particularly at different times. This mapping is very useful in locating policy work with actors and their roles in the policy process. However, this approach to policy work has been critiqued for its lack of theoretical explanation of why actors come to be positioned in these ways and how the central policy position came to be. For example, Singh et al (2013) interplay the typology with Bernsteinian insights into recontextualisation in order 'to analyse the relation between constraint (power) and agency (control) in terms of policy processes' (p 470).

The problematic relationship that we have pointed to in this entry between what policy actors do, namely, their policy work, and how that work may be conceptualised by policy researchers, is well captured by Papanastasiou (2017a). Papanastasiou (2017a) identifies a range of policy-work activities that speak to the ways in which notions of scale in policy processes are fundamental, and serve, for example, to construct actors' worlds through enabling sense-making; for example, thinking with local, regional or national-level arenas or providing the necessary analytical framework for acting upon and within the world through policy. Papanastasiou (2017a) notes that implicitly scalar arguments are deployed by participants throughout the data, yet serious consideration of scale by policy-work researchers has yet to catch up. Descriptions and explanations of policy work will therefore most likely multiply in line with researchers' developing framings of that work and the contexts within which it takes place.

Further reading

- Colebatch, H.K. (2006) The work of policy: an international survey, Lanham: Lexington Books.
- Gorur, R. (2011) Policy as assemblage, European Educational Research Journal, 10(4): 611–622.

Privatisation

Privatisation in education policy is defined and delimited in several, contested ways, where such contestations reflect ideological as much as intellectual positions. For example, the policy intermediary organisation (see entry on 'Intermediary') in England that claims to speak for the academy sector, the Confederation of School Trusts, published a statement that read: 'Setting up organisations – specialist education charities – to run and improve schools to create a better future for children is not marketisation. Nor is it privatisation. It is sensible, robust education policy, driven by a sense of urgency to bring about greater social justice' (Confederation of School Trusts, 2021, p 9). Notwithstanding such belief-based claims, there is widespread support in the literature for the claims that, first, globally, privatisation in education is increasing, although 'it shows great variability in terms of policies and modalities across different contexts' (Moschetti et al, 2020, p 371). And, second, that the definition of privatisation includes private or third-sector actors operating within the public sector (see Winchip et al, 2019).

Concerning definitions, Ball (2009b) has made frequent and important contributions to investigating and conceptualising privatisation in education policy. Ball (2009b) describes three forms of privatisation, although it is pointed out that these are non-discrete and interrelated. First is the 'recalibration' (Ball, 2009b, p 83) of public-sector institutions, who, in engaging with private companies selling educational products and services, render themselves increasingly intelligible to that private sector. Second is 'the colonisation of the infrastructures of policy' (Ball, 2009b, p 88), whereby private-sector actors work inside government and contribute to policy making through a range of roles, including 'as advisors, evaluators, service deliverers, philanthropists, researchers, reviewers, brokers, "partners", committee members and as consultants and auditors' (Ball, 2009b, p 89). They suggest tools and a language for policy making that goes on to structure how the state understands and does policy. Third is the 'privatisation of the state itself', that is, 'public services as a profit opportunity' (Ball, 2009b, p 84). The potential market is global, with privatisation recorded as happening from Ghana (Riep, 2014) to the Caribbean (Courtney and Lee-Piggott, 2022); these examples reveal another tendency, that poorer countries are particularly at risk of education privatisation, as are those that have experienced catastrophes (Fontdevila et al, 2017). Other phenomena, policy trends or events, or discourses that have been identified as enabling privatisation in education include austerity (Grimaldi, 2013) and particularly technology (Williamson, 2016b).

These three categories supplement two earlier conceptualisations, exogenous and endogenous privatisation, which were popularised by Ball (2007). Exogenous privatisation happens when private-sector actors enter and operate in formerly public education institutions and in education policy domains (see, for example, Hogan, 2015), including through procurement (Holmqvist et al, 2020) or provision. Endogenous privatisation is when public-sector actors adopt the language, methods, understandings and objectives of the private sector, sometimes referred to as corporatisation (Courtney, 2017a). Examples include the restructuring of formerly professional relationships in schools and universities through line management and their regulation through performance management. The rise of the state-funded, so-called independent model of schooling exemplifies both exogenous and endogenous forms. Called academies, free or studio schools or university technical colleges in England, charter schools in the US and *friskolor* in Sweden, structurally these schools are designed to mimic or invoke features of private schooling, such as curricular independence and power over pupil admissions, which are endogenous privatisation characteristics. However, where private-sector actors play a leading role in academy governance, including free schools (Higham, 2014), then that exemplifies exogenous privatisation. In practice, such distinctions are challenging to observe in such explicitly binarised form. These distinctions extend even to the boundary between public and private itself, which is increasingly blurred. As Cone and Brøgger (2020) note, 'the emergence of private-public assemblages forming around and beyond the states is profoundly challenging how we think of educational ownership and policymaking' (p 374). For Cone and Brøgger (2020), the concept of assemblage enables new thinking about privatisation in the European context concerning the ways in which the relationship between the private and public moves from imbrication to integration, a process in which public-services values and status are arguably retained while some operational matters are delegated to the private sector.

A further sense of privatisation concerns the shift in locus of education decision-making from the public and its democratic institutions to the family. Or justifications for political decisions are grounded in one's personal family experience. Educational matters become domestic and so are rendered private and depoliticised. The notion of privatisation is also enabled through several ideological and other discursive framings. For example, while privatisation does not explicitly form part of Sahlberg's (2011) definition of the Global Educational Reform Movement, Winchip et al (2019) insist that it is 'a fundamental objective of an approach to education reform dominated by the interests of global capital' (p 81). Mechanistically, privatisation has been enabled by, first, New Public Management, which normalised private-sector-derived methods, purposes and rationales in education and particularly what is constructed as its 'leadership'; and, second, local management of schools, which created and privileged new CEO-type roles for headteachers (Smyth, 2011). Privatisation is central to the production of the markets whose creation and privileging underpin most definitions of neoliberalism. This is because social actors' discursive and material interactions with services, phenomena, groups of people or institutions depicted and treated as *marketised* construct them as private consumers rather than public-service users.

Further reading

- Grimaldi, E. and Serpieri, R. (2013) Privatising education policy-making in Italy: new governance and the reculturing of a welfarist education state, Education Inquiry (EDUI), 4(22615): 443–472.
- Naradowski, M. and Andrada, M. (2001) The privatization of education in Argentina, Journal of Education Policy, 16(6): 585–595.

Problematisation

The dominant view of policy worlds and policy making is one in which objective evidence, impartial facts and value-free science guides the formulation of policy problems and the provision of policy solutions. According to education policy sociologists (Ozga, 2021), this pragmatic view of policy worlds and policy making as sites of rational calculus and planning reflects the ascendency and dominance of logical positivism and functionalism to the political process, namely '"objective", value-free methods for the writing and reading of policy' (Olssen et al, 2004, p 2) and, relatedly, 'the persistence of rationalistic policy methodologies that claim to solve problems' (Webb, 2014, p 2). This includes the empiricism of the 'policy sciences' with its emphasis on using deductive methods of reasoning for producing knowledge about society.

The emergence and popularity of randomised controlled trials (RCTs) in education policy research (Connolly et al, 2018) is one example of this. RCTs aim to produce rigorous assessments of the technical-practical application of specific interventions and programmes with a view to producing cost-benefit analyses that can be used to shape important policy decisions. In effect, positivistic methods 'construct policy problems in ways that match the answers they already have available' (Gale, 2001, p 384). Moreover, the commitment to policy making and policy change as a problem-solving science not only leads researchers to overestimate their own understanding or the rationality of policy making and policy actors but has the effect of obscuring the 'authoritative allocation of values' (Prunty, 1985, p 136) through which policy problems and their solutions are given meaning as unique products of political influence, agitation or control. As Gale (1994) reminds us, 'the preoccupation with policy as problem solving attempts to take policy making out of the realm of politics and into the realm of techniques in order to avoid conflict between differing values' (p 277).

From a poststructuralist and social constructivist perspective, policy making and policy worlds are actively constructed and transformed through the provision of meaning. According to Clarke et al (2015), 'policy, then, can be conceived as a particular setting in which meanings are made, installed, naturalised, normalised, and, of course, contested' (p 20). On this basis, a post-positivist or anti-foundationalist approach to policy research means stressing the 'theoretical, cultural and socio-political setting' (Grace, 1995, 12) guiding formulations of policy problems and their solutions. This requires adopting sociological, interpretive and 'historically-informed [*sic*] research' (Ozga, 2021, p 291) that combine unique interpretive frameworks (frame analysis, rhetorical analysis and policy narration, for example) to represent policy making and policy worlds as discursive spaces for the struggle over meaning (Fischer and Gottweis, 2013). This also means paying close attention to the effects of these struggles over meaning as practices from which problematisations emerge.

In the spirit of this approach, Bacchi (2012) draws on Foucauldian-inspired poststructural analysis to understand how specific behaviour, phenomena and processes acquire the provisional conceptual identity of policy problems and as objects of intervention, improvement, management or control (also see Wilkins and Gobby, 2022). Bacchi (2012) uses the term 'problem representation' (p 4) to capture the contingent relations and regularities underpinning specific forms of problematisation across space and time. 'Comparisons of problematisations', according to Bacchi (2012), 'highlight the specific combinations of factors and relations that allow something to become a "problem" in one situation and not in another' (p 6). In contrast to the pragmatism and empiricism of the policy sciences which aim to 'establish the ontology, preexistent "nature", or a priori existence of specific thoughts and (best) practices' (Webb, 2014, p 373), and therefore make things cohere in such a way that problems appear to us as self-evident, universal or given, Bacchi (2012) seeks to grasp the discursive and nondiscursive arrangements that give coherence to different forms of problematisation. Stacey (2017) applies the same anti-metaphysical, anti-transcendental philosophy to show how teachers come to be constructed through education policy in New South Wales, Australia as obstacles to the future competition of its education system and therefore a 'problem to be tackled' (p 787).

In a similar approach that seeks to trace the multiplicity of problematisations through a 'methodological investment in indeterminacy' (Koopman, 2018, p 193), Gale (1994) analyses university entrance policy in Queensland, Australia to capture the dynamics of emergence that characterise the articulation and mobilisation of social facts as problems to be governed, namely the ways in which problematisation occurs through 'particular selection and ordering of elements and events that appeared as troublesome' (p 231). Adopting the same anti-foundationalist approach to studies of education policy, Ideland (2021) considers how private actors represent and give meaning to school problems in certain ways so that specific solutions can be sold to schools as interventions leading to repair or improvement. This methodology is described by Webb (2014) as 'policy problematisations', namely 'attempt[s] to identify conditions and registers in which problems and solutions have been articulated and practiced (enacted)' (p 370). At the same time, a commitment to methodological indeterminacy means identifying 'conditions and registers that disqualify parallel (i.e. rival, contradictory) thoughts, practices, and enactments' (Webb, 2014, p 370).

Further reading

- Bacchi, C. (1999) Women, policy and politics: the construction of policy problems, London: SAGE.
- Whitburn, B., Moss, J. and O'Mara, J. (2017) The policy problem: the National Disability Insurance Scheme (NDIS) and implications for access to education, Journal of Education Policy, 32(4): 467–479.

Q

Queer policy analysis

Queer policy analysis comes from queer theory, which itself draws on diverse intellectual and activist strands, not all of which are internally coherent. This might not matter; queer theory's principal definitional criterion is that normative definitions are to be resisted and problematised, including its own, and so ambiguity is a central feature. The field's semantic adoption of 'queering' to complement 'queer theory' reflects and results from the conceptual instability of the noun form. Using 'queer' as a verb foregrounds a particular disposition that produces oppositional, subversive and/or liberatory actions. In this entry, attention is drawn to some of the major ways in which queering has been operationalised in thinking about and practising education research and policy. These strands are considered alongside their conceptual antecedents and contributors, as well as the consequent implications for policy.

In an interview, Connell (Rasmussen et al, 2014) provides a 'capsule definition' (p 340) of queer theory that may usefully be unpacked and developed:

> [B]y queer theory I understand an approach, originating from lesbian and gay intellectuals, that deconstructs the binaries within which 'lesbian' and 'gay' themselves were defined; that sees gender as performatively produced, not the expression of a fixed reality or essence; that sees conventional gender as heteronormative, not just patriarchal; that understands consciousness and identity through analysis of subjectification within discourse. (Rasmussen et al, 2014, p 340)

First, therefore, queer theory problematises binaries. Here, it reveals its activist foundations in the lesbian and gay movement which contained the first such binaries to be disrupted. Foucault (1976) argued that turning 'homosexual' from an act into an identity was purposively undertaken in order to construct and constrict those so named as objects of power in abjection of the normatively positioned yet fragile heterosexual. Drawing on Foucault's (1976) deconstructionist arguments as well as on Derrida's (Derrida and Houdebine, 1973) insights concerning binary oppositions, queer theory aimed to destabilise the ontological labels of gay, lesbian or straight, as well as to problematise their compulsory association with particular ideas about masculine and feminine (the heteronormative matrix). This strand concerns most obviously identities, particularly relating to sex and sexuality (see, for example, Courtney, 2014), especially in relation to individual experiences and lives. To understand such lives, Halberstam (1998) proposed 'a queer methodology', which is 'a scavenger methodology that uses different methods to collect and produce information on subjects who have been deliberately or accidentally excluded from traditional studies of human behaviour ... it refutes the academic compulsion toward disciplinary coherence' (p 13). This individualising possibility within queer theory has implications for interrogating education policy that advertently or otherwise serves to construct and/or reproduce such marginalised identities. For example, in England, the schools' inspectorate Ofsted includes inspection criteria focusing on promoting respect for legally defined and protected characteristics. These protected characteristics include sexual orientation as well as gender reassignment and race (Ofsted, 2019). A queer policy reading might trouble the apparent stability of these groups or challenge their deficit positioning. When queered, this stability and deficit become illusory, revealing only the reified and embodied outcomes of political power.

Second, and relatedly, queer theory aims to disrupt power relations. This might be because these relations are seen as problematic because they are predicated on binarised or fixed categories, or because they are sustained by processes of normalisation. This is a larger intellectual project than that sketched out earlier since it moves beyond the individual to consider the structural. For instance, queering homosexual identities may go on to trouble identity categories per se, showing how all are 'unstable and socially contested' (Lugg and Murphy, 2014, p 1185). The deconstructive work that troubles binaries also lends itself well to the identification and disruption of normalising and othering power relations, and consequently an important methodological branch of queer theory opened up that achieves this not empirically but textually (see, for example, Sedgwick, 1990). However, this approach may be critiqued for its distancing from the subjects whose liberation is a normative objective of queer theory.

The object of queer inquiry, or 'queertique' (Duarte, 2021, p 2), can be anything where power functions to hierarchise and normalise. Consequently, the education field has seen contributions that queer entire suites of related concepts and practices such as educational leadership (Rottmann, 2006) and education policy (Lugg and Murphy, 2013). However, owing to queer theory's origins, its objects have tended to focus somewhat more narrowly on 'stigmatisation and erasure' (Lugg and Murphy, 2013, p 183) in relation to individuals' minoritised sexual and gender identities within particular contexts. Sometimes, queering aims at liberating the individual while problematising the structural (Martino et al, 2019; Duarte, 2021). For example, Duarte (2021) problematises the binarisation of research into qualitative and quantitative modes. Duarte (2021) argues that these binaries require subversion to illuminate more profound truths about the research focus, as well as to accommodate the queer subjectivity of the researcher. Such approaches offer great potential to the field of policy studies.

Further reading

- Jagose, A. (1996) Queer theory: an introduction, New York: New York University Press.
- Richardson, D., McLaughlin, J. and Casey, M.E. (eds) (2006) Intersections between feminist and queer theory, Basingstoke: Palgrave Macmillan.

R

Rationality

The concept of rationality is central to policy formulation and implementation. Rationality refers to the quality or expectation of being logical, reasonable or scientific, and therefore points to a set of universal definitions and appropriate standards against which the usefulness of policy decisions in achieving certain goals and outcomes can be judged to be internally consistent, valid, reliable, even replicable. This view of policy decisions or advice as rational presents an ideal representation of policy as evidence-driven, namely that the policy process is a scientific or apolitical practice structured around hypothesis testing that uses value-free knowledge to generate contextual or causal explanations for social change. Leaving aside the idea that policy is evidence- or fact-based, which is arguably false in some cases, there is the notion that the rationality of the policy process can be traced to its proclivity for and demonstration of science.

But science has a communicative context according to Andrews (2007) since scientific knowledge requires both consensus and authority in order to be considered legitimate. In other words, scientific knowledge claims never exist intrinsically and independent of human activity, but rather emerge through their relation to other sources of authority or processes of legitimation and consensus formation that determine their 'politicisation' and role in the policy-making process. Moreover, even assuming that the policy process is evidence-based and scientific in the Enlightenment sense of universal and value-free, it is important to separate out the rationality of the policy process (the means by which policy makers assimilate perfect information into policy decisions so that they are fair or accurate) and the rationality of the policy actor. This is because, as Dunleavy (1991) reminds us, some people may 'operate through intransitive preference orderings' (p 249) or exercise their decision-making through emotional attachments and ethical commitments not captured by a standard or comprehensive rationality that privileges forms of instrumental choice. Moreover, according to Bevir and Brentmann (2007), economistic models of rationality are inadequate for making sense of the ways in which diverse rationalities combine in unique ways to produce iterations of local reasoning and individual experience.

To make sense of this separation, Goldthorpe (1998) distinguishes between 'subjective' and 'objective' rationality, where subjective rationality is thought to correlate with a person's beliefs and objective rationality resembles 'the standard rationality that utility theory would presuppose' (p 171). Within public choice theories, for example, the rational actor is a person who organises their actions and decisions through optimising preferences in a consistent and logical fashion, typically in ways that serve to maximise self-advantage and self-interest. On this basis, the rational actor refers to 'people [who] have sets of well-informed preferences which they can perceive, rank and compare easily' (Dunleavy, 1991, p 3). Bowe et al (1994) demonstrate how a similar conception of rationality underpins the discourse of parental choice in education, a 'positivistic tradition which promotes a methodology that requires "responsible" choosers to undertake a rational, logical, criterion/factor-based approach placing factors in a hierarchical relation to each other' (p 70). Yet evidence shows that individuals do not share the capacity (or willingness) to calculate the expected benefits and costs of their actions in ways that are commensurate with a utilitarian conception of the rational actor or what David et al (1997) calls an 'autonomous, empowered and asocial rationality' (p 401). In some cases, governments have intervened to supply the trigger or support (called 'nudging', see Thaler and Sunstein, 2008) to compel such behaviour where it does not exist.

In this description, the implied rationality that comes with calculating and optimising decisions is a normative one: it presents a model of rational human behaviour considered to be rationally superior by virtue of being organised around preferences that are deliberative, logically consistent, reflective and rule-bound. In contrast, behaviour that lacks such modulation or self-restraint, namely so-called irrational, rapid, automated or unconscious drives, or which corresponds to preference orderings not captured by economic models of decision-making, are denigrated as counter-intuitive or non-rational. This is what Haye et al (2018) call the emergence of a 'biological rationality', 'the ideal of an effective micro-politics of a self-mastered subject' (p 192). From the perspective of behavioural psychology, neurobiology, neuroeconomics, social cognition or preference theory, emotion may be considered the antithesis of rational. Yet, from a discursive psychology perspective, 'emotion can be understood to constitute a powerful rhetorical ploy for constructing alternative forms of reasoning based on the social or moral treatment of human need; as part of a cultural or gender repertoire; or as a condition for subverting the apparatus of economic rationalisation itself' (Wilkins, 2013, p 403). In other words, 'we need a model which can provide space for non-reflexive as well as reflexive forms of agency, for acting on impulse as well as on the basis of conscious intent and calculation' (Hoggett, 2001, p 43).

As Duncan and Edwards (1999) acknowledge, individual decision-making cannot be reduced to individualistic forms of economic rationalisation since, in the case of single mothers seeking paid work through entering the labour market, it involves difficult choices about what is best for others, namely the child, and therefore emerges from complex 'socially negotiated rationalities' (p 117). Similarly, Bauman (1993) encourages us to challenge the modernist impulse to reduce all action to expressions of means-end rationality and instead to 'restore legitimacy to the "inexplicable", nay irrational, sympathies and loyalties which cannot "explain themselves" in terms of their usefulness and purpose' (p 33).

Further reading

- Hodgson, D. (2011) Policy rationalities and policy technologies: a programme for analysing the raised school-leaving age in Western Australia, Journal of Education Policy, 26(1): 115–130.
- Lim, L. (2014) Ideology, rationality and reproduction in education: a critical discourse analysis, Discourse: Studies in the Cultural Politics of Education, 35(1): 61–76.

Regime

The term regime is one of the most popular concepts used by education policy researchers to make sense of the context or history within which education systems and structures are made and unmade through relations and practices of governing. In this sense, regime may connote a variety of discursive and material forces which are historically and geopolitically situated and therefore irreducible in content and form to other emergent forces that resemble a regime. Some regimes may be imagined as national, regional or local, for example, while others may be imagined at the level of the supranational and global. Regimes therefore can be broadly construed as 'governing arrangements' (Wilson, 2000, p 255) consisting of 'ideas, institutional arrangements, and interests' (May, 2014, p 4). Yet regime tends to be asserted more than it is critiqued as a concept or operationalised within a strict framework of understanding. Education is typically talked about in general terms as shaped by 'disciplinary regimes' (Thomson and Pennacchia, 2016, p 88) and 'inspection regimes' (Perryman, 2006, p 150), for example. Such polyvalence is indicative of a very slippery concept which typically emerges through academic writing in passing (articulated but not clarified in any meaningful sense).

When articulated to describe education policy configurations and movements, the term regime is often used in seemingly passive terms to describe a unifying structure, resultant formation or form of structuration and governance, namely something predetermined by law or legislation as composed of 'mutually accepted decision-making procedures and agreed upon rules for action' (Wilson, 2000, p 256). Here regime signifies the endurance of certain logics, traditions, beliefs or discourses held together and imagined collectively as hegemonic projects or governmental rationalities that influence individual action, namely 'regimes, policies, or practices grip or hold a subject fast' (Howarth, 2010, p 301). The implication of using regime in such a passive sense is that it is elevated to something intuitive, normative, agreed upon and ordinary, even omnipotent: 'identified as the cause of a wide variety of social, political and economic changes' (Clarke, 2008, p 135). On the other hand, regime is sometimes used in active terms to reference an assemblage or assembling activity in which various disparate elements cohere (or not) through the provision of negotiations, translations, accommodations and revisions that are historically, culturally and politically unique. Far from being represented in passive terms as 'background' or a pre-emptive or constitutive force, here the active use of regime connotes plurality, emergence and provisional settlements or 'relational historical blocs' (Howarth, 2010, p 313).

As Lingard et al observe (2013), testing regimes based on high-stakes national census testing are a global phenomenon where their replication and standardisation across nation-states is made possible by new forms of meta-policy driven by the Organisation for Economic Co-operation and Development's Programme for International Student Assessment; the International Association for the Evaluation of Educational Achievement's Trends in International Maths and Science Study and Progress in International Reading and Literacy Study. Yet, despite the omnipresence of testing regimes globally and any presumption of universality and uniformity, the nation, argues Lingard et al (2013), continues to play an important role in the 'rescaling of contemporary politics' (p 549) required to ensure the rearticulation of these global logics at the regional and local levels.

In some cases, regimes are represented as a collection of complementary provisos, directives and guidelines designed to shape ethical, moral or legal practices. Dickhaus (2010), for example, describes external quality-assurance policies in higher education as 'regulatory regimes' (p 257) and 'accountability regimes' (p 258). Dickhaus (2010) uses the concept of regime in passive and active terms, both to describe the ubiquity of quality-assistance policies in higher education at the global level and to point to the role of 'structure, agency, discourses and scales in creating compromises' (p 267). Adopting a Gramscian conception of hegemony, Howarth (2010) observes that 'a regime, practice or policy holds sway over a set of subjects by winning their consent or securing their compliance' (p 317). From this perspective, regimes, be they economic, cultural or political, are negotiated settlements for resolving disagreements or holding disagreements apart. It is therefore important to remain sceptical of any view of regimes as retaining a structural or internal coherence, since regimes are rather more like a facile synthesis that substitutes contingency or discourse for truth. Regimes, in other words, are held together through 'transformism, negotiation, compromise and bargaining' (Howarth, 2010, p 317). Hence Foucault (1977) describes discursive formations as 'regime[s] of truth', namely dynamic spaces that do not simply translate struggles or systems of domination. Rather, they function as sites for struggles over meaning and the provisional resolution of ideological dilemmas for the purpose of displacing, reactivating, contesting, refusing and revising various norms and values.

From a spatial or scalar perspective that takes seriously the open-endedness of these struggles as the changing products of contingent sites, practices and connections, the endurance of regimes of truth can be understood as part of the everyday labour of social actors engaged in the work of spatialisation, of scalar work, of boundary spanning and inter-regional and international coordination. In this sense, regimes are the product of multiple determinations of space and scale. As Ball (2013) observes, 'the fitting together of disparate techniques, processes, practices and relationships within a regime of truth [forms] a grid of power which operates in many different ways from many different points' (p 124). In some cases, scalar regimes function to facilitate interaction and coordination between subnational, national and international actors in order to bring about new forms of political control and economic protection. Through a study of post-socialist reforms in the Caribbean, Jules (2013) highlights the role of 'trans-regional regimes' to the governing work of creating vital, albeit fragile relays between the peoples of various small states in order to help imagine and mobilise a vision of the 'ideal Caribbean person' or the 'neo-Caribbean citizen' (p 271). Regimes, in this sense, can be conceptualised as essential components of governing, according to May (2014): 'They are the means for converting policy desires into actions that deliver benefits, regulate activities, redistribute resources, and impose burdens' (p 4).

Further reading

- Jochim, A.E. and May, P. (2010) Beyond subsystems: policy regimes and governance, Policy Studies Journal, 38(2): 303–327.
- Zembylas, M. (2023) Theorizing the affective regime of 'best practice' in education policy, European Educational Research Journal, 22(2), 281–294.

Regulation

In a broad sense, social regulation refers to 'multiple processes, contradictory and sometimes conflictual, orienting actors' conduct and the definition of the rules of the game in a social or political system' (Maroy, 2009, p 67). On a juridical and political understanding, regulation is defined as 'the totality of institutional arrangements and control mechanisms and the framing of actions by a recognised political authority' (Maroy, 2009, p 67). Political authority can be located at different levels and scales of public action from the local to the supranational. The regulating mechanisms of political authority may include, among others, rules, legislation, incentives, procedures, market mechanisms, evaluation devices, hierarchical control, standards, and cognitive or normative schemes of reference. Political regulation can also be accompanied by market regulation, institutional regulation and autonomous regulation by local actors. Regulation is not equivalent or reducible to institutional arrangements or regulative measures, however, since it emerges through interactions between these and the situated actions of actors.

Reflecting on changes in the ideals and mechanisms of regulation since the post-Second World War period, Ozga (2009) distinguishes between two forms of regulation: direct and indirect. Direct regulation can be understood within a classical model of authority as centralised, vertical and hierarchical. Indirect regulation suggests its opposite, that is, authority that is decentralised, horizontal and networked (Rhodes, 1996). A comparable typology of regulation is also offered by Maroy (2009), who differentiates between a 'bureaucratic-professional model' and a 'post-bureaucratic model'. The former model locates regulation in bureaucratic rules. In the case of education, a bureaucratic-professional model grants the teaching profession collective power over pedagogical issues and working conditions. The latter model incorporates features of an 'evaluative state model' and 'quasi-market model' that effectively reduces teacher autonomy. Maroy (2009) points to evidence of partial convergence across several countries that have implemented a 'post-bureaucratic model' of regulation. These convergences are only partial because said models are recontextualised and hybridised following geopolitically specific path dependencies. Maroy (2009) therefore demonstrates the polyvalence and contingency of regulation as a concept and research tool since it can be used to reference the dynamics of governance in the broadest sense (see entry on 'Governance') or more narrowly to refer to top-down relations of power.

West and Nikolai (2017) also understand regulation in relation to other forms of authority such as school inspection and funding. Through their comparative research on the expansion of private schools in England, Sweden and Eastern Germany, West and Nikolai (2017) specify the multiple and divergent rules shaping school governance in these countries, including admissions, teachers' qualifications, teachers' pay and conditions, and curriculum. West and Nikolai (2017) observe that differences in the rules steering these domains translate into differences in the regulation of private schooling which in turn partially explains their differentiated routes pursuing similar types of education reform.

Ozga (2009) also points to the contradictory movement of regulation through a study of the development of governance in England. Ozga (2009) argues that changes in the regulation of schools under these developments appear as deregulation but are in fact marked by strong central steering through evaluation and performance monitoring. Ozga (2009) contrasts these reforms with the post-Second World War governance model captured in the metaphor of 'partnership' and polycentric models of power sharing. To maintain partnership, the policy process during this time was the preserve of bargaining between politicians 'informed (and sometimes strongly steered) by administrators at central and local government levels, all of whom shared a set of (often implicit) assumptions about the appropriate provision of education' (Ozga, 2009, p 150). Similar models of governance, described by Ranson (2008) as a 'complex, "polycentred" division of power and responsibility' (p 204), can be traced to mainland Europe (see 'bureaucratic-professional model' by Maroy [2009]) where regulation was secured through agreement on common assumptions and general rules about provision, shared norms and values, as well as through processes of incorporation of (selected) interests through consultative processes (Maroy, 2009). Since the 1980s, publicly funded education services across Europe, North America, South America and Asia have experienced a shift towards decentralisation, marketisation and choice. However, the governing of decentralised school systems is now secured through other means that reflect the partnership model but are held together through policy instruments, such as standards, evaluation and data production, all of which strengthen the role of central authorities and dismantle or undermine the bargaining power of local and regional authorities in many cases. Vertical regulation, therefore, is exercised through indirect means, particularly through steering by data production/use, corporate and consumer models of accountability, and self-regulation through performativity. Increasingly, the role of the local and regional authorities in some cases is effectively reduced to a nodal actor in the circulation and application of data between schools and state authorities.

Further reading

- Berkovich, I. (2019) Process implementation perspective on neoliberal regulation: a comparative analysis of national curricula and standards-based reforms in the USA and Australia, Globalisation, Societies and Education, 17(5): 593–609.
- Maroy, C. (2009) Convergences and hybridization of educational policies around 'post-bureaucratic' models of regulation, Compare, 39(1): 71–84.

Resistance

Education research on resistance has a rich theoretical tradition in critical sociology and poststructuralist scholarship that has contributed to different understandings of resistance and methods for studying it. For some education researchers, resistance connotes visible social movements, collectives or associations, typically those can be considered institutionalised or popularised, while for others it is performed and embodied through subversive, often fleeting and temporary practices that remain elusive albeit ubiquitous. Courpasson and Vallas (2016) attribute seminal importance to James Scott's study of peasant societies that describes how everyday acts of resistance are largely performed in the form of 'infrapolitics' that conceal defiant beliefs while simultaneously staging compliance. While such everyday acts of resistance do not retain the promise of immediate dramatic change to the status quo, they retain the capacity to initiate and sustain pressure for change over long periods of time, including piecemeal, cumulative or incremental resistance over decades (Courpasson and Vallas, 2016). Scott's work on peasant societies has been criticised for focusing on the material side of domination, however, as well as romanticising resistance by identifying (and equating) resistance with mundane practices and minor gestures (Courpasson and Vallas, 2016). Nevertheless, Scott's work has helped to nuance understandings of the different forms of resistance that may occur, and the context-dependent histories and relationships upon which they rely as modes of articulation.

Complementing such work, the Foucauldian approach to power and resistance signifies two important interventions in debates about domination and agency. First, domination is not (only) performed through state repression or ownership of land/labour but is a diffuse process of subjugation that works subtly on individual subjectivity. Second, power should be conceptualised in dynamic terms as generative and sticky since it is not exclusively concerned with the usurpation of freedom but the transformation of human beings into subjects of freedom. This means, in effect, an analytical shift away from the simple axis of the domination/resistance relationship (McKee, 2009) to take account of the self-determining and context-creating activity of social actors. By way of Foucault, Rose (1999) and others (Burchell et al, 1991) have adopted a governmentality approach to explore the means by which different governments enjoin citizens to perform certain freedoms and responsibilities (see entry on 'Governmentality'). These perspectives bring into question the notion of oppositional intentions and actions as exterior to power. For example, some individual actions may appear at first as an index of defiance but can end up strengthening rather than weakening elements of the status quo. Certeau's influential work on the 'art of the weak' also demonstrates how subjects of domination may creatively deploy existing discourses through bricolage (see entry on 'Bricolage') but without necessarily changing the order of things. Nevertheless, such acts remind us of the 'limits of power's domain' (Courpasson and Vallas, 2016, p 7) and the relational constitution of domination and resistance as two sides of the same coin.

Courpasson and Vallas (2016) also offer helpful summaries of existing taxonomies and definitions of resistance, but warn that such heuristics carry certain biases and assumptions. A common feature of these typologies of resistance is to stress 'a defiant or contentious intent on the part of the resisters' (Courpasson and Vallas, 2016, p 5). Some taxonomies move away from dualistic accounts, however, to examine resistance along a continuum of openness, scale and intent. Though these classifications may be considered illuminating for differentiating between the diverse forms that resistance may take, they appear to be based on key assumptions that equate authentic or real resistance with forms of individualised conscious awareness, in effect disregarding those forms of resistance which might be considered too fleeting and elusive to be subject to adequate temporal-spatial or historical constructions of social action. As already outlined, the definition of resistance varies dramatically according to different ontological assumptions about power and agency. At the same time, as Thomson (2008) points out, theorisations of resistance should always be developed through empirical examples that go beyond any exclusive focus on reification (excessive theorising) to point to possibilities for change.

Thomson's (2008) study of headteachers, for example, usefully combines empirical observations with applied postcolonial theory to show the complexities of simulation, specifically the simultaneity of resistance and compliance that occurs when headteachers selectively refuse some aspects of the imposed policy in a limited space for action. Here, Thomson (2008) demonstrates how headteachers engaged in acts of public criticism openly confess 'their refusal to comply, presumably inviting sanctions' (Thomson, 2008, p 92). But rather than romanticise these actions as examples of resistance, Thomson (2008) insists that they need to be understood as part of a simultaneity of positions within a field of power that traverses the domination/resistance bifurcation. This is because these actions, as evidenced by Thomson (2008), are deployed using specific forms of strategic calculation based on the appraisal of the political context as well as confidence in the existence of collective support. Gvirtz and Narodowski (1998) offer another conceptually nuanced account of resistance through their investigation of political oppression affecting the content of teaching material during the military dictatorship of Perón in Argentina. In this macro-political context, Gvirtz and Narodowski (1998) observe how direct opposition by teachers through public protests or trade unions carried serious risks. Building on Foucault, Gvirtz and Narodowski (1998) then go on to show the ways in which teachers disguised their resistance as mundane pedagogical practices. A number of oppositional practices emerged as a result of these contradictory practices of concealed resistance, namely active depoliticisation of teaching content from above, on the one hand, and a strategic refusal of such actions by teachers, on the other hand, who omitted such content or exercised sloppy grading of politicised material. Gvirtz and Narodowski (1998), therefore, foreground the contextuality of resistance, its diverse forms and the significance of pedagogy as a space for granular forms of opposition.

Further reading

- Longmuir, F. (2019) Resistant leadership: countering dominant paradigms in school improvement, Journal of Educational Administration and History, 51(3): 256–272.
- Zembylas, M. (2021) The affective dimension of everyday resistance: implications for critical pedagogy in engaging with neoliberalism's educational impact, Critical Studies in Education, 62(2): 211–226.

Rhetorical analysis

A key focus of rhetorical analysis (or rhetorical criticism) concerns the symbolic artefacts of language and communication (metaphors, tropes, repertoires, imagery) used in discursive and textual practices to organise and deploy strategies of persuasion and incitement (Edwards et al, 2004, p 3). In this sense, rhetorical analysis is not a study of the content of language and communication (considered empty talk) or the organisation of 'facts' around manipulation and lies. Rather, rhetorical analysis shifts the focus towards explaining the idiosyncratic nature of persuasion and influence as a function of the context, purpose and imagined audience of texts and speech. Policy viewed as text and discourse, for example, implies that language construction is not only stipulative (consisting of groups of statements that are bound to and generative of context) and iterative (capable of producing new meaning through appropriation and rearticulation) but is regulative (designed to contain the possibilities for marking out the discursive boundaries that define reality or truth). From a rhetorical analysis position, policy texts can be studied for their regulative function as pragmatic, engaged attempts to activate and incite subjects as bearers of specific roles, obligations and responsibilities that extend to functions of the state including policy implementation. From this perspective, policy texts and speech can be understood to carry certain dialogic, anticipatory and ideological usages (Billig, 1996) aimed at producing and imagining spaces through which to articulate reform. The study of policy texts and speech as rhetorical devices therefore enables researchers: to explain their context and function as discursive formations that seek to actively constitute rather than simply reflect social reality (Fischer, 2003b); to trace the various 'communities of consent and dissent' (Britzman, 2000, p 36) resulting from these formations, that is, the (dis)connections between imagined and real audiences; and to make explicit any tensions, struggles and contradictions resulting from these discursive formations as successful or failed attempts at creating particular kinds of subjects, in effect making possible new ways to imagine alternative courses of action and response (Winton, 2013). To this end, Winton (2013) frames rhetorical analysis as a method of critical discourse analysis in education policy studies and policy sociology (see entry on 'Critical discourse analysis').

There are several categories or units of analysis that underpin rhetorical analysis, including exigence, construction of audience and the use of persuasive genres, among others. Exigence signifies the problem that demands urgent response. Education policies texts can be understood as a response to perceived problems (or as constructions of problems, sometimes called problem representation, see Bacchi [1999]), with the identified problem in turn providing a legitimate context for policy response and intervention. Identified problems are sometimes presented through the mechanism of 'crisis narratives', for example, which 'provide an imperative for policy action and therefore invest situations with political importance, almost regardless of the relative weight of evidence and analysis by all concerned' (Edwards et al, 2004, p 132). In other words, the 'problems' and 'crises' documented in some policy texts do not necessarily reflect a pre-existing reality but carve out the spaces through which governments can frame and justify policy response. As a result, policy texts emerge as productive spaces in which the field of possibilities and problems are negotiated to frame (and exclude) different policy options (Ball, 1990).

Exigence also signifies the practice through which policy audiences are imagined with the aim to develop communities of consent between policy makers and the recipients of policy. For these communities of consent to be made possible in practice, policy texts must simultaneously construct policy options on the basis of reality, as perceived by the recipients of policy, and reconstruct it through various exigencies to affect said reality so that it complements government policy goals. In their policy analysis of education digitalisation rhetoric in Finland, Saari and Säntti (2018) show how in a decentralised system of education that values teacher autonomy, policy texts simultaneously appeal to the formal autonomy of local actors (heads of education departments, principals and teachers) while actively reconfiguring that autonomy for different purposes, namely expanded digital education reform in the Finnish school system. More specifically, as

Saari and Säntti (2018) demonstrate, policy texts as rhetorical devices work to legitimate digital education reforms through the construction of exigencies of loss competitiveness and outdatedness which are organised as inevitable outcomes facing Finnish schools that do not adopt these reforms. At the same time, Saari and Säntti (2018) focus on associative and dissociative argumentation techniques to document some of the tensions and struggles underpinning these policy interventions, which include rolling out reforms that effectively undermine Finnish teachers' commitments to progressivism and professionalism.

Through a study of Character Matters!, a policy initiative of a school board in Ontario, Canada, Winton (2013) adopts a view of policy as rhetoric to show how policy actively works to create spaces in which sameness can be imagined and managed across difference to produce new policy communities. Winton (2013) highlights the ways in which differences between individuals and groups (in this case, parents and teaching staff) are minimised in order that their interests may be translated into shared responsibility for policy implementation. To secure the compliance of teachers in particular, Winton (2013) observes rhetorical moves towards praising teachers on the one hand and presenting the policy as flexible and uncomplicated to implement on the other hand. To deconstruct how policy as rhetoric functions to construct an imagined audience, Winton (2013) documents the various discursive resources (tropes, imagery, repertoires) mobilised from the choice of pronouns to the use of metaphors and absence of definitions. Here, Winton (2013) emphasises policy texts and speeches as persuasive discursive genres consisting of groups of statements, evaluations and arguments specifically designed and deployed to appeal to the audience's reason (logos), emotion (pathos) or confidence in the author (ethos). Winton (2013) observes, for example, how the policy initiative Character Matters! appeals to reason (logos) through articulating rationally organised arguments that good citizens require character education as a cornerstone of a civil society. These appeals to reason (logos) are also overlaid with explicit references to pathos (emotion) through discussions of student safety and risk avoidance. Ethos, observes Winton (2013), is constructed on the basis of claims to community support, endorsements by external actors, references to similarly successful programmes elsewhere and the establishment of the board as an authority.

Further reading

- Eleveld, A. (2012) The role of rhetoric and affect in policy changes: the case of Dutch life course policy, Critical Policy Studies, 6(3): 282–303.
- Nuttall, J., Henderson, L., Wood, E. and Trippestad, T.A. (2022) Policy rhetorics and responsibilization in the formation of early childhood Educational Leaders in Australia, Journal of Education Policy, 37(1): 17–38.

S

Scalar policy analysis

Similar to spatial policy analysis, which theorises space in terms of epistemology rather than a geographical/territorial fixity, scalar policy analysis is the study of the importance of scale to the socio-political work of maintaining relations across time and space through creative practices of mediation, translation, assemblage, recontextualisation and hybridisation. Here, scales such as transnational, national, regional and local can be theorised in dynamic terms as 'parts of multiple scalar and (also de-)territorial transformations, in which governmental power is constantly created or (de-)stablised' (Hartong, 2018, p 2). This has given rise to a very specific field of study – the 'politics of scale' – which seeks to make sense of socio-political crises and developments both global and (sub)national from the perspective of scalar practices that shape the way in which discrete objects, relations and actors are held together and made to influence each other. Political economy scholars working in the field of scalar policy research, for example, note that scalar practices, such as globalisation or neoliberalism, work by enabling the interests and actions of elite groups of transnational actors to pursue new means of capital accumulation and class power through the rescaling or upscaling of work and consumption (see Harvey, 2005). Scalar practices, in other words, 'establish and stabilise unequal relations within the capitalist world system' (Kaiser and Nikiforova, 2008, p 539).

Here scalar practices refer to a variety of discursive and non-discursive techniques used by different actors and organisations to achieve political and economic ends through new forms of 'territorialisation, place-making and network formation' (Pemberton and Searle, 2016, p 78), be they governments using 'scale' to reimagine regional and local projects and spaces that accommodate the shift to governance or social-movement activists using 'scale' to facilitate interaction and coordination between subnational, national and international actors. As Fraser (2010) argues, different actors and organisations articulate and produce scale 'to create some sort of advantage, to establish associations, connections, or solidarities across social divides, or to represent their interests (to be heard or seen) amidst oppressive or otherwise difficult conditions' (p 332). In this sense, the success (or failure) of political projects can be traced to the aptitude and skills of different social actors to draw on available resources and translate complicated narratives to effectively carry out what Fraser calls (2010) 'scalecraft' (p 332). Scalecraft, scaleness or scale-making (the ability to carve out new imaginary socio-political relations through an appeal to concepts of locality, regionality, nationality or otherwise) therefore hinges on the capacity of actors and organisations to effectively negotiate (and resolve, if only provisionally and tendentially) the tensions and ambivalences that prevent such relations being imagined in the first place. Scalecraft therefore is a contingent event whose fragility is constantly exposed by the tensions and contradictions flowing through pre-existing value systems and cultures. The long-term sustainability of any scale-making project, imagined in terms of regionalisation, Europeanisation or globalisation, for example, depends on 'the skill and artisanal dimension of scalar practices, such as jumping scale, rescaling, or the practice of maintaining the effectiveness of a social movement's operations at multiple scales' (Fraser, 2010, p 335).

Criticisms of scalar policy analysis relate mainly to the ways in which some researchers reify scales as 'relatively stable platforms' (Kaiser and Nikiforova, 2008, p 537) or, through reducing 'the social' to an imprint of scales, treat 'sociocultural relations as appendages to capitalist production' (p 539). Another related criticism of scalar policy analysis is its narrow focus on 'results (convergence)' (Hartong, 2018, p 2) at the expense of any focus on the problematic alignments and assemblage work that give rise to these results. But these criticisms mainly relate to political economy approaches that appear to overestimate the constitutive effects of scalar practices in different spaces and places and among different peoples. To overcome the limits of these types of engagements with scalar thinking, where scales appear fixed and bounded, Kaiser and Nikiforova (2008) propose a poststructural framing of scale to attend to important questions of 'how signification and resignification work' (p 541). Through the analytical lens of performativity, Kaiser and Nikiforova (2008) insist on opening up that analytical space in which people can be found refusing, resisting and translating the interpellative work of scalar practices at the level of everyday resignification. As Verger et al note (2020) through their study of test-based accountability reforms in two Spanish regions, Madrid and Catalonia, social actors inhabit and perform 'multiple relationships that reconstitute such programs in different scales' (p 145). Hartong (2018), for example, demonstrates how digital data are themselves scalar practices in the ongoing production of 'global-local policy mobilities' (p 136). Here, digital data function as inscription devices not only for rendering the incalculable calculable, but also for making national systems vulnerable to capture (and control) by global entities. In a similar vein, Lingard and Rawolle (2011) highlight the movement towards global systems of assessment (as evidenced by the rise of Organisation for Economic Co-operation and Development's Programme for International Student Assessment, PISA) as an example of 'the rescaling of authority' (p 490) in which the politics of nation-building is nestled within a much wider complex picture of transnational policy making.

Wilkins (2017) also shows how governments use scalar practices to influence how governance is practised within devolved school systems. Highlighting recent changes to the English school system under successive government reforms to supplant the traditional authority of local governments with the new authority of multi-academy trusts (publicly funded independent sponsors of schools), Wilkins (2017) characterises these trends as scalar practices designed to shift power towards those that are 'complimentary and supplementary to the will of government' (p 182). In some cases, the delegation of authority in schools in these contexts can result in 'scalar tensions', according to Papanastasiou (2017b), whereby school principals and governors engage in the complex discursive work of responding to different constructions of 'the local' and 'local need'.

Further reading

- Lieshout, M., Dewulf, A., Aarts, N. and Termeer, C. (2012) Doing scalar politics: interactive scale framing for managing accountability in complex policy processes, Critical Policy Studies, 6(2): 163–181.
- Marston, S., Jones, J. and Woodward, K. (2005) Human geography without scale, Transactions of the Institute of British Geographers, 30: 416–432.

Silence

Silence may be imposed upon individuals or a community through policy and policy making, either advertently or otherwise. In this sense, it implies removal from political decision-making or consideration since 'speech is what makes man [*sic*] a political being' (Arendt, 1958, p 27) and political participation is referred to metaphorically as having a voice or 'speaking out … telling it like it is' (Patton, 1989, p 29). Viewed differently, silence may be adopted agentically as a strategic response to a policy and the discursive terrain it produces. Even those constructed as policy makers may use silence as a holding measure during the policy process. The case of Angela Merkel (Former Chancellor of Germany) demonstrates that this sort of silence can be effected by saying nothing even while talking. From this perspective, silence in these contexts is productive. Silence may be produced and it 'can effectively be the site of our doing and becoming' (Brito Vieira et al, 2019, p 444).

Policy may serve to silence certain actors and/or their constituencies or communities. This can be through suppressing their contribution to the policy-making process. One example concerns the establishment in England in 2000 of the National College for School Leadership (NCSL) by the New Labour government. Intended to be the sole source of sanctioned knowledge about and for school leaders, the NCSL actively silenced potentially critical voices through commissioning and publishing research almost exclusively from ideologically compliant academics (Gunter, 2012). This approach to silencing potential policy contributors was repeated more explicitly by a later, Conservative-led government when the then UK Education Secretary called critics of his reform agenda 'the enemies of promise' and 'the Blob' (Gove, 2013). This aggressive pathologising of critical voices was a very loud form of silencing. A second way in which actors or communities can be silenced is through constructing policies that do not serve or actively contradict their interests. For instance, public health policies in the US in the early 1980s did not recognise the growing AIDS epidemic, leading to higher rates of mortality than might otherwise have been achieved. As the activist movement Act Up put it, Silence = Death (see Patton, 1989). In a sense, all policy making silences someone or something through normal processes of problem-identification or construction. Framing an issue as a potential problem to be solved through policy intervention involves including some elements and omitting or silencing others. There is, however, a valid debate concerning the distinction between omission and silencing, where the latter may be understood as purposive, 'an active pursuit undertaken by self-defined guardians of orthodoxy to preserve the integrity of a ... position that benefits ... the most powerful' (Grayson, 2010, p 1013).

Silence can also be deployed (or produced) as a tactic with diverse objectives in the policy process. In a critical exchange with colleagues (Brito Vieira et al, 2019), Jung noted that these objectives include maintaining the availability of several policy options, which serve as a distraction from certain policy ideas or a focus on others.

Silence in policy making may also serve symbolic purposes. For instance, Jung points out that it may signify a 'deliberate refusal to play along in a language game' (Brito Vieira et al, 2019, p 426) whose rules disadvantage the player choosing silence. More widely, symbolic silences can indicate 'either acceptance or refusal, in- or exclusion, or the openness to further negotiation' (Brito Vieira et al, 2019, p 426). This range speaks to a more general point about silence: its interpretation is unlikely to mirror its producer's intentions. Indeed, if silence is not recognised as significant and agentic, then it was not produced at all (Gray, in Brito Vieira et al, 2019). As Brummett (1980) explains, 'silence becomes strategic only when talk is expected' (p 289). This positions the production of silence as relational, and hence political since power relations will inevitably interpose to mediate action and interpretation. The meaning of a minister's silence on a policy matter is qualitatively different to that of the most junior advisor. This opens the space for silence to conceal 'epistemic injustice' (Gray, in Brito Vieira et al, 2019, p 434), both because of the challenge of interpretation and the fact that 'we cannot reliably distinguish a silence that is freely chosen from silence that is involuntary' (p 434). On the other hand, Brito Vieira (Brito Vieira et al, 2019) observes in silence 'the possibility of practising freedom *within*, and in resistance *to*, a hegemonic discourse, which makes us what we are while confining us to determinate vocabularies of self-articulation' (p 444, original emphasis). In this way, silence can be constitutive of identities, subjectivities and practices. This applies to groups as much as individuals since 'we make silence together. ... We speak in turns, but silence can only be meaningfully produced and maintained among and between people' (Brito Vieira, in Brito Vieira et al, 2019, p 445).

Further reading

- de St Croix, T. (2011) Struggles and silences: policy, youth work and the National Citizen Service, Youth and Policy, 106: 4359.

- Dingli, S. (2015) We need to talk about silence: re-examining silence in International Relations theory, European Journal of International Relations, 21(4): 721–742.

Social network analysis

Social network analysis describes and analyses emerging realities that are increasingly marked by growing and diverse interrelations of organisational or individual actors operating at and communicating across multiple levels and scales, from the local to the supranational. Actors in social network analysis might also be used to connote objects or events, depending on the empirical focus and questions shaping the research design. Put simply, a social network refers to a set of actors connected by and productive of relationships, communications and interactions (Finnigan et al, 2018). These actors are sometimes characterised as nodes in a network whose connections (or lack of) are defined by ties, edges or links. In some cases, the flow of interaction or points of contact between nodes in a network is open, limited or constrained owing to how social relationships and communications are organised within a particular network. Some networks are more open-ended than others, for example, with blurred edges and fuzzy boundaries that span multiple organisations and actors, government and non-government authorities, to create imbricated spaces. Social network analysis therefore is premised on the assumption that the capacity of actors to exert influence or change within a given network is relationally constructed on the basis of the configuration of relationships, communications and interactions within a given network. From a social network perspective, agency, whether it be understood in relation to human or non-human actors, is relationally rather than individually defined. Social network analysis, therefore, concerns the nature of interactions between actors (or nodes) as elements in the formation of networks.

In educational settings like schools and school systems, where government and non-government influence is exercised indirectly and at a distance through inscription devices like performance indicators and data-driven monitoring and surveillance systems, the social network perspective is useful for tracing how influence (and non-influence) is determined by the social embedding of actors as nodes in a network (Kolleck, 2016). In policy research more generally, the social network perspective is helpful for examining phases of the policy cycle as nodes in the formation of networks (Finnigan et al, 2018). Before the term 'network' became popular, a similar phenomenon was referenced using terms such as epistemic communities or policy sub-systems, among others. Yet the concept of network is doing something analytically different here, namely tracing the channels of formal and informal influence that move through and between discrete entities to explain the formation of things as endogenous and exogenous in nature. A social network perspective is therefore appropriate for investigating how policy rationalities and technologies are formulated or governed at the intersection of various levels and scales of authority from the local to the global. Moreover, social network analysis allows for the flow or interruption of connections between actors to be measured using quantitative graphic metrics and visually represented through graphical displays to capture the density, size, volume and opacity of connected nodes in a given network.

While the concept of networks has garnered attention among geographers and economists for some time, the rise of globalisation, network governance and New Public Management, together with the accompanying dynamics of privatisation and externalisation that flow from and enable these configurations (Menachy and Verger, 2019), has invigorated attention among education policy scholars interested in the logic of networks as organising principals for education reform and development. New Public Management, for example, is a strategy in subordinating politics to economic evaluations through the provision of 'output controls … private-sector styles of management practice [and] greater discipline and parsimony in resource use' (Hood, 1991, pp 4–5), with the effect that more formal autonomy is granted to municipal authorities and schools to make decisions about budget allocation, strategic planning and (in some countries) teacher pay and working conditions. But New Public Management is also akin to 'meta-policy' (Wilkins et al, 2024) since it echoes and redeems the priorities of various global advocacy networks, philanthropic organisations and supranational entities like the World Bank who continually promote quality improvement and effectiveness of management of control systems as mechanisms for ensuring good governance among schools and school systems. In this context, social network analysis is useful for showing how policy ideas travel within and across various geopolitical spaces (or not) according to the density and opacity of connected nodes in a national-global network.

There are multiple methods and sources of evidence gathering used in social network analysis to trace the intensity of relations between nodes in a network, from questionnaires and interviewing to citation mapping and social media resources. There are also various theoretical perspectives and heuristics used to supplement and enhance social network analyses of policy, from social capital theory and cognitive social structure theory to diffusion theory and the advocacy coalition framework (Kolleck, 2016; Finnigan et al, 2018). A key methodological focus of social network analysis, however, is the use of mathematical concepts and quantitative methods. This includes the adoption of key concepts like centrality, used to describe the capacity of actors to enable flows in a network that serve their own interests. Other concepts include central actors (those who are more likely to exert influence on the generation of relationships in a network) and peripheral actors (those with limited capacity or willingness to exert influence). Other related concepts include degree centrality and eigenvector centrality with the former acting as an index for the number of ties between actors in a network and the latter adding weight to a particular tie depending on the intensity of the connectedness between actors in a network. Actors in a network can also be construed as brokers whose purpose is to mediate connections between actors and shape information or resource flows. Social network analysis also uses different visual techniques such as sociograms to portray the properties of networks, such as the density of the network and the positionality, distribution and connectedness of ties.

Further reading

- Baek, C., Hörmann, B., Karseth, B., Pizmony-Levy, O., Sivesind, K. and Steiner-Khamsi, G. (2018) Policy learning in Norwegian school reform: a social network analysis of the 2020 incremental reform, Nordic Journal of Studies in Educational Policy, 4(1): 24–37.
- Schuster, J., Jörgens, H. and Kolleck, N. (2021) The rise of global policy networks in education: analyzing Twitter debates on inclusive education using social network analysis, Journal of Education Policy, 36(2): 211–231.

Spatial policy analysis

Spatial policy analysis is the study of imaginaries of place/space as dynamic sites for the configuration of power and the organisation, performance and negotiation of practices and identities. Rather than viewing place/space as 'backdrop, location or passive context' (Clarke, 2019, p 195), or as a territorially bounded, discrete, fixed entity lacking agency or prescribed limited agency by wider powers, spatial policy analysis encourages us to think about 'space relationally' (Massey, 2004, p 5) as historically changing products of contingent sites, practices and connections. Space/place, be it imagined through the bounded nation, the local pub or the international community, are products of the labour of boundary making, of spatialisation and spatial identities. The result, what we might call the 'container model of space' (Clarke, 2019, p 196), is the discursive product of struggles and negotiations over representations of space/place. This means that different meanings and categories of scale and scalar representations and logics – such as the 'local', 'regional', 'national' – are similarly ambiguous owing to their variability as contingent expressions for the ways in which diverse elements come together (or not) to form a provisional unity of difference we might call government or the state. Spatial policy analysis therefore represents a move away from reification/ abstraction in order to preserve a more complicated view of the fragility and emergence of things. Closely related to this is an appreciation for the open-endedness of struggles over hegemony, where power has to be continually worked for through conflict negation, resolution, negotiation or 'repeated recalibration and reinvention' (Peck and Theodore, 2015, p 25). In a radical move that avoids reducing social change to a residual effect of hegemonic projects, spatial policy analysis opens up possibilities for thinking differently and positing alternatives to the present.

This type of relational thinking introduces a topological conception of space/ place as 'enabling attention to how certain forms of reach mobilise power across space, bringing apparently "distant" agents and agencies into close contact' (Clarke, 2019, p 205). It represents a shift away from cartographic and topographical representations of space and place as bounded, homogeneous and unchanging, including 'universalising/essentialising propositions implicit in some of the evocations of the meaningfulness of place' (Massey, 2004, p 7). Space/ place, for example, offer up essential discursive resources for the mobilisation of 'people like us' and 'people like them', of outsiders and insiders, of local culture or local history. In other words, space/place constitute important signifying practices and interpretive repertoires through which 'sense-making practices' emerge (Papanastasiou, 2019, p 3). The imagining of space/place also gives rise to new ways of governing and managing populations and domains, often affectively through the appeal to place-and-space-based forms of belonging and attachment. This might include mobilising imaginaries of space/place to facilitate new modes of governing, namely the shift from government to governance, which, despite its appeal to ad hoc experimentation and democratisation of policy, develops on the condition that fields of policy transfer are 'socially and institutionally constructed' (Peck and Theodore, 2015, p 26), that is, mobilised within 'intersubjective frames of reference and institutionalised centers of authority' (p 26) that advance the strategic interests of larger powers.

At the same time, it is important not to present a diminished view of the local as (only) an instantiation of effects of larger powers occurring somewhere else. In Massey's (2004) view, these historically and culturally unique constructions should not be construed exclusively through the lens of international relations and political science literature as products of globalisation, in which there is 'a diminished understanding of the potential of local agency' (p 11). Instead, they can be viewed as time-space sensitive imaginings of difference, sameness and otherness that constitute themselves as well as actively contribute to how 'the global is constituted, invented, coordinated, produced' (Massey, 2004, p 11). The ontological-political implications of thinking relationally about space and place are therefore far-reaching: through recognising the agency of the local, as not simply a bearer or imprint of wider global-capitalist forces but as significant discursive resources for reimagining, reworking and challenging those forces, people may be mobilised to 'avail themselves of the imaginative resources [used] to reconstruct it' (Massey, 2004, p 7). Poole et al. (2020), for example, demonstrate how, despite the responsibilities of local policy makers to adhere to implementation of government-mandated policy, it is translated and recontextualised 'according to spatial dimensions such as geographic location, population density, and local school district leaders' understandings of local spatial realities' (p 124).

In the field of education policy, spatial policy analysis has played an important role in advancing our understanding of how policy emerges through spatialising practices. Gulson and Witzenberger (2022) use the example of the Australian main education technology trade show, EduTech, to show how space/place provides important discursive resources for the mobilisation of new types and sites of expertise, authority and technology – what are called 'topologies of policy' (p 146). These policy spaces, Gulson and Witzenberger (2022) argue, seek to not only 'legitimise the use of AI [artificial intelligence] within education' (p 157) but generate relations of dependency between education technology sellers and education providers in order to future-proof the continuing influence of automated education technologies on the workflow of education practitioners and administrators. Similarly, Lawn and Lingard (2002) draw on spatial policy analysis to show the multiple interacting forces that flow vertically (through transnational agenda setting and negotiation) and horizontally (through national system administrators and policy networks) to engender imaginary spaces for a Europeanisation of education policy. Lawn and Lingard (2002) draw our attention to the fragile relays 'between state and EU offices, between agencies and subcontractors, between academics and policy managers, between experts and officials, and between voluntary and public sector workers' (p 292) who, collectively, negotiate possibilities for extranational policy spaces.

Further reading

- Brenner, N. (2004) New state spaces: urban governance and the rescaling of statehood, Oxford: Oxford University Press.
- Stevenson, H., Milner, A., Winchip, E. and Hagger-Vaughan, L. (2019) Education policy and the European semester: challenging soft power in hard times, in L. Tett and M. Hamilton (eds) Resisting neoliberalism in education: local, national and transnational perspectives, Bristol: Policy Press, 211–224.

T

Temporal policy analysis

In policy studies that draw on a positivist epistemology, time is treated as an objectively existing, fixed and independent variable. Pralle (2006) exemplifies this perspective through research into how and why interest-group conflicts alter in terms of their patterns of engagement and their strategies. Pralle (2006) argues that *as time passes*, opposing groups in a conflict are more likely to move from an expansion versus containment to a direct-engagement model. DeLeo (2016) adopts a similar framing in noting that the 'imposition of time constraints can heighten conflict' (p 6). Writing of his own work, but arguably with wider resonance across positivist-informed policy studies, DeLeo (2016) describes time as 'both an important context – a frame … as well as a potential catalyst' (p 7). Nonetheless, there are limits in this framing to the malleability of time; even the tactics of 'extending deadlines or "buying time"' (DeLeo, 2016, p 16) do not move time from being an independent variable into socially constructed terrain.

There is, however, a significant literature in policy studies which, through its post-positivist epistemologies, constructs time and temporality as contextually experienced, 'institutionally structured and caught within complex webs of social networks, relations and inequalities' (Bennett and Burke, 2018, p 914). Social actors live time differentially; their experiences are mediated by hierarchising power structures including race, class and gender (Bennett and Burke, 2018). Drawing on Heidegger, Bennett and Burke (2018) argue that 'experiences of time are … intensely *relational*' (p 915, original emphasis); they are constitutive of context, social encounters and consequently of identities. Temporalities are embodied and distinctive. Lapping (2017) and Thompson and Cook (2014), drawing on Deleuze's theorisation of time, are able to go further in stating that time does not itself exist, but constitutes through synthesis a present that alone exists, and that only 'just as long as the contracted relations between the contemplated elements brought together in the assemblage' (Lapping, 2017, p 910). Synthesis of time, for Deleuze, takes three forms: synthesis of habit, of memory and of novelty. Thompson and Cook (2014) summarise habit as referring to 'gestures, movements and actions that are the synthesis of earlier events' (p 706). These gestures, events and actions are contracted 'into a (living) present' (Thompson and Cook, 2014, p 706), but in a way that is future-oriented. The synthesis of memory means that 'the pure past is the creation of a memory of that past' (Thompson and Cook, 2014, p 706), that is, the past is created after its passing. Synthesis of novelty is the only one not to concern repetition (Thompson and Cook, 2014) and opens up possibilities for new futures.

Socially constructionist conceptualisations of time and temporality position positivist framings as problematic. This is not simply a matter of epistemology;

researchers have identified a collocation of fixed-variable thinking about time with problematic normative ideas concerning life trajectories and acceptable identities, practices or bodies (Pillow, 2015; Bennett and Burke, 2018). For instance, Bennett and Burke (2018) identify the way in which meritocratic discourses in higher education reduce time to 'notions of "effective time management skills"' and their logic 'presents a rigid and linear notion of [students'] potential which privileges fixed, developmental timeframes' (p 917) or 'hegemonic timescapes' (p 918). Students who do not fit into this timescape are constructed as problems. Pillow (2015) notes a similar effect through a 2015 study of teen mothers and their relationship with the education system. In defying heteronormative expectations of the 'right time' to procreate, they are rendered 'out of time' (Pillow, 2015, p 55) by policy.

Post-positivist conceptualisations of temporality may also provide the means to remedy or mitigate some of these identified issues. For instance, Pillow (2015) develops Halberstam's notion of queer time to disrupt the heteronormative logic of what is termed the conventional temporality in policy studies. Queer time comes from queer theory (see entry on 'Queer policy analysis') and seeks to disrupt the normalising discourses that sustain inequitable power relations. It achieves this by centring knowledge produced by and for the marginalised in ways that collapse accepted categories and assumptions. Queer time enables Pillow (2015) to ask, 'how can we work from the knowings of the teen pregnant body without wanting to fix this body and assign this body in time?' (p 61). Thompson and Cook (2014) use Deleuze's conceptualisation of time in order to identify and theorise a key problem with contemporary education policy making, that superficially new interventions reconstruct the problems of the past repeatedly and also the failings of past policies.

Further reading

- Deleuze, G. (1994) Difference, repetition, New York: Columbia University Press.
- Hayes, A. and Findlow, S. (2020) The role of time in policymaking: a Bahraini model of higher education competition, Critical Studies in Education, 61(2): 180–194.

Think tank

Think tanks operationalise and normalise the politicisation of research evidence (Kauko, 2022), since while an explicit political or ideological agenda is not a definitional criterion of think tanks, they do all aim to have political *impact*. Pautz (2011) defines think tanks beyond this aim as being non-governmental institutions, with no formal authority to make decisions, but which instead engage in advocacy, the development and maintenance of policy networks and the provision of research-based expertise to policy makers. Ball and Exley (2010) view think tanks as more than simply network developers and maintainers, however. For Ball and Exley (2010), think tanks are a key constituent feature of those networks and serve to operationalise them. The rise of these networks in policy making and governance exemplifies a shift in how policy gets done, as well as 'in the nature of the state' (Ball and Exley, 2010, p 151). Specifically, policy networks instantiate 'the emergence of new state modalities, with a shift away from government towards forms of polycentric governance, where policy is produced through multiple agencies and … sites of discourse generation' (Ball and Exley, 2010, p 151). From this perspective, think tanks are one constituent agency of many, whose significance lies as much in their relationship with other 'nodes' (Ball and Exley, 2010, p 152) in the policy network as in what they themselves may or may not do. Following this argument, the importance of Pautz's (2011) contested insistence that think tanks do not lobby is dissolved since think tanks are tightly imbricated with other policy actors who do lobby. Further, Ball and Exley (2010) note that the policy entrepreneurs within these networks are highly mobile, moving from think tank to government to academia. In this sense, think tanks are 'at least to some degree [composed of] "insiders" compared with those firmly outside the policy loop' (Ball and Exley, 2010, p 154). These observations in effect refute Pautz's claims regarding think tanks' externality and independence.

Think tanks' objective of having political impact is largely and increasingly achieved at the time of writing. Ball and Exley (2010) and Kauko (2022) both identify evidence of the multiple direct and indirect ways in which think tanks successfully competed with other sources of policy influence, such as 'local authorities, teaching unions and the civil service, and academia' (Ball and Exley, 2010, p 152) to provide an evidence base for the academy programme in England in the early 2000s. This shift is largely attributable to successive governments' privileging think tanks over other sources of knowledge. Justifications range from the slow speed at which they complained that academia functions (Kauko, 2022), or its over-specialisation in subjects, to the so-called inertia and conformism of the civil service (Ball and Exley, 2010).

Many think tanks operate supranationally as key actors in the Global Education Reform Movement (GERM), where they advocate and provide evidence for GERM-associated policies regarding, for instance, the so-called autonomy of schools and their leaders, accountability regimes and the standards agenda. A consequence of the networked nature of think tanks is that they are susceptible to capture by corporate interests, hence their important role in legitimising the movement and insertion of GERM-related policies. Think tanks are able to frame their inquiries around a 'what-works' paradigm whose seductive objectiveness and simplicity may well produce policy-ready answers, but which do not address the complex interplay of interests and context that universities are more likely to bring to bear through their examinations (Auld and Morris, 2016). The way in which many think tanks produce these simplified and politicised policy solutions follows a pattern, which serves to reinforce the think tanks' reputation, strengthen their argument through restricting the analytical focus and undermine alternative perspectives. The final identification of so-called 'best practices' often reflects nothing more than self-imposed methodological flaws and prior beliefs (Auld and Morris, 2016).

Arguments have been advanced that the role of think tanks extends beyond reproducing the legitimacy for contemporaneously hegemonic projects, such as GERM. Their role additionally might involve 'chang[ing] the political climate so that in time the proposed policies would come to be seen as logical and appropriate' (Haughton and Allmendinger, 2015, p 1682). Think tanks are therefore particularly consequential 'in the rare circumstances when the hegemonic status of a "paradigm" such as Keynesianism or monetarism falters' (Pautz, 2011, p 427). In this sense, think tanks may act as policy entrepreneurs who seek to establish 'new programmatic ideas' (Verger, 2012, p 111) or a discursive reframing of the social world into a space composed of new problems and tailored solutions. Neoliberalism's successor is, in this reading, liable to be currently extant and contained in fringe think tanks' brochures and pamphlets, just as the Black Papers (see Bantock, 1977) set out the agenda for neoliberalism in the dying days of welfarism in the UK.

Further reading

- Stahl, J. (2016) Right moves: The conservative think tank in American political culture since 1945, Chapel Hill: The University of North Carolina Press.
- Williamson, B. (2021) Psychodata: disassembling the psychological, economic, and statistical infrastructure of 'social-emotional learning', Journal of Education Policy, 36(1): 129–154.

Topology

Increasingly, education policy scholars at the time of writing are turning their attention to adopting topology as a conceptual and methodological lens for theorising and empirically documenting education policy making as topological. The relevance of topology to studies of education policy is in part related to the observation that policy making is no longer restricted to, and therefore the exclusive product of, power relations and negotiations occurring within nationally confined borders. As Simon et al (2009) observe, methodological statism and nationalism as units of analysis assume 'a fixed linkage between government and territory in a single nation' (p 38). The rise of trade liberalisation, transnational capital accumulation and technologically driven social connectivity across the globe since the 1990s implies something different, however, namely that politics and authority can no longer be studied from a single vantage point or isolated entity such as the nation-state or government. The turn to 'regionalisation', 'Europeanisation' and 'globalisation' as units and methods of analysis for the study of policy making helps to better situate these processes within multi-causal and multi-directional relations as translocal, mobile and networked (Ramirez et al, 2016; Robertson, 2016). In other words, policy making is better understood as co-constructed by a diverse array of actors (human and non-human) spanning multiple scales and levels of influence flowing between and through the local and the global, with the effect that policy is mobile as well as morphs on the move. Thus, topology functions as both empirically based observations of the nature of globalised education policy marked by networking and relationality (Gulson et al, 2017) and as epistemological and methodological propositions for situating the study of these conditions.

Topological thinking can be contrasted with topographical understandings of society and culture. This distinction is well captured by Harvey (2012): '[i]n topographical mapping, the boundaries of state power appear as commensurate with a clearly defined territorial boundary, and such categorical mappings are echoed in the spatially nested structures of administrative division' (p 77). Topologisation, on the other hand, draws attention to multiple new spatial figures where borders 'do not coincide with the edges of a demarcated territory, and where it is the mutable quality of relations that determines distance and proximity, rather than a singular and absolute measure' (Harvey, 2012, pp 77–78). Thus, topological culture, economy and politics are marked by 'spatio-temporal continuities' (Lury et al, 2012) and function not through 'essential properties, such as archetypes, values or norms, or regional location' (Lury et al, 2012, p 5) but by engendering and multiplying relations, connectedness and continuity among disparate entities. The topological characteristics of space and time mean that they are emergent rather than fixed external frameworks. Distant points, such as entities or events, can become proximal categorically as well as spatially and temporally. Thus, discontinuities may be turned into continuities by establishing equivalences or similitudes through commensurate qualities of categorising and different forms of visualisation.

To this end, Lingard et al (2014) have illustrated how metrics, models, calculations and comparisons, which compose modern regimes of education governance, facilitate the topological turn in politics with a focus on conceptions of 'what is near or connected and what is distant or disconnected' (p 713). New data infrastructures in particular 'create and sustain dynamic political and moral spaces' that are essential for understanding the topological becoming of education processes and events (Lingard et al, 2014, p 713). Similarly, digitalisation enables novel connections across spaces, creating possibilities for power to operate through and across territories by establishing (novel) similarities or marking contrasts. These technologies and infrastructures simultaneously create new possibilities for steering and the exercise of power over others at great distances and across multiple scales, the types of steering that may have previously been considered beyond (topographical) reach (Lewis et al, 2015). The Organisation for Economic Co-operation and Development, for example, has successfully extended the influence of its policies through discourses and instruments such as rankings and reports. Gulson and Sellar (2019) focus on the space-making practices of these initiatives, in particular, the topological potential of data infrastructures to create new power topologies in education through 'physical manifestations of data in education spaces (e.g. data visualisations); the introduction of a new generation of information management systems and education software; rapidly increasing capacities for data analysis; and bringing in new actors to provide the technical expertise required to develop and maintain the infrastructure' (p 357).

Adopting the analytic of topology, Saari (2022) adds to this literature by focusing on education policies that envision creative learning environments and new school architectures, albeit taking a slightly different approach by capitalising on the notion of 'topological reflexivity' to capture those modes of thinking and acting upon policies designed to enhance topological configurations. In the case of Saari's (2022) study, topological reflexivity can be considered a process that is at once descriptive and prescriptive since it categorises capital or labour as 'mobile' while simultaneously normalising these categorisations as 'domestic' or 'institutional', thus helping to embed them within organisations as familiar logics and practices. Saari (2022) also notes the ways in which topological reflexivity is performed and enabled through affective registers that function to incite behaviour change.

Further reading

- Decuypere, M., Hartong, S. and van de Oudeweetering, K. (2022) Introduction—space-and time-making in education: towards a topological lens, European Educational Research Journal, 21(6): 871–882.
- Hartong, S. (2018) Towards a topological re-assemblage of education policy? Observing the implementation of performance data infrastructures and 'centers of calculation' in Germany, Globalisation, Societies and Education, 16(1): 134–150.

Transfer

The concept of 'educational transfer' is central to comparative and international education studies of the movement of ideas, actors, projects, technologies and practices through international and global spaces. This includes an empirical focus on the various activities and networks that come together (or not) to support their circulation and recontextualisation at multiple levels and scales as well as across different sectors (for example, from the criminal justice system to education, see Taylor, 2018). Historically, debates on educational transfer first emerged in fields of educational administration where the focus concerned normative and logistical arguments centred around whether or not policy transfer across national borders and education systems was possible and even desirable. Opinions on this issue were varied among different education reformers and researchers at the time, with some insisting that education policy and practice can be viewed as acontextual and acultural, and therefore open to flexible transfer to other contexts. This view of education policy and practice as acontextual and acultural can be traced to a set of core technocratic beliefs and political and economic ambitions that envisage education systems across the globe as similar, interchangeable structures of relations and practices that can be adapted to serve and benefit from a universal (scientific) problem-solving rationality. This universal perspective of education development largely dominates the worldviews of international, intergovernmental organisations like the World Bank and the Organisation for Economic Co-operation and Development who forecast future education challenges on the basis of certain teleologies (that education should follow an indefinite growth model borrowed from economic theory), scientific precepts (that the value of education can be measured, tested and verified using meta-analysis and deductive logic) and metaphysical ideations (that the purpose of education is intimately connected with employability and job flexibility, skills acquisition and positional advantage and mobility in changing labour markets). Similar perspectives can also be traced to some comparative education researchers who use applied science approaches to examine the development of educational institutions and systems as technical achievements or failures of output controls and quality improvement instruments.

In contrast to the applied scientific approach to policy transfer described previously, there is an interpretive strand of comparative and international education that borrows from critical realist, constructivist and other critical policy approaches to empirically trace the outcomes of policy transfer as overdetermined by the dynamics of macro convergence and microvariation trends. In this framing, policy transfer is understood to occur through context-specific path dependencies and geopolitical accommodations and translations. The dynamics of these processes are described using a variety of concepts, including diffusion, imposition and lesson drawing, all of which connote explicit and implicit mechanisms of transfer. In the same interpretive tradition, some education researchers distinguish between models of soft transfer (where policy transfer is enabled through dissemination, technical assistance and provision of expertise) and hard transfer (where policy transfer develops on the basis of coercion, sanctions and loan conditionalities).

Marxist dependency theory, for example, lends itself to a macro-level theory of hard transfer since it approaches policy transfer as developing through imposition and domination, such as mechanisms of imperialism, colonialism and the perpetual inequality of geopolitical power relations and wealth. Similarly, neo-institutionalist theories focus on macro-level convergence theories to explain policy transfer as the diffusion of a common world educational culture. In both cases, macro-level perspectives are used to explain policy transfer through a focus on the dominating character of certain socio-political and cultural structures and the logic of valorisation implicit to these structures, be it private sector management, profit-extraction, marketisation and/or commercialisation. In contrast, micro-level perspectives shift the focus towards explaining policy transfer through the dynamic interactions between actors operating within specific path dependencies, therefore highlighting those 'institutional orders and social relations outside the immediate logic of valorisation [that] typically have their own values and norms, bases of social inclusion or exclusion, their own forms of structured conflict' (Jessop, 2016, p 11). Some approaches also combine macro- and micro-levels of analysis, such as self-referential social systems theory and critical realist approaches that use systems theory to understand the different kinds of institutional dynamics (resources, capacity and frameworks) that 'create the incentives (or disincentives) for the effective implementation of technical solutions' (Gillies, 2010, p 37).

Micro theories of policy transfer therefore focus on the incentives (and disincentives), culturally and politically understood, that drive the adoption, transformation, hybridisation or rejection of wider globally circulating discourses, with a focus on concepts of 'educational borrowing and lending' and 'externalisation'. For instance, externalisation and sociologic refer to a system's intra-societal reflection processes which are thought to produce supplementary meanings that then transform exogenous models, ideas or catchwords into more familiar terms, thus contributing to policy transfer but also changing the object of transfer along the way. These intra-societal reflection processes, which can be applied to understandings of different levels and scales of organisation from the individual schools to the nation-state, rely on concepts of diffusion, imposition and lesson drawing to study different aspects of selectivity and learning among actors in these networks and their diverse confrontations with and accommodations of wider globally circulating discourses. Lesson drawing, for example, is used to explain any deliberate effort at policy transfer on the part of actors, yet these accommodations are always understood in relation to motive, interests and incentive. Understood in another way, while globally diffuse patterns of governance may be evidenced across multiple countries, it is important to understand the contingency of social formations and structurations as unique products of disparate motives and interests (Wilkins et al, 2024).

Further reading

- Cowen, R. (2009) The transfer, translation and transformation of educational processes: and their shape-shifting?, Comparative Education, 45(3): 315–327.
- Silova, I., Rappleye, J. and Auld, E. (2020) Beyond the western horizon: rethinking education, values, and policy transfer, in G. Fan and T. Popkewitz (eds) Handbook of education policy studies, Singapore: Springer, 3–29.

Translation

Despite strong evidence of policy convergence in the way that many education systems across the globe govern themselves using comparative-competitive frameworks, test-based accountabilities and consumer logics, pointing to the consolidation of what Mundy et al (2016) call 'new global policy spaces for education' (p 2), research on policy translation highlights the complicated distribution and assemblage of global patterns of rule in the context of geopolitically sensitive networks, connections and flows (Silova, 2012; Beech and Artopoulos, 2016; Wilkins et al, 2019, 2024). Translation studies of policy therefore document the role of values systems, political–administrative structures, and historical or cultural traditions and commitments as sensitising framings through which global patterns of rule are reorganised to complement the novel arrangement of different geopolitical settlements. While translation approaches to policy studies go beyond a concern with linguistic translation as function or outcome of policy transfer and implementation, practices of translation can be broadly conceptualised as discursive. Clarke et al (2015), for example, describe policy translation as linguistic practices in the sense that it involves rendering contentious political problems into matters of technical proficiency or efficiency, in effect subjugating politics to problem-solving sciences so they are more amenable to capture by statistical mapping and prediction, intervention and even control. These are strategies of 'depoliticisation', according to Clarke (2008), that work to 'conceal the problems and conflicts of politics behind an appeal to forms of knowledge and varieties of technical expertise' (p 142).

While language plays a central role in policy translation, it is not sufficient to making policy move. The study of policy as translation is also about tracing the material-discursive labour of moving policy. This may include a focus on the mundane, quotidian practices through which policy articulation functions as a reflex of the situated commitments and priorities of different epistemic communities, organisations and networks. Policy translation therefore has as its analytical and empirical focus the labour of socially situated actors engaged in everyday dilemmas of grafting and holding together disparate elements to forge new hegemonic alignments and forms of agency. As Li (2007) observes, 'what appears to be rational landscape design or "management" is the serendipitous outcome of everyday practices that have quite disparate motives' (p 13). To this end, the notion of translation is sometimes used synonymously with enactment or recontextualisation. These concepts are mobilised to achieve different kinds of analytical work but principally are united by their shared refusal of a view of policy transfer as a linear, smooth process of transplantation from one point to another. They also problematise binary understandings of transfer, resulting, for instance, in either acceptance of or resistance to policy. Translation, on the contrary, highlights the contextual, changing and conflictual nature of policy movement as 'transformation, negotiation, and enactment' and as a 'politically infused process of dislocation and displacement' (Lendvai and Stubbs, 2009, p 677). On this description, studies of policy translation complement a poststructural, relational framing of power 'where power is understood as a temporal, fluid and interactive process, working through distortions, displacement and transformation resulting in a constant inscription and re-inscription of power relations' (Lendvai and Stubbs, 2009, pp 676–677). The focus on relationality within studies of policy translation also has implications for theorisation of actors whose identities are not understood to prefigure translation but rather emerge as co-productions of policy processes.

The translation approach can be traced to the sociology of translation tradition (Callon, 1986), in particular Latour's (1986) translation model of power which offers an alternative to the diffusion or networked model of power as distribution (see entry on 'Diffusion'). Here, Latour's (1986) translation model assumes that power is a consequence of a collective action as it relies on an intense activity of enrolling and mobilising actors as the bearers and performers of various roles and actions. Translation, in other words, precedes the kinds of reifications of power and resultant formations found in abstractions such as networks, structures or systems. Translation is, rather, the study of the discursive-material labour of fixing, fitting and arranging conditions in ways that allow relations of power and their abstractions to take hold and endure. One detailed programme of action for this analysis is presented by Grimaldi and Barzanò (2014) who, drawing on Callon (1986), map how global policy ideas of merit are assembled and re-assembled through socio-material practices.

Further reading

- Dickhaus, B. (2010) The selectivity of translation: accountability regimes in Chilean and South African higher education, Globalisation, Societies and Education, 8(2): 257–268.
- Wilkins, A., Collet-Sabé, J., Gobby, B. and Hangartner, J. (2019) Translations of new public management: a decentred approach to school governance in four OECD countries, Globalisation, Societies and Education, 17(2): 147–160.

U

Unbundling

Powered by the growth of for-profit activities, marketisation, massification and a perceived gap between higher education degrees and the demands of an ever-changing labour market, unbundling is a process of disentanglement based on the notion that higher education teaching, administration and management are akin to commercial services or products that can be divided or combined in different ways. McCowan (2017, p 736) distinguishes between two types of unbundling. The first type of unbundling occurs through the disaggregation of services or products that were previously delivered or sold together. The second type of unbundling refers to a 'no-frills' model where a product is stripped of its non-essential parts so it can be acquired by (and integrated into) other delivery forms and services. Advocates of unbundling view these developments as not only desirable but inevitable given the diverse needs and changing aspirations of individuals, the requirements to make products and services more accessible to a wider range of users, and the pressures on service providers to make their products and delivery mechanisms more cost-efficient and effective. Critics, however, argue that unbundling not only transforms but undermines the values, functions and modes of interaction traditionally performed by higher education institutions and their workers. From this perspective, unbundling is the unravelling of traditional forms of higher education, albeit affecting higher education systems across the globe at different rates and scales through varying intensities and differential effects (McCowan, 2017; Ivancheva et al, 2020).

There are various examples of unbundling across different phases and sectors of education, albeit higher education at the time of writing has emerged as the main site for its innovation and dissemination. A key focus for researchers working this area is the realisation, application and effects of unbundling on curriculum, the academic profession, policy reform, and interactions between public and private institutions and actors (Ivancheva et al, 2020). More concrete examples include the growing division between professionals and organisations involved in the design, delivery or assessment of courses (for example, Massive Open Online Courses; the introduction of low-cost degree courses; the outsourcing of administrative, information and communication technology, and managerial tasks to sub-contractors; the growth of teaching-only institutions; the separation of teaching from research; the expansion of distance education and multi-campus universities; and the emergence of new divisions of labour among academic and non-academic personnel). Regarding the latter, Macfarlane (2011) observes that unbundling displaces the figure of the 'all-round academic' traditionally charged with holistic integration of research and teaching and design and delivery of pedagogical activity from content to assessment. These developments in the recalibration of academic work are paralleled by the rise of 'para-academics' (Macfarlane, 2011), such as skills advisors, tutors or learning technologists, all of whom are responsible for disentangled, distributed tasks.

For McCowan (2017), unbundling places new demands on higher education institutions to organise themselves as a response to values and preferences for personalisation and individual choice, as well as market-driven determinations of short-term customer orientation and satisfaction. Unbundling is typically rationalised on the grounds that service providers must make strides towards redressing the wider inequalities in society that make it disproportionately more difficult, in some cases financially impossible, for some people to access educational opportunities, thus intensifying demands and legitimacy for provision of low-cost degrees and easy-to-access and participate in individual courses. At the same time, unbundling not only risks falling short of these aims but reproducing wider systemic inequalities. This is because, depending on the context, low-cost courses or degrees can receive little actual recognition by employers despite the promise of improved employability. In terms of functions, one of the main consequences of unbundling includes the disaggregation and fragmentation of degree programmes and the hollowing out of a holistic conception of learning and knowledge. Learning delivered through short-term, individually selected, competence-oriented courses are predominantly transmission-based and mono-directional. In this way, unbundling recalibrates the practices of curriculum, pedagogy and learning in profound ways. Moreover, by focusing on core functions such as basic instruction, unbundling may devalue other central functions such as group-based and mutual learning, collaboration and critical arguing and thinking. These fundamental changes to the interactive component of education, considered by many to be essential to learning, not only make education more amenable to commercial (re)packing and digitalisation but, for some, represent the integration of education within the wider demands of society. McCowan (2017), for example, uses the term 'hyperporosity' to describe the now fuzzy boundary between education and society and the opportunities it creates for external actors, such as governments and industry, to influence higher education.

The effects of unbundling are still ongoing and under investigation as different higher education institutions and sectors across the globe come under increased pressure to subsidise their finances through improved commercialisation, platformisation and digital repacking and delivery of services. Increasingly, too, education researchers are turning their attention to processes of rebundling, such as integration between mentoring and employer engagement or teaching and administrative duties. It can be speculated that universities that perform well in international higher education rankings might enjoy more leverage as a result and retain their traditional bundled structures and practices, leading to new national and global divisions between institutions. Ivancheva et al (2020) therefore call on researchers to study the meaning-making practices of actors involved in unbundling processes and how the ongoing digitalisation and platformisation of higher education further solidify these trends in the marketisation of higher education and its subsumption to the logic of capital.

Further reading

- Cliff, A., Walji, S., Mogliacci, R.J., Morris, N. and Ivancheva, M. (2022) Unbundling and higher education curriculum: a cultural-historical activity theory view of process, Teaching in Higher Education, 27(2): 217–232.
- Komljenovic, J. (2019) Making higher education markets: trust-building strategies of private companies to enter the public sector, Higher Education, 78(1): 51–66.

V

Visual methods

Visual methods and visual analysis refer to tools and technologies used for generating and analysing data about the social world. Typically, visual methods make use of non-verbal modes of representation and/communication in order to supplement or compensate for traditional verbal or text-based approaches to data generation and sense making. Visual methods make use of a wide range of digital and non-digital artefacts to generate data about the social world, including maps, diagrams, photographs, video footage, collage and drawings (Radley and Taylor, 2003; Copeland and Agosto, 2012; Wilkins, 2012). Visual methods such as photo elicitation, auto-photography and participatory mapping are therefore particularly useful in creative and arts-based research and learning but also when working with research participants who, for whatever reason, cannot engage in conventional forms of data generation which rely on speech or written forms of communication. Through enabling people to communicate their perspectives and experiences through visual forms of representation, visual methods help to generate new knowledge and forms of meaning making, especially among 'hard to reach' groups (Delgado, 2015). In some instances, visual methods have been used to great effect as a supplement to interviews as a way to prompt memory and reduce misunderstandings between interviewer and interviewee (Harper, 2002). Central to visual methods, however, is an appreciation for the context in which visual artefacts of any description (maps, photographs, drawings) are produced, with the implication that visual artefacts cannot be read as neutral or unmediated reflections of 'objective truth' but rather emerge through an interpretive framework made possible by the producer and viewer.

In the 20th century, visual anthropologists primarily used documentary photography and film as supplementary artefacts for supporting empirical claims about the nature of the social world (Edwards, 1992), in what can be described as 'realist ethnography'. In the 1970s and 1980s, these documentary and realist traditions of early visual methods came to be displaced by postmodernist, critical theory and cultural studies perspectives and concerns about the discursive composition and effects of the visual image, specifically its social and political function as a vehicle for affirming, contesting and concealing claims to power and ideology. This deconstructive approach to visual analysis, what might be termed a visual culture approach, emphasised the polysemic nature of visual images, namely the idea that visual images have the capacity to communicate multiple meanings depending on the situated context of the viewer. The implication here is 'that the recipient [of the image is also] a co-creator of it' (Eagleton, 2003, p 96). This led to a burgeoning, and now popular, interest in the wider social and political context in which visual images are produced, disseminated and consumed (Pink, 2005).

Visual methods have been used by education researchers to study the movement and translation of global education policy, with a unique focus on the affective and discursive role of the visual and of mediatisation more generally as a central component to policy dissemination and policy translation. Adhikary et al (2018), for example, observe how Teach for Bangladesh (TfB), a non-government organisation and offshoot of Teach for All/America, makes strategic use of social media, videos and photos to enable local institutionalisation of globally circulating policy discourses aimed at 'vernacularising' or translating policy initiatives borrowed from TfB through the provision of 'cosmopolitan, globally glamorous, emotionally propulsive' (p 655) ideas and perspectives, in effect making them attractive and meaningful to specific local audiences as potential customers of their graduate programme. In a similar vein, Berkovich and Benoliel (2019) employ a visual discourse analysis to document the visual representational practices of the Organisation for Economic Co-operation and Development (OECD) to consider 'representations of teaching and teachers achieved by the visual resources used in OECD covers' (p 133). Berkovich and Benoliel (2019) conclude that, despite the appeal to liberal discourses of racial and gender diversity, 'the [visual] organisation actually holds a conservative view of gender roles and has an Eurocentrism/ Whiteness bias' (p 142). Decuypere and Landri (2021) offer up similar analytical work albeit through a visual digital analysis with a focus on the 'platformisation' of European educational spaces made possible by websites. Here Decuypere and Landri (2021) reflect on the capacity of websites to articulate and combine various types of information (numbers, measures, recommendations) through the provision of online interactive visualisation tools, thus highlighting these websites as normative spaces and assemblages that perform specific operations that include 'co-constructing policy spaces and consequential (popularised) spaces of action' (p 867).

Adopting a 'videological analysis', Koh (2009, p 294) demonstrates how Singaporean education policy texts are visually mediated through televisual images. Focusing on one specific documentary produced in Singapore in 2000, Learning Journeys, and the education policy message upon which it is based, 'Thinking Schools, Learning Nation' (TSLN), Koh (2009) points to the significance of mediatisation to imposing 'a top-down, selected perspective of how "TSLN" policy is realised at the ground' (p 294). Combining a policy assemblage approach with visual network analysis, Lunde and Ottesen (2021) use the open-source platform Gephi to build and analyse a visualisation of the relationships between policy actors as nodes in a network or assemblage, as imagined in two key policy documents from Ireland and Norway. The benefit of this visual network analysis is it allows Lunde and Ottesen (2021) to colour-code regions according to the priorities for policy actors set out in these documents, thus enabling Lunde and Ottesen (2021) to capture visually how some actors are able to partake in multiple practices given their position at the interface of different regions and their 'potential to steer the educational direction to enhance multiple governance mechanisms at once, such as assessment and evaluation' (p 208).

Further reading

- Decuypere, M. (2016) Diagrams of Europeanization: European education governance in the digital age, Journal of Education Policy, 31(6): 851–872.
- Nguyen, X.T. and Mitchell, C. (2012) On the use of visual methodologies in educational policy research, South African Journal of Education, 32(4): 479–493.

W

World culture theory

Central to world culture theory (sometimes called world polity theory, world systems theory or world system analysis) is the claim that the development and emergence of education systems, policies and practices within nation-states is isomorphic and can be explained by wider systemic changes occurring at the international and global level where 'rationalised myths' (Silova and Brehm, 2015, p 12) perpetuated by world culture scripts/models come to bear upon and influence national and subnational policy contexts. In this sense, world culture theorists are less concerned with the role of unique path tendencies, organisational logics and value systems to the formation of education systems, nor do they take seriously the context-sensitive, micro-political strategies through which national policy frameworks are adapted in the context of regional and local developments and the contradictions and tensions flowing from these untidy convergences and problematic alignments. Instead, world culture theorists adopt the lens of methodological globalism (or 'regionalisation' and 'Europeanisation') to locate and explain the development of education systems according to trends considered to be generalisable and evidence of policy borrowing and policy transfer.

However, in order for a country to be amenable to statistical capture within this model of generalisation, it must have 'already committed itself to the modern nation-state institutional apparatus' (Rappleye, 2015, p 59) and therefore modelled itself according to a meta-policy or globally circulating discourse shared by other countries, that is, 'world models [that] are a derivative of the dominant global position of the West' (Rappleye, 2015, p 66). One implication of this is that world culture theory is often accused of normative commitments to epistemic communities and organisations originating in the Global North, giving rise to postcolonial critiques of the Eurocentrism of world culture theory (see Takayama, 2015). This might include a narrow technical focus on using metrics, performance indicators and output measurements to calculate teaching quality, school management, inputs and infrastructure, and learner preparation. In turn, the adoption of these policy instruments makes it possible for schools and school systems to be located within relations of equivalence where they are made to appear to be comparable and commensurate with each other. World culture theory also suggests that the spread of meta-policy evidenced by comparable changes in the configuration of education systems across the world is an indication of 'consensus over shared meaning' (Meyer et al, 1997, p 169). The assumptions here are of policy enactment as mimetic processes. Worse, it produces an account that 'denies agency and reflective action within civil society' (Silova and Brehm, 2015, p 10).

Critics point out that world culture theory lacks a context-sensitive appreciation for the resilience and capacity of nation-states to resist and transform global policy tendencies, either through refusal or repackaging and rearticulation through the 'inherited institutional landscape' (Brenner et al, 2010, p 185) of national and subnational spaces and political projects. This does not mean adopting a position that assumes 'a fixed linkage between government and territory in a single nation' (Simon et al, 2009, p 38), since doing so would sidestep important engagements with the questions of the globalisation of education policy in favour of upholding presumptions about the structural coherence and determination of education policy at the national and subnational level. Instead, it means emphasising the unevenness and variegation of global education policy through a focus on the role of intermediating actors, networks and projects in the formation of global patterns of education governance, specifically the ways in which policy 'moves' and 'travels' and comes to be revised and inflected within unique historical and geopolitical settings (Wilkins et al, 2024). Closely related to this is the idea that any evidence of policy convergence may only be a form of window dressing, 'thus leading to no real "adoption" and thus little substantive change in social and educational conditions' (Rappleye, 2015, p 66). Moreover, through attributing importance to the epistemic work of international organisations as the key movers for social change, world culture theory assumes 'a rationalised culture in which progress is actively sought' (Stromquist, 2015, p 130).

In this sense, world culture theory may be accused of perpetuating and legitimising the norm that certain world models are hegemonic and omnipresent or even omnipotent – what Silova and Brehm (2015) call the 'telos of world of culture theory' (p 10). Moreover, since it assumes a degree of shared meaning or sense making among those who take up these policies, 'the enactment of a policy text is also read de facto as something enacted consensually' (Rappleye, 2015, p 78), in effect undermining a view of policy worlds as the outcome of political influence, agitation, coercion or control. By the same token, developmentalist and conflict theories have been criticised for failing to explain the success of global hegemonic projects as world models or world polity in the management of national education systems. Some world cultural theorists, however, adopt the concept of 'discourse coalitions' (Schriewer, 2000, p 73) to explain such phenomena in terms of the selection, retention and combination (or co-articulation) of power struggles and ideologies to secure hegemony.

More recently, however, world culture theorists have moved beyond some of the functionalist, reductionist language that characterised earlier work to adopt a 'political-realist orientation' and dialectical approach that combines macro-phenomenology with neo-institutionalism to acknowledge that 'the relative influence of culture, politics and economics, for example, is to investigate their interaction within ongoing social conflicts over the goals, structures, workings and outcomes of education systems' (Griffiths and Arnove, 2015, p 103). This turn to dynamic concepts of friction, translation, adoption and appropriation includes a sharper focus on the complicated distribution and diffusion of patterns of global education governance to take account of the 'on-going processes of morphing' (Schulte, 2012, p 475) that produce comparable, yet uneven and untidy developments of similar world culture models. On the other hand, some researchers claim that recent iterations of world culture theory, with its emphasis on 'scientific' methodology and positivist language to explain (mostly) neoliberal projects (Silova and Brehm, 2015), fails to underscore the fragility of such projects and therefore the possibilities for alternative models.

Further reading

- Ramirez, F.O. (2012) The world society perspective: concepts, assumptions, and strategies. Comparative Education, 48(4): 423–439.
- Sobe, N.W. (2015) All that is global is not world culture: accountability systems and educational apparatuses, Globalisation, Societies and Education, 13(1): 135–148.

References

Adams, B.E. (2020) Decentralization and policy experimentation in education: the consequences of enhancing local autonomy in California, Publius: The Journal of Federalism, 50(1): 30–54.

Adams, P. (2016) Education policy: explaining, framing and forming, Journal of Education Policy, 31(3): 290–307.

Addey, C. and Piattoeva, N. (eds) (2022) Intimate accounts of education policy research: the practice of methods, London: Routledge.

Adhikary, R.W. and Lingard, B. (2017) A critical policy analysis of 'Teach for Bangladesh': a travelling policy touches down, Comparative Education, 54(2): 181–202.

Adhikary, R.W., Lingard, B. and Hardy, I. (2018) A critical examination of Teach for Bangladesh's Facebook page: 'social-mediatisation' of global education reforms in the 'post-truth' era, Journal of Education Policy, 33(5): 632–661.

Ahmed, S. (2004a) The cultural politics of emotion, New York: Routledge.

Ahmed, S. (2004b) Affective economies, Social Text, 22(2): 117–139.

Aikens, K., McKenzie, M. and Vaughter, P. (2016) Environmental and sustainability education policy research: a systematic review of methodological and thematic trends, Environmental Education Research, 22(3): 333–359.

Alasuutari, P. (2015) The discursive side of new institutionalism, Cultural Sociology, 9(2): 162–184.

Alasuutari, P. and Qadir, A. (2019) Epistemic governance: social change in the modern world, Cham: Palgrave Macmillan.

Amiel, M., Yemini, M. and Kolleck, N. (2022) Questioning the rhetoric: a critical analysis of intergovernmental organisations' entrepreneurship education policy, European Educational Research Journal, 21(5): 756–777.

Anderson, B. (1991) Imagined communities: Reflections on the origin and spread of nationalism. London: Verso.

Anderson, B. and McFarlane, C. (2011) Assemblage and geography, Area, 43(2): 124–127.

Anderson, K.T. and Holloway, J. (2020) Discourse analysis as theory, method, and epistemology in studies of education policy, Journal of Education Policy, 35(2): 188–221.

Andrews, M. (2007) Exploring cross-cultural boundaries, in D.J. Clandinin (ed) Handbook of narrative inquiry: mapping a methodology, Thousand Oaks: SAGE, 489–511.

Appadurai, A. (1996) Modernity at large: cultural dimensions of globalization, Minneapolis: University of Minnesota Press.

Apple, M.W. (2013) Can education change society?, New York and Abingdon: Routledge.

Archer, M.S. (1984) Social origins of educational systems, London: SAGE.

Arendt, H. (1958) The human condition (2nd edn), Chicago: University of Chicago Press.

Auld, E. and Morris, P. (2016) PISA, policy and persuasion: translating complex conditions into education 'best practice', Comparative Education, 52(2): 202–229.

Avelar, M., Nikita, D.P. and Ball, S.J. (2018) Education policy networks and spaces of 'meetingness': a network ethnography of a Brazilian seminar, in A. Verger, M. Novelli and H.K. Altinyelken (eds) Global education policy and international development: new agendas, issues and policies, London: Bloomsbury Academic, 55–57.

Bacchi, C. (1999) Women, policy and politics: the construction of policy problems, London: SAGE.

Bacchi, C. (2000) Policy as discourse: what does it mean? Where does it get us?, Discourse: Studies in the Cultural Politics of Education, 21(1): 45–57.

Bacchi, C. (2012) Why study problematizations? Making politics visible, Open Journal of Political Science, 2(1): 1–8.

Bacchi, C. (2016) Problematizations in health policy: questioning how 'problems' are constituted in policies, SAGE Open, 6(2).

Bacchi, C. and Goodwin, S. (2016) Poststructural policy analysis: a guide to practice, New York: Springer Nature.

Bailey, P.L.J. (2013) The policy dispositif: historical formation and method, Journal of Education Policy, 28(6): 807–827.

Bailey, P.L.J. (2015) Consultants of conduct: new actors, new knowledges and new 'resilient' subjectivities in the governing of the teacher, Journal of Educational Administration and History, 47(3): 232–250.

Baiocchi, G., Graizbord, D. and Rodríguez-Muñiz, M. (2013) Actor-network theory and the ethnographic imagination: an exercise in translation, Qualitative Sociology, 36(4): 323–341.

Bajenova, T. (2019) Rescaling expertise in EU policy-making: European think tanks and their reliance on symbolic, political and network capital, Globalisation, Societies and Education, 17(1): 61–77.

Baker, T. and McGuirk, P. (2017) Assemblage thinking as methodology: commitments and practices for critical policy research, Territory, Politics, Governance, 5(4): 425–442.

Ball, S.J. (1990) Politics and policy making in education: explorations in policy sociology, London: Routledge.

Ball, S.J. (1993) What is policy? Texts, trajectories and toolboxes, Discourse: Studies in the Cultural Politics of Education, 13(2): 10–17.

Ball, S.J. (1994) Researching inside the state: issues in the interpretation of elite interviews, in D. Halpin and B. Troyna (eds) Researching education policy: ethical and methodological issues, London: Falmer Press, 107–120.

Ball, S.J. (1995) Intellectuals or technicians? The urgent role of theory in educational studies, British Journal of Educational Studies, 43(3): 255–271.

Ball, S.J. (1997) Policy sociology and critical social research: a personal review of recent education, British Educational Research Journal, 23(3): 257–274.

Ball, S.J. (2000) Performativities and fabrications in the education economy: towards the performative society, Australian Educational Researcher, 27(2): 1–23.

Ball, S.J. (2003) The teacher's soul and the terrors of performativity, Journal of Education Policy, 18(2): 215–228.

Ball, S.J. (2007) Education plc: understanding private sector participation in public sector education, London: Routledge.

Ball, S.J. (2008) New philanthropy, new networks and new governance in education, Political Science, 56(4): 747–765.

Ball, S.J. (2009a) The governance turn!, Journal of Education Policy, 24(5): 537–538.

Ball, S.J. (2009b) Privatising education, privatising education policy, privatising educational research: network governance and the 'competition state', Journal of Education Policy, 24(1): 83–99.

Ball, S.J. (2013) Foucault, power and education, New York: Routledge.

Ball, S.J. (2016) Following policy: networks, network ethnography and education policy mobilities, Journal of Education Policy, 31(5): 549–566.

Ball, S.J. (2017) Laboring to relate: neoliberalism, embodied policy, and network dynamics, Peabody Journal of Education, 92(1): 29–34.

Ball, S.J. (2021) Response: policy? Policy research? How absurd?, Critical Studies in Education, 62(3): 387–393.

Ball, S.J. and Exley, S. (2010) Making policy with 'good ideas': policy networks and the 'intellectuals' of New Labour, Journal of Education Policy, 25(2): 151–169.

Ball, S.J., Maguire, M., Braun, A. and Hoskins, K. (2011) Policy actors: doing policy work in schools, Discourse, 32(4): 625–639.

Ball, S.J., Maguire, M., Braun, A., Hoskins, K. and Perryman, J. (2012a) How schools do policy: policy enactments in secondary schools, London: Routledge.

Ball, S.J., Maguire, M., Braun, A., Perryman, J. and Hoskins, K. (2012b) Assessment technologies in schools: 'deliverology' and the 'play of dominations', Research Papers in Education, 27(5): 513–533.

Bangura, Y. (1997) The concept of policy dialogue and gendered development: understanding its institutional and ideological constraints, African Journal of Political Science, 2(2): 53–92.

Bansel, P. (2015a) A narrative approach to policy analysis, in K. Gulson, M. Clarke and E. Bendix Petersen (eds) Education policy and contemporary theory: implications for research, Oxon: Routledge, 183–194.

Bansel, P. (2015b) The subject of policy, Critical Studies in Education, 56(1): 5–20.

Bantock, G. (1977) An alternative curriculum, in C.B. Cox and R. Boyson (eds) Black paper 1977, London: Maurice Temple Smith Ltd, 78–86.

Barber, M. (2007) Instruction to deliver: Tony Blair, the public services and the challenge of delivery, London: Methuen.

Barnett, C. (2005) The consolations of 'neoliberalism', Geoforum, 36(1): 7–12.

Bartlett, L. and Vavrus, F. (2016) A vertical case study of global policy-making: early grade literacy in Zambia, in K. Mundy, A. Green, B. Lingard and A. Verger (eds) The handbook of global education policy, Malden, MA: Wiley Blackwell, 554–572.

Bauman, Z. (1993) Postmodern ethics, Oxford: Blackwell.

Beech, J. and Artopoulos, A. (2016) Interpreting the circulation of educational discourse across space: searching for new vocabularies, Globalisation, Societies and Education, 14(2): 251–271.

Béland, D. and Howlett, M. (2016) The role and impact of the multiple-streams approach in comparative policy analysis, Journal of Comparative Policy Analysis: Research and Practice, 18(3): 221–227.

Bender, T. (2010) Reassembling the city: networks and urban imaginaries, in I. Farías and T. Bender (eds) Urban assemblages: how actor-network theory changes urban research, New York: Routledge, 303–323.

Bennett, A. and Burke, P.J. (2018) Re/conceptualising time and temporality: an exploration of time in higher education, Discourse, 39(6): 913–925.

Bennett, C.J. (1991) What is policy convergence and what causes it?, British Journal of Political Science, 21(2): 215–233.

Bennett, C.J. and Howlett, M. (1992) The lessons of learning: reconciling theories of policy learning and policy change, Policy Sciences, 25(3): 275–294.

Bensimon, E. and Marshall, C. (2003) Like it or not: feminist critical policy analysis matters, The Journal of Higher Education, 74(3): 337–349.

Berkovich, I. and Benoliel, P. (2019) Understanding OECD representations of teachers and teaching: a visual discourse analysis of covers in OECD documents, Globalisation, Societies and Education, 17(2): 132–146.

Berkovich, I. and Benoliel, P. (2020) Marketing teacher quality: critical discourse analysis of OECD documents on effective teaching and TALIS, Critical Studies in Education, 61(4): 496–511.

Berkovich, I. and Benoliel, P. (2021) Framing the role of the school leader in OECD documents: a critical analysis, Globalisation, Societies and Education, 19(1): 41–54.

Bevir, M. (2010) Rethinking governmentality: towards genealogies of governance, European Journal of Social Theory, 13(4): 423–441.

Bevir, M. and Trentmann, F. (2007) After modernism: local reasoning, consumption, and governance, in M. Bevir and F. Trentmann (eds) Governance, consumers and citizens: agency and resistance in contemporary politics, Hampshire and New York: Palgrave Macmillan, 165–190.

Biesta, G. and Burbules, N.C. (2003) Pragmatism and educational research, Lanham: Rowman & Littlefield.

Billig, M. (1996) Arguing and thinking: a rhetorical approach to social psychology, Cambridge: Cambridge University Press.

Blackmore, J. (2014) Cultural and gender politics in Australian education, the rise of edu-capitalism and the 'fragile project' of critical educational research, Australian Educational Researcher, 41(5): 499–520.

Blackmore, J. (2022) Governing knowledge in the entrepreneurial university: a feminist account of structural, cultural and political epistemic injustice, Critical Studies in Education, 63(5): 622–638.

Blasco, M.C. and Vargas, C.A. (2011) Educational policy, anthropology, and the state, in B.A.U. Levinson and M. Pollock (eds) A companion to the anthropology of education, Chichester: Wiley-Blackwell, 368–387.

Bonnett, M. (1999) Education for sustainable development: a coherent philosophy for environmental education?, Cambridge Journal of Education, 29(3): 313–324.

Boossabong, P. and Chamchong, P. (2019) The practice of deliberative policy analysis in the context of political and cultural challenges: lessons from Thailand, Policy Studies, 40(5): 476–549.

Bourke, T. and Lidstone, J. (2015) What is plan B? Using Foucault's archaeology to enhance policy analysis, Discourse: Studies in the Cultural Politics of Education, 36(6): 833–853.

Bowe, R., Ball, S. and Gold, A. (1992) Reforming Education and Changing Schools, London: Routledge.

Bowe, R., Gewirtz, S. and Ball, S. (1994) Captured by the discourse? Issues and concerns in researching parental choice, British Journal of Sociology of Education, 15(1): 63–78.

Brain, K., Reid, I. and Boyes, L.C. (2006) Teachers as mediators between educational policy and practice, Educational Studies, 32(4): 411–423.

Braun, A., Ball, S.J., Maguire, M. and Hoskins, K. (2011) Taking context seriously: towards explaining policy enactments in the secondary school, Discourse: Studies in the Cultural Politics of Education, 32(4): 585–596.

Brenner, N., Peck, J. and Theodore, N. (2010) Variegated neoliberalization: geographies, modalities, pathways, Global Networks, 10(2): 182–222.

Brenner, N., Madden, D.J. and Wachsmuth, D. (2011) Assemblage urbanism and the challenges of critical urban theory, City, 15(2): 225–240.

Brent Edwards, D. (2013) International processes of education policy formation: an analytic framework and the case of plan 2021 in El Salvador, Comparative Education Review, 57(1): 22–53.

Brito Vieira, M., Jung, T., Gray, S.W.D. and Rollo, T. (2019) The nature of silence and its democratic possibilities, Contemporary Political Theory, 18(3): 424–447.

Britzman, D. (2000) 'The question of belief': writing poststructural ethnography, in E.A. St. Pierre and W. Pillow (eds) Working the ruins: feminist poststructural theory and methods in education, New York: Routledge, 27–40.

Brøgger, K. (2016) The rule of mimetic desire in higher education: governing through naming, shaming and framing, British Journal of Sociology of Education, 37(1): 72–91.

Brøgger, K. and Staunæs, D. (2016) Standards and (self)implosion: how the circulation of affects accelerates the spread of standards and intensifies the embodiment of colliding, temporal ontologies, Theory and Psychology, 26(2): 223–242.

Brown, C.P. (2007) Examining the streams of a retention policy to understand the politics of high-stakes reform, Education Policy Analysis Archives, 15(9): 1–28.

Brown, P.R. (2020) Understanding barriers to new approaches: a case study from Australian remote indigenous policy, Critical Policy Studies, 14(4): 408–425.

Bruff, I. (2014) The rise of authoritarian neoliberalism, Rethinking Marxism: A Journal of Economics, Culture and Society, 26(1): 113–129.

Brummett, B. (1980) Towards a theory of silence as a political strategy, Quarterly Journal of Speech, 66(3): 289–303.

Bryman, A. (2008) The end of the paradigm wars, in P. Alasuutari, L. Bickman and J. Brannen (eds) The SAGE handbook of social science research methods, London: SAGE, 13–25.

Burchell, G., Gordon, C. and Millar, P. (eds) (1991) The Foucault effect: studies in governmentality, Hemel Hempstead: Harvester Wheatsheaf.

Burgess, C., Bishop, M. and Lowe, K. (2022) Decolonising Indigenous education: the case for cultural mentoring in supporting Indigenous knowledge reproduction, Discourse: Studies in the Cultural Politics of Education, 43(1): 1–14.

Burrows, R. (2012) Living with the H-index? Metric assemblages in the contemporary academy, The Sociological Review, 60(2): 355–372.

Butler, J. (1990) Gender trouble: feminism and the subversion of identity, New York: Routledge.

Callon, M. (1986) Some elements of a sociology of translation: domestication of the scallops and the fishermen of St Brieuc Bay, in J. Law (ed) Power, action and belief: a new sociology of knowledge?, London: Routledge and Kegan Paul, 196–223.

Camphuijsen, M.K., Møller, J. and Skedsmo, G. (2021) Test-based accountability in the Norwegian context: exploring drivers, expectations and strategies, Journal of Education Policy, 3(5): 624–642.

Candido, H.H.D. (2020) Datafication in schools: enactments of quality assurance and evaluation policies in Brazil, International Studies in Sociology of Education, 29(1–2): 126–157.

Carr, E. (2010) Enactments of expertise, Annual Review of Anthropology, 39: 17–32.

Carstensen, M.B. (2015) Institutional bricolage in times of crisis, European Political Science Review, 9(1): 139–160.

Carusi, F.T., Rawlins, P. and Ashton, K. (2018) The ontological politics of evidence and policy enablement, Journal of Education Policy, 33(3): 343–360.

Carvajal, J.F.P. (2022) Advocacy NGOs and the neoliberal manufacture of the street voice, Journal of Education Policy, 37(5): 723–734.

Carvalho, L.M. (2012) The fabrications and travels of a knowledge-policy instrument, European Educational Research Journal, 11(2): 172–188.

Cavanagh, S.L. (2006) Spinsters, schoolmarms, and queers: female teacher gender and sexuality in medicine and psychoanalytic theory and history, Discourse: Studies in the Cultural Politics of Education, 27(4): 421–440.

Chabbott, C. (2003) Constructing education for development, New York: RoutledgeFalmer.

Chase, S.E. (2017) Narrative inquiry: toward theoretical and methodological maturity, in N.K. Denzin and Y.S. Lincoln (eds) The Sage handbook of qualitative research (5th ed), Los Angeles: SAGE, 546–560.

Chen, S. (2016) Dawning of hope: practice of and reflections on indigenous teacher education in Taiwan, Policy Futures in Education, 14(7): 943–955.

Chung, J., Atkin, C. and Moore, J. (2012) The rise and fall of the MTL: an example of European policy borrowing, European Journal of Teacher Education, 35(3): 259–274.

Clarke, J. (2004) Subjects of doubt: in search of the unsettled and unfinished. Paper prepared for CASCA annual conference, London, Ontario, 5–9 May.

Clarke, J. (2008) Living with/in and without neo-liberalism, Foccal, 51: 135–147.

Clarke, J. (2019) Developing a spatial social policy: taking stock and looking to the future, in A. Whitworth (ed) Towards a spatial social policy: bridging the gap between geography and social policy, Bristol: Policy Press, 195–209.

Clarke, J., Bainton, D., Lemdvai, N. and Stubbs, P. (2015) Making policy move: towards a politics of translation and assemblage, Bristol: Policy Press.

Coburn, C.E. (2004) Beyond decoupling: rethinking the relationship between the institutional environment and the classroom, Sociology of Education, 77(3): 211–244.

Cohen, M., March, J. and Olsen, J. (1972) A garbage can model of organizational choice, Administrative Science Quarterly, 17(1): 1–25.

Colebatch, H.K. (2006) What work makes policy?, Policy Sciences, 39(4): 309–321.

Collier, S.J. and Ong, A. (2005) Global assemblages, anthropological problems, in S.J. Collier and A. Ong (eds) Global assemblages: technology, politics, and ethics as anthropological problems, Malden, MA: Blackwell, 3–21.

Cone, L. and Brøgger, K. (2020) Soft privatisation: mapping an emerging field of European education governance, Globalisation, Societies and Education, 18(4): 374–390.

Confederation of School Trusts (2021) A bridge to the future, Nottingham: Confederation of School Trusts.

Connolly, P., Keenan, C. and Urbanska, K. (2018) The trials of evidence-based practice in education: a systematic review of randomised controlled trials in education research 1980–2016, Educational Research, 60(3): 276–291.

Cooper, A. (2014) Knowledge mobilisation in education across Canada: a cross-case analysis of 44 research brokering organisations, Evidence and Policy, 10(1): 29–59.

Cooper, A. and Shewchuk, S. (2015) Knowledge brokers in education: how intermediary organizations are bridging the gap between research, policy and practice, Policy Analysis Archives, 23(118): 1–8.

Cooper, D. (1998) Governing out of order: space, law and the politics of belonging, London: Rivers Oram Press.

Copeland, A.J. and Agosto, D.E. (2012) Diagrams and relational maps: the use of graphic elicitation techniques with interviewing for data collection, analysis, and display, International Journal of Qualitative Methods, 11(5): 513–533.

Courpasson, D. and Vallas, S. (2016) Resistance studies: a critical introduction, in D. Courpasson and S. Vallas (eds) The SAGE handbook of resistance, London: SAGE, 1–28.

Courtney, S.J. (2014) Inadvertently queer school leadership amongst lesbian, gay and bisexual (LGB) school leaders, Organization, 21(3): 383–399.

Courtney, S.J. (2015) Corporatised leadership in English schools, Journal of Educational Administration and History, 47(3): 214–231.

Courtney, S.J. (2016) Post-panopticism and school inspection in England, British Journal of Sociology of Education, 37(4): 623–642.

Courtney, S.J. (2017a) Corporatising school leadership through hysteresis, British Journal of Sociology of Education, 38(7): 1054–1067.

Courtney, S.J. (2017b) The courtier's empire: a case study of providers and provision, in H.M. Gunter, D. Hall and M.W. Apple (eds) Corporate elites and the reform of public education, Bristol: Policy Press, 177–189.

Courtney, S.J. (2020) Why you should reject entrepreneurial leadership, in J.S. Brooks and A. Heffernan (eds) The school leadership survival guide: what to do when things go wrong, how to learn from mistakes and why you should prepare for the worst, Charlotte: Information Age Publishing, 409–421.

Courtney, S.J. and Gunter, H.M. (2015) Get off my bus! School leaders, vision work and the elimination of teachers, International Journal of Leadership in Education: Theory and Practice, 18(4): 395–417.

Courtney, S.J. and Gunter, H.M. (2017) Privatizing leadership in education in England: the multiple meanings of school principal agency, in D. Waite and I. Bogotch (eds) The Wiley international handbook of educational leadership, Malden, MA: Wiley-Blackwell, 295–310.

Courtney, S.J. and McGinity, R. (2020) Conceptualising constructions of educational-leader identity, in A. Heffernan and R. Niesche (eds) Researching identity and subjectivity in educational leadership, London: Routledge, 8–23.

Courtney, S.J. and Lee-Piggott, R. (2022) Time to turn the tide: privatisation trends in education in the Caribbean, Brussels: Education International.

Courtney, S.J. and McGinity, R. (2022) System leadership as depoliticisation: reconceptualising educational leadership in a new multi-academy trust, Educational Management Administration and Leadership, 50(6): 893–910.

Courtney, S.J., McGinity, R. and Gunter, H.M. (2018) Introduction: theory and theorising in educational leadership, in S.J. Courtney, R. McGinity and H.M. Gunter (eds) Educational leadership: Theorising professional practice in neoliberal times, London: Routledge, 1–11.

Courtney, S.J., Gunter, H.M., Niesche, R. and Trujillo, T. (2021a) Introduction: taking critical perspectives and using critical approaches, in S.J. Courtney, H.M. Gunter, R. Niesche and T. Trujillo (eds) Understanding educational leadership: critical perspectives and approaches, London: Bloomsbury, 1–11.

Courtney, S.J., Gunter, H.M., Niesche, R. and Trujillo, T. (eds) (2021b) Understanding educational leadership: critical perspectives and approaches, London: Bloomsbury.

Czarniawska, B. (1997) Narrating the organization: dramas of institutional identity, Chicago: University of Chicago Press.

Dahlstedt, M. (2009) Governing by partnerships: dilemmas in Swedish education policy at the turn of the millennium, Journal of Education Policy, 24(6): 787–801.

Dahlstedt, M. and Fejes, A. (2019) Shaping entrepreneurial citizens: a genealogy of entrepreneurship education in Sweden, Critical Studies in Education, 60(4): 462–476.

Dale, R. (1994) Applied education politics or political sociology of education? Contrasting approaches to the study of the recent education reform in England and Wales, in D. Halpin and B. Troyna (eds) Researching education policy: ethical and methodological issues, London: Falmer Press, 31–41.

David, M., Davies, J., Edwards, R., Reay, D. and Standing, K. (1997) Choice within constraints: mothers and schooling, Gender and Education, 9(4): 397–410.

Davies, J.S. (2012) Network governance theory: a Gramscian critique, Environment and Planning A, 44(11): 2687–2704.

Davies, J.S. and Spicer, A. (2015) Interrogating networks: towards an agnostic perspective on governance research, Environment and Planning C: Government and Policy, 33(2): 223–238.

Davies, P. (2004) Sociology and policy science: just in time?, British Journal of Sociology, 55(3): 447–450.

Davis, E.R., Wilson, R. and Dalton, B. (2020) Another slice of PISA: an interrogation of educational cross-national attraction in Australia, Finland, Japan and South Korea, Compare, 50(3): 309–331.

Dean, M. (1998) Risk, calculable and incalculable, Soziale Welt, 49: 25–42.

DeBeer, Y. (2015) Policy archaeology: digging into special education policy in Ontario, 1965–1978, Qualitative Research Journal, 15(3): 319–338.

DeBray, E., Hanley, J., Scott, J. and Lubienski, C. (2020) Money and influence: philanthropies, intermediary organisations, and Atlanta's school board election, Journal of Educational Administration and History, 52(1): 63–79.

Decuypere, M. and Landri, P. (2021) Governing by visual shapes: university rankings, digital education platforms and cosmologies of higher education, Critical Studies in Education, 62(1): 17–33.

Decuypere, M., Grimaldi, E. and Landri, P. (2021) Introduction: critical studies of digital education platforms, Critical Studies in Education, 62(1): 1–16.

DeLeo, R.A. (2016) Time and the management of policy conflict: issues, actors and institutions in the Boston biolaboratory controversy, Critical Policy Studies, 10(1): 3–20.

Deleuze, G. (1992) What is a dispositif? in Michel Foucault: Philosopher, translated by T.J. Armstrong, Hertfordshire: Harvester Wheatsheaf, 159–168.

Delgado, M. (2015) Urban youth and photovoice: visual ethnography in action, Oxford: Oxford University Press.

Derrida, J. and Houdebine, J.-L. (1973) Interview: Jacques Derrida, Diacritics, 3(1): 33–46.

de Sousa Santos, B. (2006) Globalizations, Theory, Culture and Society, 23(2–3): 393–399.

Deutsch, K.W. (1966) The nerves of government, New York: The Free Press.

Diamond, P. (2021) What Michael Barber's appointment tells us about Whitehall reform and the 'science' of delivery, British Politics and Policy at LSE, January.

Dickhaus, B. (2010) The selectivity of translation: accountability regimes in Chilean and South African higher education, Globalisation, Societies and Education, 8(2): 257–268.

Dillon, M. and Lobo-Guerrero, L. (2008) Biopolitics of security in the 21st century: an introduction, Review of International Studies, 34(2): 265–292.

Dobbins, M. (2017) Exploring higher education governance in Poland and Romania: re-convergence after divergence?, European Educational Research Journal, 16(5): 684–704.

Dodge, M. and Kitchin, R. (2007) The automatic management of drivers and driving spaces, Geoforum, 38(2): 264–275.

Douglas, M. (1992) Risk and blame: essays in cultural theory, London and New York: Routledge.

Duarte, B.J. (2021) Situating subjectivities in the macrosocial policy context: critical/queer multifocal policy research, Journal of Education Policy, 36(5): 691–707.

Dubois, V. (2009) Towards a critical policy ethnography: lessons from fieldwork on welfare control in France, Critical Policy Studies, 3(2): 221–239.

du Gay, P. (2003) The tyranny of the epochal: change, epochalism and organizational reform, Organization, 10(4): 663–684.

Duggan, J. (2021) The co-productive imagination: a creative, speculative and eventful approach to co-producing research, International Journal of Social Research Methodology, 24(3): 355–367.

Duménil, G. and Lévy, D. (2004) Capital resurgent: roots of the neoliberal revolution, Cambridge, MA: Harvard University Press.

Duncan, S. and Edwards, R. (1999) Lone mothers, paid work and gendered moral rationalities, London: Macmillan.

Dunleavy, P. (1991) Democracy, bureaucracy and public choice: economic explanations in political science, Hertfordshire: Harvester Wheatsheaf.

Eacott, S. (2017) School leadership and the cult of the guru: the neo-Taylorism of Hattie, School Leadership and Management, 37(4): 413–426.

Eagleton, T. (2003) After theory, New York: Basic Books.

Edwards, E. (ed) (1992) Anthropology and photography 1860–1920, New Haven: Yale University Press.

Edwards, D.B. Jr., Le, H. and Sustarsic, M. (2020) Spatializing a global education phenomenon: private tutoring and mobility theory in Cambodia, Journal of Education Policy, 35(5): 713–732.

Edwards, R., Nicoll, K., Solomon, N. and Usher, R. (2004) Rhetoric and educational discourse: persuasive texts?, London and New York: RoutledgeFalmer.

Enright, E., Kirk, D. and Macdonald, D. (2020) Expertise, neoliberal governmentality and the outsourcing of health and physical education, Discourse: Studies in the Cultural Politics of Education, 41(2): 206–222.

Escobar, O. and Elstub, S. (2017) Forms of mini-publics: an introduction to deliberative innovations in democratic practice, newDemocracy Foundation, Research and Development Note 4.

Espeland, W.N. and Sauder, M. (2007) Rankings and reactivity: how public measures recreate social worlds, The American Journal of Sociology, 113(1): 1–40.

Espeland, W.N. and Sauder, M. (2016) Engines of anxiety: academic rankings, reputation, and accountability, New York: Russell Sage Foundation.

Eta, E.A. and Mngo, Z.Y. (2020) Policy diffusion and transfer of the Bologna Process in Africa's national, sub-regional and regional contexts, European Educational Research Journal, 20(1): 59–82.

Evans, J. and Davies, B. (2012) Embodying policy concepts, Discourse: Studies in the Cultural Politics of Education, 33(5): 617–633.

Fairclough, N. (2013) Critical discourse analysis and critical policy studies, Critical Policy Studies, 7(2): 177–197.

Fataar, A. (2006) Policy networks in recalibrated political terrain: the case of school curriculum policy and politics in South Africa, Journal of Education Policy, 21(6): 641–659.

Fay, B. (1975) Social theory and political practice, London: Allen & Unwin.

Fenwick, T. and Edwards, R. (2011) Considering materiality in education policy: messy objects and multiple reals, Educational Theory, 61(6): 709–726.

Fetterman, D.M. (2010) Ethnography (3rd edn), Thousand Oaks: SAGE.

Finkelstein, N.D. and Grubb, W.N. (2000) Making sense of education and training markets: lessons from England, American Educational Research Journal, 37(3): 601–631.

Finnigan, K.S., Luengo-Aravena, D.E. and Garrison, K.M. (2018) Social network analysis methods in educational policy research, in C. Lochmiller (ed) Complementary research methods for educational leadership and policy studies, Cham: Palgrave Macmillan, 231–252.

Fischer, F. (2003a) Beyond empiricism: policy analysis as deliberative practice, in M.A. Hajer and H. Wagenaar (eds) Deliberative policy analysis: understanding governance in the network society, Cambridge: Cambridge University Press, 209–227.

Fischer, F. (2003b) Reframing public policy: discursive politics and deliberative practices, Oxford: Oxford University Press.

Fischer, F. and Forester, J. (eds) (1993) The argumentative turn in policy analysis and planning, Durham, NC: Duke University Press.

Fischer, F. and Gottweis, H. (2013) The argumentative turn in public policy revisited: twenty years later, Critical Policy Studies, 7(4): 425–433.

Fitzgerald, T. and Gunter, H.M. (2008) Contesting the orthodoxy of teacher leadership, International Journal of Leadership in Education, 11(4): 331–340.

Fontdevila, C., Verger, A. and Zancajo, A. (2017) Taking advantage of catastrophes: education privatization reforms in contexts of emergency, in T. Koinzer, R. Nikolai and F. Waldow (eds) Private schools and school choice in compulsory education: global change and national challenge, Wisebaden, Germany: Springer VS, 223–244.

Foucault, M. (1972) The archaeology of knowledge, translated by A.M. Sheridan Smith, London: Tavistock.

Foucault, M. (1976) Histoire de la sexualité, 1: La volonté de savoir (History of Sexuality, 1: The Will to Know), Paris: Gallimard.

Foucault, M. (1977) Discipline and punish: the birth of the prison, translated by A. Sheridan, New York: Pantheon.

Foucault, M. (1980) The confession of the flesh, in C. Gordon (ed) Power/knowledge: selected interviews and other writings, Hassocks: Harvester Press, 194–228.

Foucault, M. (1981) The order of discourse, in R. Young (ed) Untying the text: a post-structuralist reader, London: Routledge and Kegan Paul, 48–78.

Foucault, M. (1982) The subject and power, Critical Inquiry, 8(4): 777–795.

Foucault, M. (1991) Remarks on Marx: conversations with Duccio Trombadori, translated by R.J. Goldstein and J. Cascaito, New York: Semiotext.

Foucault, M. (1998) Nietzsche, genealogy, history, in D.F. Bouchard (ed) Language, counter-memory, practice: selected essays and interviews, Ithaca: Cornell University Press, 139–164.

Foucault, M. (2000) Power, volume three: essential works of Foucault, 1954–1984, translated by R. Hurley and J.D. Faubion, New York: New York Press.

Foucault, M. (2002) So is it important to think?, in J.D. Faubion (ed) Michel Foucault. Power, vol 3, London: Penguin Books, 454–458.

Foucault, M. (2008) The birth of biopolitics: lectures at the Collége de France, 1978–79, Basingstoke: Palgrave.

Fraser, A. (2010) The craft of scalar practices, Environment and Planning A: Economy and Space, 4(2): 332–346.

Freeman, R. (2007) Epistemological bricolage: how practitioners make sense of learning, Administration and Society, 39(4): 476–496.

Freire, P. (1970) Pedagogy of the oppressed, New York: Continuum.

Fussey, P. and Roth, S. (2020) Digitizing sociology: continuity and change in the internet era, Sociology, 54(4): 659–674.

Fylkesnes, S. (2019) Patterns of racialised discourses in Norwegian teacher education policy: whiteness as a pedagogy of amnesia in the national curriculum, Journal of Education Policy, 34(3): 394–422.

Gabriel, R. and Paulus, T. (2015) Committees and controversy: consultants in the construction of education policy, Educational Policy, 29(7): 984–1011.

Gale, T. (1999) Policy trajectories: treading the discursive path of policy analysis, Discourse: Studies in the Cultural Politics of Education, 20(3): 393–407.

Gale, T. (2001) Critical policy sociology: historiography, archaeology and genealogy as methods of policy analysis, Journal of Education Policy, 16(5): 379–393.

Gale, T. (1994) Story-telling and policy making: the construction of university entrance problems in Australia, Journal of Education Policy, 9(3): 227–232.

Galvin, D.J. and Hacker, J.S. (2020) The political effects of policy drift: policy stalemate and American political development, Studies in American Political Development, 34(2): 216–238.

Gaus, N. and Hall, D. (2017) Corporate elites and higher education reform: the corporatisation of academic life in Indonesia, in H.M. Gunter, D. Hall and M.W. Apple (eds) Corporate elites and the reform of public education, Bristol: Policy Press, 75–87.

Geller, H.A. and Johnston, A.P. (1990) Policy as linear and nonlinear science, Journal of Education Policy, 5(1): 49–65.

Genieys, W. and Smyrl, M. (eds) (2008) Elites, ideas, and the evolution of public policy, Basingstoke: Palgrave Macmillan.

Gewirtz, S. and Ozga, J. (1990) Partnership, pluralism and education policy: a reassessment, Journal of Education Policy, 5(1): 37–48.

Giddens, A. (2002) Runaway world: how globalization is reshaping our lives, London: Profile Books.

Gilardi, F. (2010) Who learns from what in policy diffusion processes? American Journal of Political Science, 54(3): 650–666.

Gillborn, D. (2008) Conspiracy? Racism and education: understanding race inequality in education, Abingdon and New York: Routledge.

Gillies, J. (2010) The power of persistence: education system reform and aid effectiveness, Washington, DC: USAID.

Gobby, B. (2013) Principal self-government and subjectification: the exercise of principal autonomy in the Western Australian Independent Public Schools programme, Critical Studies in Education, 54(3): 273–285.

Gofen, A. (2014) Mind the gap: dimensions and influence of street-level divergence, Journal of Public Administration Research and Theory, 24(2): 473–493.

Goldthorpe, J. (1998) Rational action theory for sociology, The British Journal of Sociology, 49(2): 167–192.

Gonzalez, F.E. (1998) Formations of Mexicananess: Trenzas de identidades multiples (Growing up Mexicana: braids of multiple identities), Qualitative Studies in Education, 11(1): 81–102.

Goodwin, N. (1996) Governmentality in the Queensland Department of Education: policies and the management of schools, Discourse: Studies in the Cultural Politics of Education, 17(1): 65–74.

Gorski, P.C. and Zenkov, K. (eds) (2014) The big lies of school reform, New York: Routledge.

Gorur, R. (2014) Towards a sociology of measurement in education policy, European Educational Research Journal, 13(1): 58–72.

Gorur, R. (2015a) Assembling a sociology of numbers, in K. Hamilton, B. Maddox and C. Addey (eds) Literacy as numbers: researching the politics and practices of International Literacy Assessment, London: Cambridge University Press, 1–16.

Gorur, R. (2015b) Producing calculable worlds: education at a glance, Discourse: Studies in the Cultural Politics of Education, 36(4): 578–595.

Gorur, R. (2015c) Situated, relational and practice-oriented: the actor-network theory approach, in K. Gulson, M. Clarke and E. Bendix Petersen (eds) Education policy and contemporary theory: implications for research, London: Routledge, 87–98.

Gorur, R. and Dey, J. (2021) Making the user friendly: the ontological politics of digital data platforms, Critical Studies in Education, 62(1): 67–81.

Gorur, R., Hamilton, M., Lundahl, C. and Sjödin, S.E. (2019a) Politics by other means? STS and research in education, Discourse: Studies in the Cultural Politics of Education, 40(1): 1–15.

Gorur, R., Sorensen, E. and Maddox, B. (2019b) Standardizing the context and contextualizing the standard: translating PISA into PISA-D, in M. Prutsch (ed) Science, numbers and politics, Cham: Palgrave Macmillan, 301–329.

Gove, M. (2013) I refuse to surrender to the Marxist teachers hell-bent on destroying our schools: Education Secretary berates 'the new enemies of promise' for opposing his plans, The Daily Mail, 23 March. Available at: https://www.dailymail.co.uk/debate/article-2298146/I-refuse-surrender-Marxist-teachers-hell-bent-destroying-schools-Education-Secretary-berates-new-enemies-promise-opposing-plans.html

Grace, G. (1995) School leadership: beyond education management. An essay in policy scholarship, London: Routledge.

Grace, G. (1998) Critical policy scholarship: reflections on the integrity of knowledge and research, in G. Shacklock and J. Smyth (eds) Being reflexive in critical educational and social research, London: Falmer Press, 204–220.

Gray, J. (2007) Enlightenment's wake: politics and culture at the close of the modern age, London: Routledge.

Grayson, K. (2010) Dissidence, Richard K. Ashley, and the politics of silence, Review of International Studies, 36(4): 1005–1019.

Greenfield, T.B. and Ribbins, P. (eds) (1993) Greenfield on educational administration: towards a humane science, London: Routledge.

Greer, S.L. (2006) The politics of divergent policy, in S.L. Greer (ed) Territory, democracy and justice: regionalism and federalism in western democracies, Basingstoke: Palgrave Macmillan, 157–174.

Gregory, D. (1994) Geographical imaginations, Oxford: Blackwell.

Grek, S. (2009) Governing by numbers: the PISA 'effect' in Europe, Journal of Education Policy, 24(1): 23–37.

Grek, S. (2013) Expert moves: international comparative testing and the rise of expertocracy, Journal of Education Policy, 28(5): 695–709.

Griffen, Z. (2022) The 'production' of education: the turn from equity to efficiency in U.S. federal education policy, Journal of Education Policy, 37(1): 69–87.

Griffiths, J., Vidovich, L. and Chapman, A. (2009) Policy 'partnerships'? Power dynamics in curriculum reform, Journal of Educational Administration and History, 41(2): 193–208.

Griffiths, T.G. and Arnove, R.F. (2015) World culture in the capitalist world-system in transition, Globalisation, Societies and Education, 13(1): 88–108.

Grimaldi, E. (2013) Old and new markets in education: austerity, standards and ICT as pushes towards privatisation(s) in Italy, European Educational Research Journal, 12(4): 425–446.

Grimaldi, E. and Ball, S.J. (2021) Paradoxes of freedom: an archaeological analysis of educational online platform interfaces, Critical Studies in Education, 62(1): 114–129.

Grimaldi, E. and Barzanò, G. (2014) Making sense of the educational present: problematising the 'merit turn' in the Italian eduscape, European Educational Research Journal, 13(1): 26–46.

Grimaldi, E. and Landri, P. (2019) Tackling early school leaving and the governing of educational transitions in Italy, Comparative Education, 55(3): 386–403.

Gronn, P. (2003) Leadership: who needs it? School Leadership and Management, 23(3): 267–291.

Guimarães, S. (2015) The teaching of Afro-Brazilian and indigenous culture and history in Brazilian basic education in the 21st century, Policy Futures in Education, 13(8): 939–948.

Gulson, K.N. (2007) Neoliberal spatial technologies: on the practices of educational policy change, Critical Studies in Education, 48(2): 179–195.

Gulson, K.N. and Webb, P.T. (2012) Education policy racialisations: Afrocentric schools, Islamic schools, and the new enunciations of equity, Journal of Education Policy, 27(6): 697–709.

Gulson, K.N. and Webb, P.T. (2017a) Education policy and racial biopolitics, Bristol: Bristol University Press.

Gulson, K.N. and Webb, P.T. (2017b) Mapping an emergent field of 'computational education policy': policy rationalities, prediction and data in the age of artificial intelligence, Research in Education, 98(1): 14–26.

Gulson, K.N. and Sellar, S. (2019) Emerging data infrastructures and the new topologies of education policy, Environment and Planning D: Society and Space, 37(2): 350–366.

Gulson, K.N., Lewis, S., Lingard, B., Lubienski, C., Takayama, K. and Webb, P.T. (2017) Policy mobilities and methodology: a proposition for inventive methods in education policy studies, Critical Studies in Education, 58(2): 224–241.

Gulson, K.N. and Witzenberger, K. (2022) Repackaging authority: artificial intelligence, automated governance and education trade shows, Journal of Education Policy, 37(1): 145–160.

Gunter, H.M. (2012) Leadership and the reform of education, Bristol: Policy Press.

Gunter, H.M. (2016) An intellectual history of school leadership practice and research, London and New York: Bloomsbury.

Gunter, H.M. (2019) The politics of public education, Bristol: Policy Press.

Gunter, H.M. and Mills, C. (2017) Consultants and consultancy: the case of education, Cham: Springer.

Gvirtz, S. and Narodowski, M. (1998) The micro-politics of school resistance: the case of Argentine teachers versus the educational policies of Peron and Evita, Discourse: Studies in the Cultural Politics of Education, 19(2): 233–241.

Haas, P. (1992) Introduction: epistemic communities and international policy coordination, International Organisation, 46(1): 1–35.

Hacker, J.S. (2004) Privatizing risk without privatizing the welfare state: the hidden politics of social policy retrenchment in the United States, American Political Science Review, 98(2): 243–260.

Hacker, J.S. and Pierson, P. (2010) Winner-take-all politics: public policy, political organization, and the precipitous rise of top incomes in the United States, Politics and Society, 38(2): 152–204.

Halberstam, J. (1998) Female masculinity, Durham, NC: Duke University Press.

Hall, D., Gunter, H.M. and Bragg, J. (2013a) Leadership, New Public Management and the re-modelling and regulation of teacher identities, International Journal of Leadership in Education, 16(2): 173–190.

Hall, D., Gunter, H.M. and Bragg, J. (2013b) The strange case of the emergence of distributed leadership in schools in England, Educational Review, 65(4): 467–487.

Hall, P.A. (1993) Policy paradigms, social learning, and the state: the case of economic policymaking in Britain, Comparative Politics, 25(3): 275–296.

Hamann, E.T. and Rosen, L. (2011) What makes the anthropology of educational policy implementation 'anthropological'? in B.A.U. Levinson and M. Pollock (eds) A companion to the anthropology of education, Chichester: Wiley-Blackwell, 461–477.

Hamilton, M. (2017) How international large-scale skills assessments engage with national actors: mobilising networks through policy, media and public knowledge, Critical Studies in Education, 58(3): 280–294.

Hamilton, M. and Hillier, Y. (2007) Deliberative policy analysis: adult literacy assessment and the politics of change, Journal of Education Policy, 22(5): 573–594.

Hammersley, M. (1994) Ethnography, policy making and practice in education, in D. Halpin and B. Troyna (eds) Researching education policy: ethical and methodological issues, London: Falmer Press, 145–160.

Hardy, I., Heikkinen, H., Pennanen, M., Salo, P. and Kiilakoski, T. (2021) The 'spirit of the times': fast policy for educational reform in Finland, Policy Futures in Education, 19(7): 770–791.

Harper, D. (2002) Talking about pictures: a case for photo elicitation, Visual Studies, 17(1): 13–26.

Hartmann, E. and Komljenovic, J. (2021) The employability dispositif, or the re-articulation of the relationship between universities and their environment, Journal of Education Policy, 36(5): 708–733.

Hartong, S. (2015) Global policy convergence through 'distributed governance'? The emergence of 'national' education standards in the US and Germany, Journal of International and Comparative Social Policy, 31(1): 10–33.

Hartong, S. (2016) Between assessments, digital technologies and big data: the growing influence of 'hidden' data mediators in education, European Educational Research Journal, 15(5): 523–536.

Hartong, S. (2018) Towards a topological re-assemblage of education policy? Observing the implementation of performance data infrastructures and 'centers of calculation' in Germany, Globalisation, Societies and Education, 16(1): 134–150.

Hartong, S. (2021) The power of relation-making: insights into the production and operation of digital school performance platforms in the US, Critical Studies in Education, 62(1): 34–49.

Hartong, S. and Piattoeva, N. (2021) Contextualizing the datafication of schooling: a comparative discussion of Germany and Russia, Critical Studies in Education, 62(2): 227–242.

Harvey, D. (2005) A brief history of neoliberalism, Oxford: Oxford University Press.

Harvey, P. (2012) The topological quality of infrastructural relation: an ethnographic approach, Theory, Culture and Society, 29(4–5): 76–92.

Hatcher, R. and Tryona, B. (1994) The 'policy cycle': a Ball by Ball account, Journal of Education Policy, 9(2): 155–170.

Haughton, G. and Allmendinger, P. (2015) Think tanks and the pressures for planning reform in England, Environment and Planning C: Government and Policy, 34(8): 1676–1692.

Hauptman Komotar, M. (2022) Comparative higher education research in times of globalisation of higher education: theoretical and methodological insights, European Educational Research Journal, 21(4): 645–657.

Hay, S. and Kapitzke, C. (2009) Industry school partnerships: reconstituting spaces of educational governance, Globalisation, Societies and Education, 7(2): 203–216.

Haye, A., Matus, C., Cottet, P. and Niño, S. (2018) Autonomy and the ambiguity of biological rationalities: systems theory, ADHD and Kant, Discourse: Studies in the Cultural Politics of Education, 39(2): 184–195.

Heclo, H. (1974) Modern social politics in Britain and Sweden: from relief to income maintenance, New Haven: Yale University Press.

Heimans, S. (2012) Coming to matter in practice: enacting education policy, Discourse: Studies in the Cultural Politics of Education, 33(2): 313–326.

Hendriks, C.M. (2007) Praxis stories: experiencing interpretive policy research, Critical Policy Studies, 1(3): 278–300.

Hepworth, K. (2014) History, power and visual communication artefacts, Rethinking History, 20(2): 280–302.

Herweg, N., Huß, C. and Zohlnhöfer, R. (2015) Straightening the three streams: theorising extensions of the multiple streams framework, European Journal of Political Research, 54(3): 435–449.

Higgins, S. and Novelli, M. (2020) Rethinking peace education: a cultural political economy approach, Comparative Education Review, 64(1): 1–20.

Higham, R. (2014) 'Who owns our schools?' An analysis of the governance of free schools in England, Educational Management Administration and Leadership, 42(3): 404–422.

Hogan, A. (2015) Boundary spanners, network capital and the rise of edu-businesses: the case of News Corporation and its emerging education agenda, Critical Studies in Education, 56(3): 301–314.

Hoggett, P. (2001) Agency, rationality and social policy, Journal of Social Policy, 30(1): 37–56.

Holland, D. and Lave, J. (2001) History in person: an introduction, in D. Holland and J. Lave (eds) History in person: enduring struggles, contentious practices, intimate identities, Sante Fe: School of American Research Press, 3–36.

Holmqvist, D., Fejes, A. and Nylander, E. (2020) Auctioning out education: on exogenous privatisation through public procurement, European Educational Research Journal, 20(1): 102–117.

Honig, M.I. (2004) The new middle management: intermediary organizations in education policy implementation, Educational Evaluation and Policy Analysis, 26(1): 65–87.

Hood, C. (1991) A public management for all seasons? Public Administration, 69(1): 3–19.

Howarth, D. (2010) Power, discourse, and policy: articulating a hegemony approach to critical policy studies, Critical Policy Studies, 3(3–4): 309–335.

Howlett, M. (2019) Moving policy implementation theory forward: a multiple streams/critical juncture approach, Public Policy and Administration, 34(4): 405–430.

Howlett, M. and Migone, A. (2013) Policy advice through the market: the role of external consultants in contemporary policy advisory systems, Policy and Society, 32(3): 241–254.

Howlett, M., Mukherjee, I. and Koppenjan, J. (2017) Policy learning and policy networks in theory and practice: the role of policy brokers in the Indonesian biodiesel policy network, Policy and Society, 36(2): 233–250.

Hsieh, C.-C. (2016) A way of policy bricolage or translation: the case of Taiwan's higher education reform of quality assurance, Policy Futures in Education, 14(7): 873–888.

Huencho, V.-F. (2021) Implementation of indigenous public policies and tensions to governance: evidences from the Chilean case, Critical Policy Studies, 15(2): 209–222.

Huitema, D., Jordan, A., Munaretto, S. and Hilden, M. (2018) Policy experimentation: core concepts, political dynamics, governance and impacts, Policy Sciences, 51(2): 143–159.

Hunkin, E. (2016) Deploying Foucauldian genealogy: critiquing 'quality' reform in early childhood policy in Australia, Power and Education, 8(1): 35–53.

Hupe, P. (2014) What happens on the ground: persistent issues in implementation research, Public Policy and Administration, 29(2): 164–182.

Ideland, M. (2021) Google and the end of the teacher? How a figuration of the teacher is produced through an ed-tech discourse, Learning, Media and Technology, 46(1): 33–46.

Ingold, K. (2011) Network structures within policy processes: coalitions, power, and brokerage in Swiss climate policy, Policy Studies Journal, 39(3): 435–459.

Ingold, K. and Varone, F. (2012) Treating policy brokers seriously: evidence from the climate policy, Journal of Public Administration Research and Theory, 22(2): 319–346.

Introna, L.D. (2016) Algorithms, governance, and governmentality: on governing academic writing, Science, Technology, and Human Values, 41(1): 17–49.

Ivancheva, M.P., Swartz, R., Morris, N.P., Walji, S., Swinnerton, B.J., Coop, T. and Czerniewicz, L. (2020) Conflicting logics of online higher education, British Journal of Sociology of Education, 41(5): 608–625.

Janks, H. (1997) Critical discourse analysis as a research tool, Discourse: Studies in the Cultural Politics of Education, 18(3): 329–342.

Jann, W. and Wegrich, K. (2006) Theories of the policy cycle, in F. Ficher, G.J. Miller and M.S. Sidney (eds) Handbook of public policy analysis: theory, politics and methods, New York: CRC Press, 43–62.

Jessop, B. (2010) Cultural political economy and critical policy studies, Critical Policy Studies, 3(3–4): 336–356.

Jessop, B. (2016) Primacy of the economy, primacy of the political: critical theory of neoliberalism, in U. Bittlingmayer, A. Demirovic and T. Freytag (eds) Handbuch Kritische Theorie [Handbook of critical theory], Berlin: Springer, 1–13.

Jessop, B. and Sum, N.-L. (2016) What is critical? Critical Policy Studies, 10(1): 105–109.

Jobér, A. (2022) Dressed for success: making an appearance at an educational technology event, in C. Addey and N. Piattoeva (eds) Intimate accounts of education policy research: the practice of methods, New York and London: Routledge, 77–90.

Johansson, H. and Hvinden, B. (2005) Welfare governance and the remaking of citizenship, in J. Newman (ed) Remaking governance: peoples, politics and the public sphere, Bristol: Policy Press, 101–118.

Jules, T.D. (2013) Ideological pluralism and revisionism in small (and micro) states: the erection of the Caribbean education policy space, Globalisation, Societies and Education, 11(2): 258–275.

Kaiser, R. and Nikiforova, E. (2008) The performativity of scale: the social construction of scale effects in Narva, Estonia, Environment and Planning D: Society and Space, 26(3): 537–562.

Kakabadse, A.P., Kakabadse, N.K. and Kouzmin, A. (2011) From local elites to a globally convergent class: a historical analytical perspective, in A.P. Kakabadse and N.K. Kakabadse (eds) Global elites: the opaque nature of transnational policy determination, Basingstoke: Palgrave Macmillan, 1–37.

Kallo, J. (2021) The epistemic culture of the OECD and its agenda for higher education, Journal of Education Policy, 36(6): 779–800.

Kauko, J. (2022) Politics of evidence: think tanks and the Academies Act, British Educational Research Journal, 48(6): 1232–1253.

Kay, A. and Baines, D. (2019) Evolutionary approaches to the concept of drift in policy studies, Critical Policy Studies, 13(2): 174–189.

Kenway, J. (1990) Gender justice? Feminism, state theory and educational change, Discourse: Studies in the Cultural Politics of Education, 11(1): 55–76.

Kerber, W. and Eckardt, M. (2007) Policy learning in Europe: the open method of co-ordination and laboratory federalism, Journal of European Public Policy, 14(2): 227–247.

Kincheloe, J. (1991) Educational historiographical meta-analysis: rethinking methodology in the 1990s, International Journal of Qualitative Studies in Education, 4(3): 231–245.

King, P.J. and Roberts, N.C. (1992) An investigation into the personality profile of policy entrepreneurs, Public Productivity and Management Review, 16(2): 173–190.

Kingdon, J. (1984) Agendas, alternatives and public policies, Boston: Little Brown and Company.

Klijn, E.A. (2012) New public management and governance: a comparison, in D. Levi-Faur (ed) The Oxford handbook of governance, Oxford: Oxford University Press, 206–218.

Koh, A. (2009) The visualization of education policy: a videological analysis of Learning Journeys, Journal of Education Policy, 24(3): 283–315.

Kolleck, N. (2016) Uncovering influence through social network analysis: the role of schools in education for sustainable development, Journal of Education Policy, 31(3): 308–329.

Kooiman, J. (2003) Governing as governance, London: SAGE.

Koopman, C. (2018) Problematization in Foucault's genealogy and Deleuze's symptomatology: or, how to study sexuality without invoking oppositions, Angelaki, 23(2): 187–204.

Kosunen, S. and Hansen, P. (2018) Discursive narratives of comprehensive education politics in Finland, European Educational Research Journal, 17(5): 714–732.

Krishnan, A. (2009) What are academic disciplines? Some observations on the disciplinarity vs. interdisciplinarity debate, NCRM Working Paper Series.

Lambert, K., Alfrey, L., O'Connor, J., and Penney, D. (2021). Artefacts and influence in curriculum policy enactment: Processes, products and policy work in curriculum reform, European Physical Education Review, 27(2): 258–277.

Landri, P. (2018) Digital governance of education: technology, standards and Europeanization of education, London: Bloomsbury.

Lange, B. and Alexiadou, N. (2010) Policy learning and governance of education policy in the EU, Journal of Education Policy, 25(4): 443–463.

Lapping, C. (2017) The explosion of real time and the structural conditions of temporality in a society of control: durations and urgencies of academic research, Discourse, 38(6): 906–922.

Lascoumes, P. and Le Galès, P. (2004) Gouverner par les Instruments (Governing by Instruments), Paris: Presses de Sciences Po.

Lasswell, H.D. (1971) A pre-view of policy sciences, New York: American Elsevier.

Latour, B. (1986) The powers of association, in J. Law (ed) Power, action and belief: a new sociology of knowledge?, London: Routledge and Kegan Paul, 264–280.

Law, J. (2004) After method: mess in social science research, London: Routledge.

Law, J. and Singleton, V. (2014) ANT, multiplicity and policy, Critical Policy Studies, 8(4): 379–396.

Lawn, M. (2013) Voyages of measurement in education in the twentieth century: experts, tools and centres, European Educational Research Journal, 12(1): 108–119.

Lawn, M. and Lingard, B. (2002) Constructing a European policy space in educational governance: the role of transnational policy actors, European Educational Research Journal, 1(2): 290–307.

Laws, D. and Forester, J. (2007) Learning in practice: public policy mediation, Critical Policy Studies, 1(4): 342–370.

Le Galès, P. (2016) Performance measurement as a policy instrument, Policy Studies, 37(6): 508–520.

Leithwood, K. and Jantzi, D. (2005) A review of transformational school leadership research 1996–2005, Leadership and Policy in Schools, 4(3): 177–199.

Lemke, T. (2007) An indigestible meal? Foucault, governmentality and state theory, Distinktion: Scandinavian Journal of Social Theory, 8(2): 43–64.

Lemke, T. (2015) New materialisms: Foucault and the 'government of things', Theory, Culture and Society, 32(4): 3–25.

Lendvai, N. and Stubbs, P. (2009) Assemblages, translation, and intermediaries in southeast Europe, European Societies, 11(5): 673–695.

Lerner, D. and Lasswell, H.D. (eds) (1951) The policy sciences: recent developments in scope and method, Stanford: Stanford University Press.

Levin-Waldman, O.M. (2005) Welfare reform and models of public policy: why policy sciences are required, Review of Policy Research, 22(4): 519–539.

Lewin, K.M. (2011) Policy dialogue and target setting: do current indicators of education for all signify progress?, Journal of Education Policy, 26(4): 571–587.

Lewis, S. (2021) The turn towards policy mobilities and the theoretical-methodological implications for policy sociology, Critical Studies in Education, 62(3): 322–337.

Lewis, S. and Hogan, A. (2019) Reform first and ask questions later? The implications of (fast) schooling policy and 'silver bullet' solutions, Critical Studies in Education, 60(1): 1–18.

Lewis, S., Sellar, S. and Lingard, B. (2015) PISA for schools: topological rationality and new spaces of the OECD's global educational governance, Comparative Education Review, 60(1): 27–57.

Lewis, S.J. and Russell, A.J. (2011) Being embedded: a way forward for ethnographic research, Ethnography, 12(3): 398–416.

References

Li, T.M. (2007) Practices of assemblage and community forest management, Economy and Society, 36(2): 263–293.

Liasidou, A. (2009) Critical policy research and special education policymaking: a policy trajectory approach, Journal for Critical Education Policy Studies, 7(1): 107–130.

Lingard, B. (2006) Globalisation, the research imagination and deparochialising the study of education, Globalisation, Societies and Education, 4(2): 287–302.

Lingard, B. (2016) Think tanks, 'policy experts' and 'ideas for' education policy making in Australia, The Australian Educational Researcher, 43(1): 15–33.

Lingard, B. and Rawolle, S. (2004) Mediatizing educational policy: the journalistic field, science policy, and cross-field effects, Journal of Education Policy, 19(3): 361–380.

Lingard, B. and Rawolle, S. (2011) New scalar politics: implications for education policy, Comparative Education, 47(4): 489–502.

Lingard, B., Martino, W. and Rezai-Rashti, G. (2013) Testing regimes, accountabilities and education policy: commensurate global and national developments, Journal of Education Policy, 28(5): 539–556.

Lingard, B., Sellar, S. and Savage, G.C. (2014) Re-articulating social justice as equity in schooling policy: the effects of testing and data infrastructures, British Journal of Sociology of Education, 35(5): 710–730.

Lipsky, M. (1980) Street-level bureaucracy: dilemmas of the individual in public services, New York: Russell Sage Foundation.

Lubienski, C. (2018) The critical challenge: policy networks and market models for education, Policy Futures in Education, 16(2): 156–168.

Lúcio, J. and Neves, T. (2010) Mediation in local educational governance: the educating cities movement in a Portuguese town, European Educational Research Journal, 9(4): 484–497.

Lugg, C.A. and Murphy, J.P. (2013) Skipping away from inanity: towards a whimsical queering of educational policy, Texas Education Review, 1: 179–195.

Lugg, C.A. and Murphy, J.P. (2014) Thinking whimsically: queering the study of educational policy-making and politics, International Journal of Qualitative Studies in Education, 27(9): 1183–1204.

Lunde, I.M. and Ottesen, E. (2021) Digital technologies in policy assemblages in Ireland and Norway: a visual network analysis, European Educational Research Journal, 20(2): 193–211.

Lury, C., Parisi, L. and Terranova, T. (2012) Introduction: the becoming topological of culture, Theory, Culture and Society, 29(4–5): 3–35.

Lyotard, J.-F. (1984) The post-modern condition: a report on knowledge, Manchester: Manchester University Press.

Macfarlane, B. (2011) The morphing of academic practice: unbundling and the rise of the para-academic, Higher Education Quarterly, 65(1): 59–73.

MacIntyre, A. (2013) After virtue. Revelation, London and New York: Bloomsbury.

Madison, D.S. (2011) Critical ethnography: method, ethics, and performance (2nd edn), London: SAGE.

Maguire, M. and Braun, A. (2019) Headship as policy narration: generating metaphors of leading in the English primary school, Journal of Educational Administration and History, 51(2): 103–116.

Maguire, M., Hoskins, K., Ball, S.J. and Braun, A. (2011) Policy discourses in school texts, Discourse: Studies in the Cultural Politics of Education, 32(4): 597–609.

Marcus, G.E. and Saka, E. (2006) Assemblage. Theory, Culture and Society, 23(2–3): 101–106.

Maroy, C. (2009) New modes of regulation of education systems, Compare: A Journal of Comparative and International Education, 39(1): 67–70.

Maroy, C., Pons, X. and Dupuy, C. (2017) Vernacular globalisations: neo-statist accountability policies in France and Quebec education, Journal of Education Policy, 32(1): 100–122.

Martino, W., Airton, L., Kuhl, D. and Cumming-Potvin, W. (2019) Mapping transgender policyscapes: a policy analysis of transgender inclusivity in the education system in Ontario, Journal of Education Policy, 34(3): 302–330.

Masschelein, J. (2004) How to conceive of critical educational theory today?, Journal of Philosophy of Education, 38(3): 351–367.

Massey, D. (2004) Geographies of responsibility, Geografiska Annaler: Series B, Human Geography, 86(1): 5–18.

May, P.J. (1992) Policy learning and failure, Journal of Public Policy, 12(4): 331–354.

May, P.J. (2014) Implementation failures revisited: policy regime perspectives, Public Policy and Administration, 30(3–4): 277–299

Mazur, A.G. (2016) Policy analysis: feminist comparative policy, in D.A. Bearfield and M.J. Dubnick (eds) Encyclopaedia of public administration and public policy, New York: Taylor & Francis, 2526–2532.

McCann, E. (2011) Veritable inventions: cities, policies and assemblage, Area, 43(2): 143–147.

McCowan, T. (2017) Higher education, unbundling and the end of the university as we know it, Oxford Review of Education, 43(6): 733–748.

McFarlane, C. (2011) Assemblage and critical urbanism, City, 15(2): 204–224.

McGinity, R. (2017) Political and corporate elites and localised educational policy-making: the case of Kingswood Academy, in H.M. Gunter, D. Hall and M.W. Apple (eds) Corporate elites and the reform of public education, Bristol: Policy Press, 191–202.

McKee, K. (2009) Post-Foucauldian governmentality: what does it offer critical social policy analysis?, Critical Social Policy, 29(3): 465–486.

McKenzie, M. and Aikens, K. (2021) Global education policy mobilities and subnational policy practice, Globalisation, Societies and Education, 19(3): 311–325.

McKenzie, M., Bieler, A. and McNeil, R. (2015) Education policy mobility: reimagining sustainability in neoliberal times, Environmental Education Research, 21(3): 319–337.

McLendon, M.K. and Cohen-vogel, L. (2008) Understanding education policy change in the American states: lessons from political science, in B.S. Cooper, J.G. Cibulka and L.D. Fusarelli (eds) Handbook of education politics and policy, New York: Routledge, 30–51.

Menachy, F. and Verger, A. (2019) The value of network analysis for the study of global education policy: key concepts and methods, in R. Gorur, S. Sellar and G. Steiner-Khamsi (eds) World yearbook of education 2019: comparative methodology in an era of big data and global networks, Abingdon: Routledge, 117–131.

Merkus, S. and Veenswijk, M. (2017) Turning New Public Management theory into reality: performative struggle during a large-scale planning process, Environment and Planning C: Politics and Space, 35(7): 1264–1284.

Merriam Webster Dictionary (nd) Definition of automation. Available at: https://www.merriam-webster.com/dictionary/automation

Meyer, J. and Rowan, B. (1977) Institutionalized organizations: formal structure as myth and ceremony, American Journal of Sociology, 83(2): 340–363.

Meyer, J., Boli, J., Thomas, G. and Ramirez, F. (1997) World society and the nation-state, The American Journal of Sociology, 103(1): 144–181.

Michael, M. (2017) Actor-network theory: trials, trails and translation, London: SAGE.

Milana, M. (2016) Global polity in adult education and UNESCO: landmarking, brokering and framing policy, Globalisation, Societies and Education, 14(2): 203–226.

Miller, P. and Rose, N. (1990) Governing economic life, Economy and Society, 19(1): 1–31.

Miller, P. and Rose, N. (2008) Governing the present: administering economic, social and personal life, Cambridge: Polity.

Minh Ngo, T., Lingard, B. and Mitchell, J. (2006) The policy cycle and vernacular globalization: a case study of the creation of Vietnam National University – Hochiminh City, Comparative Education, 42(2): 225–242.

Mintrom, M. and Norman, P. (2009) Policy entrepreneurship and policy change, Policy Studies Journal, 37(4): 649–667.

Mirowski, P. (2009) Postface: Defining neoliberalism, in P. Mirowski and D. Plehwe (eds) The road from Mont Pèlerin: the making of the neoliberal thought collective, Cambridge, MA: Harvard University Press, 417–456.

Mol, A. (1999) Ontological policy: a work and some questions, in J. Law and J. Hassard (eds) Actor Network Theory and after, Oxford: Blackwell, 74–89.

Molla, T. (2021) Critical policy scholarship in education: an overview, Education Policy Analysis Archives, 29(2): 1–26.

Montecinos, V. (1993) Economic policy elites and democratization, Studies in Comparative International Development, 28(1): 25–53.

Moschetti, M., Martinez Pons, M., Bordoli, E. and Martinis, P. (2020) The increasing role of non-State actors in education policy-making: evidence from Uruguay, Journal of Education Policy, 35(3): 367–393.

Müller, M. and Schurr, C. (2016) Assemblage thinking and actor-network theory: conjunctions, disjunctions, cross-fertilisations, Transactions of the Institute of British Geographers, 41(3): 217–229.

Mundy, K., Green, A., Lingard, B. and Verger, A. (2016) The globalisation of education: key approaches and debates, in K. Mundy, A. Green, B. Lingard and A. Verger (eds) The handbook of global education policy, Malden, MA: Wiley Blackwell, 1–20.

Nay, O. (2012) How do policy ideas spread among international administrations? Policy entrepreneurs and bureaucratic influence in the UN response to AIDS, Journal of Public Policy, 32(1): 53–76.

Newman, J. (2007) Governance as cultural practice: text, talk and the struggle for meaning, in M. Bevir and F. Trentmann (eds) Governance, consumers and citizens: agency and resistance in contemporary politics, Hampshire and New York: Palgrave Macmillan, 49–68.

Nichols, N. and Griffith, G.I. (2009) Talk, texts, and educational action: an institutional ethnography of policy in practice, Cambridge Journal of Education, 39(2): 241–255.

Nudzor, H.P. (2009) Re-conceptualising the paradox in policy implementation: a post-modernist conceptual approach, Discourse: Studies in the Cultural Politics of Education, 30(4): 501–513.

Ochs, K. and Phillips, D. (2002) Comparative studies and 'cross-national attraction' in education: a typology for the analysis of English interest in educational policy and provision in Germany, Educational Studies, 28(4): 325–339.

Ofsted (2019) Guidance: education inspection framework, London: Crown Copyright.

Olmedo, A. (2017) Something old, not much new, and a lot borrowed: philanthropy, business, and the changing roles of government in global education policy networks, Oxford Review of Education, 43(1): 69–87.

Olmedo, A. and Wilkins, A. (2017) Governing through parents: a genealogical enquiry of education policy and the construction of neoliberal subjectivities in England, Discourse: Studies in Cultural Politics of Education, 38(4): 573–589.

Olmedo, A., Bailey, P.L.J. and Ball, S.J. (2013) To infinity and beyond …: heterarchical governance, the Teach for All network in Europe and the making of profits and mind, European Educational Research Journal, 12(4): 492–512.

Olssen, M., Codd, J. and O'Neill, A.-M. (2004) Education policy: globalization, citizenship and democracy, London: SAGE.

O'Neill, A.M. (2015) The New Zealand experiment: assessment-driven curriculum – managing standards, competition and performance to strengthen governmentality, Journal of Education Policy, 30(6): 831–854.

Ong, A. (2007) Neoliberalism as a mobile technology, Transactions of the Institute of British Geographers, 32(1): 3–8.

Oplatka, I. (2004) The characteristics of the school organization and the constraints on market ideology in education: an institutional view, Journal of Education Policy, 19(2): 143–161.

O'Reilly, M. and Kiyimba, N. (2015) Advanced qualitative research, London: SAGE.

Ozga, J. (1987) Studying education through the lives of policy makers: an attempt to close the micro-macro gap, in S. Walker and L. Barton (eds) Changing policies, changing teachers: new directions for schooling, Buckingham: Open University Press, 138–150.

Ozga, J. (2000) Policy research in educational settings: contested terrain, Buckingham: Open University Press.

Ozga, J. (2009) Governing education through data in England: from regulation to self-evaluation, Journal of Education Policy, 24(2): 149–162.

Ozga, J. (2021) Problematising policy: the development of (critical) policy sociology, Critical Studies in Education, 62(3): 290–305.

Ozga, J. and Jones, R. (2006) Travelling and embedded policy: the case of knowledge transfer, Journal of Education Policy, 21(1): 1–17.

Paananen, M. and Grieshaber, S. (2022) Policies of interlude and interruption: stories of governance as an assemblage, Journal of Education Policy, 38(3): 367–385.

Papanastasiou, N. (2017a) How does scale mean? A critical approach to scale in the study of policy, Critical Policy Studies, 11(1): 39–56.

Papanastasiou, N. (2017b) The practice of scalecraft: scale, policy and the politics of the market in England's academy schools, Environment and Planning A: Economy and Space, 49(5): 1060–1079.

Papanastasiou, N. (2019) The politics of scale in policy: scalecraft and education governance, Bristol: Policy Press.

Parreira do Amaral, M. and Zelinka, J. (2019) Lifelong learning policies shaping the life courses of young adults: an interpretative analysis of orientations, objectives and solutions, Comparative Education, 55(3): 404–421.

Patton, C. (1989) Power and the conditions of silence, Critical Quarterly, 31(3): 26–39.

Pautz, H. (2011) Revisiting the think-tank phenomenon, Public Policy and Administration, 26(4): 419–435.

Peck, J. and Theodore, N. (2015) Fast policy: experimental statecraft at the thresholds of neoliberalism, Minneapolis: University of Minnesota Press.

Pemberton, S. and Searle, G. (2016) Statecraft, scalecraft and urban planning: a comparative study of Birmingham, UK, and Brisbane, Australia, European Planning Studies, 24(1): 76–95.

Pereyra, M.A., Luzón, A., Torres, M. and Torres-salinas, D. (2018) PISA as a social media event: powering the 'logics of competition', in S. Lindbland, D. Petterson and T.S. Popkewitz (eds) Education by the numbers and the making of society: the expertise of international assessments, Abingdon: Routledge, 149–165.

Perrotta, C., Gulson, K.N., Williamson, B. and Witzenberger, K. (2021) Automation, APIs and the distributed labour of platform pedagogies in Google Classroom, Critical Studies in Education, 62(1): 97–113.

Perry, L.B. and Tor, G. (2008) Understanding educational transfer: theoretical perspectives and conceptual frameworks, Prospects, 38(4): 509–526.

Perryman, J. (2006) Panoptic performativity and school inspection regimes: disciplinary mechanisms and life under special measures, Journal of Education Policy, 21(2): 147–161.

Perryman, J. (2009) Inspection and the fabrication of professional and performative processes, Journal of Education Policy, 24(5): 611–631.

Perryman, J., Ball, S.J., Braun, A. and Maguire, M. (2017) Translating policy: governmentality and the reflective teacher, Journal of Education Policy, 32(6): 745–756.

Phelps, A., Durham, J. and Wills, J. (2011) Education alignment and accountability in an era of convergence: policy insights from states with individual learning plans and policies, Education Policy Analysis Archives, 19(31): 1–33.

Phillips, D. (2000) Learning from elsewhere in education: some perennial problems revisited with reference to British interest in Germany, Comparative Education, 36(3): 297–307.

Phillips, D. (2006) Investigating policy attraction in education, Oxford Review of Education, 32(5): 551–559.

Phillips, D. and Ochs, K. (2003) Processes of policy borrowing in education: some explanatory and analytical devices, Comparative Education, 39(4): 451–461.

Piattoeva, N. (2015) Elastic numbers: national examinations data as a technology of government, Journal of Education Policy, 30(3): 316–334.

Piattoeva, N. and Boden, R. (2020) Escaping numbers? The ambiguities of the governance of education through data, International Studies in Sociology of Education, 29(1–2): 1–18.

Piattoeva, N. and Saari, A. (2022) Rubbing against data infrastructure(s): methodological explorations on working with(in) the impossibility of exteriority, Journal of Education Policy, 37(2): 165–185.

Piattoeva, N., Klutas, A. and Suominen, O. (2019) Making and mobilizing contexts in policy and research, in R. Gorur, S. Sellar and G. Steiner-Khamsi (eds) World yearbook of education 2019: comparative methodology in an era of big data and global networks, Abingdon: Routledge, 202–218

Piazza, P. (2019) Antidote or antagonist? The role of education reform advocacy organizations in educational policymaking, Critical Studies in Education, 60(3): 302–320.

Pillow, W. (2003) 'Bodies are dangerous': using feminist genealogy as policy studies methodology, Journal of Education Policy, 18(2): 145–159.

Pillow, W.S. (2015) Policy temporality and marked bodies: feminist praxis amongst the ruins, Critical Studies in Education, 56(1): 55–70.

Pink, S. (2005) Doing visual ethnography, London: SAGE.

Pitton, V.O. and McKenzie, M. (2022) What moves us also moves policy: the role of affect in mobilizing education policy on sustainability, Journal of Education Policy, 37(4): 527–547.

Player-Koro, C., Rensfeldt, A.B. and Selwyn, N. (2018) Selling tech to teachers: education trade shows as policy events, Journal of Education Policy, 33(5): 682–703.

Plehwe, D. (2009) Introduction, in P. Mirowski and D. Plehwe (eds) The road from Mont Pèlerin: the making of the neoliberal thought collective, Cambridge, MA: Harvard University Press, 1–42.

Plowright, D. (2011) Using mixed methods: frameworks for an integrated methodology, London: SAGE.

Pollard, V. and Vincent, A. (2022) Micro-credentials: a postdigital counternarrative, Postdigital Science and Education, 4: 843–859.

Poole, W., Fallon, G. and Sen, V. (2020) Privatised sources of funding and the spatiality of inequities in public education, Journal of Educational Administration and History, 52(1): 124–140.

Popkewitz, T. (1991) A political sociology of educational reform: power/knowledge in teaching, teacher education, and research, New York: Teachers College Press.

Popkewitz, T. (1996) Rethinking decentralization and state/civil society distinctions: The state as a problematic of governing, Journal of Education Policy, 11(1): 27–51.

Poppema, M. (2009) Guatemala, the Peace Accords and education: a post-conflict struggle for equal opportunities, cultural recognition and participation in education, Globalisation, Societies and Education, 7(4): 383–408.

Posch, P. (1999) The ecologisation of schools and its implications for educational policy, Cambridge Journal of Education, 29(3): 341–348.

Power, M. (2013) The apparatus of fraud risk, Accounting, Organizations and Society, 38(6–7): 525–543.

Pralle, S. (2006) Branching out, digging in: environmental advocacy and agenda setting, Washington, DC: Georgetown University Press.

Pressman, J.L. and Wildavsky, A. (1973) Implementation: how great expectations in Washington are dashed in Oakland, Berkeley: University of California Press.

Priem, K. and Fendler, L. (2019) Shifting epistemologies for discipline and rigor in educational research: challenges and opportunities from digital humanities, European Educational Research Journal, 18(5): 610–621.

Prince, R. (2012) Policy transfer, consultants and the geographies of governance, Progress in Human Geography, 36(2): 188–203.

Pring, R. (2012) Putting persons back into education, Oxford Review of Education, 38(6): 747–760.

Prunty, J. (1985) Signposts for a critical educational policy analysis, Australian Journal of Education, 29(2): 133–140.

Raaper, R. (2017) Tracing assessment policy discourses in neoliberalised higher education settings, Journal of Education Policy, 32(3): 322–339.

Rabinow, P. (2003) Anthropos today: reflections on modern equipment, Princeton: Princeton University Press.

Radley, A. and Taylor, D. (2003) Images of recovery: a photo-elicitation study on the hospital ward, Qualitative Health Research, 13(1): 77–99.

Raffnsøe, S., Staunæs, D. and Bank, M. (2022) Affirmative critique, Ephemera, 22(3): 183–217.

Raffo, C. and Gunter, H.M. (2008) Leading schools to promote social inclusion: developing a conceptual framework for analysing research, policy and practice, Journal of Education Policy, 23(4): 397–414.

Ralston, S. (2021) Higher education's micro credentialing craze: a postdigital-Deweyan critique, Postdigital Science and Education, 3(1): 83–101.

Ramirez, F.O., Meyer, J.W. and Lerch, J. (2016) World society and the globalisation of education policy, in K. Mundy, A. Green, B. Lingard and A. Verger (eds) The handbook of global education policy, Malden, MA: Wiley Blackwell, 43–63.

Ranson, S. (2008) The changing governance of education, Educational Management Administration and Leadership, 36(2): 201–219.

Ranson, S., Arnott, M., McKeown, P., Martin, J. and Smith, P. (2005) The participation of volunteer citizens in school governance, Educational Review, 57(3): 357–371.

Rappleye, J. (2015) Revisiting the metaphor of the island: challenging 'world culture' from an island misunderstood, Globalisation, Societies and Education, 13(1): 58–87.

Rasmussen, M.L., Gowlett, C. and Connell, R. (2014) Interview with Raewyn Connell: the cultural politics of queer theory in education research, Discourse: Studies in the Cultural Politics of Education, 35(3): 335–346.

Ratner, H., Andersen, B.L. and Madsen, S.R. (2018) Configuring the teacher as data user: public-private sector mediations of national test data, Learning, Media and Technology, 44(1): 22–35.

Rawolle, S. and Lingard, B. (2008) The sociology of Pierre Bourdieu and researching education policy, Journal of Education Policy, 23(6): 729–741.

Rawolle, S. and Lingard, B. (2015) Bourdieu and doing policy sociology in education, in K.N. Gulson, M. Clarke and E. Bendix Petersen (eds) Education policy and contemporary theory: implications for research, London and New York: Routledge, 15–26.

Regalsky, P. and Lauri, N. (2007) 'The school, whose place is this'? The deep structures of the hidden curriculum in indigenous education in Bolivia, Comparative Education, 43(2): 231–251.

Rhodes, R.A.W. (1996) The new governance: governing without government, Political Studies, 44(4): 652–667.

Rickinson, M. and McKenzie, M. (2021) Understanding the research-policy relationship in ESE: insights from the critical policy and evidence use literatures, Environmental Education Research, 27(4): 480–497.

Riep, C.B. (2014) Omega School Franchise in Ghana: 'affordable' private education for the poor or for-profiteering? in G. Walford, I. Macpherson and S. Robertson (eds) Education, privatisation and social justice: case studies from Africa, South Asia and South East Asia, Didcot: Symposium Books, 259–276.

Rixecker, S.S. (1994) Expanding the discursive context of policy design: a matter of feminist standpoint epistemology, Policy Sciences, 27(2): 119–142.

Roberts, N.C. and King, P.J. (1991) Policy entrepreneurs: their activity structure and function in the policy process, Journal of Public Administration Research and Theory, 1(2): 147–175.

Roberts-Mahoney, H., Means, A.J. and Garrison, M.J. (2016) Netflixing human capital development: personalized learning technology and the corporatization of K-12 education, Journal of Education Policy, 31(4): 405–420.

Robertson, J. and Tisdall, E.M. (2020) The importance of consulting children and young people about data literacy, Journal of Media Literacy Education, 12(3): 58–74.

Robertson, S.L. (2016) The global governance of teachers' work, in K. Mundy, A. Green, B. Lingard and A. Verger (eds) The handbook of global education policy, Malden, MA: Wiley Blackwell, 275–290.

Rogers, E.M. (2003) Diffusion of innovations, New York: Free Press.

Rönnberg, L. (2017) From national policy-making to global edu-business: Swedish edu-preneurs on the move, Journal of Education Policy, 32(2): 234–249.

Rose, N. (1999) Powers of freedom: reframing political thought, Cambridge: Cambridge University Press.

Rose, N. (2017) Still 'like birds on the wire'? Freedom after neoliberalism, Economy and Society, 45(3–4): 303–323.

Rottenburg, C. (2013) The rise of neoliberal feminism, Cultural Studies, 28(3): 418–437.

Rottmann, C. (2006) Queering educational leadership from the inside out, International Journal of Leadership in Education, 9(1): 1–20.

Rutkowski, D.J. (2007) Converging us softly: how intergovernmental organizations promote neoliberal educational policy, Critical Studies in Education, 48(2): 229–247.

Saari, A. (2012) The map is the territory: educational evaluation and the topology of power, European Educational Research Journal, 11(4): 586–600.

Saari, A. (2022) Topologies of desire: fantasies and their symptoms in educational policy futures. European Educational Research Journal, 21(6): 883–899.

Saari, A. and Säntti, J. (2018) The rhetoric of the 'digital leap' in Finnish educational policy documents, European Educational Research Journal, 17(3): 442–457.

Sabatier, P.A. (1988) An advocacy coalition framework of policy change and the role of policy-oriented learning therein, Policy Sciences, 21(2–3): 129–168.

Sahlberg, P. (2011) The fourth way of Finland, Journal of Educational Change, 12(2): 173–185.

Sahlgren, O. (2023) The politics and reciprocal (re)configuration of accountability and fairness in data driven education, Learning, Media and Technology, 48(1): 95–108.

Sahlin, K. and Wedlin, L. (2008) Circulating ideas: imitation, translation and editing, in R. Greenwood, C. Oliver, K. Sahlin and R. Suddaby (eds) The SAGE handbook of organisational institutionalism, London: SAGE, 218–242.

Saint-Martin, D. (1998) The new managerialism and the policy influence of consultants in government: an historical–institutionalist analysis of Britain, Canada and France, Governance, 11(3): 319–356.

Salter, M.B. (2008) Imagining numbers: risk, quantification, and aviation security, Security Dialogue, 39(2–3): 243–266.

Sander, I. (2020) Critical big data literacy tools: engaging citizens and promoting empowered internet usage, Data and Policy, 2: e5.

Savage, G.C. (2020) What is policy assemblage? Territory, Politics, Governance, 8(3): 319–335.

Savage, G.C. and O'Connor, K. (2019) What's the problem with 'policy alignment'? The complexities of national reform in Australia's federal system, Journal of Education Policy, 34(6): 812–835.

Savage, G.S., Gerrard, J., Gale, T. and Molla, T. (2021) The politics of critical policy sociology: mobilities, moorings and elite networks, Critical Studies in Education, 62(3): 306–321.

Scheurich, J.J. (1994) Policy archaeology: a new policy studies methodology, Journal of Education Policy, 9(4): 297–316.

Schmidt, V. (2008) Discursive institutionalism: the explanatory power of ideas and discourse, Annual Review of Political Science, 11: 303–326.

Schriewer, J. (2000) Comparative education methodology in transition: towards a science of complexity? in J. Schriewer (ed) Discourse formation in comparative education, Frankfurt am Main: Peter Lang, 3–52.

Schulte, B. (2012) World culture with Chinese characteristics: when global models go native, Comparative Education, 48(4): 473–486.

Sedgwick, E.K. (1990) Epistemology of the closet, Berkeley: University of California Press.

Sellar, S. (2015a) Data infrastructure: a review of expanding accountability systems and large-scale assessments in education, Discourse, 36(5): 765–777.

Sellar, S. (2015b) A feel for numbers: affect, data and education policy, Critical Studies in Education, 56(1): 131–146.

Selwyn, N. (2013) Rethinking education in the digital age, in K. Orton-Johnson and N. Prior (eds) Digital sociology: critical perspectives, London: Palgrave Macmillan, 197–209.

Selwyn, N. (2016) 'There's so much data': exploring the realities of data-based school governance, European Educational Research Journal, 15(1): 54–68.

Selwyn, N., Hillman, T., Eynon, R., Ferreira, G., Knox, J., Macgilchrist, F. and Sancho-Gil, J.M. (2020) What's next for Ed-Tech? Critical hopes and concerns for the 2020s, Learning, Media and Technology, 45(1): 1–6.

Selwyn, N., Hillman, T., Bergviken Rensfeldt, A. and Perrotta, C. (2023) Digital technologies and the automation of education: key questions and concerns, Postdigital Science and Education, 5: 15–24.

Shahjahan, R.A., Bylsma, P.E. and Singai, C. (2022) Global university rankings as 'sticky' objects and 'refrains': affect and mediatisation in India, Comparative Education, 58(2): 224–241.

Shaw, K.M. (2004) Using feminist critical policy analysis in the realm of higher education, The Journal of Higher Education, 75(1): 56–79.

Shipan, C.R. and Volden, C. (2008) The mechanisms of policy diffusion, American Journal of Political Science, 52(4): 840–857.

Shiroma, E.O. (2014) Networks in action: new actors and practices in education policy in Brazil, Journal of Education Policy, 29(3): 323–348.

Shore, C. and Wright, S. (1997) Policy: a new field of anthropology, in C. Shore and S. Wright (eds) Anthropology of policy: critical perspectives on governance and power, London: Routledge, 3–30.

Silova, I. (2012) Contested meanings of educational borrowing, in G. Steiner-Khamsi and F. Waldow (eds) World yearbook of education 2012: policy borrowing and lending in education, New York: Routledge, 229–245.

Silova, I. (2021) Facing the Anthropocene: comparative education as sympoiesis, Comparative Education Review, 65(4): 587–616.

Silova, I. and Brehm, W.C. (2015) From myths to models: the (re)production of world culture in comparative education, Globalisation, Societies and Education, 13(1): 8–33.

Simon, M., Olssen, M. and Peters, M. (2009) Re-reading education policies. Part 1: the critical education policy orientation, in M. Simon, M. Olssen and M. Peters (eds) Re-reading education policies: a handbook studying the policy agenda of the 21st century, Rotterdam: Sense Publishers, 1–35.

Singh, P. (2015) Performativity and pedagogising knowledge: globalising educational policy formation, dissemination and enactment, Journal of Education Policy, 30(3): 363–384.

Singh, P., Thomas, S. and Harris, J. (2013) Recontextualising policy discourses: a Bernsteinian perspective on policy interpretation, translation, enactment, Journal of Education Policy, 28(4): 465–480.

Singh, P., Heimans, S. and Glasswell, K. (2014) Policy enactment, context and performativity: ontological politics and researching Australian National Partnership policies, Journal of Education Policy, 29(6): 826–844.

Smith, R. (2017) The emergence of the quantified child, Discourse: Studies in the Cultural Politics of Education, 38(5): 701–712.

Smyth, J. (2010) Speaking back to educational policy: why social inclusion will not work for disadvantaged Australian schools, Critical Studies in Education, 51(2): 113–128.

Smyth, J. (2011) The disaster of the 'self-managing school': genesis, trajectory, undisclosed agenda, and effects, Journal of Educational Administration and History, 43(2): 95–117.

Smyth, J. (2012) Policy activism: an animating idea with/for young people, Journal of Educational Administration and History, 44(3): 179–186.

Sobe, N.W. (2018) Problematizing comparison in a post-exploration age: big data, educational knowledge, and the art of criss-crossing, Comparative Education Review, 62(3): 325–343.

Sobe, N.W. and Kowalczyk, J. (2018) Context, entanglement and assemblage as matters of concern in comparative education research, in J. McLeod, N.W. Sobe and T. Seddon (eds) World yearbook of education 2018: uneven space-times of education: historical sociologies of concepts, methods and practices, London: Routledge, 197–204.

Souto-Otero, M. and Beneito-Montagut, R. (2016) From governing through data to governmentality through data: artefacts, strategies and the digital turn, European Educational Research Journal, 15(1): 14–33.

Spreen, C.A. (2004) Appropriating borrowed policies: outcomes-based education in South Africa, in G. Steiner-Khamsi (ed) The global politics of educational borrowing and lending, New York: Teachers College Press, 101–113.

Springer, S. (2015) Postneoliberalism? Review of Radical Political Economies, 47(1): 5–17.

Srivastava, P. and Baur, L. (2016) New global philanthropy and philanthropic governance in education in a post-2015 world, in K. Mundy, A. Green, B. Lingard and A. Verger (eds) The handbook of global education policy, Malden, MA: Wiley Blackwell, 433–448.

Stables, A. (2003) School as imagined community in discursive space: a perspective on the school effectiveness debate, British Educational Research Journal, 29(6): 895–902.

Stacey, M. (2017) The teacher 'problem': an analysis of the NSW education policy Great Teaching, Inspired Learning, Discourse: Studies in the Cultural Politics of Education, 38(5): 782–793.

Stankiewicz, L. (2022) Discourse, resistance and organization: critical discourse analysis of the 'revolt of the humanities' in Poland, Discourse: Studies in the Cultural Politics of Education, 43(3): 483–495.

Staunæs, D. (2018) 'Green with envy:' affects and gut feelings as an affirmative, immanent, and trans-corporeal critique of new motivational data visualizations, International Journal of Qualitative Studies in Education, 31(5): 409–421.

Steiner-Khamsi, G. (2014) Cross-national policy borrowing: understanding reception and translation, Asia Pacific Journal of Education, 34(2): 153–167.

Stoker, G. (1998) Governance as theory: five propositions, International Social Sciences Journal, 50(155): 17–28.

Stone, D. (2017) Understanding the transfer of policy failure: bricolage, experimentalism and translation, Policy and Politics, 45(1): 55–70.

Strang, D. and Meyer, J.W. (1993) Institutional conditions for diffusion, Theory and Society, 22(4): 487–511.

Stromquist, N.P. (2015) Explaining the expansion of feminist ideas: cultural diffusion or political struggle?, Globalisation, Societies and Education, 13(1): 109–134.

Suárez, D.F. and Bromley, P. (2016) Institutional theories and levels of analysis: history, diffusion, and translation, in J. Schriewer (ed) World culture re-contextualised: meaning constellations and path-dependencies in comparative and international education research, London: Taylor & Francis, 139–159.

Sugiyama, N.B. (2013) Theoretical debates on policy diffusion: a motivations approach, in Diffusion of good government: social sector reforms in Brazil, Notre Dame, IN: Notre Dame Press, 24–49.

Sutoris, P. (2018) Ethically scaling up interventions in educational development: a case for collaborative multi-sited ethnographic research, Comparative Education, 54(3): 390–410.

Swist, T., Magee, L., Phuong, J., & Sweeting, D. (2017) The labour of communicating publics: Participatory platforms, socio-technical intermediaries and pluralistic expertise, Communication and the Public, 2(3): 210–225.

Takayama, K. (2012) Exploring the interweaving of contrary currents: transnational policy enactment and path-dependent policy implementation in Australia and Japan, Comparative Education, 48(4): 505–523.

Takayama, K. (2015) Provincialising the world culture theory debate: critical insights from a margin, Globalisation, Societies and Education, 13(1): 34–57.

Takayama, K. and Apple, M.W. (2008) The cultural politics of borrowing: Japan, Britain, and the narrative of educational crisis, British Journal of Sociology of Education, 29(3): 289–301.

Tamboukou, M. (1999) Writing genealogies: an exploration of Foucault's strategies for doing research, Discourse: Studies in the Cultural Politics of Education, 20(2): 201–217.

Tamboukou, M. and Ball, S.J. (2003) Genealogy and ethnography: fruitful encounters or dangerous liaisons?, in M. Tamboukou and S.J. Ball (eds) Dangerous encounters: genealogy and ethnography, Bern: Peter Lang, 1–36.

Taylor, E. (2018) Student drug testing and the surveillance school economy: an analysis of media representation and policy transfer in Australian schools, Journal of Education Policy, 33(3): 383–397.

Taylor, S. (1997) Critical policy analysis: exploring contexts, texts and consequences, Discourse: Studies in the Cultural Politics of Education, 18(1): 23–35.

Taylor, S. (2004) Researching educational policy and change in 'new times': using critical discourse analysis, Journal of Education Policy, 19(4): 433–451.

ten Dam, G.T.M. and Volman, M.L.L. (1995) Feminist research and educational policy, Journal of Education Policy, 10(2): 209–220.

Thaler, R. and Sunstein, C. (2008) Nudge: improving decisions about health, wealth and happiness, Harmondsworth: Penguin.

Thompson, G. and Cook, I. (2014) Education policy-making and time, Journal of Education Policy, 29(5): 700–715.

Thomson, P. (2008) Headteacher critique and resistance: a challenge for policy, and for leadership/management scholars, Journal of Educational Administration and History, 40(2): 85–100.

Thomson, P. (2014) Field, in M. Grenfell (ed) Pierre Bourdieu: key concepts, Stocksfield: Acumen, 65–80.

Thomson, P. and Pennacchia, J. (2016) Disciplinary regimes of 'care' and complementary alternative education, Critical Studies in Education, 57(1): 84–99.

Tikly, L. (2003) Governmentality and the study of education policy in South Africa, Journal of Education Policy, 18(2): 161–174.

Tilleczek, K. (2012) Policy activism with and for youth in transition through public education, Journal of Educational Administration and History, 44(3): 253–267.

Torgerson, C.J. and Torgerson, D.J. (2001) The need for randomised controlled trials in educational research, British Journal of Educational Studies, 49(3): 316–328.

Torgerson, D. (2019) Lasswell in the looking glass: a 'mirror' for critical policy studies, Critical Policy Studies, 13(1): 122–130.

Troyna, B. (1994) Critical social research and education policy, British Journal of Educational Studies, 42(1): 70–84.

Vakirtzi, E. and Bayliss, P. (2013) Towards a Foucauldian methodology in the study of autism: issues of archaeology, genealogy, and subjectification, Journal of Philosophy of Education, 47(3): 364–378.

Van Dijk, T.A. (1993) Principles of critical discourse analysis, Discourse and Society, 4(2): 249–283.

van Lieshout, M., Dewulf, A., Aarts, N. and Termeer, C. (2012) Doing scalar politics: interactive scale framing for managing accountability in complex policy processes, Critical Policy Studies, 6(2): 163–181.

Van Poeck, K. and Lysgaard, J.A. (2015) The roots and routes of environmental and sustainability education policy research, Environmental Education Research, 22(3): 305–318.

Verger, A. (2012) Framing and selling global education policy: the promotion of public-private partnerships for education in low-income contexts, Journal of Education Policy, 27(1): 109–130.

Verger, A. and Skedsmo, G. (2021) Enacting accountabilities in education: exploring new policy contexts and theoretical elaborations, Educational Assessment, Evaluation and Accountability, 33(3): 391–401.

Verger, A., Fontdevila, C. and Zancajo, A. (2017) Multiple paths towards education privatization in a globalizing world: a cultural political economy review, Journal of Education Policy, 32(6): 757–787.

Verger, A., Fontdevila, C. and Parcerisa, L. (2019) Reforming governance through policy instruments: how and to what extent standards, tests and accountability in education spread worldwide, Discourse, 40(2): 248–270.

Verger, A., Prieto, M., Pagès, M. and Villamor, P. (2020) Common standards, different stakes: a comparative and multi-scalar analysis of accountability reforms in the Spanish education context, European Educational Research Journal, 19(2): 142–164.

Wagenaar, H. (2006) Interpretation and intention in policy analysis, in F. Fischer, G. Miller and M. Sidney (eds) The handbook of public policy analysis: theory, politics and methods, Boca Raton: CRC Press, 429–422.

Wagner, P., Weiss, C.H.W., Wittrock, B. and Wollmann, H. (eds) (1991) Social sciences and modern state, Cambridge: Cambridge University Press.

Waldow, F. (2009) Undeclared imports: silent borrowing in educational policy-making and research in Sweden, Comparative Education, 45(4): 477–494.

Wals, A.E.J. and Benavot, A. (2017) Can we meet the sustainability challenges? The role of education and lifelong learning, European Journal of Education, 52(4): 404–413.

Walters, W. (2012) Governmentality: critical encounters, Abingdon: Routledge.

Ward, I. (2015) Media influence on public policy, in B. Head and K. Crowley (eds) Policy analysis in Australia, Bristol: Policy Press, 183–197.

Webb, P.T. (2014) Policy problematization, International Journal of Qualitative Studies in Education, 27(3): 364–376.

Webb, P.T. and Gulson, K.N. (2015) Policy, geophilosophy and education, Rotterdam: Sense Publishers.

Weible, C.M., Sabatier, P.A. and McQueen, K. (2009) Themes and variations: taking stock of the advocacy coalition framework, Policy Studies Journal, 37(1): 121–140.

Weick, K.E. (1976) Educational organizations as loosely coupled systems, Administrative Science Quarterly, 21(1): 1–19.

Weiler, K. (2008) The feminist imagination and educational research, Discourse: Studies in the Cultural Politics of Education, 29(4): 499–507.

West, A. and Nikolai, R. (2017) The expansion of 'private' schools in England, Sweden and Eastern Germany: a comparative perspective on policy development, regulation, policy goals and ideas, Journal of Comparative Policy Analysis: Research and Practice, 19(5): 452–469.

Wetherell, M. (2001) Themes in discourse research: the case of Diana, in M. Wetherell, S. Taylor and S.J. Yates (eds) Discourse theory and practice, London: SAGE, 14–28.

Wetherell, M. (2003) Racism and the analysis of cultural resources in interviews, in H. Berg, M. Wetherell and H. Houtkoop-Steenstra (eds) Analysing race talk: multidisciplinary approaches to the interview, Cambridge: Cambridge University Press, 11–30.

Wetherell, M. and Edley, N. (1999) Negotiating hegemonic masculinity: imaginary positions and psycho-discursive practices, Feminism and Psychology, 9(3): 335–356.

Wheelahan, L. and Moodie, G. (2021) Analysing micro-credentials in higher education: a Bernsteinian analysis, Journal of Curriculum Studies, 53(2): 212–228.

Wilder, M. and Howlett, M. (2014) The politics of policy anomalies: bricolage and the hermeneutics of paradigms, Critical Policy Studies, 8(2): 183–202.

Wilkins, A. (2012) School choice and the commodification of education: a visual approach to school brochures and websites, Critical Social Policy, 32(1): 70–87.

Wilkins, A. (2013) Libertarian paternalism: policy and everyday translations of the rational and the affective, Critical Policy Studies, 7(4): 395–406.

Wilkins, A. (2016) Modernising school governance: corporate planning and expert handling in state education, London and New York: Routledge.

Wilkins, A. (2017) Rescaling the local: multi-academy trusts, private monopoly and statecraft in England, Journal of Educational Administration and History, 49(2): 171–185.

Wilkins, A. (2018) Neoliberalism, citizenship and education: A policy discourse analysis, in A. Peterson, G. Stahl and H. Soong (eds) The Palgrave Handbook of Citizenship and Education, Basingstoke: Palgrave, pp 141–153.

Wilkins, A. (2019) The processual life of neoliberalisation: permutations of value systems and normative commitments in a co-operative trust setting, International Journal of Inclusive Education, 23(11): 1180–1195.

Wilkins, A. (2021) Deconstructing governance: perspectives in post-positivist thinking, in M.A. Peters and R. Heraud (eds) Encyclopedia of educational innovation, Singapore: Springer.

Wilkins, A. (2023a) Publics in education: Thinking with Gunter on plurality, democracy and local reasoning, in T. Fitzgerald and S.J. Courtney (eds) Critical education policy and leadership studies: The intellectual contributions of Helen M. Gunter, Cham, Switzerland: Springer.

Wilkins, A. (2023b) Mapping the field: education policy research and theory, in A. Wilkins (ed) Policy foundations of education, London: Bloomsbury, 9–32.

Wilkins, A. and Gobby, B. (2020) Governance and educational leadership, in S. Courtney, H. Gunter, R. Niesche and T. Trujillo (eds) Understanding educational leadership: critical perspectives and approaches, London: Bloomsbury, 309–322.

Wilkins, A. and Gobby, B. (2022) Objects and subjects of risk: a governmentality approach to education governance, Globalisation, Societies and Education. https://doi.org/10.1080/14767724.2022.2114073

Wilkins, A., Collet-Sabé, J., Gobby, B. and Hangartner, J. (2019) Translations of New Public Management: a decentred approach to school governance in four OECD countries, Globalisation, Societies and Education, 17(1): 147–160.

Wilkins, A., Collet-Sabe, J., Esper, T., Gobby, B. and Grimaldi, E. (2024) Assembling New Public Management: Actors, networks and projects, in D.B. Edwards, A. Verger, K. Takayama and M. McKenzie (eds) Researching global education policy: diverse approaches to policy movement, Bristol: Policy Press.

Williams, D.G. (2011) Public deliberation and dialogue in public management, in R.A. Lohmann and J. Van Til (eds) Resolving community conflicts and problems: public deliberation and sustained dialogue, New York: Columbia University Press, 254–263.

Williams, R. (2015 [1976]) Keywords: a vocabulary of culture and society (3rd edn), Oxford: Oxford University Press.

Williamson, B. (2012) Centrifugal schooling: third sector policy networks and the reassembling of curriculum policy in England, Journal of Education Policy, 27(6): 775–794.

Williamson, B. (2014) New governing experts in education: policy labs, self-learning software, and transactional pedagogies, in T. Fenwick, E. Mangez and J. Ozga (eds) Governing knowledge: comparison, knowledge-based technologies and expertise in the regulation of education, London: Routledge, 218–230.

Williamson, B. (2015) Governing software: networks, databases and algorithmic power in the digital governance of public education, Learning, Media and Technology, 40(1): 83–105.

Williamson, B. (2016a) Digital education governance: data visualization, predictive analytics, and 'real-time' policy instruments, Journal of Education Policy, 31(2): 123–141.

Williamson, B. (2016b) Silicon startup schools: technocracy, algorithmic imaginaries and venture philanthropy in corporate education reform, Critical Studies in Education, 59(2): 218–236.

Williamson, B. (2018) Big data in education: the digital future of learning, policy and practice, London: SAGE.

Williamson, B. (2019) Startup schools, fast policies, and full-stack education companies: digitizing education reform in Silicon Valley, in K.J. Saltman and A.J. Means (eds) The Wiley handbook of global educational reform, Medford: Wiley, 283–306.

Williamson, B. (2021) Digital policy sociology: software and science in data-intensive precision education, Critical Studies in Education, 62(3): 354–370.

Williamson, B. and Eynon, R. (2020) Historical threads, missing links, and future directions in AI in education, Learning, Media and Technology, 45(3): 223–235.

Williamson, B., Bayne, S. and Shay, S. (2020) The datafication of teaching in higher education: critical issues and perspectives, Teaching in Higher Education, 25(4): 351–365.

Wilson, C.A. (2000) Policy regimes and policy change, Journal of Public Policy, 20(3): 247–274.

Winchip, E., Stevenson, H. and Milner, A. (2019) Measuring privatisation in education: methodological challenges and possibilities, Educational Review, 71(1): 81–100.

Winton, S. (2013) Rhetorical analysis in critical policy research, International Journal of Qualitative Studies in Education, 26(2): 158–177.

Wodak, R. and Meyer, M. (2009) Critical discourse analysis: history, agenda, theory, and methodology, in R. Wodak and M. Meyer (eds) Methods for critical discourse analysis, London: SAGE, 1–33.

Wood, L.A. and Kroger, R.O. (2000) Doing discourse analysis: methods for studying action in talk and text, London: SAGE

Wright, N. (2001) Leadership, 'bastard leadership' and managerialism: confronting twin paradoxes in the Blair education project, Educational Management Administration and Leadership, 29(3): 275–290.

Wright, N. (2003) Principled 'bastard' leadership? A rejoinder to Gold, Evans, Earley, Halpin and Collarbone, Educational Management Administration and Leadership, 31(2): 139–143.

Yanow, D. (2007) Interpretation in policy analysis: on methods and practice, Critical Policy Studies, 1(1): 110–122.

Yates, L., Connolly, P. and Torrance, H. (2011) Engaging science policy: from the side of the mess, British Journal of Sociology of Education, 32(3): 467–482.

Yeatman, A. (ed) (1998) Activism and the policy process, Sydney: Allen & Unwin.

Yu, H. (2018) Shaping the educational policy field: 'cross-field effects' in the Chinese context, Journal of Education Policy, 33(1): 43–61.

Zamudio, M.M., Russell, C., Rios, F. and Bridgeman, J.L. (2011) Critical race theory matters: education and ideology, New York and Abingdon: Routledge.

Index